GENESIS 37–50

CLAUS
WESTERMANN

GENESIS 37–50

A Commentary

Translated by
John J. Scullion S.J.

AUGSBURG PUBLISHING HOUSE
MINNEAPOLIS

GENESIS 37–50
A Commentary

First published 1982 by Neukirchener Verlag, Neukirchen-Vluyn, in the Biblischer Kommentar Series.

First published in English 1986 by Augsburg Publishing House in the USA and in Great Britain by SPCK, Holy Trinity Church, Marylebone Road, London NW1 4DU.

Library of Congress Cataloging in Publication Data

Westermann, Claus.
  GENESIS 37–50.

  Bibliography: p.
  Includes indexes.
  1. Bible.   O. T. Genesis XXXVII-L—Commentaries.
I. Title.
BS1235.3.W3713   1986   222′.11077   85-26802
ISBN 0–8066–2197–4

The paper used in this publication meets the minimum requirements of American National Standard for Information Sciences—Permanence of Paper for Printed Library Materials, ANSI Z39.48-1984.

∞™

Manufactured in the U.S.A.   APH 10-2546

1   2   3   4   5   6   7   8   9   0   1   2   3   4   5   6   7   8   9   0

To the British Academy
in Gratitude for Awarding
the Burkitt Medal 1977 for Biblical Studies

Contents

9

Contents

Contents

Translator's Preface

Professor Westermann worked on his commentary on Genesis for almost 25 years. It is the most comprehensive and profound commentary on this great book since Hermann Gunkel's pioneering work at the beginning of this century.

The translation was spread over seven years amid full programs of lecturing and administration and several lengthy periods of hospitalization. My relief and joy on completing it were balanced by the sober reflection that I should do it all over again and much better. I can only apologize for its inadequacies and hope that, despite them, Professor Westermann's great contribution to biblical studies will become known to a wide audience in the English-speaking world.

The following points should be noted regarding the translation of this volume:

1. The translation of the Hebrew text of Genesis is deliberately rather literal but attempts in every case to convey Professor Westermann's nuances.

2. Quotations from other parts of the Old Testament, the Apocrypha, and the New Testament are from the Revised Standard Version of the Bible, copyright 1946, 1952, and 1971 by the Division of Christian Education of the National Council of Churches.

3. The spelling of all personal, proper, and place-names from the Bible follows the usage of the Revised Standard Version.

4. Abbreviations of the biblical books are those of the RSV, Common Bible.

I would refer the reader to volume 2, *Genesis 12–36,* for all abbreviations.

Again, I thank Mrs. Leonie Hudson whose manuscript was of that same high standard as those of the previous volumes which drew such praise from the publishers. Shirley Sullivan assisted with the proofreading, and my colleague, Brian Moore S.J., was ready to help at any stage. My thanks are due to both.

Finally, I would note what a pleasure it has been to deal with the publishing firms, Augsburg, Minneapolis, and SPCK, London. Their courtesy, consideration, and encouragement have meant much.

John J. Scullion S.J.
Newman College
(University of Melbourne)
887 Swanston Street,
Parkville, Vic. 3052
Australia

Introduction to the Joseph Story

Literature on the History of the Exegesis of Genesis 37–50

J. Wellhausen, *Die Composition des Hexateuch und der historischen Bücher* (1876-78; 1963⁴). B. D. Eerdmans, *Alttestamentliche Studien I: Die Komposition der Genesis* (1908). H. Gunkel, "Die Komposition der Joseph-Geschichten," ZDMG 76 NF 1 (1922) 55-71. O. Eissfeldt, "Stammessage und Novelle in den Geschichten von Jakob und seinen Söhnen," FRLANT 35 NF 19 (1923) 56-77 = KS I (1962) 84-104. H. Gressmann, "Ursprung und Entwicklung der Joseph-Sage," FRLANT 36 NF 19 (1923) 1-55. W. Rudolph, "Die Josephgeschichte," in P. Volz and W. Rudolph, *Der Elohist als Erzähler*, BZAW 63 (1933) 145-184. M. Noth, *A History of Pentateuchal Traditions* (1948; 1966³; Eng. 1972). H. Brunner, "Die Weisheitsliteratur," HO I,2 (1952) 90-110. G. von Rad, "Josephsgeschichte und ältere Chokma," VT.S 1 (1953) 120-127 = ThB 8 (1958; 1965³) 272-280. A. Jepsen, "Zur Überlieferungsgeschichte der Vätergestalten," WZ(L) 2/3 (1953/54) 265-281. M. Buber, *Die fünf Bücher der Weisung I* (1954). C. T. Fritsch, " 'God Was with Him': A Theological Study of the Joseph Narrative," Interp. 9 (1955) 21-34. O. Kaiser, "Stammesgeschichtliche Hintergründe der Josephgeschichte. Erwägungen zur Vor- und Frühgeschichte Israels," VT 10 (1960) 1-15. H. Cazelles, "Patriarches," DBS VII (1961) 81-156. M. Gan, "The Book of Esther in the Light of the Story of Joseph in Egypt" [in Hebr.], Tarb. 31 (1961/62) 144-149. S. Mowinckel, "Erwägungen zur Pentateuchquellenfrage," NTT 65 (1964) 61ff. L. Ruppert, *Die Josepherzählung der Genesis: Ein Beitrag zur Theologie der Pentateuchquellen* (diss. Würzburg) SAM 11 (1965). F. V. Winnett, "Re-Examining the Foundations," JBL 84 (1965) 1-19. C. Westermann, *Die Josepherzählung der Genesis*, CPH 5,1 (1966) 11-118. H. Prang, *Formgeschichte der Dichtkunst* (1968). R. N. Whybray, "The Joseph Story and Pentateuchal Criticism," VT 18 (1968) 522-528. J. L. Crenshaw, "Method in Determining Wisdom Influence upon 'Historical' Literature," JBL 88 (1969) 129-142. D. B. Redford, *A Study of the Biblical Story of Joseph (Genesis 37-50)*, VT.S 20 (1970) O. H. Steck, *Die Paradieserzählung*, BSt 60 (1970). R. de Vaux, *The Early History of Israel I* (1971; Eng. 1978) 291-320. W. Brueggemann, "Life and Death in Tenth-Century Israel," JAAR 40 (1972) 96-109. H. Schulte, "Die Entstehung der Geschichtsschreibung im Alten Israel," BZAW 128 (1972). G. W. Coats, "The Joseph Story and Ancient Wisdom: A Reappraisal," CBQ 35 (1973) 285-297. E. I. Lowenthal, *The Joseph Narrative in Genesis* (1973). G. W. Coats, "Redactional Unity in Genesis 37–50," JBL 93 (1974) 15-21. R. N. Whybray, *The Intellectual Tradition in the OT*, BZAW 135 (1974). A. Meinhold, "Die Gattung der Josephsgeschichte und des Estherbuches: Diasporanovelle II," ZAW 88 (1976) 72-93. C. Westermann, *Genesis 12–50: Erträge der Forschung* (1975) 56-68. G. W. Coats, *From Canaan to Egypt: Structural and Theological Context for the Joseph Sto-*

ry, CBQMS 4 (1976). H. Donner, *Die literarische Gestalt der alttestamentlichen Josephgeschichte* (1976). E. Otto, "Die 'synthetische Lebensauffassung' in der frühköniglichen Novellistik Israels," ZThK 74 (1977) 371-400. P. D. Miscall, "The Jacob and Joseph Stories as Analogies," JSOT 6 (1978) 28-40. H. Seebass, "Erwägungen zum altisraelitischen System der zwölf Stämme," ZAW 90 (1978) 196-219; *Geschichtliche Zeit und theonome Tradition in der Joseph-Erzählung* (1978). F. Crüsemann, *Der Widerstand gegen das Königtum*, WMANT 49 (1978). R. Davidson, *Genesis 12–50*, CBC (1979). I. Willi-Plein, "Historische Aspekte der Josephgeschichte," *Henoch 1* (1979) 305-331. H. C. Schmitt, *Die nichtpriesterliche Josephgeschichte*, BZAW 154 (1980).

Other Literature on Genesis 37–50

A. Wächter, *Josephs Geschichte nach Genesis, Targum des Onkelos und der Jûsof-Sure des Koran* (1878). L. A. Rosenthal, "Die Josephgeschichte, mit den Büchern Ester und Daniel verglichen," ZAW 15 (1895) 278-284; 17 (1897) 125-128. P. Riessler, "Zu Rosenthals Aufsatz," ZAW 16 (1896) 182. J. Marquart, "Chronologische Untersuchungen," PhS 7 (1899) 637-720; 677-700. H. Winckler, *Geschichte Israels in Einzeldarstellungen II* (1900) 67-77. C. Steuernagel, Die Einwanderung der israelitischen Stämme in Kanaan (1901). A. H. Sayce, *Joseph and the Land of Egypt* (1904). E. König, "Is Joseph Forever Lost to Us as a Real Historic Person?" MethR (1905) 345-350. B. Luther, *Die Josephgeschichte* (1906) 141-154, 287-293. A. C. Welch, *The Story of Joseph* (1913) E. Weber, "Vorarbeiten zu einer künftigen Ausgabe der Genesis," ZAW 34 (1914) 199-218. W. Bousset, *Die Geschichte eines Wiedererkennungsmärchens* (1916). H. Gunkel, "Jakob," PrJ 176 (1919) 339-362, 346-348. J. Horovitz, *Die Josepherzählung* (1921). H. Gunkel, *Die israelitische Literatur* (1923; 1963). S. Luria, "Die ägyptische Bibel (Joseph- und Mosesage)," ZAW 44 (1926) 94-135. S. Rubin, *Biblische Probleme I: Die Josephgeschichte in neuer Beleuchtung* (1931). V. Laridon, "De historia Joseph (Gn 37–50)," CBrug 39 (1939) 21-33. E. W. Heaton, "The Joseph-Saga," ET 59 (1947/48) 134-136. B. Reicke, *Die kultischen Hintergründe der Josepherzählung* (1948). S. Herrmann, "Die Königsnovelle in Ägypten und in Israel: Ein Beitrag zur Gattungsgeschichte in den Geschichtsbüchern des AT," WZ(L) 3 (1953) 51-62. G. von Rad, *Die Josephsgeschichte*, BSt 5 (1954; 1964⁴). S. Morenz, "Joseph in Ägypten," ThLZ 84 (1959) 401-416. P. Montet, *Das alte Ägypten und die Bibel*, BiAr IV, ed. A. Parrot (1960). J. Vergote, *Joseph en Egypte. Genèse chapitre 37–50 à la lumière des études égyptologiques récentes* (1959). I. L. Seeligmann, "Hebräische Erzählung und biblische Geschichtsschreibung," ThZ 18 (1962) 305-325. J. Maigret, L'Histoire de Joseph," BTS 53/54 (1963) 2-4. J. Vergote, "Joseph, le Patriarche," Cath. 6,25 (1965) 965-970. H. W. Wolff, "The Kerygma of the Yahwist," *Interp.* 20 (1966) 131-158. B. S. Childs, "The Birth of Moses," JBL 84 (1965) 109-122. B. J. van der Merwe, "Joseph as Successor of Jacob," Fests. T. C. Vriezen (1966) 221-232. L. Ruppert, Göttliches und menschliches Handeln. Form und Inhalt der Josephgeschichte," BiKi 21 (1966) 1-7. N. M. Sarna, *Understanding Genesis* (1966) 211-227. R. G. Collingwood, *The Idea of History* (1967) 231-249. H. Werner, *Joseph. Weiser und Seher*, ExBib 3 (1967). I. Jerusalmi, *The Story of Joseph* (1968). R. Martin-Achard, "Problèmes soulevés par l'étude de l'histoire biblique de Joseph (Genèse 37–50)," RThPh 2 (21) (1972) 94-102. L. R. Fisher, "The Patriarchal Cycles," AOAT 22 (1973) 59-65. T. L. Thompson and D. Irvin, "The Joseph and Moses Narratives," in *Israelite and Judean History*, ed. J. H. Hayes and J. M. Miller (1977). J. A. Loader, "Esther as a Novel with Different Levels of Meaning," ZAW 90 (1978) 417-421. H. Engel, *Die Vorfahren Israels in Ägypten: Forschungsgeschichtlicher Überblick über die Darstellungen seit Richard Lepsius 1849*, FTS 27 (1979).

Literary Criticism: P. Leander, "Einige Bemerkungen zur Quellenscheidung der Josephgeschichte," ZAW 17 (1897) 195f. J. Dahse, "Textkritische Studien II," ZAW 28 (1908) 1-21, 161-173. H. A. M. Wiener, *The Answer of Textual Criticism to the Higher Criticism of the Story of Joseph* I (1910). B. Jacob, *Quellenscheidung und Exegese im Pentateuch* (1916). C. R. North, "Pentateuchal Criticism," in *The OT in Modern Study*, ed. H. H. Rowley (1951) 48-83. H. Segal, *The Pentateuch: Its Composition and Its Authorship* (1967). O. Keel and M. Küchler, *Synoptische Texte aus Genesis I-II*, BibB 8,2 (1970-71). H. W. Wolff, "The Elohistic Fragments in the Pentateuch," *Interp.* 26 (1972) 158-173.

Tales and Myths: E. Stucken, *Astralmythen derHebräer, Babylonier und Ägypter: Religionsgeschichtliche Untersuchungen V* (1899-1907). H. Winckler, *Abraham als Babylonier, Joseph als Ägypter: Der Weltgeschichtliche Hintergrund der biblischen Vätergeschichten auf Grund der Keilschriften dargestellt* (1903). A. Jeremias, *Das AT im Lichte des Alten Orients* (1904; 1930⁴) 372-386. D. Völter, *Ägypten und die Bibel. Die Urgeschichte Israels im Licht ägyptischer Mythologie* (1904; 1909⁴). P. Jensen, *Das Gilgamesch-Epos in der Weltliteratur I* (1906-1928) 269-384. D. Völter, *Die Patriarchen Israels und die ägyptische Mythologie* (1912; 1921²) 80-90. W. F. Albright, "Historical and Mythical Elements in the Story of Joseph," JBL 37 (1918) 111-143. H. G. May, "The Evolution of the Joseph-Story," AJSL 47 (1930/31) 83-93. J. Herrmann, "Sagenhafte Motive in der biblischen Josephsgeschichte," ORPB 30 (1931) 137-143. K. H. Bernhardt, "Anmerkungen zur Interpretation des *KRT*-Textes von Ras Schamra-Ugarit," WZ(G) 5 (1955/56) 101-121. R. Graves and R. Patai, *Hebrew Myths: The Book of Genesis* (1964). E. Brunner-Traut, *Altägyptische Märchen: Die Märchen der Weltliteratur* (1965²). M. Lüthi, "Familie und Natur im Märchen," Fests. K. Ranke (1968) 181-195. C. Grottanelli, "Spunti comparativi nella storia di Giuseppe," OrAnt 15 (1976) 115-140.

Egyptian Background: G. Ebers, *Aegypten und die Bücher Mose's. Sachlicher Commentar zu den ägyptischen Stellen in Genesis–Exodus I* (1868). J. Lieblein, "Mots egyptiens dans la Bible," PSBA 20 (1898) 204ff. E. Miketta, "Die literarhistorische und religionsgeschichtliche Bedeutung der ägyptischen Eigennamen der Josephsgeschichte," BZ 2 (1904) 122-140. F. Zimmermann, "Agyptologische Randglossen zum AT," ThG 5 (1912) 357-361. M. A. Gardiner, "New Literary Works From Egypt," JEA 1 (1914) 100-106. A. S. Yahuda, *Die Sprache des Pentateuch in ihren Beziehungen zum Ägyptischen I* (1929); *Les récits bibliques de Joseph et de l'Exode confirmés à la lumière des monuments égyptiens* (1940). W. F. Elgerton, "The Government and the Governed in the Egyptian Empire," JNES 6 (1947) 152ff. W. F. Albright, "Some Important Discoveries: Alphabetic Origins and the Idrimi Statue," BASOR 118 (1950) 11-20. W. S. Smith, "The Relationship between Egyptian Ideas and OT Thought," JBR 19 (1951) 12-15. J. A. Wilson, "Egyptian Myths, Tales, and Mortuary Texts," ANET (1955; 1969²) 23-25. J. M. A. Janssen, "Egyptological Remarks on the Story of Joseph in Genesis," JEOL 14 (1955/56) 63-72. O. Eissfeldt, review: "J. Vergote, Joseph en Egypte," OLZ 55 (1960) 39-45. E. Fickel, "Die alttestamentliche Josephsgeschichte im Lichte der ägyptischen Forschung," BiLe 1 (1960) 138-140. S. Herrmann, "Joseph in Ägypten," ThLZ 85 (1960) 827-830. H. Donner, "J. Vergote, *Joseph en Egypte*," BiOr 18 (1961) 44-45. E. Atir, "Zur Frage der Beziehung zwischen der biblischen Joseferzählung und der ägyptischen Brüdererzählung" [in Hebr.], BetM 11,3 (1965/66) 3-8.

Wisdom: A. Causse, "Sagesse égyptienne et sagesse juive," RHPhR 9 (1929) 149-169. J. Fichtner, *Die altorientalische Weisheit in ihrer israelitisch-jüdischen Ausprägung*, BZAW 62 (1933). B. Gemser, "The Instructions of 'Onchsheshonqy and Biblical Wisdom Literature," VT.S 7 (1960) 102-128. D. A. Hubbard, "The Wisdom Movement and Israel's Covenant Faith," TynB 17 (1966) 3-33. G. von Rad, *Wisdom in Israel* (1970; Eng. 1972). H. D. Preuss, "Erwägungen zum theologischen Ort alttestamentlicher Weisheitsliteratur," EvTh 30 (1970) 393-417. R. Gordis, *The Social Background of Wisdom Literature*, esp. "Poets, Prophets and Sages" (1971) 160-197. J. L. Crenshaw, "Wisdom," in *OT Form Criticism*, ed. J. H. Hayes (1974) VI 225-264. A. Caquot, "Israelite Perceptions of Wisdom and Strength in the Light of the Ras Shamra Texts," Fests. S. Terrien (1978) 25-33.

In Later Literature: V. Gravowski, *Die Geschichte Josefs nach einer syrischen Handschrift* (1889). H. Speyer, *Die biblischen Erzählungen im Qoran* (1931; 1961²). B. Murmelstein, *Die Gestalt Josephs in der Agada und die Evangeliengeschichte*, Angelos 4 (1932). H. Y. Priebatsch, *Die Josephgeschichte in der Weltliteratur* (1937). H. Sprödowsky, *Die Hellenisierung der Geschichte von Joseph in Agypten bei Flavius Josephus* (diss. Greifswald, 1937). V. Vikentier, "Le dernier conte de Shaharazade . . . et ses sources anciennes," BFA, Cairo (1955) 111ff. A. W. Argyle, "Joseph the Patriarch in Patristic Teaching," ET 67 (1955/56) 199-201. E. Hilscher, "Der biblische Joseph in orientalischen Literaturwerken," MIOF 4 (1956) 81-83. J. Zandee, "Josephus contra Apionem: An Apocryphic Story of Joseph in Coptic," VigChr 15 (1961) 193-195. G. T.

Armstrong, *Die Genesis in der alten Kirche: Justin, Irenaeus, Tertullian* (1962). H. A. Brongers, *De Josefsgeschiedenis bij Joden, Christenen en Mohammedanen: Een theologische, historische en literaire studie* (1962). L. Beeston, *Baidawi's Commentary on Surah 12 in the Qur'an* (1963). A. van Seeters, "The Use of the Story of Joseph in Scripture" (diss. Richmond, 1965). D. Arenhoevel, "Die Gestalt des Joseph in der Überlieferung des AT," BiKi 21 (1966) 8-10. A. M. Goldberg, "Joseph in der Sicht des Judentums der Antike," BiKi 21 (1966) 11-13. S. Raeder, "Die Josephsgeschichte im Koran und im AT," EvTh 26 (1966) 169-190. R. Y. Ebied and M. J. L. Young, "An Unknown Arabic Poem on Joseph and his Brothers," JAOS (1974) 2-7. E. Richard, "The Polemical Character of the Joseph Episode in Acts 7," JBL 98 (1979) 255-267.

1. The History of the Exegesis of Genesis 37–50

For details see especially L. Ruppert (1965); also H. Cazelles (1961), C. Westermann (1975), H. Seebass (1978), and H. C. Schmitt (1980), listed in bibl., section 1, above.

One must distinguish three stages in the history of the exegesis of the Joseph story. The first is determined by the traditional ecclesiastical view which makes no distinction between what happened and its transmission in writing. One line of Jewish interpretation right up to the present day is closely akin to this view: B. Jacob, *Komm.* (1934; 1974[2]); M. Buber (1954); E. I. Lowenthal (1973); and others. But while Jewish interpretation has for the most part kept to the plain meaning of the text, Christian interpretation has from early times supported an allegorical sense. F. Delitzsch, for example, reproduces Pascal's explanation, *Komm.* 1852, 1887[5]: "Jesus Christ is prefigured in Joseph, his father's favorite, sent by the father to his brothers, the guiltless one sold by his brothers for twenty pieces of silver and so become their Lord. . . .. Such is the Church's vital portrayal of the Joseph story from time immemorial." The mythical explanation is close to the allegorical, even though it belongs to the second stage. With the rise of the history of religions and the study of myth, the figure of Joseph was explained mythically (C. Westermann, 1975, pp. 56f.); but this explanation has been abandoned completely. The Joseph story is no myth.

The second stage is determined by the literary-critical thesis of source division. The text of chs. 37–50 is divided up among the pentateuchal sources J, E, and P and blocks are ascribed to each.

The tribal-history explanation also belongs to this stage. For O. Eissfeldt (1923) it follows from the literary-critical explanation; O. Kaiser (1960), a recent supporter of this thesis, also adheres to the source theory. The tribal explanation is also accepted by H. Seebass (1978) and I. Willi-Plein (1979). However, a consensus is gradually forming that only a few texts in Gen. 37–50 refer to Israelite tribes and their history.

The third stage, which is the present state of the study of the Joseph story, began with the recognition that the story gives the impression of a unified whole, thus differing from chs. 12–25 and 25–36 which consist of individual narratives. H. Gunkel (1922) and H. Gressmann (1923) were the first to recognize this, and this view has to a large extent prevailed. Nevertheless, there is an element of uncertainty here; for a long time scholars did not succeed in reaching agreement about the nature and form of the whole (H. Gunkel described chs. 37–50 as a story [*Sage*], a tale [*Märchen*], a short story [*Novelle*] or even at times a cycle of stories; there is a similar vacillation in H. Gressmann's terminology); and further, H. Gunkel, G. von Rad, and others adhere to the source division. They do not raise the question of how the division into two (or three) sources is related to the "short story" as a whole. Did J and E each write short stories which were synthesized into one by R? Or, if the single short story was only the result of the synthesis, is R its author? G. von Rad has brought a further qualification to the Joseph story by discovering its sapiential character. He discusses this in detail in his essay in 1953: "The Joseph story with its obvious didactic thrust belongs to the ancient wisdom teaching" (VT.S 1 [1953] 126 = ThB 8 [1965³] 279; Eng. "The Joseph Narrative and Ancient Wisdom" in *The Problem of the Hexateuch. . .* [1966] 292-300). But how can the Joseph story be a short story and at the same time belong to the wisdom teaching? This raises the question of its composition and structure which alone can tell what it means.

More recent exegesis is mainly concerned with the problems which emerge from the history of the exegesis of chs. 37–50. There is the question of the origin and growth of layers which are explained from the standpoint of literary criticism and tradition history and, over against this, the origin and growth of the literary unity; then there is the form-critical question and the determination of the genre; finally there is the question of the composition, how the whole was formed from the parts.

A. The Literary-Critical and the Traditio-Historical Problem

An instinctive reaction of J. Wellhausen to source division in chs. 37–50 is based on the validity of this division in the rest of Genesis: "One suspects that this section, like the rest, is a synthesis of J and E; our earlier results impose this solution and would be profoundly affected were it not demonstrable (*Die Composition. . .* [1876–78] 52). W. Rudolf refers to this remark (1933), and several other defenders of the unity, e.g., H. Donner (1976), have recalled it. Gunkel and Gressmann also put source criticism in question by acknowledging that chs. 37–50 are independent of chs. 12–25 and 25–36 and exhibit the qualities of unity. It became impossible therefore to avoid the question whether the Joseph story as a short story, a creation out of "a single mold," was still compatible with source division (R. N. Whybray, 1974; H. Donner, 1976).

1) Studies that adhere to the source theory take in essence three directions: *(a)* O. Kaiser and L. Ruppert stay with classical source division; both follow H. Gunkel in this, as does H. Schulte also (1972). *(b)* H. Schulte and H. Seebass (1978) unite source division with a traditio-historical explanation. For H. Schulte two written stages, identical with J and E, follow on four oral stages; for H. Seebass tribal traditions, later transformed into family history, are the basis of the Joseph story (similar to O. Eissfeldt). *(c)* One group represents the expansion theory and tends toward the theory of literary unity. D. B. Redford (1970) sees the original Joseph story in the Reuben version (close to E) which was later expanded by the Judah version (close to J); this was later expanded by a third layer, the reworking by the editor of Genesis, who added further parts. Both versions arose between 650 and 550. So too H. C. Schmitt (1980), who reverses the process: he sees the original Joseph story in the Judah layer (in the period of David and Solomon) reworked by the Reuben layer (in the exilic or postexilic period). A. Jepsen (1953-54) and S. Mowinckel (1964) agree with W. Rudolf (1933) and want only to modify his conclusion. F. V. Winnett (1965) is also close to the thesis of literary unity. Both the Reuben and Judah versions recur in all of these, but differently each time.

2) W. Rudolf (1933) supported the thesis of literary unity with good arguments, above all with the argument that the Joseph story gives the impression of being the "creation of a single mind" (accepted by G. von Rad). He understands the doublets as a deliberate literary device of the author (so previously H. Gunkel; taken over by D. B. Redford, H. Donner, and others), and thinks that the unevennesses are better explained as additions. The reason Rudolf went almost unnoticed for so long was partly that his argumentation remained far removed from and independent of source division, and that he did not demonstrate the unity from the composition of the whole.

R. N. Whybray (1968) saw the contradiction between G. von Rad's thesis that Gen. 37–50 was the work of a *single* mind (like W. Rudolf) and his adherence to source theory. If Gen. 37–50 is "a short story through and through," then it cannot be a synthesis of pieces from several sources. R. de Vaux agrees (1971; Eng. 1978); he had earlier supported source division (RB 53-56 [1946-49]; 72 [1965]; ThD 12 [1964] 227-240), as had I (lit. above). H. Donner (1976) also gives his approval to R. N. Whybray's "either/or"; he takes up the most important objections against the source theory and settles for unity. Individual additions, however, are like chs. 12–36 and susceptible to source division. Donner does not raise the question of the composition of the whole; he does not go beyond the general classification of the Joseph story as a short story. A number of scholars have recently supported the thesis of literary unity without giving detailed reasons: W. Brueggemann (1972); E. Otto (1977); F. Crüsemann (1978); I. Willi-Plein (1979); R. Davidson (1979). Recent scholarship shows a marked tendency to the unity thesis.

B. The Literary Form

H. Gunkel arrived at a new understanding of the literary form of Gen. 37–50. This is apparent when he writes: "After all this we can no longer really call this narrative a folk story (*Sage*); it is a short story (*Novelle*)." The oldest version of the Joseph story, according to H. Gressmann, is a tale of adventure; a non-Israelite royal tale has been transferred to Joseph and expanded into a short story. Gressmann thus understands "short story" in deliberate contrast to a cycle of stories; the individual parts never existed independently but are organic members of a whole. G. von Rad took up this new approach of Gunkel and Gressmann. He sees the Joseph story as "an organically constructed narrative from beginning to end, no single part of which can have had an independent existence and separate tradition." In another place, however, he restricts this to chs. 37; 39–47; and 50. von Rad thus recognized something special about the composition that Gunkel and Gressmann had not seen so clearly: the Joseph story is arranged in individual scenes, each with its own exposition, climax, and conclusion. He thereby indicates the consequences of this new understanding: if Gen. 37–50 is described as a short story distinct from a folk story or tale, then it is a unity, conceived and planned as an articulated whole by a single mind, and it developed as a written piece. At the same time, von Rad discovered and emphasized the sapiential character of the story (1953). But how are the wisdom teaching and the short story related to each other? (G. W. Coats also raises this question.) Moreover, the material has been given the theological designation "story of divine guidance"; and it is not immediately clear how this relates to the other two designations. I wrote in the *Calwer Predigthilfen* in 1966: "The designation 'story of divine guidance' does not express clearly enough what is specific to this story. It does not deal with individual people who are guided by God in a wonderful way but rather . . . with a community, the family of Jacob. It begins with the shattering of peace in the family and reaches its goal with the restoration of peace.''

D. B. Redford (1970) goes back to H. Gressmann, describing the Joseph story as a tale/short story. The basic motif is that of the boy who has a dream of future greatness. R. de Vaux issues a reservation about the oft-used designation *novel* or *short story*; it is a self-contained piece and undoubtedly a polished work of art, but this does not mean that everything in it ''was invented by the author'' (*The Early History*. . . 1, p. 296). A. Meinhold (1975) qualifies chs. 37–50 as a ''short story from the diaspora'' and wants to demonstrate that it has the same structure as the book of Esther; both belong to the period of the exile and were written for the Jews in the diaspora. E. Otto (1977) considers the Joseph story to be an example of Israelite ''confrontation literature'' (following the Egyptologist H. Brunner) which is concerned with the problem of the suffering of the just one.

C. The Question of the Composition

In the fourth part of his essay of 1922 H. Gunkel discerned and appropriately designated the main lines of the Joseph story. It is woven out of two main motifs. The narrative of Joseph's fate at the hands of his brothers forms the framework: ''a purely family story.'' Something of another kind is introduced with the ''experiences of Joseph in Egypt.'' They rest on an independent tradition but have been assumed into the overall structure in such a way that the story as it now stands would be inconceivable without this inset. H. Gressmann had also discerned this double articulation. He distinguished a family story and a political story. He also saw correctly that the text on the death and last will and testament of Jacob is really part of the Jacob story. It was only in 1974 that G. W. Coats resumed once more these insights of Gunkel and Gressmann. His inquiry into the composition takes as its starting point the final form of the text, that is, chs. 37–50 as a whole. This does not form a structural unity but a collection of traditions about Jacob and his sons which deals with the descent of Jacob and his family into Egypt. Gen. 38 and 47:28-50 are expansions of the actual Joseph story (so too H. Gressmann). In his study of 1976, Coats agrees with Westermann and de Vaux that the main line is concerned with a family event and leads from a shattering of the peace to reconciliation. From this story there develops another in chs. 39–41, ''a political legend,'' which deals with the proper use of power. Coats sees the sapiential character, which G. von Rad ascribes to the whole of the Joseph story, as valid only for chs. 39–41. F. Crüsemann (1978, pp. 146-149) agrees in essence with Coats but sees a tighter link between the two parts of chs. 37–50 and goes even further in opposition to Gunkel and Gressmann. The conflict in the family itself also exhibits a political aspect in the question of whether a brother should lord it over his brothers (so too C. Westermann), the basic conflict of the era in which the Joseph story arose. The solution also must have its political aspect. The reconciliation of Joseph with his brothers presupposes the acknowledgment of the matter against which the brothers had revolted at the beginning. The royal policy about supply, to which chs. 39–41 lead up, is the matter that makes the reconciliation possible. It justifies Joseph's position of authority and gives an answer to the question about the monarchy.

Further assays on the problem of the composition of the Joseph story may be found in L. Ruppert, R. N. Whybray, O. H. Steck (pp. 120ff., n. 291), E. Otto, H. Seebass, I. Willi-Plein (all in bibliog. above). The theological meaning of the story will be dealt with in the conclusion.

2. The Composition of Genesis 37–50

Chapters 37–50 form a coherence inasmuch as ch. 37 deals with Joseph as a boy and ch. 50 reports his death. One can in the broad sense call them the Joseph story (G. W. Coats: "a redactional unity"). The narrative begins with a conflict between Joseph and his brothers that affects the father as well (ch. 37). Chs. 45ff. narrate the reconciliation between Joseph and his brothers and his reunion with his father. What still follows in chs. 46–50, can only be the conclusion to the climax in ch. 45; but it is too long as a conclusion. Some parts of these chapters can belong to the conclusion, but others not necessarily so; they have no immediate relationship to the narrative span of chs. 37–45f. They can be the conclusion of a Jacob story inasmuch as they all concern Jacob; 46:1-7 in particular suggest this—a text which by its own very different quality stands apart from what has preceded. The same holds for ch. 48. This is confirmed by the occurrence of P in chs. 37–50. The texts ascribed to the priestly writing occur in 37:1-2 and in chs. 46–50; they are missing from 37:3 through ch. 45. Moreover, P is fitted into 37:1-2 and chs. 46–50 in the same way as in chs. 12–36. All P passages deal with Jacob, even though Joseph is mentioned often in them. P thereby confirms that chs. 46–50, without the texts that belong to the conclusion of the Joseph story, are part of the Jacob story.

It follows that we have in chs. 37–50 a Joseph story in the stricter sense (chs. 37 and 39–45, with parts of chs. 46–50) and a conclusion to the Jacob story (in ch. 37 and parts of chs. 46–50). The P passages in chs. 37 and 46–50 belong to the latter.

It is only the Joseph story in the stricter sense that forms an unbroken unity without gaps, such as many scholars have underscored. The peculiar content, the literary and stylistic qualities that distinguish it from the rest of the patriarchal story (chs. 12-36), are valid only in this restricted sense. There are certain consequences that follow from this understanding of the composition of chs. 37–50.

1. M. Noth's explanation of the development of the Joseph story (*A History of Pentateuchal. . .* 1948; 1966[2]; Eng. 1972, pp. 208-213), which has been widely accepted, can no longer be sustained. His point of departure is confirmed, namely, that "it does not actually belong to any one of the fundamental themes, . . .nor does it belong to the 'patriarchal' theme . . .nor is it related, on the other hand, to the theme of 'guidance out of Egypt' "; but his conclusion that it "represents the broad and artistic narrative development of a cluster of themes" is not correct. It has as its basis the question: "Jacob and his sons went down to Egypt (Josh. 24:4); how might that have come about?" (p. 209). But in fact the conclusion of the Jacob story contained in chs. 37 and 46–50 tells how Jacob came to Egypt; the Joseph story in the narrower sense presupposes this conclusion (so too R. de Vaux, *The Early History. . .* 1 [1971; Eng. 1978] 293-295).

2. The two late insertions, chs. 38 and 49, are not additions to the Joseph story but belong to the conclusion of the Jacob story. Thus understood they are more meaningful and comprehensible.

3. A difficulty that has weighed upon the exegesis of ch. 37 is thereby solved. Source division found its strongest arguments in this chapter—different names for the same persons, doublets, contradictions; it is at the same time the only chapter before chs. 46–50 in which P occurs. An explanation of both peculiarities would be that the beginning of the Joseph story in the narrower sense in ch. 37 is joined with elements of the Jacob story. There are in fact two threads running side by side in this chapter, both dependent on the Joseph story being moored here in the Jacob story. A further difficulty in ch. 37 thus finds its solution: if the Joseph story arose as an independent narrative, it must have an exposition which introduces the principal persons in a circumstantial clause or in an introductory passage qualified by circumstantial clauses. Such an introductory passage (or clause) is missing; the sentences from P in 37:1-2 are but a poor substitution. The narrative begins immediately in v. 3 with the action. It follows therefore that the author of the Joseph story makes use of the Jacob story available to him as his exposition; this is where the principal persons came from—Jacob, his sons, the youngest son Joseph, the scene. A further narrative is told here about the family with which the Jacob story had been concerned. The author thereby shows his intention of continuing this story in his own independent narrative which he inserts here into the patriarchal story.

4. The consequence for chs. 46–50 is as follows: in 46:1-5 the language shows signs of a difference; it is close to that of chs. 12–36. There occur itineraries, instructions from God, and a promise—which are found elsewhere only in the patriarchal story. Further, there is an itinerary in 46:6-7 (P) and a genealogical list in 46:8-27 (P). The language of the itinerary and the genealogy and this kind of promise are strange to the Joseph story and not suited to it in style. This alone is enough to demonstrate that these texts do not belong to the Joseph story; the same holds for 48:1-19, 21-22.

It follows, therefore, that the conclusion of the Jacob story in chs. 37 and 46-50 has as its subject the question how Jacob comes to Egypt with his family (so too G. W. Coats)—but this is not the subject of the Joseph story in the narrower sense. Ch. 46 followed here on ch. 37. Jacob comes to Egypt and finds his lost son, Joseph, there. This conclusion of the Jacob story contains very little of what is narrated in chs. 39–45. This thereby confirms that the Joseph story in the stricter sense is an insertion into the Jacob story, that it arose independently of it, and that it was artistically interwoven with it in chs. 37 and 46–47.

5. This result is confirmed by the priestly texts from ch. 46 on. Gen. 46:6-7 (itinerary) and vv. 8-27 (genealogy) have been added to 46:4-5; Jacob comes to Egypt. There he blesses the Pharaoh (47:5b-10). Then follow the details about his life-span (47:28 and vv. 29-31?), his death (49:28b-33), and his burial (50:12-14). Chs. 46–50 therefore report Jacob's journey to Egypt, his last will, death, and burial in two parallel threads, one of which is P. This is just as in the case of the rest of the patriarchal story. P accordingly has functioned as the framework of chs. 37–50 by means of 37:1-2 and 50:12-14.

6. Tribal elements are found only in those parts that belong to the Jacob story; consequently, the thesis that the Joseph story is in essence a tribal story is no longer tenable.

7. Finally, it is here that the (variant) repetition of the interpretive passage 45:5-8 in 50:17-21 finds its explanation. Its original setting is solely the climax of the narrative in 45:5-8. The author of the story repeats it in 50:17-21 so as to bind

the conclusion of the Jacob story, into which he has inserted his own narrative, more firmly with his Joseph story; he thus frames the conclusion of the Jacob story in the interpretive passage, thereby giving it even greater weight.

3. The Composition of the Joseph Story in the Stricter Sense (Gen. 37; 39–45f.)

The Joseph story in the stricter sense is given its direction by the duple construction that appears in the two scenes of action. It is a family story into which a "political narrative" (H. Gressmann) is inserted. The narrative span from the impending rift in the family of Jacob in ch. 37 to the healing of the breach in chs. 45f. is a family narrative; the political narrative consists of the restoration of peace through Joseph's rise to a high civil office at the Egyptian court from which he planned and carried out an economy of supply which enabled the family of Jacob to survive (chs. 39–41). The conclusion of the Jacob story, which provides the basis for this and which deals with Jacob's coming to Egypt, was able to say this in a few sentences. This brief narrative sequence was available to the author; it underwent at his hands two expansions, chs. 39–41 and 42–45, in accordance with the principle of doubling that governs the narrative. Joseph's rise is constructed into a story of its own (G. W. Coats: "a story within a story"). Its background is the familiar tale-motif of the rise of the youngest to power and wealth (this is not the motif of the Joseph story as a whole, as D. B. Redford thinks). This first expansion is determined entirely by royal motifs and presupposes the setting and atmosphere of the royal court. Family motifs are completely absent and all roles have a political direction.

In the second expansion, chs. 42–45, family (ch. 37) and political (chs. 39–41) motifs are joined together. This is achieved by means of a contrived role play. The brothers appear in the role of petitioners whose life and death depend on the will of the potentate (cf. 12:10–20); the youngest brother plays the role of the "representative" who has at his disposal the limitless power of the Pharaoh, which can give life and take it away. This second expansion is prolonged into two journeys for the brothers, chs. 42 and 43–45, thus heightening the tension and leading to its final resolution in ch. 45.

This climax is followed by the conclusion in chs. 46–47 in which the Joseph story is interwoven with the conclusion of the Jacob story. The father who had been stricken by the conflict in ch. 37 sees his son again and can now die in peace.

The construction shows that the Joseph story itself is a unity. The two large expansions, chs. 39–41 and 42–45, together with the buildup of the tension by means of the two journeys, chs. 42 and 43–45, reveals the plan of an artist. The plan would be destroyed by division into two sources. The duple construction is the result of reflection which brings the family life-style into relationship with that of the monarchical state. It corresponds to two paths which the history of Israel has followed, that of the patriarchal period and that of the beginning of the monarchy. The transition to the monarchy was accompanied by the question, May and ought a brother rule over his brothers (37:8)? One line of thought in Israel, critical of the monarchy, passionately denied this. It is this question, hotly disputed at the time, that lies behind the binary aspect of the Joseph story. Something must be said about it here in the context of the patriarchal story (F. Crüsemann, 1978). It is to be noted that the Joseph story presents the question of the relationship of the monarchy to the old order in narrative form. This presupposes a time when narrative was still of predominant importance as a form of tradition; the Joseph story also presupposes an obvious proximity to the patriarchal stories into which it was inserted. Hence it is more likely that the story had its origin in the period of David and Solomon than in the 6th or 5th centuries (D. B. Redford and others).

4. The Literary Form of the Joseph Story

Because chs. 37–50 constitute a redactional unity, one can inquire about the form or literary type only of the Joseph story in the proper sense, without the parts belonging to the Jacob story. It has been described as a tale or a tale/short story. But its composition leads to the conclusion that the author understands it as an expansion of the patriarchal story; he wants to narrate something that happened within Jacob's family, between Joseph and his brothers, something that concerned the ancestors of the people of Israel. Well-known motifs were used, in particular the motif of the rise of the youngest brother, which also occurs in another form in chs. 25–36. H. Gunkel was the first to describe the Joseph story as a ''short story'' (*Novelle*; but see B. Luther, 1906, bibliog. above), a description accepted with enthusiasm by G. von Rad. It put the emphasis on the independence and unity of the story as well as on its artistic style and structure; hence one can understand the description; moreover, it is something different from the tale or the brief narratives of chs. 12–36. Many have accepted this designation of the Joseph story. The question must be raised, however, whether it is really correct.

Excursus: The Joseph Story as a Short Story (Novelle)

The short story (novella) had its origin in the Italian Renaissance; it was the forerunner of the German *Novelle*. The term occurs from the middle of the 18th century and is restricted to Italy and Germany. The ''novel'' of the English-speaking world corresponds to the European *Roman* (romance). Narratives which are rather short in contrast to the novel are called short stories (EBrit 16, 673-683). There is no such literary type as *Novelle* recognized in world literature (so too P. Merker, RDL 11[2] [1926-1928] and W. Stammler, ibid. 510ff.; cf. H. Prang, *Formgeschichte der Dichtkunst* [1968]). Two distinguishing marks are always alleged for the novel (*Roman*) and the short story (*Novelle*): they are fiction and they concern the individual. The *Encyclopaedia Britannica* quotes the definition of the Oxford Dictionary, ''a fictitious prose narrative'' (p. 673). H. Prang writes, ''There is almost always an individual at the center of events who is at odds with human society'' (p. 67); the EBrit, ''The oldest and commonest kind of novel is that which is based on the dominance of a single character'' (p. 675). (For further discussion of the *Novelle*, *Roman*, novel, and short story, reference should be made to the standard compendia and monographs on German and English literature.)

The distinguishing marks of fiction and the individual, however, do not hold for the Joseph story. At least it is not fiction inasmuch as it tells of people who actually lived (R. de Vaux also emphasizes this); nor is it restricted to the individual, inasmuch as it does not deal with the experiences or fate of Joseph (though many think so) but of the family of Jacob, for which Joseph acquires a particular significance. One could say that the Joseph story bears a certain resemblance to the family novel. But it is so far removed from this and the modern novel that neither of these terms should be used to describe it. However much it differs from them, it should be classified under that type of literature which covers the novel or short story, namely, belles lettres. The Joseph story is undoubtedly belles lettres; it does intend to hold the interest of its readers. The decisive difference, however, is that in this case the belles lettres aspect as well as the diverting effect on its listeners have not yet been isolated within the particular realm of aesthetics or a specifically delineated aesthetic existence; it still moves within a basically different understanding of existence which is linked indissolubly with the religious, the social, and the political. Both parts of the story have to do with the relationship of the family form of community to political society and with God's action in both; it is not a form of fiction separable from these realms. Its intention proceeds from its composition. Its basis is a simple narrative about the patriarchs. The author of the Joseph story wants to narrate a story about the patriarchs even in his expansions. The special form of this narrative is a result of the special material with which it deals. The Joseph story, too, should be called a narrative in order to preserve its continuity with the patriarchal story. The expansion requires only that it be an artistic narrative, the fruit, not of oral tradition, but of the literary plan of an artist who conceived it in written form. It is a work of art of the highest order; but the writer is not narrating something he himself invented; he is narrating a story of the patriarchs—his own fathers, and the fathers of his listeners. There is an essential difference here between the Joseph story and other literary narratives that have been handed down independently. H. Gunkel had found a similar sort of narrative in Ruth, Esther, Judith, and Tobit. D. B. Redford, p. 67, says the same, as do A. Meinhold and others. But the Joseph story differs from these in that it is built into the Jacob story and uses it as its exposition. The similarity in form is explained from the perseverence of narrative in Israel down through its history, through the exile into the postexilic period with a further flowering in the period of Judaism. However, only a few of these narratives were accepted into the canon, each for a particular reason. But Genesis remained the only *book* of narratives. The similarity in content of the book of Esther is probably to be explained from a conscious dependence of its author on this story (M. Gan, *Tarb.* 31 [1961-62] 144-149).

5. The Joseph Story and Wisdom

I am not aware of any express reference to a connection between the Joseph story and wisdom before G. von Rad's epilog in his commentary (1953; Eng. 1972[2], 433-440) and his essay of 1953. Von Rad's thesis won almost universal acceptance for a considerable time until J. L. Crenshaw (1969) and D. B. Redford (1970) raised objections (see bibliog. above). Crenshaw, to be sure, concedes sapiential influence, though not to the same extent as von Rad; the emphasis on divine providence is not peculiar to wisdom alone, and Joseph is by no means portrayed throughout as an example. Redford makes the same point and adds that Potiphar's wife is not the "loose woman" of Proverbs but the scorned woman, a well-known motif in Egyptian narrative. The key sentences in Gen. 45 and 50 would be secondary (so too G. W. Coats). E. Otto (1971) contests the sapiential character of these sentences; H. C. Schmitt distinguishes between an early and a late sapiential influence. G. W. Coats restricts the sapiential character to chs. 39–41, which he understands as a political legend with a didactic function; he denies any sapiential traits to the family narrative.

As a result of the objections raised against von Rad's assignment of the Joseph story to the wisdom category, the question about wisdom and chs. 37–50 has had to be put in a more refined manner. There is general agreement that sapiential motifs are at work in chs. 40–41. But the wisdom talk here is conditioned by the matter of the narrative. Wisdom belongs to the royal court because the king's counselor belongs there too. Only the exegesis can show if Gen. 39 is also portraying Joseph as the picture of the ideal young man. The Egyptian narrative which forms the background shows no sign of any sapiential influence, nor can ch. 39 be a standard narrative to ''warn against the loose woman'' of Proverbs because there the youth who is hankering after the loose woman is addressed and warned; rather ch. 39 is dealing with the common narrative motif of the scorned woman. The theological key sentences of chs. 45 and 50 have nothing to do with wisdom at the royal court, but are theological reflections which belong to a different realm of thought. Again, it is only the exegesis that can show whether and when and in what sense these sayings can be termed sapiential.

6. The Joseph Story and the Patriarchal Traditions

The result of the emphasis put on the uniqueness and independence of the Joseph story over against the preceding patriarchal story is that too often not enough attention has been paid to their continuity and what they have in common.

1. All people mentioned in chs. 37–45 (except chs. 39–41) have been the subject of narratives in the patriarchal story. The recognition that the Joseph story is an expansion of the Jacob story means not only that it deals with the same persons; it means also that the Joseph story is conscious of its roots in the tradition of the fathers.

2. Consequently, what is narrated about the lives of these people in chs. 37–45 (except chs. 39–41) agrees with what we know from chs. 12–36. The family determines the community structure; everyone is referred to in accordance with the position in the family: father, mother, son, brother. The form of the economy is the same; they are small-cattle nomads (as in chs. 25–36, part of the flocks is some distance from where the father lives). All the sons take part in this economy; the shepherds probably practice a limited agriculture at the same time. The life of the small-cattle shepherd is still as insecure as it was with their fathers; a severe famine threatens their existence (cf. 12:10-20); threat of hunger is a common motif. The group is still small enough for the father to act as chief; it does not wage war. As far as the evidence goes, the form of religion is the same as it was with the patriarchs.

3. Conflicts, as in the patriarchal stories, are between members of the family, especially between brothers. In both situations it is a question of priority; the conflicts give rise to a threat of murder and lead to division; but the division does not prevail. P. D. Miscall (1978, bibliog. above) has pointed to the parallels between chs. 37–45 and 25–36. In both cases the father assumes a merely passive role in the rivalry.

4. The Joseph story, however, differs in one very striking way from the patriarchal story—women scarcely appear in it; what happens takes place between the men. Can one conclude from this that from the monarchy on there was a shift in the equality between man and woman which we found in the patriarchal story, and to the disadvantage of the women?

7. The Origin and Growth of Genesis 37–50

It follows from what has been said about the composition and literary form of the Joseph story in the narrower sense that it is a unity; it therefore has one author. The obvious, self-contained plan in the narrative span from Gen. 37 to 45 demands this view. This is in accord with the result from chs. 25–36 where a similar narrative span joins chs. 27 to 33. This and the contemporaneous period of its origin (*Genesis 12–36*, on 27:1-45, Setting; on 33:1-20, Form, Setting) suggests that the Yahwist may be the author. But the Yahwist is not the author of the Joseph story. The exegesis will show that the working method and style are so basically different from that of J in chs. 12–36 that one must look for another author. The most important difference is that J put together his work out of narratives, genealogies, and itineraries that came down to him, and was the actual author only of certain introductory and concluding pieces, scenes, or links; but the author of the Joseph story composed a narrative in writing from the very beginning; he undoubtedly used several well known narrative motifs, but not traditional oral narratives.

This narrative, of independent origin, was inserted into the conclusion of the Jacob story and interwoven with it in chs. 37 and 46–47. Chs. 37 (material available to the redactor) and 46–50 arose, like the rest of Genesis, as a synthesis of several literary threads. This is very clear inasmuch as it is only in chs. 37 and 46–50 that P material has been worked in.

8. Parallels and Egyptian Background

1. There is no known parallel to the Joseph story as a whole, nor is one really conceivable. Parallels have been found only to single parts or motifs. Attention must be given to the type of parallel and its setting in the composition. There are possible literary parallels only for chs. 39–41, Joseph's rise in Egypt. The episode of Potiphar's wife has an explicit parallel in the Egyptian narrative of the two brothers (ANET 23-25); it gives a definite imprint to the very widespread motif of the scorned woman which has a number of points of contact with ch. 39. The agreement is in fact so extensive that the Egyptian story or a variant of it must have been known to the author of ch. 39. There is a whole series of narratives that are parallel to ch. 41, "the wise man as savior": disaster threatens a country, its king takes counsel from a wise man, the advice is followed, and the country is saved. But the parallel here is by way of outline; one cannot allege any particular narrative with a succession of details parallel to Gen. 41. There is, however, a parallel to ch. 40, namely, the common motif of a royal official who falls into disgrace, is put in prison and later restored to favor.

It follows that the Egyptian part, chs. 39–41, which has a special place in chs. 37–46, is colored by motifs known from Egypt and has, at least in ch. 39, a demonstrable literary parallel. It is different with the main narrative where the dominating motif is that of the youngest son who rises to power and eminence. This motif is so well known the world over in tales and narratives, and so frequent, even in the Old Testament, as to render any theory of literary borrowing superfluous. The points of contact between the story of David in 1 Sam. 16 and the Joseph story are striking; but no one would think of mutual dependence. The motif has two characteristics: the younger brother overshadows the elder (e.g., Gen. 48:12-20) and the youngest his elders. The former characterizes the Jacob-Esau story, the latter the Joseph story; aspects of the same motif in each are an indicator of the intention of the composition. It emerges clearly that the framework of chs. 37–46 is a family narrative; the main motif centers around a family relationship.

Two motifs, both widespread and both found in the Old Testament, particularly in the patriarchal story, serve to join the framework of chs. 37–46 with the central part, chs. 39–41. This is done very skillfully on both counts and is typical of the author of the Joseph story. One motif is that of the dream. The dream structure of declaration-realization forms a profound link between the life-style of the family and the kingdom; it can have significance equally in the family (ch. 37), for the courtiers (ch. 40), and for the king himself (ch. 41). Moreover, a divine power is seen or hinted at in the dreams. It is the same sustaining power that is at work in the family as well as in a monarch's kingdom. The other motif is that of famine, very important in the patriarchal story (12:10-20). It is one and the same famine that threatens Pharaoh's kingdom and is averted through Joseph's gift of divining dreams, and brings Joseph's brothers to Egypt. The result is not only to preserve Jacob's family, but also to bring it together again.

2. The Egyptian background: The scene of the action of the Joseph story in chs. 39–50 is Egypt, a fact in itself surprising. One can understand why a number of scholars have come to the conclusion that it is a short story of the diaspora like Esther. The beginning of Exodus is the point of departure: it is in Egypt that the history of the people of Israel starts. What is amazing is the completely positive and friendly portrayal of the Egyptian people and the approval of the fact that one of Israel's fathers was an important man at Pharaoh's court. This is best understood from the period of Solomon when the young Israelite monarchy had friendly relations with the Egyptian court and there was a brisk cultural exchange between them. This too is the source of the lively interest in a foreign land, its people, and its royal court.

There is no narrative in the Old Testament that reflects so immediately and vividly acquaintance with and wonder at a foreign land. The interest centers around the Pharaoh's court; in accordance with the character of the portrayal, the Pharaoh is not named. It is striking that there is no mention of the magnificent buildings, either temples or palaces. The interest is not in the architecture but rather in the institutions: Pharaoh's officers, their titles, investiture with robe, ring, and chain, court ceremonial, the king's birthday and his titles, the courtiers, priests, the chief administrator, Joseph's position and all that pertains to it. As an Egyptian official of high rank he even has magical abilities at his disposal. It is also appropriate to a court in the broad sense that there is a prison, that an official who has fallen into disgrace can be held there and brood on his fate which depends on the nod of the king. Foreigners who come to the court can receive gifts, but can also fall under suspicion as spies. Reverence for dignitaries goes beyond death by means of embalming, as one learned with amazement.

The portrayal gives the impression of a first encounter. Everything that is narrated is new to the narrator and his listeners. There is no sign of any anxiety to preserve what one has against what is foreign or any condemnation of the foreigner. The brief remark that Egyptians may not eat at table with foreigners (43:32; cf. 46:34) can only be made by those who do not know such a custom. The note fits the period of Solomon well, but is impossible for the period of the exile (against D. B. Redford and A. Meinhold).

Talk about commerce and economics is marginal. Merchants with rare spices come from Palestine to Egypt and Semitic slaves are sold to the Egyptians. There is familiarity with agriculture, viticulture, rich harvests, and a developed money economy. But there can be famine even in a land as fertile and well watered as Egypt if the Nile fails to flood. Faced with the possibility of famines, which are a much greater threat in Palestine, interest gathers around the policy of supply which the kingdom sets in operation. The foreign Egyptian comes even closer to the listener with words and proper names belonging to the Egyptian language which are often linked with rites and institutions. Reflection on the phenomenon of a foreign language is apparent in the understanding of the function of interpreters. It is only natural that the narrator's knowledge in this area is still rather restricted, that much of what is reported is inaccurate, and that many of the connections are Israelite or Semitic in general. ". . .He was not writing in Egypt for Egyptians. He wrote from the vantage-point of a Palestinian who was fascinated by his country's powerful neighbour" (R. de Vaux *The Early History*. . . 1 [1971; Eng. 1978] 301). The impression of neighboring Egypt which the narrator gives comes above all from the experience of a simple family of small-cattle breeders with no property which comes to Egypt and is exposed to all this, not knowing that one of them, a brother, has become an important official at court.

Joseph and His Brothers

Literature

Genesis 37: H. Seebass, *Der Erzvater Israel und die Einführung der Jahweverehrung in Kanaan*, BZAW 98 (1966) esp. 45f. M. Anbar, "Changement des noms des tribus nomades dans la relation d'un même événement," Bib 49 (1968) 221-232.

Genesis 37:1-4: R. Gordis, "The Text and Meaning of Hosea XIV 3," VT 5 (1955) 88-90. F. C. Fensham, "A Cappadocian Parallel to Hebrew *KUTŌNET*," VT 12 (1962) 196-198. L. Wächter, "Überlegungen zur Umnennung von *Pašḥur* in *Māgor Missābīb* in Jeremia 20,3," ZAW 74 (1962) 57-62. M. Weiss, "Einiges über die Bauformen des Erzählens in der Bibel," VT 13 (1963) 456-475. T. H. Gaster, *Myth, Legend and Custom in the OT* (1969) 215-222. C. Westermann, "Der Frieden (Shalom) im AT," *Studien zur Friedensforschung* 1 (1969) 144-177. J. Scharbert, "Der Sinn der Toledot-Formel in der Priesterschrift," Fests. W. Eichrodt (1970) 45-56. W. J. Peck, "Note on Genesis 37,2 and Joseph's Character," ET 82 (1970/71) 342f. R. E. Bee, "The Use of Statistical Methods in OT Studies," VT 23 (1973) 257-272. F. M. Cross, *Canaanite Myth and Hebrew Epic: Essays in the History of the Religion of Israel* (1973) esp. 304.

Genesis 37:5-17: T. K. Cheyne, "Occurrences of גער in the OT," ZAW 31 (1911) 315. J. Goettsberger, "Zu Genesis 37,9-11," MVÄG 22 (1917) 71-78. P. Jensen, *Die Joseph-Träume*, BZAW 33 (1918) 233-245. S. Thompson, *Motif-Index of Folk-Literature* V (1935; 1957²), "Dream of Future Greatness," 43. M. Cassirer, "The Date of the Elohist in the Light of Genesis XXXVII 9," JThS 50 (1949) 173f. E. L. Ehrlich, *Der Traum im Alten Testament*, BZAW 73 (1953). A. L. Oppenheim, "The Interpretation of Dreams in the Ancient Near East," TAPhS 46 (1956) 179-373. W. Richter, "Traum und Traumdeutung im AT: Ihre Form und Verwendung," BZ NF 7 (1963) 202-220. A. Finkel, "The Pesher of Dreams and Scriptures," RevQ 4 (1963/64) 357-370. A. Resch, *Der Traum im Heilsplan Gottes: Deutung und Bedeutung des Traums im AT* (1964). A. A. MacIntosh, "A Consideration of Hebrew גער," VT 19 (1969) 471-479. S. C. Reif, "A Note on גער," VT 21 (1971) 241-244. B. O. Long, "Prophetic Call Traditions and Reports of Visions," ZAW 84 (1972) 494-500. J. Van Seters, "The Terms 'Amorite' and 'Hittite' in the OT," VT 22 (1972) 64-81, esp. 75f. K. Jaroš, *Die Stellung des Elohisten zur kanaanäischen Religion* (1974). S. Zeitlin, "Dreams and Their Interpretation from the Biblical Period to the Tannaitic Time: An Historical Study," JQR 66 (1975/76) 1-18. M. Duvshani, "The Dreams of Joseph" [in Hebr.], BethM 4 (1976) 557-565. C. Grottanelli, "Giuseppe nel pozzo, I. Un antico tema mitico in Gen. 37,12-24 in R VI 105," OrAnt 17 (1978) 107-122. H. Seebass, "Der israelitische Name der Bucht von *Bēsān* und der Name Beth Schean," ZDPV 95 (1979) 166-172.

Genesis 37:18-28: E. Bublitz, "Ruben, Issakar und Sebulon in den israelitischen Genealogien," ZAW 33 (1913) 241-250. R. Rendtorff and K. Koch, *Studien zur Theologie der alttestamentlichen Überlieferungen* (1961). K. Koch, "Der Spruch 'Sein Blut bleibe auf seinem Haupt' und die israelitische Auffassung vom vergossenen Blut," VT 12 (1962) 396-416. P. P. Saydon, "The Conative Imperfect in Hebrew," VT 12 (1962) 124-126. M. Weiss, "Weiteres über die Bauformen des Erzählens in der Bibel," Bib 46 (1965) 181-206. G. W. Ahlström, "אדר VT 17 (1967) 1-7. S. E. Loewenstamm, "Ruben und Juda im Joseph-Zyklus" [in Hebr.], *4th World Congress of Jewish Studies 1* (1967) 69f. O. Eissfeldt, "Protektorat der Midianiter über ihre Nachbarn im letzten Viertel des 2. Jt. v. Chr.," JBL 87 (1968) 383-393. R. Bergmeier, "Das Streben nach Gewinn—des Volkes עון," ZAW 81 (1969) 93-97. G. W. Coats, "Self-Abasement and Insult Formulas," JBL 89 (1970) 14-26. J. P. Brown, "Peace Symbolism in Ancient Military Vocabulary," VT 21 (1971) 1-23. O. Keel, "Erwägungen zum Sitz im Leben des vormosaischen Pascha und zur Etymologie von פסח," ZAW 84 (1972) 414-434. S. Gevirtz, "Of Patriarchs and Puns: Joseph at the Fountain, Jacob at the Ford," HUCA 46 (1975) 33-54. H. Klein, "Verbot des Menschendiebstahls im Dekalog? Prüfung einer These A. Alts," VT 26 (1976) 161-169. W. H. Schmidt, "Jahwe in Ägypten," *Kairos* 1 (1976) 43-54 esp. 51. H. Christ, *Blutvergiessen im AT: Der gewaltsame Tod des Menschen untersucht am Wort dām,* Th.Diss 12 (1977).

Genesis 37:29-36: W. F. Otto, *Die Manen oder von der Urform des Totenglaubens* (1923; 1958²). L. Koehler, "Alttestamentliche Wortforschung," ThZ 2 (1946) 71-74. F. V. Winnett, "A Brief Comment on Genesis 37,32," BCSBS 12 (1947) 13. C. Kuhl, "Die 'Wiederaufnahme'—ein literarkritisches Prinzip?" ZAW 64 (1952) 1-11. Y. M. Grintz, "Potifar—the Chief Cook," *Lesbonenu* 30 (1965) 12-15. E. Kutsch, "'Trauerbräuche' und 'Selbstminderungsriten' im AT," ThSt 78 (1965) 23-42. J. C. de Moor, "Studies in the New Alphabetic Text from Ras Shamra, I," UF 1 (1969) 167-188. H. Gese, "Die Religion Altsyriens, Altarabiens und der Mandäer," *Die Religionen der Menschheit* 10,2 (1970).

Text

37:1 Now Jacob settled in the land where his father had sojourned, the land of Canaan.[a]

2 This is the story of Jacob. When Joseph was seventeen years old he was guarding[ab] sheep with his brothers; he was an assistant to the sons of his father's wives Bilhah and Zilpah and he brought a bad report[c] about them to his father.

3 Israel loved Joseph more than any of his other sons because he was a child of his old age; and made[a] him a sleeved tunic.

4 When his brothers saw that their father loved him more than them they hated him and could not so much as greet[a] him.[b]

5 Joseph had a dream; when he told it to his brothers [they hated him more].[a]

6 He said to them, Listen to the dream that I have had!

7 See, we were binding sheaves[a] outside in the field and my sheaf rose up and stood upright, while your sheaves gathered round and bowed down before mine.

8 His brothers said to him, Are you going to be[a] king over us and lord it over us? And so they hated him still more because of his dreams and what he had said.

9 And he had yet another dream which[a] he told to his brothers, See, I have had another dream: the sun and the moon and eleven stars were bowing down before me.

10 [a]When he told it to his father and his brothers,[a] his father rebuked him[b] and said to him, What is this dream that you have had? Am I and your mother and your brothers to bow down to the ground before you?

11 So his brothers were incensed at him; but his father pondered the matter.

12 His brothers had gone to pasture their father's sheep at Shechem.

13 Israel said to Joseph, Your brothers are minding the sheep at Shechem; come, I will send you to them. He said, I am ready.

14 Go then, he said, and see if all is well with your brothers and the sheep and bring me back word. So he sent him out of the valley of Hebron, and he came to Shechem.

15 A man met him as he was wandering in the fields and asked him, What are you looking for?

16 I am looking for my brothers, he said; tell me, please, where they are minding the flocks.

17 The man said to him, They have moved on from here. In fact I heard them[a] say, let us go on to Dothan. So Joseph went after his brothers and found them at Dothan.

18 When they saw him in the distance, and before he drew near to them, they plotted against him[a] to kill him.

19 They said to each other, Here comes this[a] dream-addict;[b]

20 now is our chance to kill him and throw him into one of these cisterns; we will say that a wild animal has eaten him! Then we shall see what use his dreams are.

21 When Reuben heard this, he tried to save[a] him from their hands and said, We must not take his life.[b]

22 [And Reuben said to them,][a] Do not shed blood! Throw him into this cistern in the wilderness, but do not lay a hand on him.[b] He planned to save him from their hands and restore him to his father.

23 Now when Joseph came up to them they took off his tunic[a] (the sleeved tunic that he was wearing).[b]

24 They took hold of him and threw him into the cistern; the cistern was empty; there was no water in it.

25a Then they sat down to eat.

25b [When they looked up, they saw a caravan of Ishmaelites coming from Gilead on their way down to Egypt with their camels carrying gum, balm, and resin.

26 Judah said to his brothers, What is to be gained[a] by killing our brother and covering up[b] his blood?

27 Come, let us sell him to the Ishmaelites and not lay our hands on him; after all, he is our brother, our own flesh! And the brothers agreed (with him).]

28a Meanwhile some Midianite merchants passed by and drew Joseph out of the cistern.

28b [They sold Joseph to the Ishmaelites for twenty silver pieces[a] and they brought Joseph down to Egypt.]

29 When Reuben came back to the cistern, Joseph was no longer in it.

30 Reuben tore his garments, went back to his brothers and said, The boy is not there! And I—where do I turn?[ab]

31 Then they took Joseph's tunic, slaughtered a goat, and dipped his tunic in the blood.

32 Then they [sent the sleeved tunic[a]] brought it to their father and said: We have found this. Do you recognize it? Is it your son's tunic or not?

33 He recognized it and said, My son's tunic[a]! A wild animal has eaten him! Joseph has been torn to pieces!

34 Then Jacob tore his garments and put sackcloth about his loins and mourned his son for many days.

35 His sons and daughters[a] tried to console him, but he would not be con-

soled and said, No, I will go down mourning to my son in the realm of the dead.[b] Thus his father wept for him.

36 Meanwhile 'the Midianites'[a] sold him [Joseph] in Egypt to Potiphar, one of Pharaoh's chamberlains, head of the bodyguard.

1a On the syntax of v. 1, L. Koehler, "Syntactica IV," VT 3 (1953) 290-305.
2ab On the construction, BrSynt §103a; רעה as 1 Sam. 16:11.   **c** On דבה, R. Gordis, VT 5 (1955) 88-90; cf. Num. 13:22; 14:36,37.
3a Not, "he often had him made. . .''; Ges-K §112h,i; correctly, Sam and Gk, ויעש.
4a On the unusual suffix in דברו, Ges-K 115c.   **b** שלום Gen. 29:6; 37:4; 37:14; 41:16; 43:23,27; 44:17.
5a The last four words are missing in the Gk; they are an addition.
7a Cf. Ps. 126:4.
8a The inf. abs. serves to strengthen questions; Ges-K §113q; BrSynt §93a.
9a Gk inserts: "to his father and. . .''
10a a—a, missing in Gk.   **b** גער, A. A. McIntosh (1969), S. C. Reif (1971), see bibliog. above.
17a Read שְׁמָעֳתִּים with Sam and Gk.
18a On the form, Ges-K §117w.
19a הלזה, as in Gen. 24:65.   **b** For this use of בעל Ges-K §128u; BrSynt §74b.
21a On the imperf. conative, P. P. Saydon, VT 12 (1962) 124-126.   **b** Double accus., Ges-K §117ll; BrSynt §94c.
22a The first three words are missing in Gk, probably an addition.   **b** As in Gen. 27:12.
23a On the double accus. Ges-K §117cc.   **b** Text uncertain; the last five words are probably an addition (D. B. Redford).
26a On בצע, H. Bergmeier, ZAW 81 (1969) 93-97.   **b** Covering blood, K. Koch, VT 12 (1962) 396-416.
28a Details of weights and measures which are taken for granted are often omitted, BrSynt §85e.
30a Compound sentence Ges-K §143a.   **b** Participle as predicate in a deliberative sentence, Ges-K §116p.
32a "Sent" stands in contradiction to "brought." A number of solutions have been proposed. D. B. Redford: "they sent the ample tunic" is an addition.
33a The addition of היא in Sam, Gk, and Syr is quite out of place; an exclamation, not a statement is intended.
35a Gk adds καὶ ἦλθον = וַיָּבוֹאוּ   **b** On שאל, L. Koehler, ThZ 2 (1946) 71-74; W. Baumgartner, ThZ 2 (1946) 233-235.
36a Following v. 28, read וְהַמְּדָיָנִים; cf. BHS.

Form

Ch. 37 forms the introduction to the Joseph story (Gen. 37; 39–45f.). There was once an independent narrative behind ch. 37, as is clear from vv. 1-2 which introduce P's conclusion to the Jacob story; this is continued in ch. 46 and in the transition, v. 36, which is in partial agreement with 39:1. There are points of contact in content, as the exegesis will demonstrate. It is not possible to reconstruct the narrative behind Gen. 37; one can only say that it was part of the Jacob tradition and dealt with a conflict within Jacob's family. Gen. 25–36 dealt with a conflict between brothers; the present narrative differs in that the participants in the conflict are the father, the brothers, and one from their number. Ch. 37 in its present form has become the introduction to the Joseph story and forms an independent part within it, carefully worked into the whole, and divided into three scenes (with a transition) in which the locale changes each time. The distinct symmetrical structure of the Joseph story appears here; the threefold division of scenes in the introduction (ch. 37) corresponds to that of the narrative as a whole:

Father's house	Fields	Father's House
Canaan (ch. 37)	Egypt (chs. 39–45)	Canaan (chs. 46–50, in part)

The first (vv. 3-11) and third (vv. 31-35) scenes take place between the father, the brothers, and Joseph; the second in the fields (after the transition in vv. 12-17) between the brothers and Joseph (vv. 18-20). The distribution of the actors in the three parts is almost the same as in the whole narrative.

The first scene (vv. 3-11) narrates the estrangement of Joseph from his brothers; the family peace is shattered. The reason given in v. 3 is sufficient for this; v. 12 could follow on v. 4. Following the narrative law of the single strand (*Einlinigkeit*, H. Gunkel) it is to be assumed that this was the only cause of the conflict in the underlying story. The further cause, the dreams in vv. 5-11, are not a necessary part of the original narrative that stands behind ch. 37, though they are of the Joseph story as a whole in which they form one of the determining motifs (two dreams on three occasions).

The second scene, vv. 18-20, narrates the crime of the brothers, the result of their hatred, v. 3. The narrator has deliberately woven two threads together here for the benefit of the listener or reader; there are clearly two different narrative courses, each of which even has a different set of names: Reuben/Judah, Ishmaelites/Midianites. The narrator makes clear to his readers, who likewise know the variants in the patriarchal narratives, that he is picking up two variants of this part of the narrative available to him. He is guided by the concern we meet everywhere in Genesis to preserve the traditional variants of the patriarchal story. He may perhaps have had a further purpose with this duplication; cf. comm. on vv. 28a, 29, 30ff.

The third scene, vv. 31-35, a unity like the first, narrates the brothers' attempt to cover up their crime by deceiving their father with an alleged misfortune.

The section "Setting" drops out in the individual chapters of the Joseph story because it is a matter of parts of a single narrative whole (see above, Intro.).

Commentary

[37:1-2] Vv. 1-2, introduction (P; corresponding to Gen. 25:19-20). The text consists of three parts: transition (v. 1), title to the conclusion of the Joseph story (the separating *toledoth* formula) (v. 2aα), and the beginning of a narrative about Joseph which breaks off after the first sentence (v. 2aβb).

The information about Jacob's dwelling place follows immediately on 36:8 in P (note about Esau's dwelling place). Whereas Edom becomes Esau's possession, Canaan remains "the land where his father sojourned" (as in 17:8; 28:4; 36:7; 47:9; Ex. 6:4; cf. L. Wächter, ZAW 74 [1962] 57-62). The sentence forms a transition; it concludes in P the story of Jacob and Esau by means of the contrast 36:8/37:1 and at the same time provides the passage to the conclusion of the Jacob story. There is an almost word-for-word correspondence in 47:27a.

[**37:2**] The introductory formula corresponds to 36:1; ch. 36 gives genealogical data only about Esau and his descendants; the story of Jacob begins anew with a narrative about his son. This *toledoth* of Jacob continues right up to his death and burial. P's narrative about Joseph begins as often in P with details about age: "When Joseph was seventeen years old. . .." This, together with the two following sentences, forms the exposition. It says first that Joseph at this age was a shepherd among the flocks with his brothers; this was in accord with the life-style of the fathers. The words immediately following, נער והוא, would be meaningless as an independent sentence "and he was (still) young" after the details about his age; they could be understood only as a gloss—which would be difficult to explain. They are to be linked, therefore, with what follows and נער is to be understood as (attendant-) boy, assistant, or apprentice shepherd as in Ex. 33:11 (F. Delitzsch, B. Jacob, G. von Rad, and others). This second sentence, that Joseph was there helping the sons of Bilhah and Zilpah (namely, Dan and Naphtali, Gad and Asher), leads into the main part of the narrative. The report that Joseph brought to Jacob did not concern all the brothers but only the four sons of Jacob's secondary wives. This then has nothing to do with the hatred of the brothers in vv. 3-11, but concerns the continuation of the rivalry between Jacob's wives (chs. 29–30) in their sons, the rivalry between the mistresses and the maidservants. דבה denotes a bad report in the story of the scouts in Num. 14:37; the scouts had something bad to say about the land. The suffix here can only mean that something bad was said about them. However, it cannot be concluded whether the bad report about the sons of the maidservants was justified or not; nor can Joseph's role be determined with certainty. Joseph's action in the context of vv. 1-2 together with vv. 3ff. is to be understood as an act of tale-bearing by which he wanted to make himself important. But this is unlikely in P who elsewhere plays down or ignores the conflict between the brothers; it is possible that in the original narrative Joseph wanted to act as mediator between the brothers (G. Jacob, E. I. Lowenthal). The narrative breaks off here (cf. 35:22). In the present context the fragment serves as substitute for the exposition.

[**37:3-4**] Vv. 3-4 narrate the circumstances that gave rise to the series of events that follow. These verses do not follow easily on v. 2. We find here the suture between the beginning of the Joseph story and the exposition which the narrator takes over from the Jacob story. The exposition needed only to introduce the family of Jacob in which the subsequent events took place. It would be better if the list of sons in 36:22b-26 followed the introductory words אלה תלדות יעקב of v. 2; according to K. Budde, R. Smend, J. Skinner, O. Procksch, J. Scharbert, and others the list was subsequently displaced after ch. 35.

Vv. 3-4 correspond to the narratives of the patriarchal story in form, style, and content. The passage is certainly a unity; it could come from J, from whom the narrator of the Joseph story could have taken it over unaltered.

[**37:3**] The change of name from Jacob (vv. 1-2, P) to Israel (v. 3, also in v. 13) can be explained from the narrative that was taken over; it was perhaps deliberate on the part of the redactor (who joined vv. 1-2 with vv. 3ff.) in order to make known the other voice that is now speaking (H. Donner, "The reasons for the change are not obvious," *Die Literarische Gestalt. . .* [1976] 39; G. W. Coats, *From Canaan to Egypt. . .* [1976] 9). The story tells of the predilection of the fa-

ther for his youngest son, the reason being that the boy was a child of his old age.
Gen. 25:28 also tells of the predilection of parents for one of the sons. The narrator accepts this reality without making any judgment. "Predilection" is not to be
understood here in a quantative sense; the reason for it is that Joseph "is a child of
his old age." When a man's life span is drawing to a close and a child is born to
him, then this is something different from the situation of a young man at the
height of his strength; the relationship to the child is something special. It would
be foolish to issue moral judgments here. The narrator reveals the significance of
this human phenomenon by introducing it at the beginning of his narrative, which
proceeds in a succession of highs and lows. But it is not the father's predilection
for Joseph that arouses the brothers' hatred; it is something else. Jacob presents
Joseph with a distinctive garment; it is this that gives rise to open conflict. כתנת
פסים does not mean "a coat of many colors" (Luther, following Gk and Vg), but
a sleeved tunic or a "tunic reaching to the extremities" (wrists and ankles)
(KBL). In 2 Sam. 13:18 it is the apparel of a princess. The garment then is not
only a fine present from the father to his beloved son; it also sets Joseph apart from
his brothers; the consequence of predilection is preference. The predilection becomes public and so the father shares the blame for the conflict that it unlooses.

With the present of the sleeved tunic the narrator introduces the motif of
the garment which he continues throughout the narrative. This presupposes the
great social significance of dress; for thousands of years it has been one of the
most striking and powerful indications of social rank. Not only the dreams, but
also the present of the garment is a matter that concerns Joseph's position with regard to his brothers.

[**37:4**] "When his brothers saw. . ." (v. 4) marks the transition from predilection to preference that gives rise to the subsequent events. The father's predilection, having now given way to preference, evokes the brothers' hatred: "they
hated him," or "they became hostile to him." The Hebrew verb שׂנא does not
mean a state or attitude but an act. Hatred directed toward someone is like the
strain in a bow; the resolution of the tension must issue into action. It is striking
that the brothers direct their hatred toward Joseph and not toward their father. The
narrator shows here a profound understanding of the human condition. He touches
on an experience that he can presuppose in his hearers: the hatred of the one
slighted is often directed not toward the one who favors unjustly, but toward the
one favored. Cain does not direct his hatred against God who preferred Abel to
him, but against Abel, in respect of whom he had been slighted.

The text of the last sentence of v. 4 is not certain. One should probably
read דַּבֶּר לוֹ with the Gk instead of דַּבְּרוֹ. But the meaning is clear: the brothers
could not bring themselves to greet him in a friendly way. Thus is expression giv-
en to the rupture of fellowship between the brothers and Joseph. Even today the
refusal to greet means the rupture of fellowship; at that time the greeting had much
more significance. It is the greeting of welcome and farewell, the inquiry after
one's health, that maintains intact the שׁלום of the community (C. Westermann, in
Studien zur Friedenforschung 1 [1969] 144-177). The peace of the house of Jacob
has been shattered. Can it be restored?

[**37:5-11**] Joseph's dreams (vv. 5-11): The narrator of the Joseph story, following
his principle of doubling, has added a second motif to the one that sets the drama

37

in motion; for him it both determines and holds together the narrative as a whole. Not only do pairs of dreams recur in chs. 40 and 41 (leading to Joseph's eleva- tion), but they also contain the element of tension—announcement- realization—that keeps the narrative moving vividly from scene to scene. Such an extensive and complicated narrative structure as found in the dream series (two dreams three times) never occurs in J; it is peculiar to the narrator of the Joseph story. So too is the heightening from the first to the third pair. The first has its set- ting in the family; the dreamer is the shepherd boy, the audience his father and brothers. The simple, basic character of the dream accords with this; it needs nei- ther explanation nor interpreter; its meaning is clear to all involved. It is the first dream that is really determinative; the second merely intensifies and expands; it is also much shorter. The three parties stand out in clear relief in the narration of the dreams: the father, the brothers, Joseph.

One can say with certainty that the reason for the brothers' hatred in vv. 3-4 belongs to the tradition available to the narrator of the Joseph story; the dreams in vv. 5-11 are his own work because they point to the future, to Joseph's eleva- tion which is unfolded in chs. 39–41.

[37:5-8] Vv. 5-6 are introductory and announce the dream; v. 7 presents the dream itself and v. 8 the reaction of the brothers. Both language and style are highly artistic: Joseph's childish boasting as he narrates his dream, the brothers' testy reaction, and in the background the sharp contrast in the matter at issue. Jo- seph describes the dream in rhythmic, almost choreographic language, regulated by verbs and with a recurrent הנה. He is full of his dream which compels him to tell it to his brothers. In contrast, his brothers' reply is a cool, almost threatening question—two verbs in closely knit parallelism marking the climax. The dream is divided into an exposition (v. 7a) and the twofold action of rising up ("mine") and bowing down ("yours"). V. 7a presupposes that the brothers have been at work in the fields bringing in the harvest; small-cattle shepherds engaged sporadi- cally in agriculture. Joseph's dream speaks for itself and needs no explanation. The brothers understood at once: it can only mean that he will rule over them, be their king: משל and מלך mean the same. The brothers state what it is all about; a brother—and he the youngest—is to rule over his brothers. It is the basic question of man (a brother) ruling over his equals (brothers), a question which agitated Is- rael in the period of the rise of the monarchy (C. Westermann, *Die Josepherzählung der Genesis*, CPH 5,1 [1966]; F. Crüsemann, WMANT 49 [1978]). It is a social order that stands in opposition to the community order of the family where the only authority is parental. The brothers (and the father too in vv. 9-11) represent the old order which they see threatened by their youngest brother's arrogance arising from his dream. The question of kingship is only hinted at, but it runs on through the narrative. Joseph has no idea what his dream has stirred; he re- mains prepossessed by his childish aspiration.

The background to the young man's dreams is a motif in narratives and tales that is very common and widespread, namely, the younger (youngest) brother overshadows the elder (older brothers). H. Gunkel and H. Gressmann provide a number of examples. D. B. Redford, pp. 88f., makes a valuable contribution by distinguishing in the motif the younger/elder aspect and the youngest/older brothers aspect. The author here reveals his technique in arranging the material, thought out to the last detail: he inserts his own Joseph story into the Jacob tradition available to him, thereby adding his motif (youngest/older brothers) to the motif of the Jacob-Esau story (younger/elder brother).

The sentence v. 8b, "And they hated him still more," is intended to join vv. 5-11 with vv. 3-4 (D. B. Redford maintains that the words are a gloss, p. 29). It comes too early here because of the plural, "because of his dreams." F. Delitzsch explains the further addition, "and because of what he had said," as "because of the brash frankness with which he spoke to them."

[37:9-11] Joseph's second dream supplements the first by including the parents as well. It is described in a single image, v. 9bβ. There are eleven stars, each corresponding to one of the brothers—not a constellation. Any mythical meaning, which a number of exegetes see here, is remote. What is stressed is the father's reaction; he is shocked and angry and rejects as sharply as the brothers the reversal of the social order that the dream threatens. Nevertheless he "ponders the matter" (as Lk. 2:19); it is a dream which can be of some significance for the future. But it is as secular as the narrative as a whole (the narrator anticipates the continuation of the narrative); there is not a word about any communication from God to Joseph in the dream.

On dreams in general, cf. lit. above. G. W. Coats, *From Canaan to Egypt* (1976) 14f., correctly criticizing W. Richter, notes in reference to the Joseph story that one must be cautious of any sort of schematization of the dreams. The author has amalgamated the dreams with his story in such a way that they can be explained only out of the context in which they now stand.

[37:12-17] A transition (vv. 12-17): Jacob sends Joseph to his brothers. What is narrated here could follow directly on vv. 3-4; nothing would be lost from the progress of the narrative. Thus it becomes even clearer that the narrator of the Joseph story has here inserted into his narrative the pervading motif of the dreams.

The next principal scene in the fields with the brothers is expanded in the transition vv. 12-17 inasmuch as the protagonists—the father, the brothers, Joseph—who in vv. 1-11 were together in Jacob's house, are now separated. The brothers have gone with the flocks to a distant pasture near Shechem (cf. chs. 30f.), while Joseph stays with his father (v. 12). After some time Jacob sends Joseph to the brothers to inquire after their well-being and that of the herds (vv. 13-14). Joseph does not find them at Shechem but, after inquiry, at Dothan (vv. 15-17). Most exegetes now accept the unity of vv. 12-17.

[37:12-14] Vv. 12-14 are the preparation for a meeting between Joseph and his brothers outside their father's domain; it is only there that the brothers' hate can be realized in action. Jacob has no idea of the danger to which he is exposing his son through the commission he gives him. Joseph accepts it; he goes to inquire after the well-being of his brothers and the flocks and bring news to his father (vv. 13-14). The word שלום is used twice (cf. 29:6); it is one of the key words in the Joseph narrative. It intimates that what should serve the interests of the peace leads to its being shattered. The animals are also included in the prosperity (שלום) of the community; it is on their well-being that that of the people depends.

In v. 13 Jacob first asks his son if he is prepared to undertake the commission; Joseph says he is ready. He too without apprehension falls in with the proposal. The location, from the valley of Hebron (sing.), is very striking because of its distance from Shechem. H. Seebass proposes an emendation to "plain of Rehabon" (ZAW 90 [1978] 196-219); others explain the difficulty by means of source division. It is more likely that v. 14b is an already independent itinerary note which originally did not belong in this context (D. B. Redford maintains that it is a gloss, p. 28; also H. C. Schmitt, p. 26).

Geographical details in ch. 37 have caused exegetes many difficulties (cf. earlier commentaries; more recently D. B. Redford, pp. 143-145; "The Locale of the E Author"; H. C. Schmitt, pp. 29-31). The difficulties of the various locales are usually solved by means of two sources or layers. However, it is to be noted that such localization is almost entirely missing in the rest of the Joseph story (46:1-7 is part of the conclusion of the Jacob story). It is to be concluded that the geographical details in ch. 37 stem from the material at hand in which one must reckon with the possibility of variants. These details have been fused into the introduction to the Joseph story and adapted in the process in such a way that their original context has not been retained; hence no conclusion can be drawn from them.

[37:15-17] This brief and vividly portrayed interlude, vv. 15-17, is meant to show how helpless Joseph is in the open, far from his father. It is of no avail to him that he is the preferred son; protection does not extend so far. He is helpless because he does not find the brothers at the place assigned; a man sees his perplexity, inquires what is the matter, and shows him the way. Now he is even further from his father. Dothan is about 12 km. from Shechem, and Joseph meets his brothers there.

[37:18-30] The brothers' deed (vv. 18-30): The brothers see Joseph coming and attack him with intent to murder (vv. 21-22). Reuben wants to prevent this and to save Joseph, so he implores the brothers not to kill him but to throw him into a cistern (vv. 23-25). As soon as Joseph arrives the brothers seize him, take off his tunic, throw him into a cistern, and sit down to eat. While they are eating, some Midianite merchants pass by, take Joseph out of the cistern, and bring him to Egypt (v. 28). Reuben then returns to the cistern and finds that Joseph is no longer there. This is a unified and self-contained course of events.

A variant, vv. 25b, 26, 27, 28b, is inserted into this narrative: the brothers see a caravan of Ishmaelites coming (v. 25b). So Judah advises the brothers to sell Joseph to them in order to prevent them from committing fratricide (vv. 26, 27a). His brothers listen to him (v. 27b), and sell Joseph to the Ishmaelites. We most certainly have a narrative variant here. Three considerations confirm this view: It is an obvious doublet with a cohesive course of events: the intention of the brothers, motivation, advice given to them, heed of the advice, Joseph goes to Egypt. The names of the brothers and the description of the caravan vary. It is scarcely possible for a variant to be so clearly defined. The narrator of the Joseph story obviously intends to let his listeners know that he has at his disposal two versions of how Joseph came down to Egypt and will let both speak. This explanation is confirmed by 40:15 and 45:4 where in retrospect it is left an open question how Joseph came down.

[37:18-20] The plot to murder (vv. 18-20): As soon as the brothers see Joseph coming (v. 18a), their hatred again flares up (v. 4). Now he is in their power and they decide to kill him (v. 18b). This plot is unfolded in vv. 19-20. First, all of them participate (v. 19a). Their hatred is given expression in their cry, "Here comes this dream-addict [or master dreamer]!" The narrator here, as in v. 23, skillfully joins the two motifs of the tunic (vv. 3-4) and the dreams (vv. 5-11). V.

20 comprises the quick decision of the brothers as Joseph approaches. They must be unanimous in their murderous plot and in their plan to conceal the murder; they will throw the corpse into a cistern and allege a disaster. They thus intend to destroy the dreams and his dreams. This is a common motif.

[37:21-22] Reuben opposes the plot. He tries (conative imperf.) to rescue Joseph from their power. He urges his brothers; the language shows his excitement. He wants to persuade them not to kill Joseph but only throw him into a cistern; for the moment he can do no more. He wants in any case to prevent murder, hence the accumulation of phrases לא נכנו נפש (as in Deut. 22:26), אל־תשפכו־דם, ''predominantly for the violent shedding of human blood, Gen. 9:6; Lev. 17:4,'' R. Rendtorff and K. Koch, *Studien zur Theologie der alttestamentlichen Überlieferungen* (1961) 145ff., and יד אל תשלחו־בו; cf. 22:12. The repeated ויאמר in vv. 21b and 22 is difficult; the first three words of vv. 22 are probably an addition. Reuben's plan to rescue Joseph is repeated once more at the end of v. 22, together with his intention ''to restore him to his father.'' Reuben thus exercises the function of the eldest brother. In the patriarchal period when groups or parts of the family were away from the father, the eldest present took over the role of the father when it was necessary; he bore responsibility for this limited time. When the group returned home, he had to answer the father's questions.

> Our notion of *responsibility* has its origin in such circumstances in an early form of society. It is a quite simple and uncomplicated concept. There is one who has to answer. Such responsibility does not arise from a sense or consciousness of responsibility, but from the fact that he is the one who has to answer. ''Only Reuben, the eldest, thinks of his father'' (B. Jacob). Language makes clear the significance of the difference between the younger and elder brothers in early civilization; many languages, e.g., Hungarian and Chinese, only have a word for the older and younger brother, and not one for brothers in general (F. Tschirsch).

[37:23-25a] As soon as the unsuspecting Joseph comes up to the brothers, they strip him of the detested tunic, seize him, and throw him into an empty cistern. They do not carry out the murder they planned; to that extent they heeded Reuben. But it is clear what will become of Joseph. He cannot get out of the cistern by himself. It is striking that there is not a word about any reaction on Joseph's part, though 42:21 says in retrospect that Joseph begged his brothers. The narrator shows his skill in that the mention of it in 42:21 has a function (M. Weiss, Bib 46 [1965] 202), whereas here it has not, inasmuch as it is part of crime to shut one's eyes to the suffering and pleas of the victim. The narrator trusts that his hearers will understand. The pause that follows is a necessary preparation for the continuation of the action. The brothers sit down to eat.

[37:25b-27, 28b] The variant, vv. 25b-27, 28b, is inserted into and smoothly adapted to the context. While they are eating, the brothers see a caravan of Ishmaelites approaching (v. 25b). There is a detailed description of their arrival, their wares, and their destination.

> The merchandise: נכאת is gum (tragacanth), צרי balm, לט resin; all three are mentioned again in 43:11 among the presents that the brothers are to take down to Egypt. The three are mentioned also in Egyptian texts; they are used in medicine and cosmetics, espe-

cially in embalming (for details cf. J. Vergote, *Joseph en Egypt.* . . [1959] 10,14; D. B. Redford, VT.S 20 [1970] 192f.). The import of such merchandise from East Jordan, the trade route through Dothan, Midianite and Ishmaelite commercial caravans—are all well attested.

The appearance of the Ishmaelite caravan suggests an idea to Judah, the eldest brother in the variant, which he proposes to his brothers (vv. 26-27). Judah too intends to save Joseph and guard his brothers against murder and the consequent "covering of his blood"; at the same time, however, he is at one with them in doing away with him. Even more clearly does he warn his brothers of the outrage of fratricide, "He is our brother, our own flesh!" The brothers agree and sell Joseph to the Ishmaelites for twenty silver pieces (v. 28b), "the average price of a young boy still growing up, Lev. 27:4f." (H. Gunkel). The Ishmaelite merchants take Joseph with them on their way down to Egypt.

[**37:28a, 29, 30**] Reuben had planned to take Joseph out of the cistern so as to restore him to his father (v. 22). But while the brothers were eating (v. 25), some Midianite merchants passed by and lifted Joseph out of the cistern. One assumes that they had heard his cries. When Reuben came to the cistern later, it was empty. In horror and distress he tears his garments, returns to his brothers, and in his despair lets them know that he wanted to rescue him from the very beginning. The description is most impressive. Reuben exclaims in the presence of his brothers, "The boy is not there! And I—where am I to turn?" One could expand Reuben's last sentence: ". . .from my father's face"; he knows that he is the one who must answer when his father asks after Joseph.

Conclusion to vv. 18-30: when the two variants, the one featuring Reuben and the other Judah, are seen side by side, it is obvious that there are two different presentations (H. C. Schmitt, BZAW 154 [1980] 23). But Reuben's alarm when he finds the cistern empty (vv. 29-30) cannot be harmonized with the Judah variant and the Ishmaelite merchants. Whatever one does to unite the two versions conceptually, two different presentations remain and the narrator has made them quite clear (also H. Donner, 1976, pp. 44f.). When vv. 25b-27, 28b are recognized as a variant, the rest of the chapter from v. 3 to the end can be seen as a unified series of events; the main thread is that Reuben is the eldest brother, and the climax is his lament in v. 29. Only then is the moving change from the murderous intent of the brothers in vv. 18-20 to Reuben's lament in v. 29b set in relief.

It is striking that the author takes this one place to portray in two variants an episode that takes place between Joseph and the brothers. The narrator often makes use of doublets to stress a motif or a step in the narrative. This may be his intention here as well. He presents then the authority of the elder brother, to be exercised in certain circumstances, as each rises to prevent the murderous deed. This is basically different from the dominion of the monarchy inasmuch as it is an authority delegated by the father to the eldest son for a limited time, demanding that it give a responsible account of itself. Thus the emphasis here on the intervention of the elder brother would be a sign that the Joseph narrative as a whole is preoccupied with the questions of dominion and authority between family and state. Conditioned and limited authority based on human responsibility and conscience is opposed to the "absolute" dominion of the king.

From the fact that there are certain points of correspondence between Reuben/Jacob and Judah/Israel, D. B. Redford posits the juxtaposition of a Judah and a Reuben layer. H. C. Schmitt follows him in this. Redford maintains that the Reuben layer is the basic one, Schmitt the Judah layer. But there is much uncertainty in both views.

[37:31-35] The third scene: The deed is concealed, vv. 31-35. The murderous intent of the brothers embraces the deed and its concealment. The deed is narrated in two variants (vv. 23-30); this last part is a unity. The brothers feign an accident (vv. 31-32) and succeed in deceiving their father. The father is deeply moved by the report; he laments and carries out the ritual of mourning (vv. 33-34). The attempts of his sons and daughters to comfort him are in vain (v. 35).

[37:31-32] Once again one should note the narrator's art. The narrator restricts himself to a narrative chain: they took. . .slaughtered. . .dipped. . .said. There is not a word about any discussion, not a word as to whether all the brothers acted together, not a word about the brothers' reaction when Reuben makes known his intention. Everything moves from the situation; the mere sequence of events sets the unalterable in sharp relief; all that remains is to conceal the deed and deceive the father. The tunic is the means of concealment; the garment motif now recurs for the third time. The brothers show the father the bloodstained tunic, the gift from the loving father. The story began with the gift. It was this that aroused the brothers' hatred and moved them to tear the cloak from Joseph, far from his father. They now bring the bloodstained tunic back to him so as to conceal what they have done. The bloodstained garment is a common motif in tale (H. Gunkel) and story as a deceptive *corpus delicti*.

The verbs in v. 32 present a difficulty: the brothers either brought the tunic themselves as the verb ויביאו says, or they sent it through another וישלחו. The contradiction is usually solved by source division. If one reads the text as a unity, two possibilities present themselves. *(a)* The brothers send the tunic by means of a messenger, and so ויביאו is to be understood personally (B. Jacob: "they sent. . . and someone brought. . ."; R. de Vaux: "they sent. . . and had it brought. . ."); *(b)* The brothers bring it themselves; so F. V. Winnett, who derives שלח in this case from another root meaning "to tear"; so too some Jewish interpreters. D. B. Redford inclines to this view (p. 29). The movement of the narrative, however, seems to me to make it impossible that the brothers send the tunic by means of messengers, especially as in that case they would not hear the father's lament. Hence either וישלחו is to be understood as "tear" with F. V. Winnett, or there are traces here of a variant, for which כתנת הפסים might speak in evidence.

[37:33] The father recognizes his son's garment. His reaction is encompassed in three moving, climactic sentences. In the first he confirms his sons' questions, v. 32b (Sam, Gk, Syr, add היא, thus misconstruing the deliberate brevity). The second draws the conclusion from the first comment, "A wild animal has eaten him!" This is the only conclusion possible for him. The brothers have succeeded with their deception. This second sentence, though still a statement, bursts into a lament: טרף טרף יוסף; the form and the repetition of the verb make it obvious that it is a standard cry of lament which was raised when someone had been attacked and torn apart by an animal. It is not possible to render the cry itself in translation. The father's lament is the climax of the narrative. These short sentences are extremely dense, mounting in intensity from one to the other, and ending with the name Joseph. Earlier interpretations which separated v. 33 into two sources destroyed thereby the narrative art of the climax.

[37:34-35] The lament breaks out and there follows a whole situation brought about by the news of Joseph's death. From now on the old man's life is marked by mourning for his youngest and much loved son. The rites of mourning are described: Jacob tears his garments (cf. 44:13) and puts on sackcloth; the last verb encompasses both: ''. . .and mourned. . ..'' Once again the garment motif is sounded. For the rites, cf. E. Kutsch, ThSt 78 (1965) 23-42 and H. Schmid, RGG³, 6, 961f., 1000. These customs are very widespread, cf. H. Gese, *Die Religionen der Menscheit* 10,2 (1970) 21,71. The hithp. form of אבל describes the situation: ''to be engaged in mourning rites, to be in mourning,'' KBL. The שׂק, a loincloth of coarse material, is worn on the bare skin. These customs are so old and widespread that their meaning can no longer be determined.

[37:35] Jacob's sons and daughters (another tradition according to which Jacob had several daughters) set out, i.e., they all rally to Jacob to console him. The verb נחם means not only that they spoke words of comfort, but rather that they wanted to bring about a change and have Jacob put an end to the rites of mourning (cf. 38:12; on נחם, C. Westermann, *Isaiah 40–66* [1976³; Eng. 1969] 33-44, on 40:1). But Jacob remains obdurate and gives his reason, v. 35b. He will remain in mourning until death. Death is described as ''going down to Sheol,'' a standard expression belonging not to the patriarchal period but to the period of narrator. Sheol appears here for the first time in Genesis; it is a non-Israelite name (cf. L. Koehler, ThZ 2 [1946] 71-74; W. Baumgartner, ibid., 233-235) and suggests wasteland, no-land, underworld (KBL). The phrase carries an appendage here, ''to my son''; death will reunite him with his son. This expectation, which gives expression to the deep grief of the one who remains behind, is obviously dependent on religious form and attitude; it occurs also in Canaanite mourning ceremonies: ''Baal is dead. . .. After Baal I'll descend into the earth'' (Baal epic, ANET 139, g. I* AB vi 24-26), as well as in many other places right down to the present. The last three words of the verse are not a doublet of v. 34b; their meaning is rather that he stayed there weeping for his son. The brothers could do away with their preferred brother, but not with the love of the father for his son. The family peace is permanently shattered.

[37:36] V. 35 brings the narrative of ch. 35 to its conclusion; v. 36 forms the transition to ch. 39; it is so similar to 39:1 that it has probably been formed from it. On the other hand, it follows immediately on v. 28a (the אתו in v. 36a is to be understood in this way; it has no antecedent). This means that the transition continues the main thread of the narrative of ch. 37, not of the variant vv. 25b-27, 28b, though the Ishmaelites appear again in 39:1. The Midianites sell Joseph in Egypt; i.e., the narrative of Joseph, his father, and his brothers goes further; the scene changes (on the transition see C. Kuhl [1952], I. L. Seeligmann [1962]; H. C. Schmitt [1980], all in bibliog. above. Schmitt is of the opinion that v. 36 was first added by the redactor who inserted ch. 38).

Purpose and Thrust

Looked at in itself, the introduction to the Joseph story, ch. 37, is a pure family narrative. As such, it follows immediately on the preceding Jacob-Esau story. It tells further of the family of Jacob. It too deals with a conflict between brothers which threatens to destroy the welfare of the family by the prospect of murder. In the former story it is a question of the rivalry between two brothers; here the father, the brothers, and the youngest brother are involved. Moreover, in the course of the narrative the eldest brother appears as the one responsible before the father over against the brothers as a group. Though what happens remains within the family circle, it already points beyond it. The monarchy comes into view in Joseph's dreams, a frightening possibility for the brothers and the father; it hints at the transition from the family to the monarchy which is unfolded in the continuation of the Joseph story in chs. 39–41. The narrator, who has experienced the reality of the Judaean-Israelite monarchy, wants to say something about the conflict between family and monarchy by means of his narrative; this is his intention in expanding the narrative of the Jacob tradition available to him. The expansion is already prepared in the introductory chapter (the narrative is still in the social realm in the traditional material of vv. 3-4). The dreams in the first part are the clearest foretaste of what, to the family's horror, may come to pass. This thread is carried on in chs. 39–41, Joseph's rise in Egypt. In the second part the brothers' crime is against brother and father alike; it demands a continuation, following the narrative structure "crime and punishment." In the third part the father's grief is portrayed in such a way that it cannot be the end. The peace of Jacob's family is broken; it will be the feared ascendancy of Joseph that will lead by many a detour to the possibility of reconciliation. But the narrator wants in this way to say something about the monarchy that the father and the brothers must also acknowledge as wholesome. Nothing is yet said in the introductory part about how the God of the fathers is at work in all this; it can emerge only in the course of events that follow.

Judah and Tamar

Literature

Genesis 38: B. Luther, "Die Novelle von Juda und Tamar und andere israelitische Novellen," in E. Meyer, *Die Israeliten*. . . (1906) 173-206. R. Hartmann, "Zu Genesis 38," ZAW 33 (1913) 76f. P. Cruveilhier, "Le lévirat chez les Hébreux et chez les Assyriens," RB 34 (1925) 524-546. U. Cassuto, "The Story of Tamar and Judah" [in Hebr.], in *J. M. Simḥoni Mem. Vol.* (1929) 93-100 = *Stud. in the Bible* (1972) 108-117. R. H. Pfeiffer, "A Non-Israelitic Source of the Book of Genesis," ZAW NF 7 (1930) 66-73. T. H. Robinson, "The Origin of the Tribe of Judah," Fests. R. Harris (1933) 265-273. J. Lewy, "Les textes paléo-assyriens et l'Ancien Testament," RHR 110 (1934) 29-65 esp. 30f. J. Mittelmann, *Der altisraelitische Levirat* (1934). M. Burrows, "Levirate Marriage in Israel," JBL 59 (1940) 23-33; "The Ancient Oriental Background of Hebrew Levirate Marriage," BASOR 77 (1940) 2-15. R. H. Pfeiffer, *Introduction to the OT* (1941; 1953²) esp. 159-167. A. L. Oppenheim, "Mesopotamian Mythology II," Or. NS 17 (1948) esp. 34. A. F. Puukko, "Die Leviratsehe in den altorientalischen Gesetzen," Fests. B. Hrozný: ArOr 17(II) (1949) 296-299. C. Lattey, "Vicarious Solidarity in the OT," VT 1 (1951) 267-274. S. Yeivin, "*Yēhūdā*": *Enṣiqlōpedyā Miqra`ēt* III (1958) 487-508. O. Eissfeldt, *Stammessage und Menschheitserzählung in der Genesis*, SAB 110,4 (1964/65). M. C. Astour, "Tamar the Hierodule. An Essay in the Method of Vestigial Motifs," JBL 85 (1966) 185-196. E. R. Leach, "The Legitimacy of Solomon. Some Structural Aspects of OT History," *Archives européennes de Sociologie*, 7 (1966) 58-101. N. H. Snaith, "The Daughters of Zelophehad," VT 16 (1966) 124-127. T. & D. Thompson, "Some Legal Problems in the Book of Ruth," VT 18 (1968) 79-99, esp. 93ff. E. R. Leach, "Genesis as Myth and Other Essays," Cape Ed. 39 (1969). S. Belkin, "Levirate and Agnate Marriage in Rabbinic and Cognate Marriage," JQR 60 (1969/70) 275-329. G. W. Coats, "Widow's Rights: A Crux in the Structure of Gn 38," CBQ 34 (1972) 461-466. R. de Vaux, "L'installation des Israelites dans le sud palestinien et les origines de la tribu de Juda," 5th *World Congress of Jewish Stud.* I (1972) 150-156. A. Phillips, "Some Aspects of Family Law in Pre-Exilic Israel," VT 23 (1973) 349-361. D. A. Leggett, "The Levirate and Goel Institutions in the OT" (diss. Amsterdam, 1974). J. W. Rogerson, *Myth in OT Interpretation*, BZAW 134 (1974) 124ff. J. A. Emerton, "Some Problems in Genesis XXXVIII," VT 25 (1975) 338-361; "An Examination of a Recent Structuralist Interpretation of Gen XXXVIII," VT 26 (1976) 79-98. C. M. Carmichael, "A Ceremonial Crux: Removing a Man's Sandal as a Female Gesture of Contempt," JBL 96 (1977) 321-336. J. Goldin, "The Youngest Son or Where Does Genesis 38 Belong," JBL 96 (1977) 27-44. J. A. Emerton, "Judah and Tamar," VT 29 (1979) 403-415. S. Niditch, "The Wronged Woman Righted: An Analysis of Gen 38," HThR 72 (1979) 143-148. C. M. Carmichael, " 'Treading' in the Book of Ruth," ZAW 92 (1980) 248-266, esp. 251.

Genesis 38:1-11: P. Koschaker, "Zum Levirat nach hethitischem Recht," RHAs 2 (1933) 77-89. C. A. Ben-Mordecai, "Chezib," JBL 58 (1939) 283-286. Y. Aharoni, "Tamar and the Roads to Elath," IEJ 13 (1963) 30-42. J. Blenkinsopp, "Theme and Motif in the Succession History (2 Sam XI 2ff.) and the Yahwist Corpus," VT.S 15 (1966) 44-57. T. C. Mitchell, "The Meaning of the Noun *htn* in the OT," VT 19 (1969) 93-112. E. Lipiński, "L'éthymologie de 'Juda,' " VT 23 (1973) 380f. E. M. Yamanchi, *Cultic Prostitution*, AOAT 22 (1973). E. Pennacchini, "Un contributo all'interpretazione die Gn 38,9," *StudHierosolymitana in onore di P. B. Bagatti* II (1975; Eng. 1976). H. C. Waetjen, "The Genealogy as the Key to the Gospel according to Matthew," JBL 95 (1976) 205-230. J. J. Stamm, "Ein ugaritisch-hebräisches Verbum und seine Ableitungen," ThZ 35 (1979) 5-9 = J. J. Stamm, *Beiträge z. hebr. u. altorient. Namenkunde: Orbis biblicus et orientalis* 30 (1980) 199-203.

Genesis 38:12-30: A. Jirku, *Die Dämonen und ihre Abwehr im AT* (1912) esp. 89. F. Zimmermann, "The Births of Perez and Zerah," JBL 64 (1945) 377f. D. Daube, "Concerning Methods of Bible-Criticism. Late Laws in Early Narratives," ArOr 17 (1949) 88-99. J. Fichtner, "Der Begriff des 'Nächsten' im AT," WuD NF 4 (1955) 23-52. A. van Selms, "The Origin of the Title 'The King's Friend,' " JNESt 16 (1957) 118-120. A. M. Dubarle, "Les Textes divers du livre de Judith," VT 8 (1958) 344-373. P. Wernberg-Møller, "Observations on the Hebrew Participle," ZAW 71 (1959) 54-67 esp. 55. T. J. Meek, "Translating the Hebrew Bible," JBL 79 (1960) 328-335. J. R. Porter, "The Legal Aspects of the Concept of 'Corporate Personality' in the OT," VT 15 (1965) 361-380. J. D. Martin, "The Forensic Background to Jeremiah III 1," VT 19 (1969) 82-92 esp. 85. H. McKeating, "Justice and Truth in Israel's Legal Practice: An Inquiry," CQR 3 (1970) 51-56. G. Ridout, "The Rape of Tamar," in *Essays in Hon. of J. Muilenburg* (1974). M. J. Buss, "The Distinction Between Civil and Criminal Law in Ancient Israel," *6th World Congress of Jewish Stud. Jerusalem* 1 (1977) 51-62. I. Robinson, "*bepetah enayim* in Genesis 38,14," JBL 96 (1977) 569. A. Phillips, "Another Example of Family Law," VT 30 (1980) 240-243.

Text

38:1 At that time Judah[a] left his brothers and went down and pitched his tent with a man from Adullam named Hirah.

2 There Judah saw the daughter of a Canaanite named Shua; he married her and went to her.

3 She conceived and bore a son and called[a] him Er.

4 She conceived again and bore a son and called him Onan.

5 She conceived yet again and bore a son and called him Shelah. 'She'[a] was in Chezib when she bore him.

6 Judah took a wife named Tamar for Er, his first-born.

7 But Er, Judah's firstborn, was wicked in Yahweh's eyes and Yahweh caused him to die.

8 So Judah said to Onan, Go to your brother's wife and do the duty of a brother-in-law[a] and raise up issue to him.

9 But Onan knew that the issue would not be his; and so whenever he went to his brother's wife he destroyed[a] his seed (by spilling it) on the ground so as not to raise[b] issue to his brother.

10 But what he did was wicked in the eyes of Yahweh and he caused him to die also.

11 So Judah said to Tamar, his daughter-in-law, Go back to your father's house as a widow until my son Shelah has grown up; for he feared that he too would die like his brothers.
So Tamar went and lived in her father's house.

12 In the course of time Shua's daughter, Judah's wife, died; after Judah had finished mourning he and his friend, Hirah the Adullamite, went up to the shearers at Timnah.

13 When Tamar was told, Your father-in-law is going up to shear his sheep in Timnah,

14 she put off her widow's clothes, veiled herself,[a] draped herself, and sat at the entrance gate to Enaim which is on the way[b] to Timnah, because she knew that Shelah had grown up and she had not been given to him in marriage.

15 When Judah saw her he thought she was a prostitute because she had veiled her face.

16 He turned off to the roadside and said, Come, let me lie with you! He did not know that she was his daughter-in-law. She answered, What will you give me to lie with me?

17 He said, I will send you[a] a kid from the flock. She answered, But give me[b] a pledge[c] until you send it.

18 He said, What sort of pledge shall I give you? She answered, Your signet ring, your cord, and the staff you carry. He gave them to her and went to her; she became pregnant by him.[a]

19 Then she rose and went home. She took off her veil and put on her widow's clothes again.

20 When Judah sent the kid by his friend the Adullamite to recover the pledge from the woman, he could not find her.

21 He asked the men of the place,[a] Where is the prostitute who used to sit by the roadside at Enaim? They said, There was no prostitute here.[b]

22 He returned to Judah and said, I did not find her; and more, the men of the place said that there was no such prostitute there.

23 So Judah said, Let her keep[a] the pledge lest we be mocked at. I did send a kid and you did not find her!

24 About three[a] months later Judah was told, Your daughter-in-law Tamar has played the prostitute and is pregnant because of[b] her conduct. Judah said, Bring her out to be burnt.

25 As she was to be[a] brought out she sent to her father-in-law saying, I am pregnant by the man to whom these belong. See if you recognize whose these are, the signet ring, the cord,[b] and the staff.

26 Judah recognized them and said, She is within her rights rather than I. Why did I not give her to my son Shelah! He had no further relations with her.

27 When the time of her bearing came, there were twins in her womb.

28 While she was giving birth one[a] of them put out a hand. The midwife took it and tied a scarlet thread on it saying, This one came out first.

29 But as soon as he drew back[a] his hand, his brother came out. She said, What a breach it is you have torn! And she[b] named him Perez.

30 Then his brother who had the scarlet thread on his hand came out; she[a] called him Zerah.

1a On the name *Judah*, E. Lipiński 1973, lit. above.

3a Read וַתִּקְרָא with Sam, TargJ; cf. vv. 4 and 5, also v. 30.

5a Read וְהָיָא with Gk; Ges-K §112uu.

8a Denominative from יבם, brother-in-law; noun and verb elsewhere only in Deut. 25:5,7.

9a Frequentative; Ges-K §159o; 112e,f,dd.   **b** Form, Ges-K §66i.

14a Read with Sam, TargO, Syr, וַתִּתְכַּס.   **b** Syr, Vg read "at the crossroad."

17a Insert לָךְ with Gk, L, Vg.   **b** Insert לִי with Syr.   **c** ערבון, a loanword from Akk; also Greek.

18a On the use of ל BrSynt §107e.

21a Read הַמָּקוֹם with Sam, Gk, Syr.   **b** בזה = "here," Ges-K §102g; BrSynt §23e; as Gen. 48:9.
23a Vg: *habeat sibi.*
24a Read with Sam כְּמִשְׁלֹשֶׁת, Ges-K §97e; BrSynt §84a.   **b** לְ, to indicate efficient cause, Ges-K §121f.
25a Asyndetic circumstantial sentence; technical term, as in Deut. 22:21, 24.   **b** Read with the versions as in v. 18.
28a Indefinite personal subject, "one," Ges-K §144d.
29a Read כַּהֲשִׁיבוֹ (Gk, A. Dillmann, H. Holzinger) or כְּמוֹ הָשִׁיב, Ges-K §164g. On the construction כ with participle, T. J. Meek 1960, lit. above.   **b** Read וַתִּקְרָא with some Mss, Sam, Syr, TargJ; cf. note on v. 3a.
30a Read וַתִּקְרָא; cf. notes on vv. 3a, 29b.

Form

Ch. 38 is a self-contained individual narrative; "there is no place where it can be fitted into the patriarchal story" (H. Holzinger). As already indicated, the narrative of Judah and Tamar has not been inserted into the Joseph story; it has nothing to do with it but rather is an insertion into the Jacob story, into its conclusion (the traditional material of Gen. 37 and chs. 46–50). A redactor has inserted it into the Jacob story so as to preserve it like other individual narratives about the sons of Jacob, e.g., Gen. 34, concerning Simeon and Levi, and the fragment 35:22-23, Reuben (so too J. Wellhausen, H. Holzinger, H. Gunkel, J. A. Emerton 1975-76, bibliog. above). Ch. 38 is unanimously attributed to J, but without sufficient reason. Linguistic grounds are sparse and the broad genealogical frame, vv. 1-2, 27-30, speaks against J. All that can be said with certainty is that ch. 38, like the other texts mentioned, has been appended because it deals with a son of Jacob. It is certain too that ch. 38 stems from oral tradition; this is particularly obvious here. Vv. 12-26 form the kernel of the narrative, vv. 1-11 and 27-30, two genealogical passages, the framework. The relative independence of vv. 1-11 and 27-30 is clear inasmuch as both parts provide details which are not necessary for the narrative in vv. 12-26 and so overload the function of the exposition and the conclusion. They are more accurately described as prehistory. The narrative is set within the frame of reports; both are clearly separated from each other even though vv. 1-11 and 27-30 are adapted to the narrative in between. The narrative needed some such detailed genealogical frame because it was circulating independently, something like the case of the book of Ruth. The reason for this is that the narrator is telling his listeners something about their ancestors. In the genealogical frame he takes up and extends what they already know; in the narrative they learn something new about them.

It is clear then that Gen. 38 is a family narrative and not in essence tribal history (so A. Dillmann, H. Gunkel, M. Noth, J. Skinner, and others). It is a narrative of the family of Judah, the family from which the tribe of Judah sprang and deals with a case of family law. In the broader sense it is the distressing situation of childlessness which often occurs in the patriarchal stories. It is not that "her womb had been closed"; rather Tamar is a young wife who has become a childless widow. The story tells how by a daring ruse she herself redresses the right which has been withheld from her by her husband's family. The present narrative differs from chs. 25 and 27 where family and tribal history are far from each other; here they are close together because the narrative is played out on Canaanite soil in the transition to sedentary life. Judah, the father of the tribe, has left his brothers (v.

1), and Tamar's sons Perez and Zerah (vv. 27-30) designate clans of the tribe of Judah which are mentioned in Num. 26:19-22. J. A. Emerton has written three enlightening essays on the history of the exegesis of ch. 38 (1975, 1976, 1979; bibliog. above). The second of these is a careful presentation and critique of E. R. Leach's attempt to explain the chapter by structural analysis (1966, 1969; bibliog. above).

Setting

The origin of the narrative must be supplemented by further specifying its locale. The oral form had its origin within the circle of the descendants of Judah and Tamar as a narrative about the ancestors. In contrast to most of the patriarchal narratives, its place or origin can be determined with certainty: it is a part of the later tribal territory of Judah in the eastern Shepelah specified by the very place-names in the narrative—Adullam, Chezib (Achzib), Enaim, and Timnah. It is possible to specify the place in this case because the event narrated takes place at the beginning of the process of sedentarization, as indicated in v. 1. J. A. Emerton is of the opinion that Gen. 38 presupposes the period of the judges and that the period of the settlement is still remembered (1975, p. 347). However, I cannot agree with Emerton when he accepts a Canaanite origin of the narrative (1979, pp. 410f., 414). If Tamar, the heroine of the narrative, is a Canaanite, she becomes nevertheless the wife of a son of Judah and thereby is the subject of the narrative insofar as she belongs to the family of Judah (it is important here that the real narrative begins in v. 12 where Tamar is a member of the family of Judah). The genealogical frame speaks against a Canaanite origin of the narrative as does the position in it of the Canaanite Hirah who is obviously subordinated to Judah. The narrative arose among the descendants of Judah and Tamar in a mixed population in which Canaanites and groups of immigrant Israelites (or Jacob-people) still lived at peace with each other and intermarried.

Commentary

[38:1-11] It is necessary to know something of what precedes the narrative in order to understand it. This could have been summarized in a few sentences; but such would have constituted a mere exposition. However, because the narrative of Judah and Tamar had been passed on independently, the introduction had to be more detailed and assume the form of a genealogy corresponding to the genealogical introduction to large narrative works. It is similar in the book of Ruth.

[38:1-5] The introductory genealogy compasses two generations, the first being vv. 1-5. V. 1 forms the redactional transition, v. 2 records Judah's marriage to a Canaanite who bears him three children (vv. 3-5).

[38:1] In v. 1 the redactor who inserted ch. 38 in this place makes the transition from the patriarchal story to a period when Judah no longer lives with his brothers. Judah is here an individual, not the representative of a tribe. Because it is a redactional passage, neither "at that time" nor "went down" can be fixed chronologically or geographically. The redactor simply presupposes that the sons of Jacob have parted from each other in the period after they have become sedentary. So he uses the terminology of the itinerary in describing the movement, וַיֵּרֶד, giving the point of departure, מֵאֵת, and its goal, וַיֵּט עַד. The abbreviated וַיֵּט (to be supplemented with אָהֳלוֹ) as well as the עַד are to be understood in the context of the terminology as referring to an actual place. But there is an adaptation here and the reference is to a person living in this place with whom Judah acts jointly, as indicated in what follows. The phraseology has been notably abbreviated; cf. v. 16 (אֵל). Adullam lies 16 km. northwest of Hebron in the Judaean hill country; according to Josh. 12:15 it was a royal Canaanite city, see also 1 Sam. 22:1; 2 Sam. 23:13; Mic. 1:15. The name Hirah occurs only in Gen. 38; it is perhaps related to Hirman (O. Procksch).

[38:2] "There Judah saw. . ." (v. 2). It is a peculiarity of the narrative art of Genesis that a succession of events is introduced by an act of perception through the senses, for the most part the sense of sight. This is usually a personal action. Everything began with Judah seeing the girl. No more need be said. The girl was the daughter of a Canaanite named Shua (elsewhere only in 1 Chron. 2:3), and Judah takes her to wife. The storyteller feels no embarrassment in narrating that the father of the tribe of Judah joins ranks with a Canaanite and marries the daughter of a Canaanite. This attests the early origin of the story; it arose at a time when nobody took scandal from it. It is different in 24:3. Gen. 24, therefore, must have arisen later than Gen. 38, a secure argument that they cannot come from the same author. It is surprising that the early link with Canaanites and marriage with them has been preserved in this narrative which has undergone a long tradition-history.

[38:3-5] The birth of three sons, vv. 3-5, is recorded entirely in the language of the genealogy: "she conceived. . .bore. . .called." It is also a sign of the antiquity of the narrative that the mother named the sons. The names occur again in the list of Israelites who came down into Egypt (46:12) and in Num. 26:19 (cf. 1 Chron. 2:3; 4:21). They do not occur elsewhere, but cf. Onam, Gen. 36:23, and the gentilitial שֵׁלָנִי (Num. 26:20; Neh. 11:15). The note about the birthplace of the third son in v. 5b (born elsewhere than the other two) shows that we are dealing with a once independent genealogy, because the information is not necessary for the narrative that follows. The place Chezib (only here) is to be equated with Achzib (Josh. 15:44; Mic. 1:14), 5 km. to the south of Adullam (M. Noth, *Das Buch Josua* [1938] 68).

[38:6-11] The next generation (vv. 6-11): Judah gives his oldest son a wife, probably a Canaanite, though no details of her origin are given. Her name is Tamar ("date palm"), later the name of a daughter of David (2 Sam. 13:1) and a daughter of Absalom (2 Sam. 14:27). The two main persons in the narrative have now been introduced, Judah in vv. 1-5 and Tamar in vv. 6-11.

[38:7] The death of Er, Judah's firstborn, is reported in v. 7 in a style corresponding to that of the genealogy with the brief remark that it was premature and hence unnatural; it was the custom to explain such a death as a punishment by God for a crime (T. and D. Thompson, VT 18 [1968] 93). The phrase וַיְמִתֵהוּ יְהוָה never occurs in J.

[38:8] Tamar has been widowed while still young and has no children. Judah, who had given her as wife to his son, is now responsible for her, i.e., for the continuation of the family of the prematurely deceased. The custom of the levirate meets this situation. It is an emergency measure which, however, has the stamp of family law and which is found also outside Israel and Canaan in similar social circumstances (O. Procksch mentions Africa, India, Persia, and Greece).

Excursus on the Levirate

(Lit. in bibliog. above): The family law custom of the levirate (brother-in-law marriage) is found only three times in the O.T., Gen. 38, Ruth, and Deut. 25:5-10. It is "that the surviving brother is obliged to beget children from his sister-in-law, the first-born of whom is regarded as the child of the deceased" (H. Gunkel ad loc.). The meaning of the custom is explained in Deut. 25:6 (cf. Gen. 38:8): "that his name may not be blotted out of Israel." It is only a secondary purpose of the levirate that the property of the deceased passes on to the one who is heir to his name, and is probably a later accretion. It is not mentioned in Gen. 38 or Deut. 25. It is clear from the few references in the O.T. that the custom could be observed in different ways according to the situation. As G. W. Coats has shown (1972, bibliog. above), Gen. 38 indicates that originally the widow had only the right to a descendant, not to marriage with the brother-in-law. The designation "brother-in-law marriage" is to this extent inaccurate. Tamar does not become Onan's wife; neither is her purpose to force Judah to marriage, but only to have a son (J. Skinner: "in early times the union was only temporary"). Deut. 25:5-10 shows that the custom met with opposition and was widely rejected; it is probably forbidden altogether in Lev. 20:21 (so A. Phillips 1973, bibliog. above).

Judah, following the custom, requires his second son Onan to raise issue to his brother. The demand is phrased in three sentences. The first, "Go in to your brother's wife," is, in the second, based on the levirate requirement, ויבם אתה. The verb is a denominative from יבם, brother of a married man, Latin *levir*, only in Deut 25:5,7; the verb occurs only here and in Deut.

[38:9-10] Onan merely goes through the motion of carrying out his father's demand; in reality he rejects his obligation toward his deceased brother; he lets his seed fall upon the ground. The narrator gives as the reason his own self-interest; he does not want to beget posterity for others. But perhaps there is already in the background an early revolt against the custom as mentioned specifically in Deut. 25:7. Onan thereupon dies and his death is explained as a punishment by God for his conduct.

[38:11] Judah has only one son left and is concerned about his survival. It is questionable whether one can say that "Judah regards Tamar as a wife who brings misfortune," A. Dillmann, A. Jirku (1912, 71, bibliog. above); rather it is stated explicitly that the deaths of Er and Onan are due to their own fault. Judah's concern for his only surviving son does not need any such basis. Judah does not yet come to any definite decision; he puts it off saying that Shelah is still too young. Tamar thereupon complies with his request to return to her father's house (cf. Lev. 22:13). It remains in the balance whether Tamar will get her right; this seems to depend on Judah as hitherto it is he alone who has made all the decisions as father of the family.

[38:12-26] The real action begins with Tamar seizing the initiative; she herself procures her right to have a son from her husband's family (vv. 12-23). Judah concedes the justice of her headstrong conduct (vv. 24-26). Whereas Judah is the main actor in vv. 1-11, it is Tamar in vv. 12-26.

[**38:12**] The introduction or transition begins skillfully after a lapse of time with an action of Judah, as if he were the main actor. In the meantime Judah's wife has died and the period of mourning has ended. The narrator says this in order to avoid the subsequent complication of a further marriage of Judah. It is characteristic of the narrative style that nothing is said of the reasons and circumstances; the sequence of narrative episodes in which the event runs its course is enough.

Judah goes up to Timnah (Josh. 15:57, 7 km. northeast of Adullam) with his friend Hirah to supervise the shearing of the sheep (cf. 31:9) and to celebrate with the shepherds the feast connected with it.

[**38:13-14**] The initiative now passes quietly to Tamar. It is only in the last sentences of vv. 13-14, again a sequence of narrative episodes, that the reasons for her taking the initiative are given. Tamar was living in her father's house with no future. She had noticed that she had been deprived of her right because Shelah had grown up in the meantime. She decided, therefore, to procure her right herself and devised a risky plan which could cost her both her honor and her life. Her opportunity comes when she hears that Judah is going up to Timnah for the shearing (v. 13). She stands dressed as a prostitute by the road which Judah must pass (as Jer. 3:2; Ezek. 16:25). בפתח עינים probably means "at the entrance gate to Enaim," a small village near Timnah; it is mentioned only here (it is perhaps the Enam of Josh. 15:34).

[**38:15-19**] Judah approaches her and proposes intercourse. She agrees and there is discussion about the price. Judah goes to her and they have intercourse. Tamar departs with the pledge she has required of him. The narrative is sober with not a word beyond the bare facts; it is taken as normal and no moral judgment is passed. The narrator thus succeeds in presenting the event solely under the aspect of Tamar's plan: a wife wants to procure her right. Accordingly the conclusion says that she conceives a child ותהר לו. From this point of view Tamar has done what justice and the death of her husband demand of her, though by means of a ruse. She has been so clever that the pledge leaves open to her the opportunity, however slim, of escaping disgrace and the death penalty and of bearing a son to her deceased husband who will be acknowledged by the family.

It is twice emphasized that Judah takes her for a prostitute (vv. 15 and 16b); no further censure is passed on him. He may be following a custom in promising her a kid as payment. In Greece and elsewhere a kid is the hetaera sacrifice in the service of the goddess of love (cf. Judg. 15:1). But Tamar requires a pledge from him because he is a stranger: his signet ring, cord, and staff. It is now possible for her to identify with certainty the father of her child. These are the insignia of a prominent man in Babylon (Herodotus) as well as in Canaan and Israel. The signet ring or cylinder seal is used to sign contracts; the staff has markings carved on it which are peculiar to the owner. The seal was carried on a cord around the neck. Insignia to the number of three are found often in Ugaritic literature (C. Gordon).

[**38:20-23**] The purpose of the brief closing scene (vv. 20-23) is to explain that the insignia remained in Tamar's possession right up to the denouement; that is just what she had planned. The episode serves further to portray Judah as an honorable man. The narrator does not regard Judah's going to a prostitute as something dishonorable; but it would have been dishonorable had Judah reneged on the payment. Hence it is expressly stated in v. 23b that he had done all to deliver the promised kid. The insignia that he leaves with her are extremely valuable. It is significant that the (apparent) prostitute זונה is here called קדשה "the consecrated" or hierodule, by Hirah, Judah's friend. This was, to be sure, the more polite designation. There will have been no clear separation between the two in the rural situation presupposed here; nevertheless, the word קדשה gives expression to something more or less accepted. Cultic prostitution, later attacked so passionately by the prophets (Hosea, Ezekiel), is still acknowledged in a mixed population. Religious prostitution had played a role among the peoples of the Near East from ancient times.

[**38:24-26**] The climax of the narrative, vv. 24-26, demonstrates the complete art of the narrator as, briefly and tensely, he directs the dramatic events toward his one point of interest, the statement of Judah that vindicates Tamar. This is the goal of the narrative.

[**38:24**] The two sentences of v. 24 are very compact. After about three months it can be seen that Tamar is pregnant. This established a misdemeanor that must be punished. Jurisdiction lies solely with the head of the family and Tamar belongs to the family of Judah. The information conveyed to Judah has the precise form of an accusation laid before a court: "Tamar your daughter-in-law has played the harlot!" The second sentence sharpens the accusation: "Further, she is pregnant because of her misconduct!" Tamar is thus accused of adultery either as Er's widow or Shelah's betrothed. According to old family law the establishment of the fact is sufficient for criminal punishment without inquiry or legal process. Judah pronounces sentence immediately, "She is to be burnt." It is introduced with, "Bring her out!" i.e., outside the gate, because the death sentence is to be carried out outside the locality (Deut. 22:21, 24). Burning was perhaps an earlier and more severe punishment for adultery; stoning was the penalty later in Israel (Deut. 22:23f.). The execution of punishment, in which "the entire community takes part" (G. von Rad), follows the legal procedure of sedentary people; v. 24 presupposes a peculiar mixed form of legal administration in accordance with the mixed population.

[**38:25**] "As she was to be brought out. . ." (v. 25): Tamar has waited until this moment. There is no word about all that she must have endured, no attempt to defend her, no plea for mercy. Nor is there any explanation as to how she was still able to send a deputation to Judah after the death sentence. It is precisely by these means that the narrator achieves the desired effect. Tamar has staked her all, chancing her honor and life, so as to get her right and prove her innocence. She takes her stand entirely on the pledge which now, at the very last moment, publicly establishes the father of the child in such a way that Judah himself has to reveal her innocence. The presentation here is close to the hero-story so characteristic of the period of the judges (cf. *Genesis 12–36*, 50-54). "Only Tamar is unmistakably praised by the narrator" (G. von Rad, p. 362, in his description of the figure of Tamar; similarly J. A. Emerton). On the presentation of the exhibits in v. 25b, H. McKeating writes: "Rarely are material exhibits in evidence and only in Gen. 38:25 could they be called convincing" (1970, bibliog. above).

[38:26] Judah, an honorable man, shows himself equal to the difficult and somewhat humiliating situation (v. 26). He states openly, "She is within her rights rather than I." He sees her conduct as justified by his own injustice, "Why did I not. . . ." Thus it is expressed with particular clarity and force that in the Old Testament "justice" is seen not from the point of view of the individual but from that of the community (K. Koch, "Gerechtigkeit," BHH 1 [1962] 548f.). So one who has injured another confesses his offense openly. The narrative reaches its climax and goal with Judah's justification of Tamar. Enough has been said; it is not necessary to narrate further what this last minute change of fortune meant for Tamar. We find an echo of the high honor in which Tamar was held in Ruth 4:12.

The narrator remarks in conclusion, v. 26b, that Judah had no further relations with Tamar. A relationship which would not have fulfilled the levirate obligation could be regarded as incest.

[38:27-30] The narrative issues into the genealogy again in the closing section (vv. 27-30); it reports the birth of twins (vv. 27, 28) and their naming (vv. 29, 30). This genealogical note is expanded by the suggestion of a dispute over precedence (vv. 28, 29). The present passage, vv. 27-30, is a parallel to 25:21b-25a which also concerns twins and the question of precedence (38:27 is almost word for word the same as 25:24). Both passages deal with a genealogical note which contains within it the beginnings of a narrative; in chs. 25ff. the narrative is continued, in 38:27-30 it remains where it is. It is clear that we have here a once independent genealogical note, because the suggestion of a dispute over precedence (vv. 28, 29) has no connection with the narrative in vv. 12-26. The close parallel between 38:27-30 and 25:21-26 is explained from the conflict between the birth of twins and the birth of the first, and this was always the occasion for a new narrative.

[38:27] It is presupposed that Tamar has been received back into her family with honor. The twins that she is expecting are legitimate, i.e., they are recognized as children of her deceased husband, fathered by a member of the family of this house.

[38:28] At the birth of the twins it is important to establish beyond dispute which of the two came first from the mother's womb. The midwife takes every precaution and identifies the first arm that comes out with a scarlet thread (cf. Josh. 2:18).

[38:29] But a complication now arises (v. 29). The first draws his hand back, והנה יצא אחיו, i.e., the other is the firstborn. The midwife admonishes him as being violent: "What a breach it is you have torn!" So, following the midwife's exclamation about his violent arrival, he is named Perez (originally, rupture of the perineum?).

[38:30] Then his brother, with the scarlet thread on his hand, is born (v. 30). He is called זרח. The name Perez is explained from the midwife's exclamation; זרח is not explained at all. It is likely that he is given a name that has to do with the scarlet thread, שני. But the name זרח does not in any way sound like it. A connection has been made with it according to the sense because the personal name זרח is identical with the noun and verb זרח = to rise or come forth; rising, shining.

There could be tones of "shining, red"; but this is farfetched. The explanation of the lack of similarity between the giving of the names is that the conclusion of the narrative of vv. 12-26 told of the birth of one son only, and his naming, Perez; J. A. Emerton writes: "The story needs the birth of a child as its climax" (1979, p. 406, bibliog. above). Ruth 4:12,18, which speaks of only one son of Tamar, supports this. Here, as in the older form of the conclusion of Gen. 38, Perez was understood only as a personal name, the son of Tamar who carries on her line that finally leads to David. This original conclusion was expanded by the tradition of the two lines of Perez and Zerah that stemmed from Judah and occur in the two lists in Gen. 46 and Num. 26:20f. (expressly designated here as two lines from Judah). Thus the genealogical appendage first acquires its tribal aspect. It is not possible to be more specific. The line of Zerah, stemming from Judah, is listed by itself in Josh. 7:1, 16-18, 24; 22:20. The name designates an Edomite line in 36:33 (cf. *Genesis 12–36*, comm. ad loc.).

G. von Rad maintains that the conclusion, vv. 27-30, is unsatisfactory because it does not say whether Tamar marries and whom she marries. G. W. Coats has explained the situation correctly: the right for which Tamar fought, according to the old custom of the levirate, concerned only a male descendant: "Juda's [sic] judgment established Tamar's right to have the child" (1972, p. 465, bibliog. above). The conclusion in its original form told only of the birth of her son Perez.

Purpose and Thrust

The originally independent narrative deals with the change of fortune of a woman in distress. She has lost her husband as a young wife and is a childless widow. Many ancient narratives deal with the distress of the childless wife. It is peculiar to this narrative that Tamar could have a child in accordance with the levirate custom; but her husband's family has withheld this right from her. The narrative might continue with Tamar imploring God's help and being rescued from her distress by God's intervention. But there is no trace of this in ch. 38. It is a secular narrative through and through and tells further how Tamar herself procures her right by a daring and clever ruse on the very edge of propriety. The narrator approves of Tamar quite openly; he sets in relief her cleverness and firmness of purpose. When Judah finally says, "She is within her rights rather than I," he thereby acknowledges that the questionable means Tamar uses to procure her right are justified and that justice is restored by them. The right is the greater good and Judah, too, submits to it.

Tamar is one of those women in the patriarchal stories who, unjustly disadvantaged, seizes the initiative herself, even in opposition to established custom and order; she revolts against their constriction like Hagar, Rebekah, Leah and Rachel, and Lot's daughters. Tamar can procure her right only by revolting against her father-in-law's authority and by behaving in a way that is a grave offense to custom. It is characteristic of the patriarchal stories that revolt against the established social order, where it is a question of injustice, is initiated by women only. And in each case the justice of such self-defense is recognized.

The narrative is secular and says nothing of God's action or speech. Tamar is certainly not presented as an "Old Testament saint" (F. Delitzsch). If one raises the question of theology, and this is not necessary for the understanding of the narrative, one can only stand behind Judah's final judgment, "She is within her rights rather than I." For Judah the right is the greater good and he must submit to it; even though it is a hard blow to his authority, he sees the right as protecting the community. He takes for granted that it is God who protects the right of the community; there is no need to state this. It is just this that makes the story of Tamar a biblical story. One can speak of God providentially protecting the life of the community without specifically mentioning it. This is also the setting of Tamar's behavior.

Gen. 38 does not mention that the son of Tamar, born from the event narrated here, is one of David's forefathers (but cf. Ruth 4); it is important, however, from the overall context of the story reported in the Old Testament. The story tells later listeners about David's ancestors, of how the line of David was preserved by the daring action of a woman who was a Canaanite by birth (T. and D. Thompson [1968] 89, bibliog. above).

Genesis 39:1-23

Joseph and His Master's Wife

Literature

Genesis 39: A. Hamada, "Stela of Putiphar," ASAE 39 (1939) 273-277. W. Kornfeld, "L'adultère dans l'Orient antique," RB 57 (1950) 92-109. J. Hempel, "Glaube, Mythos und Geschichte im AT," ZAW 65 (1953) 109-167 esp. 116. W. A. Ward, "Egyptian Titles in Genesis 39–50," BibSacr 114 (1957) 40-59. D. W. Thomas, ed., *Archaeology and OT Study* (1967). Y. D. Yohanan, ed., *Joseph and Potiphar's Wife in World Literature: An Anthology of the Story of the Chaste Youth and the Lustful Stepmother* (1968). G. Velten, "Joseph sauveur et aliénateur, Gn 39; 41; 47,13-20," ETR 46 (1971) 349-354.

Genesis 39:1-6: H. J. Heyes, *Joseph in Ägypten* (1904; 1921³). V. Aptowitzer, "Schenke und Schenkin: Zu Hammurapi #110," WZKM 30 (1917/18) 359-365. P. Katz, "Two Kindred Corruptions in the Septuagint (Gn 39,4; Jes 51,6)," VT 1 (1951) 261-266. J. Scharbert, "Das Verbum *PQD* in der Theologie des AT," BZ 4 (1960) 209-226. H. W. Wolff, "The Kerygma of the Deuteronomic Historical Work" (1961), Eng. in W. Brueggemann, *The Vitality of OT Traditions* (1975) 83-100. M. H. Pope, "Marginalia to M. Dahood's Ugaritic-Hebrew Philology," JBL 85 (1966) 455-466 esp. 459. H. D. Preuss, " '. . .ich will mit dir sein!' " ZAW 80 (1968) 139-173. C. Westermann, *Blessing: In the Bible and the Life of the Church* (1968; Eng. 1981). D. Vetter, "Jahwes Mit-Sein, ein Ausdruck des Segens," AzTh 1,45 (1971). M. J. Mulder, "Versuch zur Deutung von Sokènèt in 1 Kön I 2,4," VT 22 (1972) 43-54. L. Schmidt, "Israel ein Segen für die Völker?" ThViat 12 (1975) 135-151 esp. 139f. H. Tawil, "Hebrew צלח/הצלח, Akkadian ešēru/šūšuru: A Lexicographical Note," JBL 95 (1976) 405-413. C. Westermann, "Das Schöne im AT," Fests. W. Zimmerli (1977) 479-497.

Genesis 39:7-23: B. Landsberger, "Über die Völker Vorderasiens im 3. Jt.," ZA 35 (1924) 213-238. L. Baeck, "Der Ibri," MGWJ 83 (1939; 1963²) 66-68. B. H. Stricker, "La prison de Joseph," *Acta Or Kopenhagen* (1943) 101-137. A. M. Honeyman, "The Occasion of Joseph's Temptation," VT 2 (1952) 85-87. S. Donadoni, "La seduzione della moglie di Bata," RSO 28 (1953) 143-148. H. Otten, "Kanaanäische Mythen aus Hattusa-Bogazköy," MDOG 85 (1953) esp. 30ff. R. J. Williams, "Ancient Egyptian Folktales: The Tale of Two Brothers," UTQ 37 (1958). A. Jepsen, "Gnade und Barmherzigkeit im AT," KuD 7 (1961) 261-271. K. W. Neubauer, "Der Stamm *CHNN* im Sprachgebrauch des AT" (diss. Berlin 1964). C. J. Mullo Weir, "Mesopotamia: Nuzi," D. W. Thomas, ed., *Archaeology and OT Study* (1967) 73-86 and F. F. Bruce, "Tell El-Amarna," 3-20. G. W. Coats, "Despoiling the Egyptians," VT 18 (1968) 450-457. A. Malamat, "King Lists of the Old Babylonian Period and Biblical Genealogies," JAOS 88 (1968) 163-173. K. Koch, "Die Hebräer vom Auszug aus Ägypten bis zum Grossreich Davids," VT 19 (1969) 37-81. M. Greenberg, "Hab/Piru and Hebrews," WHJP II (1970) 188-200. I.

Willi-Plein, "חן: Ein Übersetzungsproblem. Gedanken zu Sach. XII 10," VT 23 (1973) 90-99. L. Rost, *Studien zum AT*, BWANT 6 (1974) esp. 10f. 17,24. E. Lipinski, "L' 'esclave Hebreu,' " VT 26 (1976) 120-123. W. Weinberg, "Language Consciousness in the OT," ZAW 92 (1980) 185-204 esp. 195, 203.

Text

39:1   After Joseph had been brought down[a] to Egypt [Potiphar, one of Pharaoh's chamberlains, chief of the guard][b] an Egyptian bought him from the Ishmaelites who brought him there.

2   Now Yahweh was with Joseph so that he prospered,[a] and lived[b] in the house of his Egyptian master.

3   When his master saw that Yahweh was with him and gave success to all that he did,

4   Joseph found favor in his eyes; he became his personal attendant. Then he made him administrator of his household and entrusted[a] to him all that[b] he had.

5   From the time that he entrusted his household and all that he had to him, Yahweh blessed the house of the Egyptian because of Joseph, and his blessing rested on all that he had both in house and field.

6   He[a] left all he had in Joseph's care and concerned himself personally[b] with nothing but the food he ate. Now Joseph was of fine appearance and handsome.[c]

7   After this his master's wife began to take notice of Joseph and said to him, Come, lie with me!

8   But he refused and said to his master's wife, See, with me (around) my master does not concern himself[a] with his household and has entrusted all that he has to me.

9   He himself is not greater in this house than I,[a] and he has withheld nothing from me except you, because you are his wife. How could I do anything as wicked as this and sin against God?

10   She kept asking Joseph day after day, but he refused to lie with her[a] [and to be with her].[b]

11   On one occasion when he came as usual[a] to the house to do his work, and none of the members of the household were inside,

12   she seized hold of his cloak and said, Lie with me! But he left his cloak in her hand and fled and ran from the house.

13   Now when she saw that he had left his cloak in her hand and fled from the house,

14   she called out to the men of the household and said to them, Look! He has brought a Hebrew[a] to us to sport with us; he came to me to lie with me, but I screamed out aloud.

15   When he heard my scream he left his cloak beside me and fled and ran from the house.

16   So she kept his cloak by her[a] until his master came home.

17   Then she told him her story. She said, The Hebrew slave whom you brought to us came to me to sport with me.

18   When I raised my voice and screamed he left his cloak beside me and fled from the house.

19   When his master heard what his wife had to say to him, telling him This is what your servant did to me, he was very angry.

20   So he took Joseph and had him thrown into prison where the prisoners of the king were held.[a] And there he remained.

21   But Yahweh was with Joseph and showed steadfastness to him,[a] and won him[b] the favor of the governor of the prison.

22   So the governor of the prison entrusted to Joseph all the prisoners who
     were there; everything that they[a] did there was done through him.[b]
23   The governor of the prison did not concern himself any[a] further with
     what he had[b] entrusted to him because Yahweh was with him and
     gave success to all that he did.

1a Ges-K §142b.   **b** "The royal cooks or butchers (1 Sam. 9:23f.) who had come to
be the bodyguard" (J. Skinner); cf. 2 Kings 25:8; D. B. Redford, VT.S 20 (1970) 56; also
Gen. 40:3-4; 41:10,12. On the problem of the addition, see below ad loc.
2a H. Tawil, 1976, bibliog. above.   **b** ויהי, with the meaning "he remained," H.
Gunkel.
4a J. Scharbert, 1960, bibliog. above; W. Schottroff פקד, THAT II, 466-486.   **b** Add
אשר, with three Mss and Sam, corresponding to v. 5.
6a עזב to entrust, as in Is. 10:3; Job 39:14.   **b** ידע and את, D. B. Redford, op.cit.,
53.   **c** On the construction Ges-K §128x; BrSynt §77f.
8a Sam reads מאומה as in v. 23; but מה־בבית "is good Hebrew" (H. Holzinger).
9a On the construction Ges-K §107rt; 112p; BrSynt §163a.
10a אצל = side; parts of the body can form prepositions, BrSynt §117c.   **b** The
words להיות עמה are missing in Gk[106]; perhaps an addition.
11a כהיום הזה does not mean "one day" as in Ges-K §126s, but "as usual" (A. M.
Honeyman, 1952, bibliog. above; also D. B. Redford).
14a On איש עברי, G. von Rad, comm. ad loc.; K. Koch, 1969, bibliog. above.
16a On the form, Ges-K §72ee.
20a On the construction, Ges-K §130c; BrSynt §162.
21a Cf. Ps. 40:2.   **b** The suffix in חנו refers to Joseph as object; cf. H. J. Stoebe, חן
and חסד, THAT I, A. Jepsen, 1961 and I. Willi-Plein, 1973, bibliog. above.
22a On the absence of the personal pronoun in the participial sentence see Ges-K
§116s.   **b** The last three words are missing in Gk.
23a את־כל־מאומה only here.   **b** On the construction, Ges-K §116o; 152b; BrSynt
§163a.

Form

The second part of the Joseph story begins with ch. 39: Joseph in Egypt (chs.
39–41). It is the story of advancement: Joseph, Jacob's son, who had been sold
there as a slave, became a high official in Pharaoh's service. The rise is narrated in
three scenes, chs. 39; 40; and 41. The tension arises from the succession of stages:
the first stage, advancement (vv. 2-6), is followed by an even greater fall (vv.
7-20), and the next stage (vv. 21-23) by a long period of quiet (ch. 40). Each part,
therefore, has its own proper place in the story of the advancement (chs. 39–41);
ch. 39 cannot be a later addition (so D. B. Redford, H. C. Schmitt) nor can chs.
39–41 be a synthesis of two sources or layers. With great skill the narrator is careful to shape each of the three scenes in such a way that they have the effect of a
whole (G. von Rad), each with its own arc of tension with introduction, climax,
and conclusion so that each step in each scene prepares the next. Ch. 39 in this
structure makes sense only as part of a greater whole: Joseph's ultimate audience
with Pharaoh began as narrated here. His recent fall 9 (vv. 7-20) leads to a meeting with officials of Pharaoh (ch. 40), and this in turn to Pharaoh sending for him
(ch. 41).

Ch. 39 begins with a bridge passage (v. 1) from ch. 37 and is divided into
rise (vv. 2-6), fall (vv. 7-20), and a new rise in prison (vv. 21-23). The episode in
the middle, vv. 7-20, is thus framed by the two parts vv. 2-6 and 21-23 in such a
way as to form a strong contrast to the theme of Yahweh's assistance which they

present. The individuality of the narrator stands out clearly both in this structure and in the implementation of details. He uses the device of doubling (W. Rudolf, H. Gunkel) which serves the mounting tension more than the narrative span. Joseph's twofold rise corresponds to his twofold fall. The attempt of the wife to seduce Joseph is narrated in two stages, vv. 7-9 an 10-11; the wife's accusation is made very effectively in the presence of the members of the household (vv. 13-15) and her husband (vv. 16-18).

Even the scholars who support the thesis of different sources in the Joseph story are almost unanimous in regarding ch. 39 as a unity (exceptions, J. Wellhausen, O. Procksch).

Commentary

[**39:1**] V. 1 is, as it were, the overpass spanning ch. 38 and joining directly with ch. 37; it has already begun in 37:36. Both verses provide for the insertion of ch. 38. This first verse, the overpass, which at the same time introduces ch. 39, consists of two verbal sentences: "Joseph was brought down. . .someone bought him." The first sentence resumes 37:28, "And they [the Ishmaelites] brought Joseph down to Egypt"; at the same time, it resumes the context there, namely, the fact that Joseph was sold as a slave and why this could be done. Ch. 39, therefore, presupposes ch. 37. The concluding adverbial modification, "from the Ishmaelites who brought him there," resumes 37:28b, "and they [the Ishmaelites] brought Joseph down to Egypt." It is here that one can pick up the redactional link that bypasses ch. 38. This also explains the variation "Midianites" in 37:36 and "Ishmaelites" in 39:1. The link is made even closer by the use of the verb "they sold him" in 37:36 (the same verb in 37:28) and the correlative "he bought him" in 39:1.

Only the designation of the buyer in the middle of v. 1 raises difficulties. There are three parts to this segment; it seems to be overloaded: (1) the name, (2) the profession, and (3) the racial origin. The real difficulty is that in a three-part note of this sort the איש מצרי should stand at the beginning: "An Egyptian bought him. . .." This generalizing detail is out of place at the end (J. Skinner). The only possibility left is that the text in an earlier form ran, "And an Egyptian bought him from the Ishmaelites. . .." One notices immediately that the wording of the addition is the same as in 37:36b. It is certain that it is an addition (so the majority of interpreters since A. Dillmann) because it is restricted to these two places, 37:36 and 39:1. The Egyptian is not mentioned by name in the rest of ch. 39 but only as "his Egyptian master," "Joseph's master," "his master," "the Egyptian." It is common for an unnamed secondary character in a narrative to acquire a name later, e.g., in the synoptic gospels.

The name פוטיפר occurs only in Gen. 37:36 and 39:1. The name of Joseph's father-in-law in 41:45, 50 and 46:20, פוטי פרע, is another form of the same name and means "the one whom Re gives." סריס means a eunuch, and in general a courtier, a court official (cf. D. B. Redford, op. cit., p. 30). His office is that of שר הטבחים, head of the bodyguard (טבח is actually butcher or cook, KBL).

[**39:2-6**] G. W. Coats, and before him L. Ruppert, have described vv. 2-6 as the exposition to ch. 39: "The. . . purpose for the exposition as a whole. . . is to set the stage for the major body of the scene in vss 7-20a" (CBQMS 4, 1976, 21). But with its emphasis on detail and its continuation in vv. 21-23 the passage has a function that goes beyond this. With its theme of Yahweh-with-Joseph (vv. 2, 3, 22, 23) it forms the theological entrance piece to the Joseph story which finds its counterpart at the end with the concluding words of Joseph, "God brought me here" (45:5-8; 50:17-21). Chs. 39–41 are the story of a rise, but a rise made possible because Yahweh was with Joseph. This is what the passages that frame it, 39:1-2 and 21-23, intend to say, and it is to this that the concluding words return (45:5-8; 50:17-21). Ch. 39, then, is a constitutive part of the Joseph story and is in no wise a later addition (against D. B. Redford and H. C. Schmitt). By his emphasis on detail the narrator gives weight to this theological entrance piece.

The arrangement unfolds the theological theme: Yahweh was with Joseph (v. 2); his master perceives this and draws the consequences (vv. 3-4); he makes him his household administrator (v. 4b). The result of this is that Yahweh blesses the house of the Egyptian (v. 5) who entrusts everything to Joseph (v. 6a). V. 6b is the transition to vv. 7-20. It is here that the introduction has its point of contact with the Egyptian story of the two brothers (see below on vv. 7-20) which tells that the work of the younger brother was particularly prosperous and so affected favorably his brother's property. The reason was that "the strength of a God was in him."

[39:2a] "Yahweh was with Joseph" (v. 2a), with the result that everything he undertook prospered. He was a "man of achievement."

Yahweh's (God's) assistance, blessing (v. 5), and success are part of the vocabulary of God's blessing in action; cf. C. Westermann (1968) and D. Vetter (1971), bibliog. above, with further literature. D. Vetter has gathered all passages together (p. 4); H. D. Preuss (1968) has gathered the extra-Israelite parallels; the passages in the patriarchal story are to be found in *Genesis 12–36*, comm. on 28:15. H. D. Preuss says that the promise of assistance "has become a more general formula of support" in the Joseph story (p. 156). Having regard to the ambit of God's assistance, this may be more precisely stated: originally it is God's assistance during the migration; in the Jacob-Esau story it is extended to the possession of cattle; in the Joseph story and the story of David it moves into the political domain, describing the political rise of a man. L. Ruppert cites a number of passages in *Die Josepherzählung der Genesis* (1965) 49f.; in particular 1 Sam. 18:12, 14, 28 (also 20:15) is an exact parallel to Gen 39:2-6, 21-23. They concern the rise of David and the fall of Saul: "But when Saul saw and knew that Yahweh was with David. . . [he] was still more afraid of David" (1 Sam. 18:28).

Gen. 39–41 narrates the story of Joseph's rise in Egypt and 39:2-6 (and vv. 21-23) gives the theological reason for it: God's assistance extends to the political domain of a distant land. Gen. 39, to be sure, is concerned with the lowest level; nevertheless, this first step brings Joseph into the administrative rank. It is here that the striking fact that the name Yahweh occurs only in 39:1-6 and 21-23 in the Joseph story finds its explanation. Scholars have proposed to explain it by source criticism (opposed by D. B. Redford and others) or by alleging that ch. 39 is a later addition. But this latter is more unlikely because a later writer would scarcely have replaced אלהים, used elsewhere without exception in the Joseph story, by יהוה. The explanation derives from the function of 39:2-6, 21-23 as the theological introit to the Joseph story as a whole. It is the narrator who is speaking. Only from his lips does the name יהוה fall, never from the lips of any of the actors in chs. 37-50. The narrator wants to link God's presence with Joseph to his presence with the patriarchs by taking over the fixed formula of Yahweh's assistance which is firmly rooted in the Isaac-Jacob tradition. It is the God of the fathers who is now with Joseph just as he was earlier with the patriarchs. But there are also echoes of Yahweh's presence with David, which brought about his rise, just as it did Joseph's.

[39:2b] The effect of God's support is that the newly acquired slave is not put to work out in the fields but is able to remain in the house.

[39:3-4] As in the case of Jacob, God's support affects the circle in which he moves. His master sees that Joseph has a golden touch and that success attends all that he undertakes (for Jacob, 21:22; 30:27). The narrator repeats the catchword of v. 2. The master consequently shows him special favor (v. 4), with the result that Joseph becomes his personal attendant.

The phrase וישרת אתו was earlier understood as an E fragment in a J text, e.g., H. Gunkel, O. Procksch, L. Ruppert; it was said to be typical of E, whereas עבד was typical of J. But this presupposition does not hold true because the verbs have distinctly different meanings. Only שרת can mean to minister to a person (cf. article in THAT).

The master further entrusted him with the administration of his household (v. 4b). This is narrated in two sentences: "he put him in charge of" or "he entrusted to him," פקד here as in Num. 1:50; 2 Kings 25:22f.; נתן ביד in the same sense in Gen. 30:35; 32:17; 2 Sam. 10:10. That is he made him major-domo, οἰκονόμος, Egyptian *mer-per* according to J. Vergote, *Joseph en Egypte. . .* (1959) 24ff. "One often sees an administrator of this kind in Egyptian representations with a staff or a papyrus roll in his hand" (H. Gunkel). An example of a rise from a menial position to that of household administrator is found in H. J. Heyes, *Joseph in Ägypten* (1904; 1921³) 128.

[39:5-6a] The master's decision has a prosperous effect on the welfare of the house and on his property. From the time that he appointed Joseph administrator, Yahweh has blessed the house of the Egyptian. The narrator could not say that Yahweh was also with Joseph's Egyptian master, because the "assistance" presupposes a mutual personal relationship. He uses the word ברך because this verb goes beyond personal relationship; house, cattle, and all that is created can be blessed. Gen. 33:17 also speaks of this overflowing power of the blessing, and the same בגלל is used. V. 5b unfolds the meaning of the verb: Yahweh's blessing rests on all his property both in house and field (cf. H. W. Wolff [1961; Eng. 1975] and L. Schmitt, bibliog. above).

The whole sequence of 39:2-6 is a particularly apt and clear example of the meaning of blessing in the Old Testament. Assistance and blessing belong together, though they are different. Blessing embraces both people and the rest of creation. The narrator simply presupposes that the blessing can flow over from the one whom Yahweh assists to a foreign people and adherents of a foreign religion precisely because of the one whom Yahweh assists. The power inherent in the blessing is expansive; the God of the fathers is further at work in Joseph's experience of servitude in a foreign land.

[39:6a] The blessing bestowed because of Joseph has its effect in turn on his master so that he had complete confidence in him (cf. v. 4a). He can leave everything in his hands (v. 6a) "but the food he ate." Some exegetes have understood these words as a euphemism for sexual relations (so V. Aptowitzer, WZKM 30 [1917/18] 359-365); it is probably to be interpreted with L. Ruppert as a fixed expression, a *pars pro toto* to indicate his private affairs.

[**39:6b**] V. 6b forms the transition from the introduction, vv. 2-6a, to the episode of vv. 7-20. This half-verse belongs as much to the motif "Yahweh was with Joseph" as to the motif of the scorned woman. Yahweh was also with Joseph inasmuch as he was of fine appearance and handsome (similarly with David, 1 Sam. 16:18). The wife of the Egyptian desired him because he was a handsome young man. The beauty of a person in the Old Testament was regarded primarily as something of significance in interpersonal living. It is circumstantial rather than existential (C. Westermann, Fests. W. Zimmerli [1977] 479-497); consequently it is found several times in the exposition of a narrative, as here (cf. Gen. 12:11 and 19:17, with the same phrase as 39:6b).

[**39:7-20**] The narrative of vv. 7-20 is constructed with classical simplicity. It begins with Joseph's mistress, the wife of the Egyptian, desiring him (v. 7). Her desire intensifies but is not fulfilled because Joseph rejects her (vv. 8-10). Vv. 11-12 form the climax: the woman's desire expresses itself in the seizure of his cloak; Joseph's rejection results in flight. Desire now turns to hate as she twice falsely accuses Joseph—before the domestics (vv. 13-15) and the master (vv. 16-18). The wife's desire is not fulfilled, but her false accusation is. The master listens to her accusation and throws Joseph into prison (vv. 19-20a). "And there he remained," says the conclusion (v. 20b).

   The twofold action in vv. 11-12 forms the climax of the narrative. The focal point of the first part is Joseph's rejection (vv. 8-9), of the second the wife's accusation (vv. 13-18). Action and speech in the narrative are remarkably balanced. The artistically constructed narrative achieves its desired effect in that Joseph's answer to the accusation, which the situation in fact demands, is missing in the second part. The first part is arranged in dialog form; in the second part, at the point where Joseph should answer the accusation (as in Gen. 3 and 4, *audiatur et altera pars*), there comes the sentence pronounced by the master which allows Joseph no reply. Joseph, as the guiltless victim, can only accept the punishment in silence (v. 20b). It is this silence of Joseph that speaks loudest out of the narrative. Even if 39:7-20 presupposes knowledge of the Egyptian story of the two brothers, it remains an independent work of art.

   Reference should be made to the use of the narrative technique of "repetitive speech" (H. Gunkel); it is an echo technique that repeats what has happened several times as each speaker takes up the story; the effect is that each time the events are repeated by the speaker and heard by the different addresses, they take on a fresh nuance. This technique is by no means tiresome in its effect but rather makes the narrative even more lively.

   Gen. 39:7-20 and the Egyptian story of the two brothers. The story is translated in an abridged form in ANET 23-25 following the Papyrus d'Orbiny (19th dynasty), British Museum 10183. J. Skinner (comm. ad loc.) gives the content as follows: Two brothers lived together: the elder, Anubis, had a house and a wife; the younger, Bata, worked for him in the fields. One day Bata entered the house to get seed for the sowing; his brother's wife wanted him to sleep with her. Very angry, "like a leopard in a rage," he rejected her suggestion out of loyalty to his brother who had been like a father to him, and expressed his abhorrence at the "great sin" that she wanted him to commit. He promises to say nothing and returns to his brother. Anubis comes home in the evening and discovers his wife covered with self-inflicted wounds; he listens to an account which resembles the false accusation of Joseph's mistress. Anubis tries to kill his brother, but finally becomes convinced of his innocence and kills his wife instead. Toward the end, the Egyptian story moves into the realm of mythical fantasy; this may be a later expansion.

The part of the Egyptian story related here is so like that of Gen. 39:7-20 that it must have been known to the narrator of ch. 39. It is incomprehensible that some exegetes contest this (H. Holzinger, W. Eichrodt, L. Ruppert). Apart from the parallel course of the narrative there are almost word for word points of agreement. It is said of the younger brother, who is in the service of the elder, that his work was particularly fruitful, "the strength of a God was in him," and that because of him his brother's property increased. The motive for the refusal is almost the same. Like Joseph, the brother describes the proposed adultery as a "great sin" or crime. H. Gunkel says that the Egyptian story has been transferred to Joseph, but that is not quite correct. It is not a question of a mechanical transfer with the substitution of names; rather, the narrator of the Joseph story has adapted the Egyptian story so as to make it into an independent episode which he has inserted into the broader narrative. To do this he had to change the relationship between the persons in the drama. The elder and younger brothers give way to the master and the slave whom he had made administrator of the household. This adaptation requires an alteration to the conclusion (not because the beginning of ch. 40 requires it). The master deals with him as is done with a slave who is accused by the mistress of a misdemeanor. As 39:7-20 is but an episode in the Joseph story, the necessary justification of the blameless one occurs only in the later course of the story and in an entirely different way.

H. Gunkel advances several other parallels to the motif in 39:7-20 besides the Egyptian one; T. H. Gaster presents another, a Hittite translation of a Canaanite myth (*Myth, Legend.* . . [1969] 217ff.; text trans. H. Otten, MDOG 85 [1953] 30ff.): the goddess Asherah complains to her husband Ekkunirsa that Baal tried to sleep with her whereas he had rejected her.

[**39:7-9**] After the transition formula (as in 40:1; 48:1) the action begins with the demand of the master's wife that Joseph sleep with her (v. 7). Joseph gives as the reason for his refusal his position with regard to his master and her (vv. 8,9a); he rejects as a רעה גדלה what would also be a sin against God (v. 9b).

[**39:7**] The transition formula in v. 7a, "after this it happened," can well be a caesura after the long introduction; it does not fit well; the ותשא of v. 7b would follow better directly on v. 6. A narrative begins yet again with someone "looking at" (cf., e.g., 33:1). Concrete perception takes the place of abstract "desire" (the same expression is found in Gil. VI,6: Ishtar desires Gilgamesh). The crass demand, "Come, lie with me!" is intended as the language of a mistress who can give orders to the slave; or is it that the narrator consciously and rather coarsely echoes the quite different language of lovers? "The episode presupposes a society in which the wife enjoys great freedom. . .. The legal wife is mistress of the house and is scarcely held in less regard than its master" (J. Vergote, ad loc.).

[**39:8, 9a**] Joseph refuses (vv. 8,9a). H. Gunkel's explanation that the narrator contrasts the lust of the Egyptian with the chastity of the young Israelite is mistaken, as can be seen already in the Egyptian parallel, where both parties belong to the same people. But the present narrative is in no wise concerned with contrasting two qualities. The reason for Joseph's refusal is clear: he may not, he will not commit a breach of trust (also H. Gunkel), not only because he knows very well that he would thereby put his position in jeopardy, but also because he cannot do this to his master who has promoted him and shown such confidence in him. It is the same reason as found in the Egyptian parallel. He respects the limit because he sees behind it the benevolence he has found in his master's eyes (v. 4). Joseph therefore emphasizes his responsibility: ". . .He has withheld nothing from me. . ..'' The narrator is deliberately setting side by side the responsibility of the eldest brother in ch. 37 and the responsibility of one in administrative office.

[**39:9b**] V. 9b adds a further ethical and religious valuation to the real reason, beginning: "How could I do anything as wicked. . .?" In human eyes it would be a רעה גדלה (in a similar context, 2 Sam. 13:16), i.e., something very evil, an evil deed and at the same time an offense against God. The sin against God would be the breach of trust; the trust thus broken was a gift of God ("Yahweh was with him"). Joseph wants in this way to confirm the grounds for his refusal. The ethical and the religious valuation is relevant for Egypt and Israel alike. In both places and among the majority of people of antiquity adultery is a serious crime (for the same expression in the Egyptian parallel, ANET 24, col. i); marriage is under divine protection. The reason why אלהים appears here, otherwise in vv. 1-6, 21-23, is that the Egyptian woman is being addressed.

[**39:10**] The ויהי at the beginning of v. 10 follows the ויהי in v. 7; it recurs on each occasion that the narrative resumes its course: vv. 11, 13, (15), (18), 19. The wife's first attempt at seduction is followed by others (vv. 7-9); she does not desist from her purpose, while Joseph remains firm in his refusal. There is no attempt to paint a psychological picture as the story gathers to its crisis, and it is just this that makes the movement so strong. The last two words of v. 10, להיות עמה, are missing in the Gk and are probably a gloss; they "are meant to take the place of the words that shock" (H. Gunkel). The portrayal presupposes a freedom of movement for women which is the complete opposite of the confinement of the harem.

[**39:11-12**] The crisis comes when the wife takes hold of Joseph's cloak. Joseph enters the house to go about his work as usual (כהיום הזה) literally "on a day like this," i.e., as usual); none of the household is there. The narrator thus emphasizes that Joseph was entirely blameless. Joseph's position prevents him from in a way raising his hand against the mistress and so he has no option but to flee from the house. It is wretched and dishonorable to have to flee from a woman, but there is no other way out; she is his master's wife.

[**39:13-15**] The narrator shows a masterly artistic touch here; he has no need to say a word about the inner change that takes place in the mistress of the house. We say, "Her scorned love changes to hate" (H. Gunkel). But the narrator does not even say this. The change that takes place in her is realized in what she sees. Everything had begun with seeing (v. 7). The wife had seen a handsome young man; now she sees his cloak; she realized that he had left it in her hand. "In my hand," i.e., in Hebrew also "in my power." She holds his fate in her hand. This is all said in one sentence in v. 13. But the words, though not stating as much, are a reminder of the motif of the cloak in the overall context. Once again, as in 37:31-34, Joseph's cloak is the *corpus delicti*; and once again it is the means of deception.

[39:14-15] The wife uses Joseph's cloak as proof of her accusation (vv. 14-15), which she first makes in the presence of the household. She thus has concrete evidence that she can lay before her husband for his decision. It is no difficult task for her to bring the household to her side. She wins their good will by joining with them in a covert accusation against the master of the house: ". . .he has brought a Hebrew to us to sport with us. . ..'' She now tells her lying story and so forces her husband to agree with her version; otherwise she would have to confess before the domestics that she had lied and be punished for her attempted adultery. She is clever enough to remain sufficiently close to the truth so that it is difficult to do anything about it. She makes the slight alteration that Joseph did not leave his cloak in her hand but beside her.

[39:16-18] She then lay down with Joseph's cloak beside her. This brings an effective pause into the dramatic action. She tells her husband the same story with slight variations, as is natural.

[39:19] The narrator once more introduces a pause. The master's reaction, "he was very angry," does not follow immediately on the first sentence, "When his master heard. . ."; the wife's story echoes, as it were, a third time in v. 19b, "what his wife had to say, telling him this is what your servant did to me." This is meant to give the master pause for reflection on what his wife has said and so compel him to his subsequent decision. What or who is the object of his anger is an open question, and must remain so. In any case he is angry because he has been put into such a situation (F. Delitzsch: "much rather because of the amazing situation").

[39:20] The conclusion shows that the master is acting under pressure. Were the meaning merely that he was angry with Joseph, then he would have had to summon him and give vent to his anger. He does not even do this; he cannot; he cannot let him so much as utter a word. The master of the house is also the master of the rights of those in his service. But in a case like this the master should most certainly have heard Joseph who as administrator was the second man in the house. He would thus expose not only his wife but also himself in the presence of the household. So on the mere accusation of his wife he casts into prison the man in whom he had complete trust. The nature of the punishment is a sign that he is not convinced of Joseph's guilt. The appropriate punishment for the crime would be death, or at least sale into a lower degree of servitude.

There is no mention of any reaction from Joseph. He is once again the underdog; he knows that he is exposed to his fate without redress. Nevertheless, the conclusion indicates that there is more to it. It is a "prison where the prisoners of the king were held." This is not a later gloss (A. Dillmann, D. B. Redford, and others), but necessary to the context (H. Gunkel). The phrase אסורי המלך is virtually the only occasion in the Joseph story where מלך appears instead of Pharaoh; the reason for this is that we have to do here with a technical term. The word for prison בית הסהר occurs only here, vv. 20 (twice), 21-22 (twice), 23; 40:3, 5. Together with it is found משמר, 40:3, 4, 7; 41:10; 42:17, 19, (30?); elsewhere Lev.

24:12; Num. 15:34; בּוֹר (ch. 37); 40:15; 41:14, elsewhere Jer. 38. H. Donner (*Die literarische Gestalt. . .* [1976] 40-41) has explained correctly that these different designations cannot be used as a criterion for source division (H. Gunkel, D. B. Redford). מִשְׁמָר means "custody" and is to be distinguished from בֵּית הַסֹּהַר which means "prison." The theory of two versions of Joseph in prison accepted by H. Gunkel and others is contrived. "The narrative is unified, without contradiction and without additions" (H. Donner, p. 40). Prison was something unknown in Israel; it was experienced in the Joseph story. There was no prison sentence in ancient Israel; we first hear of it in the later period of the monarchy (1 Kings 22:27; Jer. 38), and only in the context of the royal court.

There is nothing in Gen. 39 corresponding to the conclusion of the Egyptian narrative of the two brothers. The reason for this is not, as H. Gunkel says, "that the material of two stories has been subsequently amalgamated," but that the author of the Joseph narrative has adapted the Egyptian narrative to one episode of his broader context. The further fate of the wife has no function here, but the justification of Joseph does; it has a completely different outcome from the Egyptian parallel.

[39:21-23] Vv. 21-23 and vv. 2-6 form the frame of the narrative (vv. 7-20); but the frame is not merely the introduction and the conclusion; each part is colored by its own proper movement—advancement, fall, advancement. Joseph's rise in the house of the Egyptian is continued in his advancement in prison. These two parts correspond closely to each other; both are determined by the refrain, "Yahweh was with Joseph" (vv. 3,21a,23). Here too the effect is the master's favor (v. 20b); the master entrusts him with the supervision of the whole area of his responsibility (vv. 22, 23a). By way of conclusion it is once more emphasized that it is Yahweh's assistance that gives Joseph's work success (v. 23b as in vv. 2a,3). Both correspond by and large; only the explanatory sentences (vv. 3 and 5) are missing from vv. 21-23.

[39:21] The וַיְהִי introduces a new direction in the action. The preceding sentence, "and there he remained," is a conclusion to vv. 7-20. The refrain, "and Yahweh was with Joseph," is explained and expanded here by וַיֵּט אֵלָיו חֶסֶד, which has no equivalent in vv. 2-6. This is conditioned by the intervening narrative of Joseph's fall, vv. 7-20, to which the sentence refers: "and showed steadfastness to him." The same verb is found in the same context in Ps. 40:2 (Eng. v. 1) in the hymn of praise of one who has been saved: "he inclined to me and heard my cry" (against H. Gunkel who understands וַיֵּט as hiphil and translates: "he let him win favor"). The sentence has an important function in the narrator's thought. The listener senses the incongruity between the introduction and the action in vv. 7-20 where Yahweh clearly was not with Joseph; in any case he does nothing to prevent his fall. The narrator wants to say that God can be with a person even in the course of a fall; God remains loyal to him and yet again shows him his steadfastness. There is no need for detail; the word חֶסֶד and the echo of the hymn of praise is enough. Only now comes v. 21a, corresponding to v. 4a: "and won him the favor of the governor of the prison." The expression וַיִּתֵּן חֵן occurs also in Ex. 3:21; 11:3; 12:36; each time it is the favor of the Egyptians shown to the Israelites (or Moses). The narrator possibly had it in mind.

[39:22, 23a] The sequel is the same as in Potiphar's house (vv. 4b, 5a). The overseer of the prison entrusts him with his whole area of competence (vv. 22, 23a). The sentence, ''everything that they did there was done through him,'' obviously means that Joseph organized the prisoners' daily schedule. This comprises the supervision as well (v. 23a).

[**39:23b**] By way of conclusion, the narrator repeats once more that that was possible because Yahweh was with him and gave success to all that he did; he repeats the refrain not just for the sake of the framework of ch. 39, but as his theological introit to the Joseph narrative. What is said here holds for Joseph's rise as a whole.

Purpose and Thrust

Following on the story of the patriarchs we have here for the first time a narrative about a son who is forcibly separated from his family and has to live as a slave among foreigners in a foreign land. As a slave he is at the disposition of those in power; he is accused of a crime and is not even given a hearing. He has neither right nor legal counsel. He has only one resource to help him—the God of his fathers is with him. The chapter depends on this. The help works in two directions, through his submission and his demeanor. God's help means that he advances him, not in any spectacular way, but simply. Joseph is received in a friendly manner by those with whom he has to work. He is enabled to rise because ''he found favor in the eyes of his master.'' The God of his fathers is with him: this does not mean, as it does later, that God is *against* those who are ''pagans,'' but that he prospers them because of Joseph. This occurs again only after the collapse of the state of Israel: ''But seek the welfare of the city where I have sent you into exile, and pray to the Lord on its behalf. . .'' (Jer. 29:7). The welfare of the foreigners reaches its climax because of Joseph in ch. 43. God's presence with him extends into the political arena.

God's assistance has its effect on Joseph's bearing. He prospers his work. From this springs loyalty and responsibility, described in the middle part (vv. 7-20). Joseph acquires a high degree of responsibility because of the success that God confers on him. The master's wife sets herself in opposition to this by wanting to seduce him (vv. 8-9). He remains true to his master, and so true to the God of his fathers who is with him. Were he to lose the trust of his master he would lose not only his position but also God's assistance which brought him to that position: ''How could I. . . sin against God?''

This is a narrative of God's action and the comportment of a person before God taking place in simple, ordinary circumstances as daily work prospers and the friendly disposition of the authorities progresses. The prosperity is answered by competence, reliability, and unbending loyalty. These simple circumstances prepare the way to healing the shattered peace and saving many from famine. Only one passage gives a hint at what is behind it all. Joseph must experience that God's presence does not smooth the road before him; a serious fall follows the first step upwards. The refrain ''God was with Joseph'' is expanded, ''and God showed steadfastness to him,'' thus allowing us to anticipate what hardship Joseph must endure until he can say with the psalmist, ''. . .he inclined to me and heard my cry'' (Ps. 40:2[1]).

Joseph Interprets the Dreams of the Cupbearer and the Baker

Literature

Genesis 40: J. Offord, "The Princes of the Bakers and the Cup-bearers," PEFQSt 50 (1918) 139ff. A. Ungnad, "Joseph, der Tartan des Pharao," ZAW 41 (1923) 204-207. N. H. Snaith, *Notes on the Hebrew Text of Genesis XL-XLIV: Study Notes on Bible Books* (1950). E. L. Ehrlich, "Der Traum des Mardochai," ZRGG (1954) 69-74. S. Sauneron, *Les songes et leur interprétation dans l'Egypte ancienne: Les songes et leur interprétation* (1959) 17-61. E. Lorenz, *Die Träume des Pharao, des Mundschenken und des Bäckers: Psychoanalytische Interpretationen biblischer Texte*, ed. Y. Spiegel (1972).

Genesis 40:1-19: J. C. Matthes, "Bemerkungen zu einigen Stellen aus Genesis und Numeri," ZAW 31 (1911) 128-132. R. J. Zwi Werblowsky, "Stealing the Word," VT 6 (1956) 105-106. T. Horst, "Der Traum des Bäckers (Gen 40, 16-19)," BiLi 24 (1956/57) 206. E. A. Speiser, "Census and Ritual Expiation in Mari and Israel," BASOR 149 (1958) 17-25. L. Kopf, "Arabische Etymologien und Parallelen zum Bibelwörterbuch," VT 8 (1958) 161-215; 9 (1959) 247-287. Y. Kaufmann, *The Religion of Israel: From Its Beginnings to the Babylonian Exile* (1961) esp. 93f. J. J. Rabinowitz, "Neo-Babylonian Legal Documents and Jewish Law," JJP 13 (1961) 131-175. T. J. Meek, "A New Bible Translation," JBL 82 (1963) 265-271 esp. 270. J. Morgenstern, "Two Additional Notes to 'The Suffering Servant—A New Solution,' " VT 13 (1963) 321-332. S. Speier, " 'Das Kosten des Todeskelches' im Targum," VT 13 (1963) 344-345. Y. M. Grintz, "The Land of the Hebrews," OLD Jerusalem (1964) 92-102. D. B. Redford, "The 'Land of the Hebrews' in Gen XL 15," VT 15 (1965) 529-532. J. Wijngaards, "הוציא and העלה. A Twofold Approach to the Exodus," VT 15 (1965) 91-102. C. J. Labuschagne, "Teraphim—A New Proposal for Its Etymology," VT 16 (1966) 115-117. E. Zenger, "Die deuteronomistische Interpretation der Rehabilitierung Jojachins," BZ 19 (1967) 16-30 esp. 23. T. C. Vriezen, "Enkele Opmerkingen over het Woordonderzoek," *Schrift en Uitleg* (1970) 237-247. S. R. Isenberg, "On the Jewish-Palestinian Origins of the Peshitta to the Pentateuch," JBL 90 (1971) 69-81. E. C. B. MacLaurin, "Joseph and Asaph," VT 25 (1975) 27-45 esp. 28ff. H. Vorländer, "Mein Gott. Die Vorstellungen vom persönlichen Gott im Alten Orient und im AT," AOAT 23 (1975). H. Jagersma, ". . .*Ten derden Dage*. . ." (1976) esp. 18f. M. Weinfeld, "Ancient Near Eastern Patterns in Prophetic Literature," VT 27 (1977) 178-195. E. F. de Ward, "Superstition and Judgment: Archaic Methods of Finding a Verdict," ZAW 89 (1977) 1-19.

Genesis 40:20-23: E. König, *Stilistik, Rhetorik, Poetik in Bezug auf die biblische Literatur komparativisch dargestellt* (1900) 23. J. Obermann, *Ugaritic Mythology: A Study of Its Leading Motifs* (1948) esp. 20. J. Blau, "Reste des i-Imperfekts von *zkr* qal: Eine lexikographische Studie," VT 11 (1961) 81-86.

Text

40:1 Now some time after this the king's cupbearer and baker offended[a] their master, the king of Egypt.

2 The Pharaoh was angry with the two eunuchs, the cupbearer and the baker,

3 and he put[a] them in custody in the house of the chief of the guard, in the prison where Joseph was held.

4 The chief of the guard made Joseph their overseer and he attended[a] to them; they remained some time[b] in custody.

5 Then on the same night they both dreamed, each his own dream, each with its own meaning, the cupbearer and the baker of the[a] king of Egypt who were held in prison.

6 When Joseph came to them in the morning he saw that they were troubled.

7 So he asked Pharaoh's eunuchs who were in custody with him in his master's house, Why are your faces[a] downcast today?

8 They said to him, We have had a dream and there is nobody to interpret it.[a] Joseph said to them, Do not interpretations belong to God? Tell them to me, please!

9 So the head cupbearer told Joseph his dream: In my dream[a] there was a vine in front of me,

10 and there were three branches on it; as it budded[a] it blossomed[b] and its clusters ripened[c] into grapes.[d]

11 The Pharaoh's cup was in my hand and I took the grapes and squeezed them into the Pharaoh's cup and put the cup in the Pharaoh's hand.

12 Then Joseph said to him: This is its interpretation. The three branches are three days.

13 Within three days the Pharaoh will raise your head and restore you to your post and you will put the cup in the Pharaoh's hand as you used to do when you were his cupbearer.

14 But[a] remember me[b] when[c] things go well with you and please do me this favor—mention me to the Pharaoh and get me out of this house.

15 For I was abducted from the land of the Hebrews and I have done nothing here that they should put me in a dungeon.

16 When the head baker saw that the interpretation was favorable he said to Joseph: I too had a dream and in it I saw three baskets[a] of white bread on my head.

17 In the top basket were all sorts of baked goods for the Pharaoh; but the birds were eating them from the basket on my head.

18 Joseph answered: This is its interpretation. The three baskets are three days.

19 Within three days the Pharaoh will raise your head [from you[a]] and will hang you on a tree and the birds will eat your flesh from you.

20 Now the third day was the Pharaoh's birthday[a] and he gave a feast for all his servants. He raised the head of the chief cupbearer and the head of the chief baker in the presence of his servants.

21 He restored the chief cupbearer to his post and he put the cup in the Pharaoh's hand.

22 But the chief baker he hanged as[a] Joseph had said in interpreting for them.

23 But the chief cupbearer gave no further thought to Joseph and forgot him.

1a Construction, Ges-K §§128a, 129b; BrSynt §132.

3a Construction, BrSynt §§152b, 162.

4a שרת as 39:4; 2 Sam 13:17.   **b** Ges-K §139h.

5a Ges-K §129h.

7a פנים plural in meaning.

8a Sentence order, Ges-K §1520; BrSynt §99a.

9a Likewise in Mari, M. Weinfeld, VT 27 (1977) 178-195.

10a Form, Ges-K §164g.   **b** Ges-K §91e. J. Skinner, "it went up in blossom."   **c** Hiph. only here; literally, "boiled."   **d** Construction, Ges-K §143d; the asyndetic construction expresses the speed of what happened.

14a כי אם (I desire nothing else) except, Ges-K §163d; differently, J. Skinner.   **b** Perfect of confidence, already accomplished; expression of something desired as already accomplished, Ges-K §106n.   **c** Construction with כאשר, see D. B. Redford, p. 43 (schema).

16a חרי hap. leg; see comm. (trans., cf. M. Dahood BibNot 13 [1980] 14-16).

19a מעליך is missing in two Ms. and Vg; gloss after the last word of the verse (J. C. Ball, comm. 1886, H. Holzinger, H. Gunkel, O. Procksch, J. Skinner and others).

20a On the form הלדת (inf. hoph.) Ges-K §§69w,71; construction, Ges-K §121b; BrSynt §99b.

22a Construction, Ges-K §144n; E. König, 1900, bibliog. above.

Form

Ch. 40 narrates the second scene of Joseph's stay in Egypt. Joseph has suffered a serious fall; the introduction (vv. 1-4) now prepares the way for his new rise. Joseph has dealings with two court officials in prison; he explains to each the meaning of his dream (vv. 5-19), and the explanation is fulfilled (vv. 20-22). But this does not deliver him from prison. The head cupbearer, now reinstated (v. 23), forgets Joseph's request (vv. 14-15).

There is a further context in which ch. 40 is set, namely, the three pairs of dreams that determine the story. The dreams of the officials in ch. 40 point back to Joseph's dreams in ch. 37; the explanation points forward to that in ch. 41. It is easy to recognize how these three sets of dreams are distributed across the whole, and to sense the function of the motif and the tension rising to the third. The structure with its symmetry is a classical example of the author's narrative art:

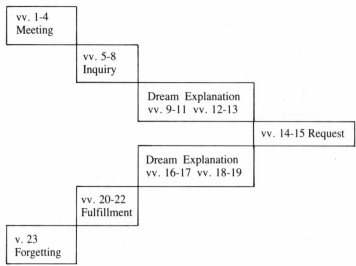

The symmetry alone is enough to show that the chapter is a unity, and the majority of exegetes acknowledge this, with slight modifications.

Literary criticism unanimously attributes the chapter to E. From the time of J. Wellhausen additions in vv. 1, 3, 4, 14, 15 were regarded as fragments from J inserted by a redactor. But W. Rudolf rightly raised the objection that there was no motive for a redactor to insert individual sentences like this, which the critics (J. Wellhausen, H. Gunkel and others) describe as superfluous in the context (H. Donner and H. C. Schmitt agree with this argument). There is not sufficient reason to infer a parallel J narrative from these incoherent fragments. This holds also for D. B. Redford's view that one must distinguish a Reuben strand from a Judah strand in ch. 40 (cf. critique of H. Donner, *Die literarische Gestalt. . .* [1976] 40, n. 82). H. C. Schmitt (BZAW 154, 1980) sees no sign of a parallel Judah strand but finds additions in vv. 1,3,5,15 which he ascribes to a reworking that presupposes a Reuben strand which wants to assimilate ch. 40 to ch. 39. It is for the exegesis to show whether all these are additions and whether they can belong to one hand. G. W. Coats (CBQMS 4 [1976] 64) accepts a unified text without additions and H. Donner, pp. 30-32, follows him in this. Both correctly presuppose that the Joseph story does not consist of parts which a redactor or editor has put together, but is the work of a single author. Nevertheless, it remains possible that individual glosses have been added later. It is to be underscored once again that the majority of exegetes understand ch. 40 to be essentially a unity.

Commentary

[**40:1-4**] Vv. 1-4 introduce the episode, bringing Joseph into contact with the two court officials. This takes place in two brief scenes. The transition formula v. 1a is followed by the first verbal sentence, ". . .offended their master. . ." (v. 1b), and the reaction of the master is followed by two further verbs: he was angry and put them into custody (v. 3). In the third scene the chief of the guard put the two royal officials under Joseph's care (v. 4a). This gives rise to the situation (v. 4b), in which the action beginning in v. 5a takes place. This is a clear and coherent sequence in which there is nothing missing and nothing superfluous. Difficulties have arisen from the different designations given to the same person in vv. 1 and 2 and apparently to the same place in v. 3; also a passage in v. 3 seems to be out of place.

[**40:1a**] The transition formula in v. 1a (found also in 15:1; 39:7; 48:1), which does not seem at first to fit the context, makes good sense when referred to the goal of vv. 1-4. It took place after these events, namely, those narrated in ch. 39, because Joseph came in contact with two of Pharaoh's officials. The transition formula is not redactional but comes from the author of the Joseph story and brings together two episodes that were once independent. This is demonstrated for Gen. 39 but is only surmised for Gen. 40. There were certainly stories in Egypt in which a court official had fallen into disfavor and was later restored to his office and dignity. The transition formula takes the place of the introduction to a narrative of this sort.

[**40:1b**] It is obviously deliberate on the part of the writer when he twice uses "king of Egypt" instead of "Pharaoh" and calls the officials simply "cupbearer" and "baker" (without שׂר); these peculiarities occur again in v. 5b, otherwise not at all ("king of Egypt" occurs again only in 41:46). With the introduction and with the start of the action in v. 5 he links the beginning of a once independent narrative with the broader context. The verb חטאו is retained for the introduction and is by no mean ''superfluous'' in the context (J. Wellhausen, H. Gunkel, and others). The whole begins with an offense by the two officials which arouses Pharaoh's anger; this is also presupposed in 41:9f.

[40:2] The Pharaoh (''before the 22nd dynasty he is always without a proper name,'' O. Procksch) becomes angry with his officials. On סריס see 37:36 and D. B. Redford, p. 51. Both are now described as שׂר so as to emphasize their standing at court. Hierarchy of rank among Pharaoh's courtiers was surprising news for Israel.

[40:3] ''He put them in custody'' (v. 3): משמר does not describe a place, namely, the prison, but a situation, detention. This means that they were under investigation, not serving a prison term. The Pharaoh has not yet come to a decision about punishment. The place of detention is ''the house of the chief of the guard'' (39:2), made more precise by אל־בית הסהר (''in the prison building''). This could be gloss (it is missing in Syr), but is not necessarily so—it designates the building in distinction from the place (משמר). The goal of the introduction comes in sight in v. 3—Joseph is detained in the same place.

[40:4] This makes possible a meeting between Joseph and the officials, because the chief of the guard who is responsible for the officials while in detention puts Joseph in charge of them (שרת used as in 39:4). The closing sentence shows clearly that what has preceded is the exposition. The situation is now ready for the action to begin.

[40:5-19] The encounter in vv. 5-8 arises out of the introduction (vv. 1-4). Joseph can perform a service for the detained officials; he has them tell him their dreams (vv. 9-11, 16-17) and interprets them (vv. 12-13, 18-19).

[40:5-8] The two officials each have a dream (v. 5); Joseph asks why they are downcast (vv. 6-7); they tell him the reason (v. 8a) and Joseph presses them to tell him what the dreams are (v. 8b).

[40:5] V. 5a follows the pattern which introduces a number of narratives. What is peculiar to the present case is that the two officials had a dream on the same night and that each dream was of particular significance (v. 5a). The last part of the verse (v. 5b) sounds very much like an appendage which is not necessary in the context (so too W. Rudolf). It is in striking agreement with v. 1, using the words cupbearer, baker, king of Egypt—words that in v. 1 are to be explained as coming from the author himself.

[40:6-7] One of Joseph's duties was to visit the two officials each morning to inquire about their needs. Once more an event begins with וירא. Joseph notices (והנם) that they are downcast. The action is set in motion by a friendly question. One can only gauge the significance of such a question when one knows what the atmosphere of a prison is. Human empathy releases the whole of what follows. It is a simple thing, an inquiry about someone's well-being, common to all people, races, and languages, that lends great significance to the Joseph story. It is not stiff formality but a lively expression of empathy with one's fellow human. Joseph saw the two prisoners and asked sympathetically why their faces were so downcast, thus opening the way that was to lead him to Pharaoh.

[**40:8a**] Both reply that they have had a dream but that there is nobody available to interpret it for them. The verb and the noun for interpreting a dream occur only in the Joseph story in the Old Testament, the verb in 40:8, 16, 22; 41:8, 12, 13, 15, and the noun in 40:5, 8, 12, 18; 41:11. "The root is common in postbiblical Hebrew and Aramaic" (D. B. Redford, p. 58). Dreams and their interpretation played a very important role in ancient Egypt. Interpretations of dreams became a specialized skill. And this is just what the courtiers say: there is no expert to interpret their dreams.

[**40:8b**] Joseph replies, "Do not interpretations belong to God?" He counters the view that only experts can explain dreams, that only the person who has studied and grasped the dream books can unravel them. If interpretation belongs to God, then he can confer this gift on whomever he pleases. So Joseph asks them to tell him their dreams. God could even give him the gift.

[**40:9-11**] The cupbearer tells his dream, introduced by v. 9a. It consists of an image and an event; the subject is the vine, then the cupbearer himself.

Both dreams are lively, miniature descriptions of life at Pharaoh's court which remind one of Egyptian art. The narrator displays all his craft here. "They are artificial dreams, i.e., what is seen in them has already been greatly stylized and raised to the dimension of the rational" (G. von Rad, *Genesis* [1972²] 371). Stylized they are in that they form a pair of contrasts, a picture of success and a picture of failure. The dream consists of an image and event (vv. 9-10), following the standard pattern of a dream narrative. The dreamer sees a vine with three branches (v. 10a); שָׂרִיג occurs only here (vv. 10,12) and in Joel 1:7; then he sees movement; the vine begins to bud (פרח) and blossom (עלתה נצה), and the clusters ripen into grapes (הבשׁילו = bring to ripeness). As a result of this extraordinary, instantaneous process the fruit of the vine is at hand to him. The cupbearer can exercise his office (v. 11). He now appears in the dream, holding Pharaoh's cup himself. He takes the grapes, squeezes them (the verb שׂחט only here) and hands the cup full of grape juice to the Pharaoh. Again there are three actions and the Pharaoh is named in each. It can remain an open question whether this second episode has been abbreviated, whether the now matured wine is meant and not just the grape juice. What is more important is that the threefold mention of the Pharaoh expresses how firmly the servant is bound to his master despite his detention.

[**40:12-13**] The interpretation that Joseph gives is in two parts: in the first he explains the three branches as three days (v. 12b); in the second he announces that the cupbearer will be reinstated in his office (v. 13). All three explanations of the dreams are divided into interpretation and announcement (40:12-13; 40:18-19; 41:26-32). Only the first part, "the three branches are three days," is an allegorical interpretation (a standard example of it) in the line of professional Egyptian dream interpretation. It is likely that the allegorical interpretation has its origin in dreams of this sort. Allegory, however, has little significance in Joseph's interpretation; he can use it, but does not need to. The emphasis is much more on the announcement in which he understands the cupbearer's dream along the lines of a parable rather than an allegory. Joseph's vital, human interest in the prisoners, shown in his questioning, necessarily includes his concern for their culpability and fate. Basic to his interpretation is his knowledge of the situation. He knows that the Pharaoh is about to come to a decision and that the two are afraid and preoccupied with this. The two contrasting dream images emerge from their very situation. Hence the introductory sentence, ''Do not interpretations belong to God?'' now appears in a new light.

''Within three days'': what he announces to the cupbearer will happen shortly. The interpretation, a short time (= three days), derives from the instantaneous process of ripening. The Pharaoh will raise his head. Literally this is a ceremonial act which takes place in audience. Because of the double meaning in vv. 19 and 20 it cannot here mean ''show favor''; the Pharaoh makes some personal gesture toward him (similarly J. J. Rabinowitz [1961], ''takes account of him''; T. J. Meek [1963], ''summon''; E. Zenger [1967], ''summon, cite'' [see bibliog. above]). In 2 Kings 25:27 also the raising of the head is a prelude to release from prison. As a consequence the Pharaoh reinstates him in office and he is able to carry out his functions once again. It is only in the last sentence of his announcement that Joseph makes a direct relationship between what was seen in the dream and what is to happen. Allegorical interpretation has no place here; the episode in the dream is put into relationship with the episode that Joseph announces. The dream is a parable of what happens.

[40:14-15] Joseph gives an interpretation favorable to the cupbearer and adds the request that he remember him when things go well with him again and mention to the Pharaoh that he is in prison and not guilty. The כִּי־אִם at the beginning is explained by the interpreter's claim to a reward. Joseph presupposes this; but he goes further, ''instead of this Joseph demands a favor'' (B. Jacob). The perfect of the two verbs can be described as *perfectum confidentiae*: ''to express facts which are undoubtedly imminent and therefore, in the imagination of the speaker, already accomplished,'' ''. . .a modal future'' (Ges-K §106n); ''only please remember'' (F. Delitzsch). Concretely, Joseph asks him to do him the favor of mentioning him before the Pharaoh (this is the meaning of the hiph. of זכר) so as to get him out of prison.

[40:15] The request is really an appeal to a higher tribunal and must have support. Both parts of v. 15 constitute this necessary support; v. 15b is not an addition (against M. Noth, D. B. Redford, and others). The first part explains that he has been reduced to a state of slavery, has become a person of diminished rights, all blamelessly, whereas previously he had been a free man. The words ''I was abducted'' are not to be made dependent on either of the two versions in ch. 37; their only function is to underscore the injustice, and for this both versions are adequate. This would be clearer if the verb were rendered by ''expel'' with L. Kopf (1958) or ''abduct'' with R. J. Zwi Werblowsky (1956; bibliog. above). ''The land of the Hebrews'' is of course anachronistic (bibliog.) The protestation of innocence follows only in v. 15b. Here it has its necessary function; it could not be alleged in the situation of 39:20-23. Here for the first time Joseph declares his innocence, using in his passionate statement the word בור to describe the prison. It is a hole, a dungeon, a place of confinement, distinct from the "official" prison, as seen from the point of view of the prisoner.

[**40:16-17**] The dream that the baker narrates is shorter and simpler in form, consisting solely of a single frame, like the second of Joseph's dreams in ch. 37 in relation to the first. The reason is that it is merely a contrast, a picture of misfortune. After the introduction, the account of the baker's dream begins in v. 16b by emphasizing the similarity. Then follows the image he saw (vv. 16b, 17a). The dream ends very quickly with the action in v. 17b in which, in contrast to the cupbearer in vv. 10f., the baker is passive.

[**40:16**] The introduction portrays with gentle irony how the baker tries to get a favorable interpretation: "I too had a dream. . . ." The picture of a baker carrying a basket on his head also occurs in Egyptian art. Here there are three baskets, in obvious parallelism to v. 10. There is no point in asking what was in the other two. The baskets are described as סלי חרי, חרי being usually rendered "baked products from wheaten flour"; so too in KBL.* The content of the basket is first mentioned in v. 17a so that it is unlikely that it is already found in v. 16b. Hence the usual translation "wicker basket" or "woven basket" (B. Jacob, E. A. Speiser following the Arabic) is to be preferred.

[**40:17a**] ". . .All sorts of baked goods for the Pharaoh": There was a highly developed industry of fine baking in ancient Egypt.

The Egyptian dictionary of Erman-Grapow gives a list of 38 sorts of cakes and 57 sorts of bread (J. Vergote, *Joseph en Egypt*. . . [1959] 37). A picture from the grave of Rameses III portrays the detailed and varied types of baking in the royal bakery. This was one of the surprising impressions that the Israelites had of the court of the Pharaoh.

[**40:17b**] V. 17b presumes that the baker is carrying out his duties for the Pharaoh's table with the baskets on his head. But he had bad luck: birds (Gen. 15:11) were eating the bread "from the basket upon my head." That the dream forbodes ill-fortune needs no explanation.

[**40:18-19**] Joseph's interpretation of this dream is also shorter. The introduction is followed by referring the three baskets to three days, as in the cupbearer's dream. The first part of the announcement in v. 19a is word for word the same as that to the cupbearer. This requires that the phrase "to raise the head" carry a neutral sense: the Pharaoh turns personally to him during an audience. The ambiguous meaning is best expressed by a literal translation. The MT follows with מעליך. One could in a pinch render ". . .will raise your head up from you"; but it is scarcely possible linguistically. The preposition does not suit the verb נשא. I think that it is quite impossible that the meaning is "behead." מעליך is certainly a gloss, a resumption of the word at the end of v. 19.

---

*See M. Dahood, Bib 62 (1981) 273-274, ". . .three baskets of white bread. . ."; BibNot 13 (1980) 14-16, Ebla, lú-ḥarí, baker of white bread, חרי = Ebla harí, Ebla ā Hebr ō, products from white flour (translator).

[**40:19b**] The second part of the verse, following "will raise your head," announces the baker's harsh fate—the death penalty by hanging. This too presupposes a detailed knowledge of the whole background of the situation. To make a parallel to the first interpretation, Joseph by way of conclusion takes up the last sentence of the dream narrative with just the slightest alteration. The announcement is all the harsher because the corpse of the one hanged is dishonored. The extreme severity of the punishment makes it certain that the baker must have committed a grave crime. It is part of the narrative art that neither the cupbearer nor the baker show any reaction to the announcement; this would have no function in the story.

[**40:23-23**] The conclusion tells how everything turned out just as Joseph had said in interpreting the dream (v. 22b). At an audience ("in the presence of his servants") on the occasion of his birthday, the Pharaoh raises the heads of both (v. 20); he reinstates the cupbearer in office (v. 21) and has the baker hanged (v. 22a). V. 23 is a transition to what follows: Joseph's request in vv. 14f. is not fulfilled.

[**40:20**] The earliest attestation that the Pharaohs celebrated their birthday with a court feast at which amnesties were granted is from the Ptolemaic period (further D. B. Redford, pp. 205ff.). But it does not necessarily follow that the present text can only have originated at that time (details, H. C. Schmitt, BZAW 154 [1980] 138f.). The author may have meant the enthronement feast (on the Pharaoh as the son of Re, H. Frankfort, *Kingship and the Gods* [1948; 1962^4] 101-139).

V. 20 shows clearly that the raising of the head at an audience refers to the ritual by which the king singles out one of his servants; he then raises the heads of both.

[**40:21-22**] The Pharaoh reinstates the cupbearer in office (this is the meaning of משקה here KBL) and had the baker hanged. All happens as Joseph had announced.

[**40:23**] This transitional sentence, v. 23, brings into perspective once more the clear structure of the chapter; it moves from the encounter in vv. 1-4 through Joseph's request in vv. 14-15 to the bitter disappointment. In the first episode Joseph's rise is followed by an undeserved fall; in the second a well-founded expectation of release is followed by disappointment. This prepares the turn of fortune in ch. 41.

Purpose and Thrust

The relationship of the three pairs of dreams to each other in chs. 37; 40; and 41 is alone sufficient to show that the Joseph story is the composition of a single author; it reveals a well-thought-out plan. The dreams in ch. 37 are comprehensible to each person concerned and need no interpretation; in fact, they are comprehensible without interpretation by a third party. But the dreams of ch. 41 require interpretation, though not that of the traditional Egyptian science of dreams. The degree of abstraction rises from the first to the third pair. This accords with the three forms of society in which the dreams take place—in a family, among the Pharaoh's servants, at the royal court.

The author who has inserted the dream motif into his narrative is at the same time a theologian in his own right. The Joseph story is entirely secular; God is rarely, but then deliberately, mentioned. Joseph says to the officials, who are unhappy because there is nobody to interpret their dreams for them, ''Do not interpretations belong to God?'' In this context the meaning is that interpretation is not limited to specialists. Joseph is saying that God's action is not confined to human institutions. This is true for the interpretation of dreams, and it is true also for worship which in Egypt was so strongly set in institutions. God is free in his action; he is thus immediately accessible. God can confer the gift of interpreting dreams on anyone; he can work on any person through another. Joseph speaks here out of his own experience. God can be with him in a foreign land, in the territory which is the preserve of foreign gods; he can affect the people of this land through him. There is no thought of competition or polemic in this action of God through Joseph, just as there was not in the case of the God of Abraham, Isaac, and Jacob. It is in accordance with the action of the God of the fathers also when the interpretation of the dreams of the cupbearer and the baker is not the result of esoteric specialization but of the sharp perception of the real situation and of empathy with one's fellow being. The religion of the God of the fathers is not confined to an isolated area; God acts and speaks directly and immediately within the whole realm of reality.

Genesis 41:1-57

Pharaoh's Dreams
and Joseph's Elevation

Literature

Genesis 41: E. Mahler, "Zu Genesis XLI," ZDMG 61 (1907) 625ff. A. Aarne and S. Thompson, *The Types of the Folk-Tale* (1928; 1964[2]). J. C. H. Lebram, "Nachbiblische Weisheitstraditionen," VT 15 (1965) 167-237. S. Niditsch and R. Doran, "The Success Story of the Wise Courtier: A Formal Approach," JBL 96 (1977) 179-193.

Genesis 41:1-36: H. Brugsch, *Thesaurus Inscriptionum Aegyptiacarum* (1883-1891); *Die biblischen sieben Jahre der Hungersnot* (1891). G. Roeder, *Urkunden zur Religion des alten Ägypten: Religiöse Stimmen der Völker* (1915; 1923[2]) esp. 177ff. J. Vandier, *La famine dans l'Egypte ancienne* (1936). J. M. A. Janssen, "Bemerkungen zur Hungersnot im Alten Ägypten," Bib 20 (1939) 69-71. J. A. Wilson, *The Burden of Egypt: The Culture of Ancient Egypt* (1951) esp. 81f. R. B. Y. Scott, "Metereological Phenomena and Terminology in the Old Testament," ZAW 64 (1952) 11-25. P. Barguet, *La stêle de la famine à Séhel: Bibliothèque d'Etude de l'Institut français d'Archéologie du Caire* 24 (1953). J. Bérard, "De la légende grecque à la Bible. Phaéton et les sept vaches maigres," RHR 151 (1957) 221f. R. de Vaux, *Ancient Israel* (1958-60; 1962). A. Finet, *Une affaire de disette dans un district du royaume de Mari* (1959). B. A. Levine, "Notes on an Aramaic Dream Text from Egypt," JAOS 84 (1964) 18-22. C. H. Gordon, *The Common Background of Greek and Hebrew Civilization* (1965) esp. 69f., 88. W. McKane, *Prophets and Wise Men* (1965) esp. 50. J. Malfroy, "Sagesse et loi dans le Deutéronome: Etudes," VT 15 (1965) 49-65. A. S. Kapelrud, "The Number Seven in Ugaritic Texts," VT 18 (1968) 494-499. W. Beyerlin, ed., *Religionsgeschichtliches Textbuch zum AT: ATD Ergänzungsreihe* 1 (1975) esp. 257.

Genesis 41:8-13: E. Kutsch, "מִקְרָא," ZAW 65 (1953) 247-253. H. M. Orlinsky, "The New Jewish Version of the Torah," JBL 82 (1963) 249-264. H. P. Müller, "Magischmantische Weisheit und die Gestalt Daniels," UF 1 (1969) 80-94; "Der Begriff 'Rätsel' im AT," VT 20 (1970) 465-489. J. MacDonald, "The Status and Role of the *Na'ar* in Israelite Society," JNES 35 (1976) 149-170.

Genesis 41:14-36: P. P. Saydon, "The Inceptive Imperfect in Hebrew and the Verb *hēhēl* 'to begin,'" Bib 35 (1954) 43-50. J. Blau, "Adverbia als psychologische und grammatische Subjekte/Praedikate im Bibelhebräisch," VT 9 (1959) 130-137. D. T. Tsumura, *The Ugaritic Drama of the Good Gods—A Philological Study* (Diss. Brandeis, 1973-74). T. Muraoka, "The Status Constructus of Adjectives in Biblical Hebrew," VT 27 (1977) 375-379. Z. Zevit, "The Exegetical Implications of Daniel VIII 1, IX 21," VT 28 (1978) 488-491.

Genesis 41:37-46: H. Schack-Schackenburg, "Genesis 41,45," ZÄS 30 (1892) 49-50. G. Steindorff, "Weiteres zu Gen 41,45," ZÄS 30 (1892) 50f.; "Der Name Josephs Saphenat-Pa'neach," ZÄS 37 (1898) 41f. S. Landersdorfer, "Sumerisches Sprachgut im AT," BWAT 21 (1916). A. von Ow, "Joseph von Ägypten und Asenath," *Allgemeine Rundschau* 15,19 (1917) 204f. E. W. Brooks, *Joseph and Asenath* (1918). I. Slabý, "Genesis 41, 41-42 und die altägyptischen Denkmäler," BZ 16 (1922) 18-33. V. Aptowitzer, "Asenath, the Wife of Joseph—A Haggadic Literary-Historical Study," HUCA 1 (1924) 239-306. E. König, "Die sprachliche Gestalt des Pentateuch in ihrer Beziehung zur ägyptischen Sprache," JBL 48 (1929) 333-343. H. Torczyner, *Ha-lashon we-ha-Sefer*, I (1948) esp. 297f. J. Herrmann, "Zu Genesis 41,43," ZAW 62 (1950) 321. J. M. A. Janssen, "Fonctionnaires Sémites au Service de l'Egypte," CEg 26,51 (1951) 50-62. A. Rubinstein, "A Finite Verb Continued by an Infinitive Absolute in Biblical Hebrew," VT 2 (1952) 362-367. P. A. H. de Boer, "The Counsellor," VT.S 3 (1955) 42-71. N. Adcock, "Genesis XLI 40," ET 67 (1955/56) 383. J. Brand, "The Title אשר על הבית," Tarb. 36 (1955/56) 221-228. F. C. Fensham, "Genesis XLI 40," ET 68 (1956/57) 284. M. G. Girardet, "Noterella filologica: Il verbo piacere in ebraico e Genesi 6:2," Protest. 12 (1957) 168-169. K. A. Kitchen, "The Term *Nšq* in Genesis 41:40," ET 69 (1957) 30. W. A. Ward, "The Egyptian Office of Joseph," JSS 5 (1960) 144-150. W. J. P. Boyd, "Notes on the Secondary Meanings of אחר," JThS 12 (1961) 54-56. M. Ellenbogen, *Foreign Words in the OT: Origins and Etymology* (1962) esp. 5. S. Mowinckel, "Drive and/or Ride in the OT," VT 12 (1962) 278-299. A. Rowe, "The Famous Solar City of On," PEQ 94 (1962) 133-142. T. C. Vriezen, "Exode XX 2: formula de loi ou d'alliance?" RechBibl 8 (1963) 33-50 esp. 43f. C. Burchard, *Untersuchungen zu Joseph und Aseneth*, WUNT 8 (1965). J. S. Croatto, "'Abrek 'Intendant' dans Gén. XLI 43," VT 16 (1966) 113-115. E. Haulotte, *Symbolique du vêtement selon la Bible* (1966). Z. W. Falk, "Hebrew Legal Terms. II," JSS 12 (1967) 241-244. J. B. Pritchard, ed., *The Ancient Near East. Supplementary Texts and Pictures* (1969). E. Lipiński, "Recherces su le livre de Zacharie," VT 20 (1970) 304-314. B. Otzen, "Noch einmal das Wort *Trkb* auf einem Arad-Ostracon," VT 20 (1970) 239-242. W. L. Humphreys, *The Motif of the Wise Courtier in the OT* (diss. N.Y., 1970-71) 287-291. D. Sänger, "Bekehrung und Exodus. Zum jüdischen Traditionshintergrund von 'Joseph und Aseneth,' " JSJ 10 (1980) 11-36. V. Sasson, "The Word *trkb* in the Arad Ostracon," VT 30 (1980) 44-52.

Genesis 41:47-49: L. Koehler, "Kleinigkeiten (zu Gn 41,47. . .)," ZAW 52 (1934) 160. H. Junker, "Josephs Verhalten gegenüber dem ägyptischen Volke," *Pastor bonus* 53 (1942) 78-81. T. Jacobsen, "Primitive Democracy in Ancient Mesopotamia," JNES 3 (1943) 159-172. E. Drioton, "L'organisation économique de l'Egypte ancienne," CHEg 3 (1950) 197-200. D. W. Thomas, "Some Observations on the Hebrew Root חדל," VTSuppl 4 (1957) 8-16. D. Weissert, "*Wā-tā'āś ha-'araes*. . .(Gen 41,47) im Lichte der Septuaginta" [Hebr.] in *Dôrôn, Untersuchungen z. klass. Kultur* (1967) 3-6. W. Helck, *Wirtschaftsgeschichte des alten Ägypten im 3. und 2. Jt. v. Chr.* (1975).

Genesis 41:50-57: F. Zimmermann, "Some Textual Studies in Genesis (. . .Gn 41,51)," JBL 73 (1954) 97-101. K. D. Schunck, "Ophra, Ephron und Ephraim," VT 11 (1961) 188-200. J. Heller, "Noch zu Ophra, Ephron und Ephraim," VT 12 (1962) 339-341. F. Golka, "Zur Erforschung der Ätiologien im AT," VT 20 (1970) 90-98. G. S. Ogden, "Time and the Verb היה in OT Prose," VT 21 (1971) 451-469, esp. 451f.

Text

41:1   Two years[a] later the Pharaoh[b] had a dream. He was standing[c] by[d] the Nile

2   when seven cows, sleek and fat, came up out of the river and grazed among the reeds;[a]

3   then seven more cows, gaunt and lean,[a] came up out of the river after them and stood by them on the bank of the Nile.

4   The[a] gaunt and lean cows devoured the sleek and fat cows. Then the Pharaoh woke up.

5   He fell asleep again and had a second dream: seven ears of grain, full and good, were growing on one stalk;

6   then seven more ears, thin and shrivelled[a] by the east wind, grew up after them.

7   The thin ears swallowed up the seven full and good ears. Then the Pharaoh woke up; it was a dream.

8   When morning came he was troubled in mind;[a] so he sent and summoned all the magicians[b] and sages of Egypt. The Pharaoh told them his dream.[c] But there was no one who could interpret it[d] for the Pharaoh.

9   Then the head cupbearer spoke up 'to'[a] the Pharaoh: Now I must recall my fault;

10 the Pharaoh was angry with his servants and put 'them'[a] in custody in the house of the chief of the guard, me and the head baker.

11 We both, he and I, had dreams on the same night, each dream with its own particular meaning.

12 Now there was a young Hebrew with us, a slave of the chief of the guard; we told him our dream and he interpreted them for us, a special interpretation for each.

13 And it turned out just as he explained to us; I was reinstated in office and he was hanged.

14 Thereupon the Pharaoh sent and summoned Joseph. They hurriedly[a] brought him out of the dungeon; he shaved and changed his clothes and came into the Pharaoh's presence.

15 The Pharaoh said to Joseph, I have had a dream[a] and no one can interpret it for me. I have heard of you; it is said that when you hear a dream you can interpret it.

16 Joseph answered the Pharaoh, Not I, but God[a] will announce prosperity for the Pharaoh.

17 Then the Pharaoh said to Joseph, This is my dream. I was standing on the bank of the Nile[a]

18 when seven cows, sleek and fat, came up out of the river and grazed among the reeds;

19 then seven more came out, gaunt, ugly, and lean. I have never seen such ugly cows in the whole of the land of Egypt.

20 Then the seven lean and ugly cows devoured the first seven, the fat ones.

21 And though they swallowed them, there was no sign that they were in their bellies; they looked as ugly as before. Then I woke up.

22 Then[a] I saw in my dream: Seven ears of corn, full and good, were growing on one stalk;

23 then seven more ears, withered,[a] thin and shrivelled by the east wind, grew up after them.

24 The withered ears swallowed up the seven good ears. I told this to the magicians and none of them could explain it to me.

25 So Joseph said to the Pharaoh, The Pharaoh's dreams are one and the same. God has told the Pharaoh what he is going to do.[a]

26 The[a] seven good cows are seven years and the good ears are also seven years.

27 The seven gaunt and lean cows that came up after them are seven years. And the seven withered ears, shrivelled by the east wind, mean seven years of famine.

28 This is what I have said to the Pharaoh: God has let the Pharaoh know what he is going to do.

29 Seven years are coming during which there will be great plenty throughout the whole of the land of Egypt.

30 Then there will come[a] seven years of famine; all the plenty in the land

of Egypt will be forgotten and the famine will destroy the land.

31 There will be no sign of the plenty in the land because of the famine that follows, for it will be very severe.

32 That the Pharaoh has dreamt[a] twice means that God has decided the matter and will soon bring it about.

33 Now the Pharaoh should look around[a] for a wise and intelligent man and put him in charge of the country.[b]

34 The Pharaoh should appoint[a] supervisors over the land [and take one-fifth[b] of the produce of the land during the seven years of plenty][c].

35 They should collect all the produce of these good years that are coming and put the grain[a] under the Pharaoh's control, 'bringing'[b] it into the cities and guarding it.

36 This grain will serve as a reserve[a] for the land against the seven years of famine which will come in the land of Egypt. Thus the land will not be wiped out by the famine.

37 The plan pleased the Pharaoh and all his courtiers.

38 The Pharaoh said to his courtiers, Can we find a man like this who has the spirit of God?

39 The Pharaoh said to Joseph, Since God has made all this known to you, there is no one as wise and intelligent as you.

40 You will be in charge of my household and all my people will 'obey'[a] you; only from the throne shall I be greater than you.[b]

41 Then the Pharaoh said to Joseph, I hereby[a] appoint you over the land of Egypt.

42 Thereupon the Pharaoh took his signet ring from his hand and put it on Joseph's; he had him dressed in fine linen and put a chain of gold[a] around his neck.

43 He had him ride on his second chariot and the cry went before him, Abrek![a] Thus he set him[b] over the whole of the land of Egypt.

44 And the Pharaoh said to Joseph, I am the Pharaoh. Without your consent no one shall move hand or foot throughout Egypt.

45 And the Pharaoh gave Joseph the name Zephenath-paneah, and he gave him as wife Asenath, the daughter of Potiphera, priest of On. [Then Joseph went out over the land of Egypt.][a]

46 Joseph was thirty years old when he entered the service of the Pharaoh, the king of Egypt. And Joseph left the Pharaoh's presence and went through the land of Egypt.

47 The land produced an abundance of grain in the seven years of plenty.

48 He gathered up all the food of the seven years of plenty[a] in the land of Egypt and brought the grain into the cities. In each city he put the harvest from the surrounding fields.

49 So Joseph stored up large quantities of grain, like the sand of the sea, until he ceased measuring it, for it could not be measured.

50 Two sons were[a] born to Joseph before the years of famine came. Asenath, the daughter of Potiphera, priest of On, bore them to him.

51 Joseph named the firstborn Manasseh because, he said, God has made me forget[a] all my hardship and my father's house.

52 He named the second Ephraim[a] because, he said, God has made me fruitful in the land of my hardship.

53 When the seven years of plenty in the land of Egypt came to an end,

54 there began seven years of famine, as Joseph had said [and there was famine in all countries; only throughout the land of Egypt was there bread].[a]

55 When the famine spread through Egypt the people cried out to the Pharaoh for bread; and the Pharaoh said to all the Egyptians, Go to Jo-

seph and do what he tells you.

56b Then[a] Joseph had all 'reserves of grain'[b] opened and sold grain to the Egyptians, for the famine was severe in the land of Egypt.[c]

56a And the famine spread over the land.

57 And the whole 'world'[a] came[b] to Egypt to buy grain from Joseph, because the famine was severe everywhere.

1a Ges-K §131d.   **b** On the title "Pharaoh," J. Vergote, *Joseph en Egypte. . .* (1959) 45-48.   **c** On the omission of the personal pronoun in the nominal sentence, Ges-K §116s.   **d** On על meaning "by," Ges-K §119cc.

2a אחו, an Egyptian word, 41:2, 18; Job 8:11; also Ugaritic.

3a Probably here and v. 4 רקות, with some Mss and Sam; so רקות in all passages dealing with the cows, דקות in all passages dealing with the ears.

4a Gk with שבע, likewise vv. 7, 20, 24; Gk of ch. 41 shows a whole series of balancing variants.

6a Only in this chapter, vv. 6, 23, 27, passive part. qal; on the construction, Ges-K §116l.

8a On the forms, Ges-K §64b.   **b** Only here, Dan. 2:2, and Ex. 7-9(P); Gk ἐξηγητάς.   **c** Sam plur.   **d** Read sing. with Gk.

9a With Sam, read אל.

10a Read plur. with Sam.

14a Gk has ויוציאהו.

15a On the transposition of אין and its noun, Ges-K §152o; *oratio obliqua*, §157a.

16a Gk, Syr, Sam: "without God one can give no assuring answer."

17a On the construction of v. 17, J. Blau, VT 9 (1959) 494-499; T. Muraoka VT 27 (1977) 375-379.

22a The versions have ואיש שנית, perhaps correctly.

23a צנמות is missing in Gk, Vg, Syr.

25a Participle with future sense, Ges-K §116d.

26a Read הפרת with Gk, Sam.

30a On the perf. consec. announcing future events, Ges-K §112x.

32a On the construction, BrSynt §159a.

33a On the form ירא, Ges-K §75p, hh.   **b** The same formula, 41:41; Dan. 2:48, and *Ahiqar* 7:25; S. Niditsch and R. Doran, JBL 96 (1977) 179-183.

34a יעשה in the sense of "have appointed" as in 1 Kings 8:32; J. Skinner, B. Jacob.   **b** Gk translates ויחמש.   **c** See comm. below.

35a For a list of foodstuffs in Gen. 37–50, see table in D. B. Redford, VT.S 20 (1970) 173.   **b** ויתנו to be inserted, following v. 48; so BHK, H. Donner, *Die literarische Gestalt* (1976).

36a פקדון a technical term, elsewhere in OT only in Lev. 5:21, 23.

40a ישק is unexplained; Gk ὑπακούσεται, the sense is certainly correct.   **b** On the construction, Ges-K §118h; BrSynt §101.

41a Gk appends σήμερον. The sentence sounds like a fixed formula.

42a Sam without article.

43a אברך, unexplained; see comm.   **b** The infinitive abs. as the continuation of a preceding finite verb, Ges-K §113z.

45a Missing in Gk.

48a To be added following Sam, Gk; cf. v. 53.

50a Sam, Gk, Vg read plural.

51a On the form, Ges-K §52m (play on the name).

52a The etymology following פרה could be relevant to Ephraim as a territorial name; J. A. Soggin BHH 1, 420f.; K. D. Schunck (1961); J. Heller (1962), bibliog. above.

54a V. 54b is probably an addition.

56a The first sentence of v. 56 is to be read at the end of the verse.   **b** Following Gk, Syr, כל־אצרות בר.   **c** The last sentence is missing in Gk.

57a Following v. 54 it is better to read ארצות with Gk.   **b** Feminines as collective terms denoting masculine persons, Ges-K §145e; BrSynt §50e.

Form

Three patterns (series of happenings) coalesce in the artistic arrangement of ch. 41. First there is the narration of a dream, its interpretation, and the realization of subsequent events that accord with the interpretation and the dream. There are many narratives that follow this pattern, particularly when, as here, it is a king who has the dream (on the royal dream, E. L. Erlich, BZAW 73 [1953]; "Traum," RGG³ IV, 1001-1005). S. Niditsch and R. Doran (JBL 96 [1977] 179-193) have demonstrated another structure in Gen. 41:1-45; Dan. 2; and *Aḥiqar* (Syr.), following the motif index of A. Aarne and S. Thompson, "The Success of the Wise Courtier" (*The Types of Folk-Tale* [1928; 1964²] type 922). There are four points of agreement: (1) A person of lower rank is called before a person of higher rank to answer a difficult question or to solve a problem. (2) The person of higher rank puts the question that no one else has been able to answer. (3) The person of lower rank solves the problem. (4) This person is rewarded. Besides the three texts mentioned, the motif index of A. Aarne and S. Thompson contains a series of folk stories corresponding to this pattern. It is only one of many possible variants when the problem consists of a dream which cannot be explained. This is the proof that behind ch. 41 stands a narrative that was once passed on independently. The same is demonstrated for ch. 39 and is probable for ch. 40. The narrator of the Joseph story, in the section that takes place in Egypt (chs. 39-41), has skillfully joined together three episodes that go back to independent narratives. S. Niditsch and R. Doran make the narrative in Gen. 41 end with v. 45, the reward given to the person of lower rank, as in the two other parallels. But it would be arbitrary and impossible to cut off vv. 46-57 because, in the first pattern, the realization of subsequent events in accordance with the interpretation and the dream (vv. 45-57) is an essential part of the narrative.

The two patterns mentioned already do not cover the long narrative in ch. 41 as a whole. Vv. 9-13 join ch. 41 firmly with chs. 39-40, and vv. 53-57 are a preparation for chs. 42-45. The third pattern is the broader context of the Joseph story into which the narrator has inserted ch. 41 (or chs. 39-41). It belongs to the structure of the Joseph story as a whole that two other pairs of dreams precede the Pharaoh's, and that the interpreter is raised from the depths of misery because of his explanation. Further, it is part of this overall plan that the problem to be solved must be a dream (vv. 1-4; dream motif in chs. 37 and 40), indeed, the dream of a king (ch. 37). The coalescence of the three threads in ch. 41 shows clearly that the chapter is at the very center of the Joseph story, the structure of which has been thought through to the last detail.

The narrator makes subtle and varied use of the device of doubling in the details of the structure. The Pharaoh has two dreams; the narrator tells both (vv. 1-7), and the Pharaoh himself narrates them (vv. 17-24). The attempt at interpretation first miscarries (v. 8) but then succeeds (vv. 25-32). The cupbearer repeats in vv. 9-13 the events narrated in ch. 40, thus skillfully linking chs. 40 and 41. The center of the chapter comprises the Pharaoh's two dreams narrated a second time (vv. 17-24), together with Joseph's interpretation (vv. 25-32; cf. 40:12-13, 18-19). The narrator has thus succeeded in setting the heart of the narrative, a dream and its interpretation, in the center of the narrative structure. Joseph's answer to the Pharaoh is in two parts; he joins interpretation (vv. 25-32) with advice (vv. 33-36). Both win the Pharaoh's approval (vv. 37-38). His reply forms the link between the first part and the second—Joseph's elevation (vv. 37-57). The ceremonial acts of installation in office follow in vv. 41-47. Then comes the conclusion, the realization of what had been announced—the seven years of plenty (vv. 47-49) and the seven years of famine (vv. 53-57). The advice that Joseph had given the Pharaoh is followed (vv. 33-36), and the land is saved in face of the famine. There follows an additional note about Joseph's age (v. 46a), and the birth and naming of his sons (vv. 50-52).

This structure, thought through in every single detail, reveals an overall plan for the whole chapter and is a proof of its literary unity. The passages which give occasion for source division are explained in the exegesis. I would refer in particular to D. B. Redford's arguments against source division (VT.S 20 [1970]), where he makes use of those of W. Rudolf on a number of occasions (BZAW 63 [1933] 145-184).

Commentary

[41:1-7] The Pharaoh's dreams (vv. 1-7): This is the report in the 3rd person of a dream; later the same report occurs in the 1st person (vv. 17-24). The two dreams are framed by vv. 1a,4b,5a,7b, introduction and conclusion. The first dream about the cows (vv. 1b-4) is divided into an exposition (v. 1b, he was standing by the Nile) and three verbs: seven cows came up. . .grazed; seven others came up. . .stood by them. . .devoured them. The second dream is shorter, with no exposition and contains only two verbs: grew up. . .swallowed. Apart from this they are exactly parallel, differing only in their subject: seven cows/seven ears of grain.

[41:1a] The first four words of v. 1a are a transition formula following directly on 40:23. Joseph had to remain in prison for two years without anything happening. By means of the transition formula an originally independent narrative about a dream of the Pharaoh becomes an episode in the Joseph story which eventually brings Joseph into the Pharaoh's presence.

[41:1b] If one brackets the formula, the original narrative began ויחלם פרעה חלם (cf. 40:5). This makes the rhythm of the sentences smoother (two threes) and each carries its own weight: "The Pharaoh had a dream"; the narrative is about the king's dream. "He was standing by the Nile." The king is looking down on the lifeline of his realm. It is a royal dream and it concerns the kingdom.

The royal dream plays a special role among the dreams that have come down to us from the ancient near east. There are accounts of dreams of Ashurbanipal (7th cent.), Nabonidus (6th cent.), Hattusilis (15th cent.), Tuthmose IV (15th cent.), and Gilgamesh (cf. E. L. Erlich, "Traum," RGG[3] IV). The royal dreams obviously concern the kingship and the king's realm; they are comprehensible in the context of sacral kingship. The king stands in a special relationship to the divinity (C. Westermann, "Das sakrale Königtum in seinen Erscheinungsformen und seiner Geschichte," ThB 55 [1974] 291-308). It is certainly no mere chance that the Old Testament reports the dream of only one king, Solomon

(1 Kings 3), who is particularly close to the sacral kingship of the ancient near east. The king is responsible for the welfare of his land; he is also the mediator of blessing; hence he receives divine advice or messages (Strabo also reports such dreams). Dreams in the whole of the ancient world indicate the special bond between the king and the divinity.

In his dream, the Pharaoh stands by the Nile (the word יאר is of Egyptian origin and is used almost exclusively for the Nile); this gives definite orientation—the Nile is the source of the fertility of Egypt (Bonfrère already in 1625). The word for reed, אחו, is also of Egyptian origin (J. Vergote, *Joseph en Egypte*. . . [1959] 59-60).

[41:2-4] The dream begins with v. 2. Dreams of this sort are, according to E. L. Ehrlich, known as "symbolic dreams," a description which is not fortuitous inasmuch as the Greek σύμβολον refers to the juxtaposition of two objects. The Pharaoh's dreams, like those of Joseph (ch. 37) and the court officials (ch. 40), are parable-dreams, i.e., the dreamer dreams of a course of events which have a counterpart in real life; the same course of events takes place in both of the Pharaoh's dreams, so that Joseph can say that they are *one* dream. The subjects of the two dreams are cattle breeding (vv. 2-4) and agriculture (vv. 5-7), both dependent on the Nile. The cow is the grazing animal characteristic of Egypt in contrast to the sheep in Palestine. The parable tells of a bizarre happening: seven fat and seven lean cows stand side by side; the fat cows are devoured by the lean. It is just the same with the ears of grain. It is this that disturbs the Pharaoh, namely, that the seven ugly, lean ones prevail. The parable of the dreams is announcing a danger that threatens. This is further enhanced by the bizarre aspect, suitable only for a dream. The number seven occurs often in Egypt and throughout the ancient near east; cf. A. Kapelrud, VT 18 (1968) 497: "Seven was the number of fate. Seven represented the full number of blessings as well as of curses"; also D. T. Tsumura, *The Ugaritic Drama of the Good Gods* (diss. Brandeis, 1973-74): "The ritual is connected with a seven-year cycle of famine before a new period of plenty."

[41:5-7a] The second dream about the ears of grain functions to complement and confirm. Pairs of dreams of this sort occur elsewhere than Gen. 37 and 40. D. B. Redford speaks of a "weak duplicate"; in fact, its real significance derives from vv. 1-4, "devour," not from itself. Further, it is no mere chance that whereas vv. 1-4 have a distinctive Egyptian coloring, the withering wind, the sirocco, in vv. 5-7 comes from the east (קדים) in Palestine, but from the south in Egypt (cf. R. B. Y. Scott, ZAW 64 [1952] 11-25).

[41:7b] The dream is narrated as an experience of the Pharaoh (v. 1a); hence it has its appropriate conclusion. The Pharaoh wakes up and only on waking does he realize that it was a dream (an experience of everyone who has a vivid dream). The dream has made such an impression on him that he cannot shake it off or forget it.

[41:8-13] The Pharaoh now looks for an interpretation; first he is unsuccessful (v. 8) and then, with reference back to ch. 40, he sees the prospect of success (vv. 9-13).

[41:8a] The dream has disturbed the Pharaoh. The verb is פעם niph., "to trouble," only here; imitated in Dan. 2:1, 3; a similar meaning in Ps. 77:5 (Eng. v. 4), "I am so troubled that I cannot speak." That the Pharaoh is troubled is a clear sign that he suspects that the dream might presage a threat to his kingdom. He has the competent courtiers summoned, those who are skilled in the interpretation of dreams, "all the magicians and sages of Egypt."

      F. Delitzsch: "He does precisely what, according to Tacitus, *Hist.* IV, 83, king Ptolemy does in a similar situation ("he reveals his nocturnal visions to the priests of Egypt whose wont it is to interpret such things"). This accords with the designation חרטמים: "diviners who belong to the priestly caste" (A. Dillmann). The word is Egyptian in origin, *ḥr-tb*, "an epithet describing priests occupied with magic, soothsayers" (KBL); it occurs only here with this meaning and is copied in Dan. 1:20; 2:2, and Ex. 7–9, all P-passages; cf. further J. Vergote, *Joseph en Egypte.* . . (1959) 80-94; D. B. Redford, VT.S 20 (1970) 203f., "chief lector priest," as Vergote; it appears as a loan word in Akk., Demotic, Hebr., Gk. H. P. Müller (UF 1 [1969] 80-94) and H. C. Schmitt (BZAW 154 [1980] 139) attack D. F. Redford's arguments for a late dating; cf. W. L. Humphreys (1970-71, bibliog. above).

      "And all the sages" is a rather general description. There were interpreters of dreams among various groups of learned men. "It is a trait of the fairy tale when the Pharaoh summons all the wise men" (H. Gunkel); "all" can also mean "all sorts" (G. Hoberg, *Komm.* 1899; 1909²). On the "contest between the wise" as a theme of wisdom literature cf. J. C. H. Lebram, VT 15 (1965) 167-237.

[41:8b] The Pharaoh puts his dream before the interpreters; none of them can explain it to him. This does not mean that they all remained silent; interpretations were certainly proposed, "but none of them satisfied the Pharaoh" (B. Jacob). Another factor probably was that the dream seemed to foretell misfortune and no one had the courage to say so. The Pharaoh saw through the falseness of those explanations that tried to avoid this.

[41:9-13] This "contest between the wise" belonged to the independent narrative on which ch. 41 is based. The narrator of the Joseph story has deftly tied this episode to what has preceded by means of vv. 9-13 (cf. v. 1a). As it often actually happens, a similar situation reminds the Pharaoh's chief cupbearer of the scene in prison which he had forgotten. He is obviously happy to recall it because it gives him a double opportunity: to settle a debt of gratitude which he had long forgotten, and at the same time to do a favor for the Pharaoh. Vv. 10-13 are a masterly summary, brief and clear, of ch. 40 which allows the Pharaoh to learn all that is necessary.

[41:14-16] Joseph in the presence of the Pharaoh (vv. 14-16): The Pharaoh sends for Joseph, who prepares for the audience and appears before him. The Pharaoh puts the questions, Joseph answers.

[41:14] The Pharaoh has no choice but to take the opportunity offered him, a sign of how much he was troubled by his dream. He has the Hebrew slave summoned. Joseph had waited two years; now all is haste. He is hurriedly brought out of the dungeon—the same word is used as in the complaint in 40:15, בור, a subtlety that is lost when these words are assigned to another source. Despite the haste and the expectation of the assembled court, Joseph prepares himself for the audience; he cannot appear before the Pharaoh as he is. The narrator pronounces the sudden reversal of his fate in slowly moving sentences, "He shaved and changed his clothes" (in 2 Kings 25:29 Jehoiachin lay aside his prison clothes before coming into the king's presence). It is only after this well-spaced pause, which says much more than any description of Joseph's thoughts or feelings, that Joseph "came into the Pharaoh's presence"; this is the turning point in his fate; ch. 41 is the center, the climax of the Joseph story, and v. 14 is the climax of ch. 41.

[**41:15-16**] The meeting between Joseph and the Pharaoh is compressed into a short, precise, and sober dialog: "The Pharaoh said to Joseph. . .Joseph answered the Pharaoh."

[**41:15**] The Pharaoh sets him the task (part of the basic narrative) and expects a solution from him in accordance with what he has heard of him. He exaggerates Joseph's ability and at the same time expects much of him ("you understand the language of dreams," E. L. Ehrlich, op.cit.)

[**41:16**] Joseph answers the Pharaoh respectfully but firmly. He rejects a commendation that he does not deserve while at the same time expressing the certainty that the Pharaoh will get his answer (ענה). But the answer will not be a demonstration of his skill in interpreting (בלעדי = "no, not I" or "that is not for me to do"); the interpretation, like the dream, will come from God. Then comes the third part of the answer, formulated as the object of יענה; it is really a sentence in itself: what God announces to you (literally, answers) will be prosperity. Many exegetes say that the reply is "polite and proper" (O. Procksch), or something similar. But this does not compass the real meaning of Joseph's answer. It must be seen in its overall context. Joseph points out to the Pharaoh that his dreams do indeed come from God; God wants to tell him something (v. 25); hence the interpretation must also come from God; otherwise it is worthless. This reference to God as the source of the interpretation is of particular importance when the dream announces misfortune. This is what the last words are about: Even though I have to interpret tidings of misfortune to you, what God has to say to you will ultimately result in prosperity. Only now does it become clear that Joseph is cleverly preparing in v. 16 the interpretation he has to give to the Pharaoh.

G. von Rad sees in v. 16 "a passage of programmatic theological significance." H. Gunkel says that "Joseph is here an inspired person (in contrast to an interpreter of dreams)." G. von Rad speaks of a "charismatic illumination." L. Ruppert and H. C. Schmitt are of the opinion that the interpretation of dreams is equated here with prophecy. But Joseph is talking about God's word and action insofar as it is directed towards the Pharaoh and his kingdom. God wants to tell the Pharaoh something important about the future of his kingdom in the dreams; hence the interpretation belongs to him. Joseph thus appeals to the nearness of the king to God (1 Kings 3) in the context of sacral kingship.

[**41:17-24a**] Without more ado the Pharaoh now tells Joseph his dreams (for a more precise comparison between vv. 17-24 and vv. 1-7, cf. D. B. Redford, pp. 79ff.). The repetition is "colored by the Pharaoh's own personal feeling" (B. Jacob); this has a function in the Joseph story as a whole and shows itself in what the

Pharaoh emphasizes. In v. 19 he underscores the "gaunt, ugly, and lean"; never has he seen such ugly cows. In v. 21, which has no equivalent in vv. 1-7, the Pharaoh adds an observation: there is no sign that the ugly, lean cows had devoured the fat ones (Joseph takes this up in his interpretation). Both additions put the emphasis on the "ugly," the threatening. The Pharaoh's account of the dream thus forms the intermediate stage between the objective account in vv. 1-7 and Joseph's interpretation in vv. 17-24. This subjective account has already moved several steps along the way to interpretation; it senses the threat that the dream is announcing. The narrator thus gives to understand that the Pharaoh agrees with Joseph's interpretation; he suspected that the interpretation lies in this direction.

[**41:24b**] This too is the meaning of the concluding sentence, v. 24b: none of the magicians was able to give an interpretation that corresponded to the Pharaoh's suspicions.

[**41:25-32**] Joseph begins his interpretation immediately (vv. 25-32). Despite its length, the chapter is very tightly knit; the interpretation too is very densely concentrated; there is not one unnecessary word. The interpretation has four parts: (1) v. 25: the dream is one; it is an announcement; (2) vv. 26-28: "seven" means seven years—an announcement; (3) vv. 29-31: an announcement arising from the interpretation; (4) v. 32: the doubling means that this will certainly happen. The interpretation does not follow the dream point by point; it is not an allegorical or symbolic interpretation; Joseph explains the dream as a parable; he tells of something that is to happen. In all three parts (vv. 25, 26-28, 29-31) his interpretation explains what is to happen. The central part, vv. 26-31, is framed by the explanations of the numbers seven (v. 25) and two (v. 32).

[**41:25**] "The Pharaoh's dreams are one and the same." Both dreams have the same object; the fat is devoured by the lean. It is thus an assertion that this will happen and an announcement: "God has told the Pharaoh what he will do" (cf. v. 16).

[**41:26-28**] This is the only part of Joseph's interpretation that can be described as "allegorical." The number seven, four times repeated, means "something other" (allegory) than it appears to mean. The allegorical element has been inserted into the interpretation of the parable (parables often show an allegorical trait) in such a way that the two sentences in v. 25 which point to the object of the parable are resumed in vv. 26-28. In v. 26 it is a dream; in v. 29 it is an announcement.

It is obvious here that the repetitions are intended by the narrator. The same is true for other apparent doublets, e.g., vv. 30-31. Certain authors, like H. Gunkel, O. Procksch, J. Skinner, and L. Ruppert, want to attribute the doublets to two sources; more recent authors, however, understand the repetitions as intended by the narrator (W. Rudolf, B. Jacob, D. B. Redford, G. W. Coats, H. C. Schmitt).

Joseph did not need any particular skill to interpret the number seven of vv. 26-28 as seven years. Such an interpretation results from the dream itself.

H. Gunkel: "Time intervals of seven days, years, etc., are in general very common; in the OT 1 Kings 6:38; 2 Kings 11:4; Ex. 23:10f." An inscription from Elephantine of the Ptolemaic period announces a seven-year famine; it is dated back to the reign of

Djoser of the third dynasty (about 2800 B.C.); the famine was happily ended by the advice of a wise Egyptian (ANET, p. 31). D. B. Redford notes: "Ugaritic texts and the Gilgamesh epic speak of a seven-year drought" (pp. 206ff.).

[41:27-28] With the words ". . .mean seven years of famine" at the end of v. 27, the interpretation of the number seven passes quietly into the interpretation of the parable. The narrator perceives that a sound intelligence and a sharp faculty of observation are enough for Joseph to be able to interpret the dream. All the elements taken together—the persistently repeated number seven, the object of the dream, the devouring of the fat by the lean, the Pharaoh's uneasiness—all these speak clearly enough. Joseph can conclude his interpretation here (v. 28), even though he has explained only two elements of the dream. B. Jacob writes, "He passes over the self-explanatory elements. Joseph's astuteness is shown in that he can distinguish the essential from the nonessential." The sign that the real interpretation concludes with v. 28 is the narrative device of *inclusio*; vv. 25-28 are framed by the same sentence, vv. 25b,28: "God has let the Pharaoh know [has announced to] what he is going to do."

[41:29-31] What God is going to do follows in vv. 29-31. These verses have the form, not of an interpretation or an explanation, but of an announcement which throws the whole weight on to the announcement of a misfortune. Only one sentence is given to the years of plenty (v. 29), whereas five are given to the famine (vv. 30-31).

    This announcement of misfortune recalls unmistakably both in form and content the prophetic proclamation of woe. In form, it proceeds in closely knit, rhythmic language with a certain parallelism of members (e.g., vv. 30,32b). In content: v. 29a recalls "see, the days are coming when. . ..."; v. 32b resembles Is. 28:22, "For I have heard a decree of destruction from the Lord God of hosts upon the whole land," and Is. 5:19, "Let the purpose of the Holy One draw near. . .." It can remain an open question what conclusion is to be drawn from this striking resemblance between an interpretation of a dream and the prophetic proclamation of woe. Both are concerned with announcing what God is going to do. There was proclamation of this sort before the writing prophets; it is possible that there is a connection with the beginnings of "court prophecy." The early prophets in Israel directed their words above all to the king; they were not only prophets of good fortune.

    The narrator has succeeded here in integrating the interpretation of the dream into the announcement. What happened in the dream is transferred into the realm of historical reality. What the Pharaoh saw passes directly into the announcement, "famine will consume the land" (v. 31a). And the Pharaoh's remark, ". . .there was no sign. . ." (v. 21), goes over into the announcement, "there will be no sign of the plenty in the land because of the famine that follows." What Joseph says corresponds to what Pharaoh has seen and gives it meaning; moreover, it coincides with what the Pharaoh had been thinking after the dream.

[41:32] The explanation of the two parallel dreams passes over into the announcement by means of the rhythmical language; the listener thus senses that Joseph has convinced the Pharaoh because he speaks "with the fullness of power."

[41:33-36] Joseph has succeeded where the magicians and priests have failed, namely, in conveying the message of woe to the Pharaoh and thereby winning from him recognition that he has interpreted the dream correctly. But it seems that we have a glaring contradiction. In v. 16 Joseph had said that "God will announce prosperity for the Pharaoh." But what came was a message of woe. A contradiction like this cannot stand. So Joseph adds a piece of advice for the Pharaoh which will enable the land to avert the disaster that the seven years of famine portends (v. 36b). In the long run it is through Joseph's astute advice that God's message to Pharaoh in the dream serves the welfare of both him and the land.

The advice that Joseph gives the Pharaoh is as clear and precise as the interpretation of the dream. He advises the Pharaoh to take measures (v. 33) which he spells out in detail under three headings (vv. 34-35). The conclusion (v. 36) explains the purpose of the measures.

[41:33a] The ועתה indicates that Joseph is now drawing the consequences of his interpretation: "now the Pharaoh should look around"; the simple Hebrew verb ראה often carries a meaning which can only be expressed in conjunction with the attendant circumstances (cf. Ges-K §75p): "a wise and intelligent man." חכם occurs in Genesis only in 41:8, 33; in 41:8 (the sages of Egypt) it means a "scholar," in 41:33 one equipped for a difficult assignment. This is expressed through the combination נבון וחכם (cf. 1 Kings 3:12—God gives Solomon a wise and understanding heart; cf. Is. 10:13; Prov. 8:14f.; Job 12:2f.). B. Jacob makes a distinction between their meanings: נבון is one endowed the power of judgment, חכם one who evaluates experience correctly; but one cannot pin down these nuances. The "wise and intelligent" man described here is the one who is capable of planning and carrying through important economic measures. "Wisdom," therefore, is not a specialized area of intellectual operation, nor is it something learned in the schools. Joseph is a "layman"; he did not attend any school of wisdom. God has opened his eyes in the face of the reality, and it is this that enables him to do what he is doing. The way in which Joseph stands the test in interpreting the dreams shows the same. He does not interpret them after the way of the professionals, the wise men of Egypt, but as one endowed by God with insight. His interpretation is more in the fashion of popular wisdom that in the wisdom of the schools. Comparative sayings are part of popular wisdom according to Proverbs; Joseph accordingly explains the dreams as parables.

[41:33b] The Pharaoh ought to put a man like this "in charge of the country," i.e., he ought make him viceroy.

[41:34a] The appointment of supervisors (v. 34a) is not another piece of advice contradicting that in v. 33, as source division would have it, but an executive detail spelling out the basic advice already given (v. 33). The executor (יעשה, meaning "arrange") in v. 34 is also the Pharaoh; Joseph is thus astutely saying that the authority of the Pharaoh must support the measures taken by the viceroy.

[41:34b] ". . .And take one-fifth. . .." This sentence interrupts the continuity between v. 34a and v. 35, as the change in the number indicates. With W. Rudolf, D. B. Redford, and particularly H. C. Schmitt it should be regarded as a gloss (against H. Donner) inserted here to give the later expansion (47:13-26) a base in the advice that Joseph gives to the Pharaoh. Another factor in favor of this is that the taking of one-fifth is not mentioned in the execution in 41:47-49.

[**41:35**] V. 35 follows on v. 34a; the subject of ויקבצו is the supervisors in v. 34a. The task of the supervisors is to collect grain, קבץ, in the years of plenty ("all" means the surplus grain); they are to store it in granaries in the central city of each area and put it "under the Pharaoh's control," i.e., under his authority and administration as well as at his disposal. These granaries were typical of ancient Egypt, a landmark, and were well known and admired in the surrounding countries.

> For a detailed account of the "supervisors" cf. D. B. Redford, VT.S 20 (1970) 207f.; J. Vergote, *Joseph en Egypte*. . . (1959) 98-102; R. de Vaux, *The Early History*. . . I (1971; 1978) 305-307; W. Beyerlin, ATD 1 (1975) 257f. 1 Kings 9:19, which tells of the store-cities that Solomon had built, shows that Israel learned from Egypt in this matter (cf. F. Crüsemann, WMANT 49 [1978] 35).

[**41:36**] Joseph concludes his advice to the Pharaoh with the assurance that the reserve thus stored (פקדון = "left over," "reserve," a technical term; elsewhere only in Lev. 5:21, 23) can secure the country in face of the famine.

[**41:37-46**] Joseph's elevation: The fate of Joseph, the captive slave, is changed with his interpretation of the Pharaoh's dream; his elevation follows immediately. The Pharaoh and his court give Joseph their approval (vv. 37-38) and the Pharaoh puts him in charge of his household, the royal palace (vv. 39-40), and the land of Egypt (vv. 41-46).

[**41:37-38**] Joseph's advice wins the approval of the Pharaoh and his court. The Pharaoh's ready and unreserved agreement is possible only because Joseph's interpretation accords with what he himself had suspected. The Pharaoh is convinced of his ability because Joseph had the courage to announce openly the message of woe while at the same time showing how it may be met. The court agrees either because it has no alternative or simply because it does not want to oppose the Pharaoh's conviction.

The Pharaoh at once draws the consequence of his agreement; Joseph has demonstrated that he is the one whom the kingdom needs in face of the threatening situation. This is what the Pharaoh means by the question addressed to his ministers (v. 38). Joseph had said in v. 33 that the Pharaoh must appoint a "wise and intelligent" man to supervise the task. The Pharaoh cannot really mean anything else when he says, ". . .a man like this who has the spirit of God." He does not mean a particular religious endowment or qualification, but an ability for the task at hand for which God is responsible. It is not that Joseph is "inspired," as some commentaries say; it is a question of an outstanding ability in the areas of political economy and statesmanship. It is important that Joseph's reference to the action of God, who wants to tell the Pharaoh something in the dreams, is taken up by the latter in a like reference: Joseph and the Pharaoh, despite the difference in their religions, are at one in their conviction that "God" acts in history.

[41:39-40] After addressing his court in vv. 37-38, the Pharaoh now turns to Joseph. With the antecedent giving the reason, v. 39, (אחר with the meaning "because," W. J. Boyd, JThS 12 [1961] 54-56), the Pharaoh announces (אתה תהיה) that he is appointing him to a position over his household and people which will be subordinate only to that of the Pharaoh himself. The reason in v. 39 comprises Joseph's suitability for such a high appointment in the words of Joseph himself ("wise and intelligent") and of the Pharaoh: God has given him the ability for it (v. 38). There is probably a court formula behind v. 40 describing authority over the Pharaoh's household and people. It is expanded here with the words "on your mouth shall. . .." The verb is uncertain; it can only mean the power to command or make regulations for the whole people (F. Delitzsch, A. Dillmann; cf. Num. 27:21).

O. Procksch refers to the Hoad-Wilbour Papyrus from the New Kingdom which mentions a dignitary "the Privy Councillor of the royal household, superintendent of the length and breadth of the land"; H. C. Schmitt refers to the master of the palace, 2 Kings 18:18, the highest state official; cf. R. de Vaux, *Ancient Israel* (1958-60; 1962) 129-131; P. A. H. de Boer, VT.S 3 (1955) 42-71. J. H. Breasted, *Ancient Records of Egypt* (AR 1906-07), regards the office of viceroy (vizier), the Pharaoh's plenipotentiary, as the office conferred on Joseph; cf. J. Vergote, *Joseph en Egypte. . . ..* (1959) 102-114.

The verb ישק cannot mean "kiss," from נשק; there must be a textual corruption. The Gk probably gives the correct sense of the verb, no longer recognizable, with ὑπακούσεται; in the context ישפט, Syr, is also possible; KBL proposes יקשב = "attend to," which would correspond to the Gk. For further proposals, see D. B. Redford, pp. 166f.

[41:41-46] Joseph's installation in office by the Pharaoh is divided into the public act of installation, v. 41 with v. 44, introduced by vv. 41a and 44a, linked with the investiture, vv. 42-43, and the family act of conferring a new name, v. 45a, with the elevation to the nobility by marriage, v. 45b. After the installation (vv. 41-45) Joseph takes over the new office by the ritual act of traveling through the land (v. 46b). A note on Joseph's age at the time of his elevation has been subsequently inserted here (v. 46a).

[41:41] The solemn installation of Joseph as viceroy "over the whole of the land of Egypt" takes place with the words of the Pharaoh ראה נתתי אתך (v. 41), which recall the words of Yahweh at the installation of Jeremiah (Jer. 1:10). It is a misunderstanding of this installation style to regard v. 41 as a doublet of v. 40 (A. Dillmann; H. Holzinger; but differently H. Gunkel); v. 40 is the announcement. There is much attestation that Asiatic slaves came to high office in Egypt; cf. J. M. A. Janssen, CEg 26,51 (1951) 50-62; R. de Vaux, *The Early History. . .* 1 (1971; 1978) 297-301.

[41:42-43] The ancient rite of investiture is linked with the installation. It consists of the giving of a ring, clothing with a festal garment, laying on of the golden chain, and arranging for the chariot.

There is an abundance of parallels for installation in office and the accompanying investiture. The rites are similar across a broad cultural area throughout the world. Hence the parallels say no more than that the investiture narrated here is similar to many others known from elsewhere. A particularly close parallel is

Ashurbanipal's account of the installation of Necho as vassal-king of Egypt (ANET 295): "I clad him in a garment of multicolored trimmings, placed a golden chain on him (as the) insigne of his kingship, put golden rings on his hands" (7th cent. B.C.); also J. Vergote, pp. 116-134; D. B. Redford, pp. 208-226; R. de Vaux, 1, pp. 298-301. But the period cannot be established on the basis of the parallels. D. B. Redford, for example, can produce 230 examples of the conferring of a golden chain and say that the last parallels come from the seventh to the second centuries B.C.; but when he says that this favors a late dating of the Joseph story, then his conclusion is questionable. It is sufficient that the author of the Joseph story knows of such insignia and their conferring from various occasions at the royal court. The selection and combination of such elements as here can be attributed entirely to the artistic arrangement of the author. A further reason for this is that the name of Joseph does not appear among the many names of the viceroys of Egypt.

[**41:42a**] The Pharaoh takes the ring from his hand and puts it on Joseph's. The signet ring plays a similar role in Esther 3:12; 8:8; it is very often there on the occasion of the clothing of priests, e.g., Ex. 28. Many such rings have been found, a number with the names of the reigning kings. The viceroy is also the keeper of the royal seal over which he has disposal: "Documents of state are stamped with the royal seal" (H. Gunkel).

[**41:42b**] The material of the garment is fine linen, such as is seen on the images from ancient Egypt; שׁשׁ = linen is an Egyptian loanword, rendered in the Gk by βύσσος. The Pharaoh puts a golden chain around Joseph's neck. This played an important role in the court of Egypt and was the equivalent of the conferring of an order. Many paintings illustrate the rite.

[**41:43**] The chariot was at that time part of the installation in high office. It is a war chariot drawn by horses and serves as well symbolic purposes (cf. H. Weippert, "Pferd und Streitwagen," in K. Galling, BRL [1977²] 250-255; S. Mowinckel, VT 12 [1962] 278-299). We know it from a number of representations. One was discovered in the tomb of Tut-ankh-Amon. Horse and chariot are found in representations of the 18th dynasty. The second chariot refers to his position as the second man in the state; the people must pay him homage, and the heralds summon them to it with the cry, "Abrek." J. Vergote, pp. 135-141, and D. B. Redford, pp. 226-228, maintain that "Abrek" is the imperative of a verb, a Semitic loanword. The meaning is clear and was already recognized by A. Dillmann: "Heralds went before him and sounded the call to homage"; so far there has been no precise philological explanation. J. S. Croatto's derivation from the Akk. *abarikku* = "administrator" (with H. C. Schmitt and others) does not accord with the context (VT 16 [1966] 113-115).

[**41:44**] Just as v. 41 begins solemnly as an address from the Pharaoh, so too the installation closes solemnly (v. 44). Vv. 41 and 44 form its frame; v. 44 extends v. 41b in two directions. The supreme authority that Joseph receives in v. 41b means an unlimited power of command (v. 44); the consequence is that Joseph is immune in his office. His authority is restricted by the Pharaoh's sovereignty, expressed by the formula אני פרעה, corresponding to אני יהוה. It is here that it has its limits, but also its guarantee. Z. W. Falk (JSS 12 [1967] 241-244) comments on the expression ''no one shall move hand or foot'': ''A legal practice similar to the Roman *vindicatio* seems to be meant in 41:44. That no one can move hand or foot in Egypt without Joseph can describe his power over the land.''

[**41:45a**] Joseph's change of name and marriage are deliberately separated from the state ceremony of installation. Both are family matters which incorporate a member of a foreign people into the Egyptian people. Joseph receives an Egyptian name; this was common in Egypt and is attested often; cf. the list from the 13th dynasty on which details are given of Palestinian-Syrian slaves with their proper and Egyptian names (ANET Supp, 117f. = 553f.) Joseph's Egyptian name צפנת פענח has been explained by G. Steindorff: ''God speaks and he lives'' (ZÄS 30 [1892] 50f.; also H. Hoberg, *Komm.* [1899]) and has been generally accepted. It does not occur elsewhere.

[**41:45b**] The Pharaoh gives Joseph a daughter from a prominent house as wife (v. 45); she is Asenath, daughter of Potiphera, the high priest of On (Heliopolis, northeast of Cairo); he thus receives him into the Egyptian nobility. The temple at On (Egyptian Anu) was a center of sun worship, and its high priest one of the most prominent of the priests. His name is the same as Potiphar in 39:1, ''the one whom Re gave.'' The name of the daughter, Asenath, means ''the one belonging to Neith.''

   This note on Joseph's marriage provided the point of departure for the novel that originated in Philo's time, ''Joseph and Asenath'' (cf. C. Burchard, WUNT 8 [1965]; D. Sänger, JSJ 10 [1980] 11-36, on the name Asenath pp. 13f., on the goddess Neith pp. 15-20). The novel, which tells of Asenath's conversion to belief in Yahweh, is the best example of the change in attitude in the later period. The narrator of the Joseph story and his listeners found nothing scandalous in Joseph becoming the son-in-law of a priest of the god Re, in his taking a theophoric name which made him a creature of an Egyptian god, and in his participating in the Egyptian state cult in his capacity as a high official. That was possible in the period of Solomon but seems to me excluded for the post-Deuteronomic period. The same difference in religious perspective appears in the book of Daniel which in much of its content presupposes the Joseph story.

   The further sentence at the end of v. 45 is missing in the Gk. Standing as it does on its own, it scarcely makes sense and is repeated as part of a whole in v. 46b. It seems to be a scribal error here. Perhaps it is a sign that v. 46a was later inserted into the text.

[**41:46a**] The detail about Joseph's age at the time of his elevation is probably an insertion from P following on the family details in v. 45.

[**41:46b**] Now properly installed, Joseph enters on his office of viceroy at the conclusion of the audience by traveling through the territory under his authority (v. 46b). It is the symbolic act of taking possession on a large scale such as we have already seen on a small scale in Gen. 13:17; here too the action of passing through the land follows the granting of it.

In retrospect, Joseph's installation in his high office of state in Egypt is an event that we can visualize in all its details as very few others in the Bible. Every detail of the ceremony has been passed down to us in Egyptian representations, even down to the almost transparent linen garments. We can view the rings, the golden chains, and the war chariots in the museums.

[**41:47-57**] Ch. 41 began with the Pharaoh's dreams (vv. 1-7); it concludes with the realization of what Joseph had told the Pharaoh in the course of his interpretation (vv. 25-32). But this is linked with the execution of the measures that Joseph had counseled (vv. 35-36). The seven years of plenty came; Joseph had the abundance of grain gathered and stored in granaries (vv. 47-49). Then the seven years of famine came during which Joseph had the reserves of grain dealt out, not only to the Egyptians (vv. 55-56), but also to those from other countries suffering from famine (v. 57). Between these two parts there is an insertion from the conclusion of the Jacob story, the birth and naming of Joseph's two sons.

[**41:47-49**] As foretold, the land produced abundance of grain in the first seven years, literally "heaps and heaps." So Joseph was able to see that his advice was carried out and the grain collected and stored. The process of storing, which had only been mentioned in v. 35, is described in detail in v. 48b. V. 49 underscores yet again the abundance of grain stored. The image of the sand of the sea and the description of the quantity are well known from the promises of blessing.

[**41:50-52**] Both the language and content of vv. 50-52 mark them off from the contiguous material and interrupt the context. They have been transferred to their present position from the conclusion of the Joseph story, so as to follow Joseph's marriage and prepare for ch. 48.

[**41:50**] The verse reports the birth of Joseph's two sons from Asenath and is inserted into the context by means of the temporal note "before the years of famine came."

[**41:51**] The name-giving accompanies the birth as, for example, in Gen. 29:31—30:24; in 30:23f. Joseph is born and named by his mother; here it is the father who names the sons because they are to continue the traditions of the father. The names of the sons preserve the experiences of the father in a foreign land. The explanation of the name of the firstborn מנשה is: "God has made me forget [vocalization adapted to the name] all my hardship." The addition of the words ואת כל־בית אבי means that "I am far from my father's house."

[**41:52**] The explanation of the name of the second son אפרים is: "God has made me fruitful in the land of my hardship"; cf. the promises of Gen. 17:6, 20; 28:3; 48:4; Ps. 105:23f. (Jacob in Egypt). Both names are names of the praise of God as in Gen. 21:6; 29:32, 35; 30:6, 18, 20, 23. In one God is praised as the one who preserves, in the other as the one who blesses; both confirm the promise "I am with you" from 39:2-6, 21-23. Joseph is saying in these names that he understands his own story as God's action on him; the names of praise accord with this. The God of his fathers has accompanied him.

[**41:53-57**] V. 53 follows directly on v. 49. The second part of the account of the realization of what had been foretold, vv. 53-57, is at the same time a preparation for what is to follow, chs. 42-43. As Joseph had announced in his interpretation of the dream, the famine follows the seven years of plenty (vv. 53-54a). It strikes the surrounding countries; only in Egypt is there grain. At the Pharaoh's behest those who are hungry have recourse to Joseph (v. 55), whose measures now come into effect. The famine is severe, but Joseph opens the granaries and provides the land with grain (v. 56b). The famine extends beyond Egypt (v. 56a), and so the whole world comes to Joseph in Egypt to buy grain (v. 57).

The text of vv. 53-57 is disturbed in several places. Following the Gk the object of ויפתח in v. 56 is to be read as ''all reserves of grain (granaries)''; the words that stand in the MT, את־כל־אשר בהם, could be the remainder of a sentence, ''and he dealt out to the Egyptians all the grain that was in them.'' In v. 57, וכל־הארצות is to be read because of the plural verb. The sequence of sentences also raises considerable difficulties which the commentators have noted and in part corrected; in particular the statements about the famine in and outside Egypt do not stand in any clear relationship to each other. Both v. 56b (A. Dillmann) and v. 56a (H. Gunkel) in their present position interrupt a subsisting context. However, the text becomes more coherent if the sentence in v. 54b about the famine ''in all countries'' is bracketed as a subsequent insertion, and v. 56a is read at the end of v. 56 and before v. 57. This makes for a smooth and obvious continuity, with vv. 53-56 dealing with the seven years of famine in Egypt and only the conclusion (vv. 56a and 57) with the famine elsewhere.

Purpose and Thrust

This is a peculiarly modern chapter. It begins with the Pharaoh's dreams with the cows and ears of grain indicating cattle-breeding and agriculture; it concludes with statesmanlike measures taken to stockpile grain so as to protect a country against a severe famine. This is stating clearly that in certain situations the gift of blessing must be supplemented by a well-thought-out policy which can be administered only by a central authority, so as to avert a severe disaster for the whole land and the hungry.

Ch. 41 stands at the center of the Joseph story. At the beginning stood the testy question of the brothers, ''Are you going to be king over us. . .?'' At the end, the breach in the family of Jacob which arose from this question is healed; the measures that Joseph takes by virtue of his royal commission also saves the life of his family. The change of fate in the life of an insignificant slave from a foreign land leads the change of fate of a whole people faced with famine. The two lines come together the moment Joseph appears before the Pharaoh to explain his dream. At the same time two lines along which God is working coalesce. One is traced by the refrain of ch. 39: ''God was with Joseph.'' It points back to the action of the God of the fathers on Jacob, the promise of assistance (presence) to the group on its way, even in foreign parts. With Joseph, God's assistance comes to be expressed for the first time when he ''finds favor'' (39:4, 21) with those on whom he is dependent in a foreign land, and then with the Pharaoh (41:37f.). The moment that Joseph appears before the Pharaoh (41:14-16) this line coalesces with the other line along which God is working, ''to bring it about that many people should be kept alive.'' This is God's blessing at work; it embraces the whole human race and can achieve its effect even through the institution of the monarchy and its power structure (cf. ch. 37). The same God who "is with Joseph" has made an announcement to the Pharaoh in a dream; and it is this insignificant slave from a foreign land who interprets the Pharaoh's dream and so makes it possible to avert the famine. These two lines of God's action come together in the dialog between the Pharaoh and Joseph at the climax of the story; it is here that Joseph points to God's action for good in the Pharaoh's dream (41:16) and the Pharaoh acknowledges God's power at work in Joseph's wisdom (41:27f.). God's action, comprehending the families of the patriarchs and the kingdom of the Pharaoh, also links the story of the patriarchs with the story of the people of Israel and its monarchy.

In the insert about the birth and naming of Joseph's two sons (vv. 50-52), the two names, expressing the praise of God, are a witness that the great statesman in Egypt remains bound to the God of his fathers.

The First Journey of the Brothers to Egypt

Literature

Genesis 42–44: G. Dossin, "A propos du nom des Benjaminites dans les Archives de Mari," RA 52 (1958) 60-62. K. D. Schunck, *Benjamin: Untersuchungen zur Entstehung und Geschichte eines israelitischen Stammes*, BZAW 86 (1963). H. B. Huffmon, *Amorite Personal Names in the Mari Texts: A Structural and Lexical Study* (1965) esp. 20f., 175f. K. Minkner, *Die Einwirkung des Bürgschaftsrechts auf Leben und Religion Altisraels* (diss. Halle [1974]).

Genesis 42:1-5: H. Gressmann, AOB (1927²) no. 87. M. Noth, *The World of the Old Testament* (1940; 1962⁴; Eng. 1958). E. Kutsch, "Die Wurzel עצר im Hebräischen," VT 2 (1952) 57-69. J. Muilenburg, "The Birth of Benjamin," JBL 75 (1956) 194-201 esp. 198. B. S. Jackson, "The Problem of Exod. XXI 22-25 (*Ius talionis*)," VT 23 (1973) 273-304. S. E. Loewenstamm, "Exodus XXI 22-25," VT 27 (1977) 352-360.

Genesis 42:6-8: E. Gilleschewski, "Der Ausdruck עם הארץ im AT," ZAW 40 (1922) 137-142. M. Fendler, "Zur Sozialkritik des Amos: Versuch einer wirtschafts- und sozialgeschichtlichen Interpretation alttestamentlicher Texte," EvTh 33 (1973) 32-53.

Genesis 42:9-16: S. Wagner, "Die Kundschaftergeschichten im AT," ZAW 76 (1964) 255-269. F. I. Andersen, "The Socio-Juridical Background of the Naboth Incident," JBL 85 (1966) 46-57. D. Michel, "'Ămät. Untersuchung über 'Wahrheit' im Hebräischen," ABG 12 (1968) 30-57. M. R. Lehmann, "Biblical Oaths," ZAW 81 (1969) 74-92. H. P. Müller, "Notizen zu althebräischen Inschriften I," UF 2 (1970) 229-242. V. Hamp, " 'Der Herr gibt es den Seinen im Schlaf,' Ps 127,2d," Fests. J. Ziegler (1972) 71-79. F. L. Horton, "Form and Structure in Laws Relating to Women: Leviticus 18:6-18," SBLASP 1 (1973) 20-33.

Genesis 42:17-26: M. A. Canney, "The Hebrew מליץ (Prov IX 12; Gen XLII 23)," AJSL 40 (1923/24) 135-137. H. N. Richardson, "Some Notes on ליץ and Its Derivatives," VT 5 (1955) 163-179, 434-436. S. E. Loewenstamm, "The Climax of Seven Days in the Ugaritic Epos," Tarb. 31 (1961/62) 227-235. H. W. Wolff, "The Elohistic Fragments in the Pentateuch," *Interp.* 26 (1972) 158-173.

Genesis 42:27-38: J. Meinhold, *Studien zur israelitischen Religionsgeschichte I: Der heilige Rest* (1903). S. Garofalo, *La nozione profetica del 'Resto d'Israele'* (diss. Rom [1942]) esp. 197-202. E. W. Heaton, "The Root š'r and the Doctrine of the Remnant," JThS 3 (1952) 27-39. R. B. Y. Scott, "The Shekel Sign on Stone Weights," BASOR 153 (1959) 32-35. F. Michaeli, *Grammaire Hébraique et Théologie Biblique: Hommage à W.*

Vischer (1960) 145-156. E. A. Speiser, "The Verb *shr* in Genesis and Early Hebrew Movements," BASOR 164 (1961) 23-28. J. C. Greenfield, "The Etymology of אֲמַתְחַת," ZAW 77 (1965) 90-92. A. A. MacIntosh, "Psalm XCI 4 and the Root סחר," VT 23 (1973) 56-62.

Text

42:1   When Jacob learned that there was grain in Egypt [and Jacob[a] said to his sons, "Why do you stand looking at[b] each other?][c]

2   he said,[a] Listen, I have heard that there is grain in Egypt; go down and buy grain[b] for us there that we may live and not[c] have to die.

3   So Joseph's brothers, ten of them, went down to buy grain in Egypt.

4   But Benjamin, Joseph's brother, Jacob did not allow to go with his brothers for he feared some harm[a] might happen to him.

5   [So the sons of Israel came down to Egypt with the others to buy grain because there was famine in the land of Canaan.][a]

6   Now Joseph [was governor in the land: he][a] was the one who sold grain to all the people of the land. So Joseph's brothers came and bowed to the ground before him.

7   When Joseph saw his brothers he recognized them but pretended not to know them and spoke harshly[a] to them. He said to them, Where do you come from? They said, From the land of Canaan to buy food.

8   Whereas Joseph recognized his brothers, they did not recognize him.

9   Joseph remembered the dreams he had of them and said to them, You are spies! You have come to spy out the weaknesses of the land!

10   But they said to him, No, my lord, your servants[a] have come to buy food.

11   All[a] of us, we[b] are the sons of one man, we are honest people; your servants are not spies.

12   But he said to them, No,[a] you have come to spy out the weakness of the land!

13   They said, We, your servants, were twelve brothers, sons of one man in the land of Canaan. The youngest is still with our father, and one is no more.[a]

14   But Joseph said to them, It is as I have said; you are spies.

15   By this you shall be tested; by the life of the Pharaoh[a] you shall not leave this place unless your youngest brother comes here.

16   Send one of you to bring your brother; the rest of you shall remain in prison;[a] your words will be tested to see whether you have spoken the truth[b] or not. If not, by the life of the Pharaoh you are spies.

17   Thereupon he had them put in custody for three days.

18   On the third day Joseph said to them, Do this[a] and you shall live; I am a man who fears God.

19   If you are honest people, then one of your brothers[a] is to remain in custody where you are; but the rest of you can go and take grain for your hungry households.[b]

20   But you must bring your youngest brother to me so that your words may be confirmed and you shall not die. [And they did so].[a]

21   Then they said to each other, We are certainly[a] guilty with regard to our brother. We saw his anguish of heart[b] when he pleaded with us, but we did not listen. That is why this disaster has befallen us.

22   But Reuben answered them, Did I not tell you not to do the boy any wrong? But you did not listen! And his blood requires retribution.

23   They did not know that Joseph understood because he used an inter-
      preter.[a]
24   Then he turned away from them and wept. Turning back to them
      again he spoke to them.[a] He took Simeon and had him bound before
      their eyes.
25   Joseph then gave orders that their sacks be filled[a] with grain, that
      each one's money be put back in his sack, and that they be given pro-
      visions for their journey; and it[b] was done for them.
26   So they loaded their grain onto their donkeys and went off.
27   When one of them opened his sack[a] at the stopping place overnight
      to give his donkey some provender, he saw his money there at the top
      of the pack.
28   He said to his brothers, My money has been returned to me; here it[a] is
      in my pack. Their hearts sank and, trembling,[b] they turned to each
      other and said, What is this that God has done to us!
29   When they came to their father Jacob in the land of Canaan, they told
      him all that had happened to them. They said,
30   The man who is lord of the country spoke harshly to us and had us put
      in 'custody'[a] alleging that we were spying out the land.
31   But we said to him, We are honest people, we are not spies.
32   We are twelve brothers, sons of the one father. One is no more, and
      the youngest is still with our father in the land of Canaan.
33   And this man who is lord of the country said to us, By this I shall know
      if you are honest men. Leave one of your brothers with me, but take
      the 'grain'[a] that your hungry households need and go.
34   But bring your youngest brother down here to me and then I shall
      know that you are not spies but honest men. 'Then'[a] I will give your
      brother back to you and you will be free to move about[b] the country.
35   [When they emptied their sacks each found[a] a bag with his money in
      his pack. When they and their father saw the bags[b] of money, they
      were afraid.][c]
36   And Jacob their father said to them, You are making me childless! Jo-
      seph is no more and Simeon is no more and you want to take Benja-
      min as well! Everything has come upon me!
37   Then Reuben said to his father, You may kill[a] my two sons if I do not
      bring him back to you. Put him in my hands[b] and I will return him to
      you.
38   But he said, My son shall not go down with you because his brother is
      dead and he alone is left. Some harm could happen to him on the
      way.[a] Then you would bring[b] my grey hairs down to Sheol in sorrow.

1a Gk omits.   b ראה hithp.; only here with this meaning; S. R. Isenberg, JBL 90
(1971) 69-81; Ges-K §54f; BrSynt §39d; Gk translates תאחרו.   c See comm.
2a ויאמר missing in Gk   b Gk translates מעט אכל as in 43:2, perhaps
correctly.   c Construction Ges-K §109g; ולא in final sentence.
4a Elsewhere only in 44:29 and Ex. 21:22, 23.
5a See M. Noth, *The World of the Old Testament* (1940; 1962⁴; Eng. 1958), and comm.
below.
6a Sam, Syr, Targj והוא; see comm. below.
7a Cf. 1 Sam. 20:10; form, Ges-K §122q.
10a Construction, Ges-K §163a; Sam, Gk, Syr omit ו.
11a Ges-K §91f.   b Form, Ges-K §32d.
12a Construction, BrSynt §134a.

13a Ges-K §152m; BrSynt §80e.
15a On the oath, BrSynt §140c, 31b; Ges-K §93aa.
16a Ges-K §110c.   **b** THAT I 201-209.
18a Construction, Ges-K §110f; BrSynt §3.
19a Construction, Ges-K §134d; BrSynt §10b; Sam האחד.   **b** Ges-K §125h.
20a Probably a gloss.
21a BrSynt §56b.   **b** Sam בצרת; on נפש, THAT II 71-96.
23a O. Betz, BHH I (1962) 349; H. N. Richardson VT 5 (1955) 163-179, 434-436.
24a Missing in Gk Mss; could be an addition.
25a Construction, Ges-K §120f; unusual construction.   **b** Impersonal; perhaps to be read as plural.
27a Gk translates אמתחתו; cf. J. C. Greenfield, ZAW 77 (1965) 90-92.
28a Sam, Gk add הוא.   **b** Construction, Ges-K §119gg; BrSynt §29a.
30a With Gk במשמר is to be inserted, following 40:3.
33a With Gk, TargO, Syr, שבר to be inserted, as in v. 19.
34a With Gk, Syr, Vg translate ואת־.   **b** On the verb סחר, cf. Gen. 23:16; Lit. in *Genesis 12–36*, ad loc.
35a Construction, Ges-K §135p; 111g.   **b** Doubled plural, BrSynt §72a.   **c** See comm.
37a The consequence precedes the condition Ges-K §159r.   **b** על־ידי as in 1 Sam. 17:22.
38a Construction, Ges-K §159eg.   **b** As 37:35; cf. 1 Kings 2:6, 9.

Form

Ch. 42 continues the events of ch. 37 without any transition formula, thus showing chs. 39–41 to be an interlude in the main narrative. The connecting motif is the famine. The story of Jacob's family continues in ch. 42 with an episode, the outbreak of famine (cf. Gen. 12:10-20). This famine which is the cause of Jacob's concern (v. 2) is the same as the one that has struck the land of Egypt. This is the link with chs. 39–41, a link which in the plan of the Joseph story is subtle and well thought out: at the beginning of ch. 42 the famine is seen from the perspective of those who are hungry, as elsewhere in the patriarchal story; in chs. 39–41 from the perspective of a king who is responsible for his people in face of a famine to come; this is the perspective intended in the interpretation of the dream and the measures taken by the Pharaoh's minister. Thus the two main lines of the Joseph story come together in the motif that joins chs. 39–41 with the broader context of chs. 37 and 42–45: the breach in Jacob's family which is eventually to be healed, and the question of the monarchy which gives rise to the breach inasmuch as it is the monarchy that enables the family of Jacob to be saved from famine and thereby heal the breach (ch. 45).

Ch. 42 is divided into three parts: departure and journey to Egypt (vv. 1-5); experiences in Egypt (vv. 6-24); return and arrival at the father's house (vv. 26-38). The structure is in fact that of a travel report, in this case of a journey made necessary by famine so as to procure the necessities of life. Because an event of this kind is attested several times not only in the Old Testament, but also in Egypt (cf. *Genesis 12–36*, 12:10-20, Setting), there must have been many such reports. Their function was to serve as points of reference later for the same or other groups when faced with a crisis. It was very important to know where and how one got grain, especially to have regard to the attitude of those who had it. This is what Gen. 42 is about. It depends on the attitude of the authorities in the foreign land whether one obtains the grain so necessary for life (''that we may live and not have to die''). The narrator of the Joseph story could well have had such a travel report before him; but he could just as well have thought it out himself independently, because an event like this was known in a wide variety of variants. Some expressions occur only, or virtually only, in this chapter and this may favor the view that some such account was available to him: in v. 1b the hiph. of ראה with this meaning; in vv. 4 and 38 אסון (elsewhere only in Ex 21:22f.); כנים meaning ''honest people,'' vv. 11, 19, 31, 33, 34; ערות הארץ in vv. 9, 12; niph. of בחן in vv. 15, 16, only here in Gen.; מליץ = interpreter in v. 23.

This report is inserted into the Joseph story as an episode and becomes a scene in the narrative. But the potentate on whom the success of the journey of Jacob's son depends was their long-lost brother; so the report becomes a dramatic episode in the context of the narrative as a whole.

As for the unity of the chapter, the difficulties caused by contradictions are to be explained otherwise than by source division. D. B. Redford in particular, as W. Rudolf before him, correctly insists that the planned architecture of the middle part would be destroyed by separation into different sources.

Commentary

[**42:1-5**] The first part, vv. 1-5, raises formidable difficulties. Its function is clear from the threefold division. First, there is the father's request (vv. 1-2) and the consequent departure of the brothers. There is the reason for the request (v. 1a) and the communication of both reason and request to the brothers (vv. 2a,2b). Second, there is the account of the brothers' departure in accordance with the father's request, with a note about their number (v. 3) which is explained in v. 4; the father does not allow Benjamin to accompany his brothers (v. 4a), for fear that something might happen to him (v. 4b). V. 4 at the same time anticipates v. 13. Finally, one would expect a sentence reporting the arrival of the brothers in Egypt; v. 5, however, says this only in a general way, and there is no account of their arrival at their journey's end.

[**42:1a**] The ויּרא at the beginning of v. 1 cannot be the beginning of the narrative. There is no exposition telling of a famine in Canaan and giving reason for what follows as in Gen. 12:10a. This is anticipated in 41:57b, which binds chs. 42 and 41 firmly together. It is a binding of motifs; it is one and the same famine. It is typical of the narrator of the Joseph story to forge a link in this way. Faced with the famine, Jacob hears that there is grain in Egypt. For millennia Egypt has been the granary for the surrounding countries (''שבר is grain as an article of commerce,'' A. Dillmann).

[**42:1b**] Both in content and in form v. 1b gives the impression of being a foreign body. *In content:* V. 2 is the natural continuation of v. 1a, showing its result; there is no reason for the question in v. 1b after v. 1a; v. 1b presupposes a sentence in which the brothers are the subject. However, the reaction of the brothers, hinted at in the question, would be in place after the father's request to his sons (as it would be after v. 2). *In form:* The beginning of v. 1b ויאמר יעקב (Gk omits the second יעקב) does not fit in with the beginning of v. 1a ויּרא יעקב; it is a fresh start (so too

J. Skinner) which presupposes a sentence in which the brothers are the subject. In any case the text is disturbed; v. 1b is a fragment.

One can only conjecture the meaning of the question, ''Why do you stand looking at each other?'' The Gk reads, ''why do you delay?'' which accords with the sense of the MT. In the version hinted at here the brothers do not simply comply with the father's request. This may be because Joseph was sold into Egypt (so the majority of exegetes); however, it is probably because they are being sent by their father to a place where the detested monarchy (ch. 37) is all-pervading and where they are exposed to potentates (as in Gen. 12:12) before whom they must pay obeisance to get bread.

[**42:2**] V. 2a is to be read immediately after v. 1a; v. 2b gives the reason for the commission to the brothers, namely, the survival of the family, the same expression as in 43:8 and Num. 4:19.

[**42:3**] When the narrator here describes the sons of Jacob as they depart as the ''brothers of Joseph'' (v. 1b), he makes yet another link, albeit unobtrusive, between chs. 39–41 and 42 (cf. M. Weiss, VT 13 [1963] 467). The number of the brothers mentioned here presupposes the tradition of the 12 sons of Jacob; it indicates at the same time how the family of the patriarchs has grown. Abraham went down into Egypt alone; Jacob's family requires 10 men and their beasts of burden, as each now has his own family. Nevertheless, the social relationships of the patriarchal story are still presupposed; the father can still command even his adult, married sons and they obey him (even though perhaps reluctantly, v. 1b); cf. E. Kutsch, VT 2 (1952) 63.

[**42:4**] The number *ten* in v. 3 does not derive from the immediate context; the reason for it must be given, thus preparing what is to follow. Jacob does not allow Benjamin to accompany them (v. 4); he is afraid that some harm may befall him on the way. The word אָסוֹן carries overtones of a fatal accident (also in Ex. 21:22, 23; cf. B. S. Jackson, VT 23 [1973] 274f.; S. E. Loewenstamm, VT 27 [1977] 357. ''Benjamin has taken Joseph's place in his father's affection'' (J. Skinner). So the situation which was the point of departure in ch. 37 recurs. Once again there is the confrontation, father/brothers/youngest brother, the narrator at the beginning of ch. 42 thus making an immediate connection with ch. 37.

[**42:5**] After the parenthesis of v. 4 one expects, as the continuation of v. 3, a sentence reporting the arrival of the brothers in Egypt. Instead we have v. 5, of which B. Jacob says, ''Every expression in the first half of the verse is strange.'' V. 5a repeats, rather than continues, v. 3. It is strange that לִשְׁבֹּר from v. 3 is repeated, that ''Joseph's brothers'' are here ''the sons of Israel,'' and especially that the goal is not mentioned. Moreover, v. 5b is almost a repetition of Gen. 41:57b. V. 5 would follow very well immediately after 41:57b as the beginning of a new scene in the narrative. The undefined ''with the others'' of v. 5 would then refer to 41:57a, ''and the whole world came to Egypt. . ..'' This would at the same time solve the other difficulty: the goal of the journey, missing in 42:5, is mentioned in 41:57a. So 42:5 would make good sense following immediately on 41:57a:

And the whole world came to Egypt to buy grain from Joseph. So the sons of Israel also came with the others to buy grain because there was a (severe) famine throughout the land.

One can only conjecture that v. 5 originally followed on 41:57 and was later displaced to its present position replacing a sentence which reported the arrival of the brothers in Egypt. This rearrangement can explain the striking בני ישראל in 42:5. The same designation occurs in 46:5, 8, likewise in the context of a journey to Egypt, hinting already at the exodus of the בני ישראל out of Egypt. This is probably what the redactor who inserted v. 5 had in mind. E. A. Speiser, ad loc., together with D. B. Redford and H. C. Schmitt, is of the opinion that בני ישראל cannot be a criterion for source division here.

[42:6-25] The sojourn of the brothers in Egypt, vv. 6-25, forms the central part of the travel account of Gen. 42: the meeting with Joseph (vv. 6-7a); the interrogation and the measures that result from it (vv. 7b-25), leading to the arrest of the brothers in v. 17 and the arrest of Simeon in v. 24. The interrogation is followed by the former, the mitigation of the sentence by the latter. Within the complex, chs. 42–45, this first meeting with Joseph is the passage that stands in contrast to the last meeting, 45:1-16; it is this contrast that determines the whole. The narrator wants to say that the last meeting would not be possible without the first; the path to reconciliation must pass through this deep valley.

[42:6-7a] The introduction to the new scene in vv. 6-7a is short and very significant. V. 6a once again resumes 41:55f., linking ch. 42 with ch. 41. The words הוא השליט על־הארץ are a later explanatory gloss, recognizable from the twofold הוא in quick succession; שליט occurs elsewhere only in Eccles. 7:19; 8:8; 10:5.

The brothers make obeisance before the foreign lord on whom the life or death of their family now depends. This is reported soberly and without any explanatory note. The gesture of self-abasement speaks for itself. It shows what the purchase of corn in Egypt means for the brothers (cf. comm. on v. 1b). They knew that they were entering a realm where they were in the hands of potentates. They are forced to bow down before the potentate for bread. The listeners are reminded of the youngest brother's dream; what was announced there is now happening.

V. 7a consists of three short sentences in narrative succession, all with the same subject and object, but each with a different grammatical form. This very short sentence, constructed with three parts, is the climax of the whole story, bringing into sharp focus what it is all about, Joseph and his brothers: "When Joseph saw his brothers he recognized them, but pretended not to know them." The obeisance was the first action; the moment of meeting is now described from Joseph's side, all attention being concentrated on the "face to face" before even a word is spoken; it is only the next sentence that begins וידבר.

[42:7b-25] The man who controls the sale of grain surprises the brothers with an interrogation (vv. 7b-16). The brothers are defenseless against the accusation that they are spies. They are arrested and held in custody for three days (v. 17). At the end of the three days and without any reason there is a mitigation and a test is imposed (vv. 18-20). The interrogation and remand for sentence are thereby concluded; the effect on the brothers is shown by their conversation in vv. 21-22, and this in turn has its effect on Joseph (vv. 23-24a). In sharp contrast to this, the whole procedure ends with the arrest of Simeon, corresponding to v. 17, and Joseph's instructions (vv. 24aβ-25), which prepare what follows.

[42:7b-17] The interrogation proceeds in two stages, vv. 7b-11 and 12-13. Joseph concludes it by repeating the accusation that they are spies (vv. 14, 16bβ), together with his instructions that they be tested (vv. 15-16a) and with their arrest for three days (v. 17).

[42:7b-11] The first stage of the interrogation begins with Joseph's question and the brothers' reply (v. 7b). There is a parenthesis in vv. 8, 9a, and the interrogation continues in v. 9b; Joseph contests the reply that the brothers give in v. 7b and accuses them of being spies. The brothers in turn contest the accusation (v. 10a, in three parts) and repeat the purpose of their coming (v. 10b); to the charge that they are spies, they counter with what they really are; honest people, sons of one man (v. 11a). At the end they repeat again their contestation of the accusation (v. 11b).

[42:7b] The two verbs in v. 7bα belong together; he spoke harshly (or sharply) to them in the words that follow immediately. וידבר is often continued by ויאמר. This alone shows that it is not possible to separate vv. 7bα and 7bβ into two sources. The brothers respond and say where they come from, and at the same time tell the purpose of their coming.

[42:8-9a] It is not often that the narrator of the Joseph story inserts the reflections of one of the participants, as he does here. It must have a special function in the sequel to what is narrated here. The interrogation begins, ". . . .[he] spoke harshly to them." This too has its reason or explanation in Joseph's reflection. The explanation is introduced in v. 8 by a sentence which is almost a mere repetition of v. 7a; hence it could be a gloss. However, it is also possible that the narrator wants to underscore yet again that his brothers did not recognize him; this was not stated explicitly in v. 7a. Joseph remembers the dreams: the narrator wants to say that at the very moment that he saw his brothers before him, Joseph had decided to heal the breach begun at that time. The structure as a whole allows this conclusion. It is to this purpose that Joseph allows his brothers to undergo the severe trial of being at the disposition of the potentate. A quick pardon at this moment could not have led to a real solution, as the continuation shows. It is a misunderstanding of the narrative to prescind from the course of events and to judge Joseph's conduct morally, to defend it, or to gloss it over (e.g., F. Delitzsch, "pastoral, spiritual wisdom"; more strongly, B. Jacob; H. Gunkel, "he punishes and harrasses them appropriately"). But J. Skinner has seen the situation correctly when he writes: "It is unnecessary to suppose that the writers traced in all this the unfolding of a constant ethical purpose." Joseph recalls the dreams; the present scene is thereby put into the context of the beginning, and the narrative course as a whole is the basis of Joseph's harsh words to his brothers.

[42:9b] Reflecting on what happened long ago, and with the intention, as yet still concealed, of bringing healing to what has been shattered, Joseph brings an accusation against his brothers which he knows to be false. It is formulated in two sentences: "You are. . . you have come to. . . ." The second explicates the first and so underscores the accusation. There is no reason at all to regard the two sentences as doublets and to separate them into two sources, as was done earlier (also H. Gunkel). This can be clearly demonstrated here; v. 9b corresponds exactly with the answer of the brothers in v. 7bβ, which likewise has two parts. The accusation is well-founded and makes sense inasmuch as the northeastern border was particularly vulnerable to incursions, and was guarded and in part fortified. The word מרגלים occurs frequently in the OT, e.g., Josh. 2:1; 1 Sam. 26:4. On the accusation of spying, cf. J. Vergote, *Joseph en Egypte. . .* (1959) 160f.; H. C. Schmitt, BZAW 154 (1980), who rightly argues against D. B. Redford: "The accusation of spying can scarcely be directed to specific historical situations in Egypt." The "weaknesses of the land" are the places where it is vulnerable; cf. F. L. Horton, SBLASP 1 (1973) 20-33.

[**42:10-11**] The brothers' defense consists in their denial of the charge at the beginning (v. 10a) and the end (v. 11b) of their reply, the repetition of their actual intention (v. 10b), and the additional detail that they are all sons of one man. This is really the only way that the brothers can defend their honest intentions ("we are honest people"; for כן with this meaning cf. V. Hamp, Fests. J. Ziegler [1972] 72f.); the information means that they are a family unit which does not wage war and has no interest in spying. Consequently, Joseph does not ask, as he might otherwise have done, who commissioned them politically.

[**42:12-14**] The interrogator contests the brothers' assertion and repeats his accusation (v. 12); then he repeats it twice more (vv. 14 and 16bβ). The narrator thereby indicates what is characteristic of this sort of interrogation: the constant repetition of the accusation is meant to unnerve the accused and break down his resistance. This is a very telling example of how the repetition of the same sentence has a clearly recognizable function; division into different sources would destroy the impression intended by the narrator. But apart from this, the description of the interrogation shows an extraordinary appreciation of social-psychological awareness on the part of the narrator. In an interrogation of this kind, the accused is defenseless, and the interrogator can take advantage of this lack of defense and beat the accused down by persistent hammering. It is disturbing that nothing has changed down to the present day.

[**42:13**] In their helplessness the brothers can do nothing more than repeat with more detail their claim to be one family. The interrogator, who is their brother, thus learns what he wants to know. Behind the interrogation which is in the foreground, the subtle art of the narrator lets something of a different kind appear in the background. The brothers can only think, If we tell him all these details about our family, then he must believe us! But when they speak of the youngest then, without being aware of it, they open the way for Joseph to take his next step.

[**42:14-17**] The interrogation is concluded with the repetition of the accusation (v. 14). The further details given by the brothers in v. 13 include verifiable data which the interrogator seizes upon immediately: "By this you shall be tested." Once more the gentle irony comes through; the interrogator knows well that the test will acquit the brothers of the charge of spying. Now with the instructions for the test, the accusation no longer carries a threat to the brothers. So Joseph with frightening mien, with an oath by the life of the Pharaoh which frames his orders, vv. 15a and 16bβ, threatens them and arrests them: "You shall not leave this place." Only one is to be freed, in order to fetch the young brother; the others are to remain under arrest.

On the oath by the life of the Pharaoh, cf. J. Vergote, *Joseph en Egypte. . .* (1959), "La formule du serment," pp. 162-167; D. B. Redford, VT.S 20 (1970) 233f.; R. de Vaux, *The Early History. . .* 1 (1977; Eng. 1978) 309; also bibliog. above. This oath presupposes the sacral dignity of the king (see comm. on 41:1b), and is also attested in Egypt. There is no need to look for Egyptian models for the form; it corresponds to the Israelite oath by the life of the king, as in 2 Sam. 15:21 (so R. de Vaux, H. C. Schmitt).

The conclusion of the instruction in v. 16b repeats the beginning in v. 15a (inclusio) with the addition to the verb, "to see whether your words are reliable or not" (i.e., whether *you* are reliable in your words). This addition gives the listeners to suspect that there is much more to the test than the situation reveals. But the dire threat, confirmed by the oath, is there again at the end: if not, the charge of spying stands. With this threat Joseph has his brothers put into custody for three days (v. 17). This is the necessary consequence of the persistent accusation of spying (against J. Skinner, who does not see any sense in it).

[**42:18-20**] Joseph's second instruction (vv. 18-20) now follows his first, in accordance with the literary device of doubling. The purpose of the doubling is not "to fill space" (H. Gunkel); rather, the encounter between Joseph and his brothers advances a step, as vv. 21-24 show. The brothers spend three days in custody, conscious that they are utterly at the disposition of the arbitrary power of the potentate; then, without any reason that they can see, they receive new instructions from Joseph about the test. The language of the second instruction is deliberately different from that of the first and is a conscious counterpart to it inasmuch as it carries a positive meaning for the brothers. It is framed by the two verbs, ". . .you shall live. . .and not die" (vv. 18 and 20). A condition separates the verbs; nevertheless, the difference in language between the first (vv. 15-17) and second (vv. 18-20) instructions is clear. Further, the condition is formulated positively, "If you are honest people. . ." (v. 19a), and the release of the brothers shows the friendly concern of the foreign potentate for their hungry families (v. 19bα, רעבון = "hunger" only here and in Ps. 37:19 in the same sense of a period of famine; literally, "bring grain to the hunger of your houses" = bring your hungry households bread); this causes amazement and confusion among the brothers. What sort of statesman is he who allows a group of potential spies to depart freely (v. 20b)! Joseph gives the reason for the change in his orders in v. 18b: "I fear God," I am a God-fearing man. This is not to be understood as an objective statement about the piety of the foreign potentate; it is functional, giving the reason why he mitigates the measures he has taken. In the background is the widespread notion, at work in many religions, that God or the gods protects the defenseless stranger. "Fear of God" is used in the same situation in Gen. 20:11 (cf. *Genesis 12–36*, pp. 325f.).

Exegetes pass very different judgments on the sentence "I am a man who fears God." Those who prescind from the dialog setting see in it an "international religious morality'' (H. Gunkel, J. Skinner, and others); ''a moral attitude'' (H. C. Schmitt and others); ''a guarantee among men that their word is reliable'' (H. W. Wolff, *Interp.* 26 [1972] 164. L. Ruppert (*Die Josepherzählung*. . . [1965] 95ff.) and H. C. Schmitt (BZAW 154 [1980] 96f.) see it in the context of the theology of history, as in Gen. 45 and 50. D. B. Redford understands it very differently and very negatively: ''This is nothing more than an ironic cut at his brothers.'' If one understands ''I am a man who fears God'' in the context of the whole chapter, then one must allow that the brothers heard two things side by side; and this was intended. If the man fears *his* god, this would be the god who stands by the potentate; the brothers could only see this as mockery (D. B. Redford). But the language of this second instruction, above all, Joseph's concern for the brothers' hungry families at home, gives the words another echo: could it be the God who has pity on the hungry and the poor? It is just this confusing double meaning that gives the ''fear of God'' its meaning and effect in the context.

[**42:21-24**] If one regards vv. 18-20 as parallel to vv. 14-17, then v. 24b has to follow immediately on v. 20. However, a brief interlude, vv. 21-24a, has been inserted in between them, reporting a conversation (or part of it) between the brothers that Joseph ''overhears.'' After the introduction (v. 21aα) they recall what they once did to their youngest brother (v. 21aβb); then follows Reuben's contribution in v. 22, and the effect on Joseph who is listening in (vv. 23, 24a). When the interlude is seen in the context of the chapter as a whole, it suggests that the ''testing'' of the brothers is producing a change in their attitude that is by no means superficial (in contrast to ch. 37).

The experience of the brothers in Egypt up to this point has brought them to a realization for which the way perhaps had long been prepared. The passage begins, ''then they said to each other''; the narrator wants to synthesize thereby the result of a long conversation between them. The interjection אבל (as in 2 Sam. 14:5) expresses perplexity, the state in which the conversation took place. The realization is summed up in the nominal sentence, ''We are certainly guilty with regard to our brother.'' All that follows is merely a spelling out of this. It is a confession of guilt, probably in a fixed, traditional form. The confession is now developed and colored by the word צרה (vv. 21a and 21b). The punishment that they now experience fits the crime that they had once committed. ''The sinner is punished in the area in which he has sinned'' (H. Gunkel); this theme occurs often in the OT, e.g., in the prophetic oracle of judgment. It has its roots in magical thinking. V. 21aβ recalls what they did: ''We saw. . .. when he pleaded. . . we did not listen.'' They have not been able to forget that moment. They understand their present painful situation as punishment: ''That is why this disaster has befallen us.'' This means that it has dawned on them that there is a connection between the mortal peril that they themselves brought on Joseph and the mortal peril in which they now stand through no fault of their own. There is a fundamental difference between the intention of the narrator, who wants to show that the brothers understood what had befallen them as punishment for their past crime, and the interpretation of an exegete that Joseph wanted to punish his brothers.

[**42:22**] Reuben now intervenes in the discussion (cf. comm. on 37:21f.) and increases the brothers' awareness of guilt, recalling his warning which they rejected; but the discussion breaks off here.

[**42:23-24a**] The whole meeting from v. 6 on has been conducted on two levels; this becomes very clear now. The high Egyptian official becomes the brother of those suspected of spying; he almost gives himself away. He listens in; what moves him to tears is the brothers' confession, which provides the opportunity for reconciliation and healing of the breach. The narrator makes use of another institution at the court of the Pharaoh, the interpreter (מֵלִיץ is found only here with this meaning; from לִיץ = "to be a spokesman"; cf. J. Vergote, *Joseph en Egypte*. . . [1959] 168; O. Betz, "Dolmetscher," BHH I [1962] 349; H. N. Richardson, VT 5 [1955] 163-179, 434-436). The way in which he uses it as a narrative device shows that he has reflected carefully on the mechanism of bridging the language gap ("earlier narrators overlook the difference of language," H. Gunkel).

[**42:24b**] ". . .He spoke to them." The sentence is rather abrupt. What he said to them does not follow. It is missing in the Gk and is surely an addition; it is possible, too, that a sentence has dropped out. The arrest and binding of Simeon (perhaps as the oldest after Reuben) really follows on v. 20; Joseph is again the harsh Egyptian lord.

[**42:25-38**] The return and arrival at the father's house forms the third part of the travel account (vv. 25-38). The return is a part in its own right only because during it there occurs an episode which belongs to the narrative (vv. 27, 28).

[**42:25-26**] The brothers depart from Egypt without Simeon (v. 25). Joseph has had their sacks filled and their money put in with the grain. It is not in accordance with the character of the narrative when one sees as the motive for this either the intention of punishing them further (H. Gunkel) or "a sign of his deeply veiled love" (G. von Rad; similarly B. Jacob). Rather, the narrator is presenting that inextricable intertwining of harshness and readiness for reconciliation which has determined Joseph's conduct from the moment that he saw his brothers before him. This ambivalence corresponds to the division within Joseph himself: Should he make himself known to his brothers (cf. comm. on vv. 23-24a) or has the hour for this not yet come? It is just because he is so pressed to do so that he feels constrained to wait yet a while.

[**42:27-28**] On the way they pass the night at a stopping place, a "hut-like building erected along the desert road" (F. Delitzsch). מָלוֹן, "a place where one spends the night" (KBL), also Ex. 4:24 and elsewhere. There, one of the brothers discovers the money in the top of his fodder-sack. He calls his brothers and they are seized with fear.

This scene as such does not present any difficulties, though difficulties do arise when one takes v. 35 into consideration; there, all the brothers empty their sacks in the presence of their father and discover their money. This doublet (or contradiction) gave those exegetes who supported source division a strong argument that vv. 27-28 belong to J, v. 35 to E. The argument was further supported by the vocabulary: vv. 27-28 uses אמתחה, v. 35 שק. But there is a difficulty here because in v. 27 both words are used in the same sentence, obviously without distinction. To counter this, the supporters of source division have recourse to the Gk which, they say, also reads אמתחה in v. 27a. This argument, however, loses its force because of the frequent tendency of the Gk to harmonize. But the word-count is a weightier argument; אמתחה occurs (11 times, once in Gk) only in Gen. 42–44, שׂק only in 42:25, 27, 35 (twice); i.e., both words occur only in the single context of the journeys of the brothers to Egypt. It is scarcely possible then to explain this difference as a criterion for two sources in the whole of the Pentateuch. It would be a definitive indication only if the different words occurred in several contexts. Apart from the fact that the two words are used in the same sentence in v. 27 of the MT, a further word, כלי, is used together with them (42:25; 43:11); and no one would claim this as a criterion for source division. For a detailed discussion of source division in this passage, cf. D. B. Redford, VT.S 20 (1970) 150-152; H. Donner, *Die literarische Gestalt. . .* (1976) 46f. It is another question whether v. 35 is a doublet of vv. 27-28 or stands in contradiction.

The surprise and fear of the one who finds his money again (הושׁב) as he opens his fodder-sack is apparent in his cry, which has a corresponding effect on his brothers: ויצא לבם, "their hearts sank," their courage failed. The brothers had departed in the hope that they could dissipate the charge that they were spies. But already on the way home they are overtaken by another charge: You are thieves! They realize again with all its force that they are delivered up to the arbitrary decision of the potentate. This is what their reaction expresses: ". . .trembling, they turned to each other and said [the Hebrew is in narrative form, without the participle], What is this that God has done to us!" The brothers' exclamation can be understood only in the light of the confession in v. 21. It is God who is at work in the crime and punishment.

When Judah gives his account before Joseph in 43:21 and says, "When we came to the lodging place and opened our sacks," then this is not in contradiction to 42:27f. where only one of them opens his sack. The difficulty that D. B. Redford sees here is without foundation, "the strange fact that only one of the brothers' asses has to be fed at the inn" (op.cit., p. 151). The narrator in v. 27 adopts the much used device of dramatizing a scene by describing the experience of a group as that of an individual. The scene thereby comes to life—one of them finds the money in his sack; he cries out in surprise, and the brothers react. The narrative is told in this way so that the dialog form can have its effect. Both the narrator and his listeners know well that the narrative is in this way describing the discovery of the money by all the brothers. It would be quite pedantic were it to continue: then the others also opened. . . and each said, My money is here too! The Joseph story is characterized throughout by a high level of narrative art; so the narrator could expect a high degree of empathy from his listeners.

[42:29-38] The arrival at the father's house: There is a tacit comparison between this scene and the return to the father in ch. 37. The brothers arrive at the father's house (v. 29) and report to him (vv. 30-34); there follows the father's lament (vv. 36-38), which Reuben's intervention cannot alter.

[42:29] The report which they have to make to the father is linked immediately with the return. The scene that closes ch. 42 makes particularly clear how important and irreplaceable narrative was in that form of society. It is obvious that a report of this kind in a situation of this kind could not be forgotten by the participants, that it was stamped in the memory, that it was recalled and narrated again.

This continual narration gave rise quite naturally to the process of tradition (cf. *Genesis 12–36*, pp. 43-50).

[42:30-34] The brothers' report synthesizes graphically their experiences in Egypt. It is divided into their disagreeable experiences (v. 30) and a summary of their conversation with "the man"; this comprises the accusation of spying (v. 30), their contesting this (vv. 31-32), and the test ordered by the foreign lord (vv. 33-34). The brothers report only the essentials and in such a way as to cause the least distress to the father. This is the reason why at first they do not say a word about the money that has been returned. The last sentence of v. 34 is also important for the report. They do not repeat to their father the threat that the man in Egypt made; on the contrary, they underscore the benefit they expect with an exaggeration normal in narrative: "You will be free to move about the country."

[42:35] One expects now a reaction from the father; but this follows only in v. 36; v. 35 disturbs the continuity between vv. 34 and 36. The effect of the verse is abrupt; it does not fit; the ויהי between the report and the response to it as well as the whole arrangement of the sentence is maladroit, especially in the reaction of the brothers over against v. 28b. V. 35 is a subsequent addition which reveals its intent in the words המה ואביהם. The glossator supposes that the father learnt nothing from the brothers' account of the return of their money, and perhaps too, following v. 27f., that the other brothers had not yet found it.

[42:36-38] The father's answer to his sons' report is first a reaction of grief and emotion (v. 36). When Reuben intervenes to provide surety for Benjamin's safe return, Jacob changes his reply to an express refusal. This means that vv. 36-38 form a continuous whole which would be destroyed were v. 38 to be detached from vv. 36f.(E) and assigned to J (J. Wellhausen; H. Gunkel; H. C. Schmitt, and others). Vv. 36 and 38 stand together of necessity in Jacob's reply to the brothers' report; the reply is continued in v. 38, due to Reuben's intervention in v. 37. The chapter could not end with v. 37.

[42:36] Jacob's reply is introduced by "Jacob their father. . .." With the addition of "their father" the narrator makes the sons' memory of their guilt resonate with the father's grief. The reply is divided into a lament (or accusation) and its explication, "You are making me childless!" This is a terrible accusation (frequent in the prophetic pronouncements of judgment, e.g., Hos. 9:12), but certainly quite unjustified here. But the explication which names the two lost sons and the one who is threatened, contains the name of Joseph. The brothers have already confessed their guilt over their father's loss (v. 22). This is why they react as they do to Jacob's present unjust accusation. The father should certainly be protected against the loss of Benjamin so that he suffer no further grief.

[42:37] Reuben is again the speaker. His intervention shows how the attitude of all the brothers has changed from ch. 37. Reuben's offer (can one call it a guarantee?) serves only to make clear to the father this change in attitude, for what interest could Jacob have in the further loss of two of his grandsons? Reuben wants to tell his father that he will do all in his power to bring Benjamin back safe; this is what the last sentence is saying.

[**42:38**] The first part of Jacob's lament has left it an open question whether he will allow Benjamin to accompany the brothers, as the man in Egypt had demanded (''and you want to take Benjamin as well!''); but Jacob has not the heart to assent to Reuben's direct request. He refuses outright: ''My son shall not go down with you. . ..'' The reason is different from that given in v. 36. He is speaking here only of Rachel's sons, of whom only Benjamin remains; he is worried that something might happen to him (as in v. 4). It is a question again of his special love for the sons of his beloved wife. This is the reason why the lament, which brings Jacob's reply to a close, is so like that in 37:35.

Purpose and Thrust

It is significant how differently the narrator describes what the brothers did to Joseph in 37:24 and 42:21. In the former, nothing is said about Joseph's reaction as it had no function there. In the latter, when faced themselves with the fear of death, they remember; they looked on unmoved at their brother's anguish; he pleaded with them but they did not listen. The interplay of crime and punishment is built into the very existence of man. The Joseph story is saying something more. Crime and punishment do not always immediately follow each other as in Gen. 3 and 4. Punishment does not always come on the heels of the crime; guilt can accompany a person without there being punishment. One's own experience of suffering or danger of death can be recognized as punishment, bring about a change of heart, and offer the opportunity for forgiveness. But the forgiveness does not take the place of the punishment; rather, it includes within it the experience of ''punishment.'' The narrator presents this whole experience primarily in secular terms. He can then in the same narrative describe it as standing in the context of God's action: ''What is this that God has done to us!'' He goes even a step further when, in 44:16, he joins the two together: ''God has found out the guilt of your servants.'' God's action, therefore, is seen in the way in which he effects the sequence of crime and punishment in the incomprehensible ups and downs of a person's life, and thereby also gives it meaning. What they did to their brother is no longer an isolated incident which, because it disturbs them, they would like to suppress. Rather, it is with them again as part of a sequence that must have meaning solely by virtue of the fact that God is at work in it. That it must have a meaning is explicated in ch. 44.

The Second Journey of the Brothers to Egypt

Literature

Genesis 43:1-7: R. B. Y. Scott, "The Service of God," *To Honor W. A. Irwin* (1956) 132-143. O. Garcia de la Fuente, " 'David buscó el rostro de Yahweh' (2 Sam 21,1)," *Aug.* 25 (1968) 477-540. B. Porten and J. C. Greenfield, "The Aramaic Papyri from Hermopolis," ZAW 80 (1968) 216-231. J. S. Croatto, "L'article hébreu et les particules emphatiques dans le semitique de l'Ouest," ArOr 39 (1971) 389-400.

Genesis 43:8-13: C. H. Gordon, "The Accentual Shift in the Perfect with *waw* Consecutive," JBL 57 (1938) 319-325. E. Wiesenberg, "A Note on מזה in Psalm LXXV 9," VT 4 (1954) 434-439. J. J. Rabinowitz, "The Aramaic Papyri, the Demotic Papyri from Gebelên and Talmudic Sources," Bib 38 (1957) 269-274; "Demotic Papyri of the Ptolemaic Period and Jewish Sources," VT 7 (1957) 398-400; "The Susa Tablets, the Bible and the Aramaic Papyri," VT 11 (1961) 55-76. W. M. W. Roth, "Hinterhalt und Scheinflucht. Der stammespolemische Hintergrund von Jos 8," ZAW 75 (1963) 296-304. N. M. Sarna, "Ezekiel 8,17: A Fresh Examination," HThR 57 (1964) 347-352. G. Sauer, "Mandelzweig und Kessel in Jer 1,11ff.," ZAW 78 (1966) 56-61. K. D. Schunck, "Jes 30,6-8 und die Deutung der Rahab im AT," ZAW 78 (1966) 48-56. S. E. Loewenstamm, " "The Lord Is My Strength and My Glory," " VT 19 (1969) 464-470. S. B. Parker, "Exodus XV 2 Again," VT 21 (1971) 373-379. H. Margulies, "Das Rätsel der Biene im AT," VT 24 (1974) 56-76. J. Niehaus, "The Use of *lûlē* in Psalm 27," JBL 98 (1979) 88-89.

Genesis 43:14: F. Zorell, "Der Gottesname 'Šaddai' in den alten Übersetzungen," Bib 8 (1927) 115-119. A. Heidel, "A Special Usage of the Akkadian Term *šadû*," JNES 8 (1949) 233-235. L. Rost, "Die Gottesverehrung der Patriarchen im Lichte der Pentateuchquellen," VT.S 7 (1959) 346-359. A. van der Branden, "Essai de déchiffrement des inscriptions de Deir 'Alla," VT 15 (1965) 129-152. O. Eissfeldt, " '*ʾäheyäh ʾašär äʾheyäh* und *ʾĒl ʿôlām*," (1965) = KS 4 (1968) 193-198. K. Koch, "Šaddaj. Zum Verhältnis zwischen israelitischer Monolatrie und nordwest-semitischem Polytheismus," VT 26 (1976) 299-332.

Genesis 43:15-25: A. Alt, "The God of the Fathers" (1929, 1953), in *Essays in OT History and Religion* (1966) 1-66. W. H. Schmidt, *Alttestamentlicher Glaube und seine Umwelt* (1968; 1975²) §3. H. Schmid, "Jhwh, der Gott der Hebräer," Jud. 25 (1969) 257-266. J. Hoftijzer, "David and the Tekoite Woman," VT 20 (1970) 419-444.

Genesis 43:26-34: S. Mowinckel, "כְּמֻר, כמר," ZAW 36 (1916) 238f. H. Grapow, "Wie die alten Ägypter sich anredeten, wie sie sich grüssten und wie sie miteinander sprachen. III," AAB II (1943). E. F. Sutcliffe, "A Note on *ʿal, lᵉ*, and *from*," VT 5 (1955) 436-439.

P. Humbert, "Le substantif *to'ēbā* et le verbe *t'b* dans l'AT," ZAW 72 (1960) 217-237 and Fests. W. Rudolph (1961) 157-160. M. Mannati, "Les accusations de Psaume L 18-20," VT 25 (1975) 659-669. G. Robinson, "The Meaning of תֹ in Isaiah 56,5," ZAW 88 (1976) 282-284.

Text

43:1 Now the famine was still severe[a] in the land.

2 When they had used up[a] all the grain that they had brought from Egypt, their father said to them, Go back and buy us a little more grain!

3 But Judah said to him, The man expressly warned us,[a] You shall not come into my presence unless your brother is with you.[b]

4 If then[a] you allow our brother to go with us, we will go down and buy food for you.

5 But if you do not allow him, we will not go down, because the man said to us, You shall not come into my presence unless your brother is with you.

6 Then Israel said, Why have you hurt me so badly as to tell the man that you had another brother?[a]

7 They answered, The man expressly inquired of us about our family and asked, Is your father still alive? Have you another brother? We answered these questions[a] of his. How were we to know[b] that he would say, Bring your brother down here?

8 Then Judah said to Israel his father, Let the boy go with me, then we will be up and on our way so that we may live and not die, we and you and our little ones.

9 I myself will be surety for him; from my hand you shall require him; if I do not bring him back and restore him to you,[a] I shall bear the guilt[b] for ever before you.

10 Had we not delayed,[a] we had already[b] been there and back twice.

11 Then Israel their father said to them, If it must be so, then[a] do this; take some of the best products of the land in your baggage and bring them down to the man—a little balsam and honey, tragacanth gum, myrrh, pistachio nuts, and almonds.

12 Take double the silver,[a] that is, the silver also[b] that was put back in the top of your packs[c] you must take with you; perhaps it was a mistake.

13 Take your brother; up and go back to the man.

14 May God Almighty be merciful to you before the man and may he send back your other[a] brother with you, and Benjamin too. But I—I am bereaved, bereaved.[b]

15 So the men took the gift and double the amount of silver with them, and Benjamin, and set out and went down to Egypt and presented themselves before Joseph.

16 When Joseph saw Benjamin with them,[a] he said to his steward, Bring these men into the house; kill[b] a beast and make ready, for they are to eat with me at noon.

17 The man did as Joseph told him and[a] brought[b] the men into Joseph's house.

18 Now the men were afraid when they were brought into Joseph's house; they thought, It is because of the money that was put back[a] in our packs the first time that we have been brought here; he wants to overpower us and seize us and take us into slavery with our donkeys.

19   So they approached[a] Joseph's steward and spoke to him at the entrance to the house.

20   They said, Listen, my lord.[a] We came down once before to buy food.

21   When we arrived at the stopping place and opened our sacks, each found his silver in the top of his sack, the full measure;[a] we have brought it back with us.[b]

22   We have brought more silver with us to buy food. We do not know who put our silver into our sacks.

23   He answered, Rest assured, don't be afraid; your God, the God of your father, has put a treasure in your sacks. I received your silver. Then he brought Simeon out to them.

24   Then the man brought them into Joseph's house,[a] gave them water to wash their feet, and gave their donkeys fodder.

25   They had their present ready for Joseph's arrival at noon, because they had heard that they were to dine with him.

26   When Joseph entered the house, they presented him with the gifts that they had brought with them '   ',[a] and bowed to the ground before him.[b]

27   He greeted them and asked,[a] How is your old father about whom you spoke to me? Is he still alive?

28   They answered, Your servant, our father, is well and is still alive. And they bowed and prostrated themselves.[a]

29   When Joseph looked up and saw his brother Benjamin, the son of his own mother,[a] he said, Is this indeed your youngest brother about whom you spoke to me?[b] And he said, May God be gracious to you, my son.[c]

30   Joseph hurried because he was deeply moved at seeing his brother and was on the verge of tears, and he went[a] into his private room and wept.

31   Then he washed his face, went out, and controlling himself said,[a] Serve the meal.

32   Then they served him by himself and the brothers separately and the Egyptians separately, because the Egyptians may not[a] eat with the Hebrews; it is an abomination[b] to them.

33   The brothers were seated in his presence in order according to their age, from the oldest to the youngest. And they looked at each other in astonishment.

34   Then he had a portion sent[a] to each of them from what was before him; but Benjamin's portion was five times[b] larger[c] than all the others. So they drank and were merry with him.

1a כבד is a verb; same meaning in Gen. 41:31; 47:4, 13; 12:10.

2a Construction, BrSynt §163b.

3a Infin. abs. to strengthen verbal idea, Ges-K §113n; D. B. Redford, VT.S 20 (1970) 44f.   **b** Exceptive clauses introduced by בלתי, Ges-K §163c; BrSynt §144.

4a Construction with יש, BrSynt §§30b, 80q; Ges-K §116q.

6a Indirect question, Ges-K §150i; BrSynt §6bii; J. Croatto ArOr 39 (1971) 389-400.

7a על־פי as in Ex. 34:27 and elsewhere.   **b** Infin. abs. to strengthen questions, Ges-K §113q; BrSynt §93a.

9a On the construction of conditional clauses, Ges-K §159n,o.   **b** As in 1 Kings 1:21.

10a On לילא, J. Niehaus, JBL 98 (1979) 88-89.   **b** כי־עתה as in 31:42; Ges-K §159ee.

11a On אפוה, cf. Gen. 27:37; Job 9:24; 24:25.

12a Ges-K §131e,q.   **b** *Waw* explicative "namely, that too."   **c** On the form, Ges-K §§65d; 72bb; 93pp.

14a Sam and Gk as in 42:19, האחד, better.   **b** Form, Ges-K §29u; construction, Ges-K §131q.

16a Word order, BrSynt §122d; construction, BrSynt §151; Sam, Gk, Vg read differently.   **b** Form, Ges-K §65b.

17a The second האיש is missing in Gk and Syr.   **b** "Causative of *b*' both ingressive (17) and terminative (24)," E. A. Speiser.

18a Sam reads המושב as in v. 12.

19a ויגשו as Gen. 18:23; 44:18, before saying something one wants to conceal.

20a Fixed formula, perhaps elliptical; see J. Hoftijzer, VT 20 (1970) 427f.

21a The silver is weighed; J. Vergote, *Joseph en Egypt. . .* (1959) 168-171.   **b** Construction, BrSynt §159a.

24a V. 24a is missing in Gk; this is an error; cf. v. 17.

26a The second הביתה is a scribal error; so too D. B. Redford and others; it is missing in Vg.   **b** Some Gk mss. and Vg insert אפים.

27a See B. Jacob, Komm.; on ל, E. Sutcliffe, VT 5 (1955) 436-439.

28a The sentence, which Sam and Gk append, is a late marginal gloss.

29a See M. Mannati, VT 25 (1975) 665f.   **b** Gk adds להביא.   **c** Form, Ges-K §67n; BrSynt §8a.

30a The two verbs וימהר ,ויבקש, express a sequence.

31a The narrative sequence of events in quick succession describes the situation.

32a The same expression in Ex. 19:23; Num. 9:6.   **b** See also 46:34 and Ex. 8:22 for the incompatibility of Egyptians and foreigners. On תועבה, P. Humbert, ZAW 72 (1960) 217-237; and Fests. W. Rudolf (1961) 157-160.

34a Form, Ges-K §144n; Gk and Syr read plural.   **b** The number, Ges-K §134r; BrSynt §88, 101; the number five, cf. 45:22, five festal garments; five occurs frequently elsewhere in reference to Egypt.   **c** On the use of יד, G. Robinson, ZAW 98 (1976) 282-284.

Form

The second journey of the brothers to Egypt covers chs. 43–45. It is only at the end of ch. 45 that their return to their father is reported. A comparison with the structure of the account of the journey of ch. 42 shows agreement in the three parts:

Departure of the brothers	42:1-5 / 43:1-15
Sojourn in Egypt	42:6-25 / 43:16-34; 44:4—45:24
Return to the father	42:26-38 / 44:1-3; 45:25-28

The difference between the accounts is the interruption of the return to Canaan in 44:4—45:24. This brings the brothers back to Egypt and is the turning point. Without this interpolation the structures are parallel.

There is extensive agreement in the structure of chs. 42 and 43; the basis of both is that of a travel account. Hence the question arises whether we have to do here with doublets, whose *juxtaposition* would be explained by literary criticism, or whether the *succession* of the two journeys (chs. 42 and 43–45) is required by the narrative as a whole (chs. 37; 39-45f.). In favor of the juxtaposition is the fact that in ch. 42 the father is called Jacob and the oldest son Reuben, whereas in chs. 43–45 they are Israel and Judah. In favor of two successive narratives is first and formally the principle of doubling. The change from Reuben to Judah would be compatible with this because the two names are nowhere juxtaposed in chs.

42–45, but follow in sequence; that is, they do not occur together; in ch. 42 it is only Reuben, in chs. 43–45 only Judah. One could understand better the narrator giving both brothers a role in chs. 42–45 if the two names were at hand to him from ch. 37 (cf. comm. on 37:28a, 29-30). The Israel/Jacob is much more of a problem; but the mere occurrence of the two names is not an obvious argument for the juxtaposition of two sources.

Excursus: "Israel" in Genesis 37–50

D. B. Redford concludes from the material presented in his tables, pp. 131, 134f., that there were two literary layers (a Judah and a Reuben layer), because in two places in chs. 37–50 the designations *Israel* for the father and *Judah* for the oldest brother coincide. But these tables rest on a classical source-critical method of statistics which isolates a single word, and which gives a very inadequate picture. (1) It is not clear enough from the tables that the Reuben/Judah case is different from the Jacob/Israel case. The table on pp. 134ff. shows that Jacob and Israel vary in chs. 37–45 (more accurately 37–48), but that Reuben occurs only as far as ch. 42; from then on it is only Judah. (2) Further, the statistical material on "Israel," p. 131, is more complicated than the table shows. Redford notes for Israel: 37:3, 13; 42:5; 43:6, 8, 11; 45:21, 28; 46:29, 30; 47:27, 29, 31; 50:2 (the Israel-passages in ch. 48 are missing). Two of these passages, 42:5 and 45:21, drop out as a criterion for source division (according to Redford also); בני ישראל is a fixed phrase; "sons of Jacob" does not occur. Gen. 47:27 is beside the point because there ישראל is obviously a designation for the people of Israel. The table then takes on a very different appearance. There remain 11 places where Israel is the father (against 15 where he is Jacob). Two of these 11 occur in ch. 37 and 5 in chs. 46–50, that is, in the conclusion of the Jacob story. In the Joseph story proper there remain only the 3 passages in ch. 43 and 45:28 for Israel. It should be noted that the 3 passages 43:6, 8, 11 belong in a single context, the conversation between the father and his sons in 43:2-13. But if the name Israel were to be a criterion in 43:2-13 for a change in the literary layer from ch. 42 to ch. 43, then this name would have to stand in v. 2, that is, in the place where another literary layer or source begins. But the word there is אביהם which in the present context refers to the one mentioned in 42:29, 36 (this seems to be reflected in the Vg and some Gk Mss which have יעקב here). Israel in 43:6, 8, 11 could then be a later alteration, the motive for which we do not know. In any case it is no longer a conclusive criterion for source division. It would be such only if the change of names were to correspond to sequences of events running along two separate lines. This is the case in ch. 37, but not in chs. 42–43.

The criterion of the different names cannot be decisive because the name Israel in these few places can have been a subsequent insertion. What alone is decisive is whether the sequence of chs. 43–44 on ch. 42 (the second journey following on the first) can be better explained from the content of the latter as juxtaposition or as succession. If one reads the explanations of the exegetes who assign ch. 42 to E (or to a Reuben layer) and chs. 43–44 to J (or to a Judah layer), one finds that they all have one thing in common; to be able to maintain the juxtaposition, they must postulate a first journey for J, because without it chs. 43–44 are incomprehensible. Without exception they have to strike out vv. 14 and 23 in chs. 43–44, which deal with Simeon, because in ch. 42 Simeon appears only in E; in other words, these exegetes must once again postulate the succession which they contest with their thesis of juxtaposition. But if, on the contrary, one regards the sequence of chs. 42–45 as rooted in the overall plan of the writer, for whom the mounting tension from the first to the second journey is necessary, then one has no need to strike out or postulate anything.

D. B. Redford (and before him F. V. Winnett) maintains that the Reuben layer (E) is a subsequent reworking of the Judah layer (J), and H. C. Schmitt wants to prove the opposite. A comparison of the process of argumentation of the two is a further reason against the view that this part of the Joseph story arose out of two sources or strata.

We have seen that structure of ch. 43 (with 44:1-3) agrees with that of ch. 42; both have three parts, departure, sojourn, return; both are travel accounts. The differences appear only in the shape of these three parts, 43:1-5, 16-34; 44:1-3. The first part, vv. 1-5, agrees with ch. 42 in the exposition: famine, the father's commission (vv. 1-2), and the brothers' departure (v. 15). It is elaborated in vv. 3-14 which deals with Benjamin's accompanying them. This elaboration (extending even to the formulation in v. 2) refers sentence by sentence to the first journey. Vv. 1-5 therefore are clearly conceived as the departure of the brothers on a second journey, i.e., ch. 42 is presupposed. The same holds for the second part, vv. 16-34; in vv. 16-17 (Joseph sees Benjamin and gives the orders) and in vv. 18-34 (in both scenes, vv. 18-25 and 26-34) almost every sentence refers to the first journey. It is beyond doubt that the narrator intends the contrast between Joseph's reception in chs. 42 and 43. The structure of ch. 43 shows with utter certainty that the author intends a sequence in chs. 42–43.

Commentary

[**43:1-2**] The beginning, vv. 1-2, corresponds to the beginning of ch. 42; v. 1 is word for word the same as 41:57b; it is the same exposition, "the famine was severe in the land" (likewise Gen. 12:10). Gen. 43:2a differs from 42:1b, 2 in that it describes a situation that has changed. The reason for the new commission refers to the brothers' first journey down to Egypt to get grain. The grain that they had then brought is now exhausted. Jacob's commission to his sons (cf. 42:2b) likewise refers to the earlier journey: שֻׁבוּ שִׁבְרוּ, Jacob tells his sons to go and buy grain again in Egypt. J. Wellhausen's proposal (taken up by H. Gunkel) to transpose 42:38 after 43:2 cannot be sustained, because of the identical structure of the beginning of chs. 42 and 43. Every sentence in 43:1-2 refers directly or indirectly to the first journey of the brothers to Egypt. Ch. 43 certainly presupposes a first purchase of grain in Egypt.

Two stylistic observations are a further argument that 43:1-2 is a continuation of ch. 42. The pronoun of אליהם in v. 2 refers to the brothers who are mentioned in 42:38. If ch. 43 were an independent literary unit, then the noun would have to stand in place of the pronoun. The second observation is that the speaker in v. 2 is "their" father; and the same holds here; the proper name should stand; and according to literary criticism it should be "Israel." But when the name Israel is missing from the introduction to a textual unit characterized by that very name, then this criterion for source division loses a great deal of weight. If ch. 43 comes from a writer for whom the father is called "Israel," then this name should stand here at the beginning in v. 2.

[**43:3-14**] The execution of the father's commission comes only in v. 15; in ch. 42 it follows immediately on v. 2. The elaboration in 43:3-14 deals with Benjamin; is he to go with the others? It is a conversation between Judah (and his brothers) and Israel (it is only in this dialog that the name Israel occurs, vv. 6, 8, 11).

[**43:3-5**] Judah makes the brothers' consent dependent on the father's permission to allow Benjamin to go with them (vv. 3-5). He proposes the alternatives, ''If then you allow. . .'' (v. 4) and ''But if you do not allow. . .'' (v. 5); they are enclosed within the condition that ''the man'' has laid down. The literary device of *inclusio* serves to strengthen the position; Judah wants to tell his father that for him and his brothers this condition is absolutely binding. This is expressed by the verb העיד, strengthened further by the infinitive absolute; ''warn'' in the same sense occurs in Ex. 19:21, 23. It can be used as a legal term, ''warning against violation of the law by the summoning of witnesses'' (B. Jacob in detail). Without Benjamin they shall not ''see his face''; the expression is used in the context of coming from a distance (B. Porten and J. C. Greenfield, ZAW 80 [1968] 227) as well as of the audience (R. B. Y. Scott, in *To Honor W. A. Irwin* [1956] 137f.); see 2 Sam. 14:28. This definitive reply to the father's request is the deliberate counterpart to Reuben's answer in 42:37, which was followed by the father's definitive refusal (42:38). The continuation required that, in a situation different from that in 42:37f., and with the threat of famine (43:1, 2a), another brother bring forward the demand of the man in Egypt; Reuben could not overbid his offer of surety. It is this new situation that entailed a definitive demand on the father. Both Reuben and Judah were in the material available to the narrator in ch. 37. Here as there he has Judah's speech follow on Reuben's. Reuben's words had no success with the father, but Judah's made him give in; so from now on to the end Judah alone is spokesman for the brothers.

[**43:6-7**] After Judah's words the father knows that he must yield. But it is human that he cannot do so quickly. He makes the same reproach to his sons that they made to the man about Benjamin (v. 6). The narrator allows the brothers, i.e., one of them, to reply so that they can take part in the conversation; they all support Judah's demand. Excitedly they say that they had not spontaneously spoken of Benjamin but had only answered the man's detailed questions (as in Ex. 34:27; Deut. 17:10). And more, they could never have known that he would demand that Benjamin come down. This second part of the argumentation is of itself sufficient and accords exactly with the interrogation in 42:15. Many exegetes maintain that the first part is not in accord with ch. 42 because the Egyptian lord did not literally put these questions in his interrogation; but this is to misunderstand what is intended here. The course of the interrogation put the brothers under a definite constraint; first they had to reply to the allegation that they were spies (42:9-10); then they gave a more precise answer, that they belonged to the one family (42:13). It would not have been possible for them to explain to their father the precise details of the course of the interrogation. The narrator, quite deliberately and with profound insight, introduces variations.

[**43:8-10**] Judah now resumes the conversation. What he says could follow immediately on vv. 3-5. The demand made there is followed here, vv. 8-10, by the request to entrust Benjamin to him (v. 8bα) arguing that this is necessary for the survival of the family. Judah cleverly takes up the words of his father from 42:2, extending them and nicely playing them out by triply underscoring the urgency: we—and you—and our little ones (''our little ones'' as in Gen. 32:12; Num. 32:16f.). The word טף is often used for children and resonates with pity for their plight.

[**43:9**] Judah now strengthens his request to entrust Benjamin to him by offering personally to provide surety for him (v. 9). He undertakes full responsibility for him (cf. comm. on 37:28a, 29, 30). Should he not bring him back, he will for ever bear the guilt (חטאתי) before his father. The narrator does not mean a particular form of penance for his guilt; he is referring to what Judah has to say to Joseph in 44:18-34 where he declares himself ready to assume surety. Judah's surety is not a doublet of Reuben's in 42:37; the surety that the father rejected then is now set in contrast with a surety that is accepted in a different situation.

[**43:10**] V. 10 sounds like an anticlimax after Judah's moving commitment. The first time it was the father who urged them to depart; now it is Judah; he wants to get the matter over quickly before the father changes his mind.

[**43:11-14**] In his closing words, vv. 11-14, Jacob begins by submitting resignedly to necessity (v. 11a), and ends with a lament acquiescing in the inevitable (v. 14b). In between he gives his sons instructions for the journey (vv. 11b-14a).

[**43:11**] Jacob submits to the inevitable in v. 11. He wants, however, to make his contribution to the success of the journey; this is the purpose of the instructions he gives. אפוא is used here as in Job 9:24; cf. Gen. 27:37, ''if then it must be so.'' His sons are to take a present with them. It is common everywhere to bring a present to an important lord whom one is going to visit (מנחה is used here in a secular sense). He recommends that they bring with them ''the best products of the land,'' Gk καρποί. The word זמרה usually means ''song''; it can be used in this sense as ''that which is praised.'' Another meaning, ''power, strength,'' is recognized together with this (so KBL; bibliog. above). The father mentions the three products listed in 37:45, balsam, tragacanth, myrrh; also pistachio nuts and almonds. דבש נכאת probably means a syrup made from grapes, also in Ezek. 27:17; it is one of Palestine's exports and is still found in Syria with the same name, *dibs*.

[**43:12-13**] Jacob now instructs his sons to take double the amount of silver with them (vv. 12-13). It is clear to both father and sons that they must make restitution. Finally he mentions their brother Benjamin and urges them to be on their way.

[**43:14**] Jacob takes leave of his sons with the wish that God may be merciful to them ''before the man'' (v. 14).

On אל שדי, which occurs in Gen. 17:1; 28:3; 35:11; 48:3; 49:25 (correction) see *Genesis 12-36*, comm. on 17:1, Excursus. Apart from 43:14 אל שדי does not occur in J and E; many exegetes therefore trace its presence here back to a secondary reworking (also K. Koch, VT 26 [1976] 229-332), though none of them can give a reason for it. However, what K. Koch has shown to be characteristic of this designation for God fits the present passage exactly: ''The oldest evidence is that blessing is the proper mode of action of Shaddai'' (pp. 326f.), and this blessing is directed to the clan. Further, he is ''mentioned only at the solemn high points of life'' (p. 322); likewise S. Mowinckel (NTT 65 [1964] 69). That this name for God is much older than P (K. Koch, S. Mowinckel, D. B. Redford, and others) is no argument against the narrator of the Joseph story having deliberately chosen it in this passage.

The father's wish for the brothers is that God would show his mercy by releasing "the other brother" Simeon and bring Benjamin back. The *waw* adversative in v. 14b, "but I. . .," expresses how conscious Jacob is of his loss in his farewell blessing on his sons; he must live with it: "How bereaved am I! I am bereaved." The word occurs in the *qal* elsewhere only in Gen. 27:45 (Rebekah) and 1 Sam. 15:33. The כאשר cannot express a relationship between the verbs here; the repetition has a strengthening effect. Thus a better translation is, "But I—I am bereaved, bereaved!"

It creates a difficulty to assign all of v. 14, or v. 14a, to another source because of the mention of Simeon (most recently H. C. Schmitt, BZAW 154 [1980] 45). There must be a word of farewell here. Is one to assume that the redactor has struck J's farewell blessing from its context so as to substitute for it E's words of farewell (difficult because of אל שדי)? One cannot strike out v. 14a alone because v. 14b is not a continuation of v. 13.

[43:15] The brothers follow their father's advice, depart, and arrive in Egypt (v. 15).

[43:16-34] The second part of the travel account, the sojourn of the brothers in Egypt (vv. 16-34), is again divided into two parts: the brothers before the steward at the entrance to the house (vv. 16-25), and the brothers before the lord inside the house (vv. 26-34). One could give ch. 43 the title "Departure and Arrival" because everything revolves about a setting in which farewell and greeting are of the utmost importance. The journey itself is reported in a single sentence.

[43:16-25] Joseph has already prepared the reception by the steward; he gives him instructions (vv. 16-17) and has let him in on the secret. By dividing the passage into two scenes the narrator has been able to settle the matter of the silver (vv. 18-23), and allay the fear of the brothers (vv. 24-25) before their meeting with Joseph, i.e., with "the man."

[43:16-17] Joseph had expected that the brothers would return and had given orders to be informed. He now sees them as they arrive and the eleventh, who can only be Benjamin, with them (there is no need to alter the text). He instructs the steward (majordomo, J. Vergote, *Joseph en Egypt. . .* (1959 171f.) to receive them into his house for the midday meal; cf. the reception of the three men by Abraham (Gen. 18:2-5). The contrast with the earlier reception, when the first words of this man were words of suspicion, is deliberate. The steward follows instructions and brings the brothers into Joseph's house. The verb "he brought" is to be understood in the sense of "he set about. . ." or "he made preparation to bring" (translator). The repetition of the verb in v. 24 is not a doublet (so W. Rudolf, D. B. Redford); rather the two sentences frame the interruption of the action, vv. 18-23, which takes place in the courtyard. It is significant that there is no description of the house (see intro., p. 29).

[43:18-23] As soon as the brothers realize that they are to be brought into the house (v. 18a), they are seized with fear; they could be overpowered and reduced to slavery. Naturally they think at once of the money that they had found in their sacks and at the same time feel themselves exposed at the mercy of a foreign power. The narrator therefore chooses a particularly strong expression, "to overpower us and seize us"; it is perhaps a fixed formula. Here, in a foreign land, so they think, they are completely exposed to the potentates (cf. Abraham in 12:12) who can do with them what they will. "They want to take us into slavery with our donkeys," they think. The powerless fear of the defenseless is speaking here, fear for oneself and one's property.

[43:19] While they are still in the courtyard and before they are brought into the house, they approach the steward and beg for a hearing (v. 19); if only he would listen to them!

[43:20-22] The steward does listen; they have found a hearing. They can tell what really happened (vv. 20-22). They can now show him that they are "honest people" (42:11). With the utmost brevity, in this case demanded by courtesy, they justify themselves by laying the facts before him. What they have to say (one is spokesman for all) is introduced by the formula בי אדני which continues to echo their plea for a hearing. In the exposition the brothers recall their first journey (v. 20). Then they give an account of how they found the silver in their sacks (v. 21); the speaker immediately adds, We have brought it back with us! They add further that they have brought more silver for their intended purchase of grain (v. 22a). The final appendage, that they do not know how the silver came to be in their sacks, leads back once more to the main issue. It reveals the state of agitation in which they told their story.

There are some who, in the interests of source division, want to attribute the report in v. 21 to a different source from 42:27 where one brother only finds the silver; but this is to fail to notice the difference in the situation. The very brief account to the steward repeats what is essential. The difference shows just how realistic is the narrative style.

[43:23] The steward's answer comes as a complete surprise to the brothers and is the turning point (v. 23). It is introduced by שלום לכם, Peace be with you! Don't be afraid! This greeting of peace from the foreigner in this moment of mortal fear assures the brothers that in the Joseph story as a whole there is peace once more and that the breach is healed. It is just as with the greeting and assurance given in worship; the call "Do not be afraid!" is based on a perfect; so too here the meaning is that God *has* acted: "Your God, the God of your father [the ו is explicative] has. . .." Even if this perhaps is a way of covering over the facts, in the broader context of the Joseph story the steward is expressing what has really happened: God, the God of your father, has taken care of you; be at peace! The idea "God of your father" means simply "the God of your family," i.e., your God. The steward knows that the brothers belong to the one family group and so he speaks of "your God" (on the "God of the fathers" cf. *Genesis 12–36*, intro. 4, "The Religion of the Patriarchs," and bibliog. that follows). By "God who. . ." he means the deity in general, cutting across all boundaries, as did the Pharaoh in ch. 41. With a smile he says, "God. . .put a treasure in your sacks"; they can make of it what they will (מטמון is used particularly for buried treasure, e.g., Is. 45:3). The closing sentence puts the brothers definitively at rest; the steward says that he received their money. He now brings Simeon out to them, i.e., into the courtyard where the conversation took place. Thus the charge of spying is withdrawn with-

out there being any need to speak of it. One of the father's wishes has been fulfilled (v. 14).

[43:24-25] Vv. 24-25 form a bridge between the two scenes. A wordless pause is
deliberately put in here; the events themselves speak. The steward brings them
into Joseph's house; what was interrupted in v. 17 is now brought to its conclusion. This sentence is omitted in the Gk, probably because the Gk found it to be an
intrusive repetition. The brothers now enter the coolness of the house where they
can wash their feet and feed the donkeys. This simple security, the relief and re-
laxation of man and beast, this is the peace into which they are received by the
steward's greeting (v. 23). They have time and leisure to make ready the gifts that
they intend to present to the lord with whom they are to dine; for, strange to say,
they are now his guests (cf. Gen. 18; 19; 24:25, 32b).

[43:26-34] The second scene is the second meeting between Joseph and his
brothers (vv. 26-34). It is divided into the greeting (vv. 26-31) and the meal (vv.
32-34).

[43:26-31] This greeting is a miniature of artistic narrative style. To understand
it, one must know the significance of greeting in the world in which it is narrated.
For us it still remains a mere marginal matter; but for the ancient world it was of
central importance for the life-style of that community. The rites of greeting were
of great consequence for social status and relationship.
       There is a sharp contrast between this reception and the first. The first took
on a political character because of Joseph's accusation; the second is also political
inasmuch as "the man" is the lord before whom the brothers prostrate themselves; Joseph turns it into a family greeting by his questions and inquiries, which
are important in family meetings. The foreign lord thus silently withdraws the
charge of spying. The change in the nature of the greeting is effected by the word
שלום, the theme word through vv. 27 and 28. Joseph confirms the reception in
peace into his house (v. 23).

[43:26] The brothers' prostration in vv. 26 and 28 frame the greeting. The double
prostration is intentional; it is appropriate to the situation, as in ch. 33; it is a misunderstanding when H. Gunkel (and others) regards vv. 26b and 28b as doublets
and attributes them to different sources. The prostration here thus differs from that
in first meeting. Mere prostration is submission, but prostration with the presentation of gifts is homage, as in Mt. 2:11. The scene is frequent in Egyptian representations. On the form of the greeting in Egypt see H. Grapow, AAB 11 (1943)
98ff.; e.g., when the king is greeted in silence at an audience, he then says a word
of greeting.

[43:27-28] These words of Joseph complete the change (vv. 27-28). He asks
them "about their peace," i.e., he greets them by inquiring after their well-being,
the familiar manner of greeting as with Moses and Jethro in Ex. 18. He asks too
after the well-being of their old father, of whom they had spoken, and inquires
whether he is still alive. The brothers are very perplexed and take up the word
שלום in their reply; שלום sounds three times in the question and answer. They

prostrate themselves before the man (both words together also in Gen. 24:26, 48). The gesture sufficiently expresses what they feel.

[**43:29-31**] Joseph now has a special greeting for his brother Benjamin. "He looked up and saw. . ."; this is said when seeing another person introduces a further event. "The great lord only 'sees' someone when he will take notice of him" (B. Jacob). The passage presupposes a great difference in age between Joseph and Benjamin. Joseph first addresses the other brothers and asks them if this youngest brother is Benjamin; as he had done when inquiring about the father, soo too here he refers back to the first meeting with the words "about whom you spoke to me," showing the brothers his interest; he has forgotten nothing. The brothers' silence is sufficient answer. He now turns to Benjamin with a special greeting: "May God be gracious to you, my son!" This is not a common, formal greeting; it is a wish that has in mind God's personal attention (cf. Gen. 33:5, 11 and the promise in Is. 30:19, "He will surely be gracious to you. . ."; cf. v. 14). The listeners may well hear echoes of the beginning of ch. 39 when Joseph, like Benjamin now, comes to Egypt as a helpless stranger and an Egyptian bestows favor on him. The greeting is an expression of emotion which so overpowers him that he can no longer hold back his tears; to conceal them from his brothers he goes into his private room (for a description of the Egyptian house, cf. A. Erman, *Ägypten und ägyptisches Leben im Altertum* [1923] 247-258; one can still see the private room in the burial chambers of important Egyptians). There is also weeping when relatives meet in Gen. 29:11; but it draws special significance here from the course of the narrative. Joseph then resumes his role; he pulls himself together and orders the food to be brought in. The scene moves quietly into its final part, the meal.

[**43:32-34**] A meal is described in these verses which is remarkable in many respects. Its significance in the course of the narrative consists primarily in this, that it expresses the change over against the first journey of the brothers to Egypt; the brothers are now the guests of the most powerful man in Egypt after the Pharaoh! This joyful meal brings to an end the brothers' journey with all their fears and dread anxieties; hence the narrator lays particular emphasis on it by reporting a rare event that takes place. This rare event has both a national and social aspect. The brothers become aware of the Egyptian prohibition to eat at table with Canaanites. Surprise such as this at the exclusive nature of Egyptian table customs is possible only in Israel's early period. The classical Greek writers, Herodotus, Diodorus, and Strabo, still know of them. This detail, in no wise necessary for the progress of the action, is taken up only because it is a piece of surprising information for both the narrator and his listeners.

[**43:33-34a**] The other peculiarity is of a social kind. It concerns seating at table. The brothers are seated in Joseph's presence according to their age, as instructed by the steward; this too astonishes them. Further, it is not the eldest, but the youngest who is the guest of honor; on Joseph's instructions he receives a particularly large portion. There are many other examples of the special attention paid to the guest of honor in the Bible (e.g., 1 Sam. 9:23f.) and in Homer. As on a former occasion (ch. 37), the youngest is given precedence over his elders.

[**43:34b**] The last sentence, ''So they drank and were merry with him,'' brings to a high point the account of the brothers' second visit to Egypt; a sharp slump follows (ch. 44). The meeting almost arrives at a resolution (Joseph's emotion, the hints given at table); but the narrator wants all this to be a preparation for what happens in ch. 44. Reconciliation could come only as in ch. 44, not as in ch. 43.

Purpose and Thrust

Ch. 43 only has meaning as a link between the first journey in ch. 42 and the resolution in chs. 44f. If it is deprived of its place here by source division, it loses the meaning which the narrator has given it by his setting. What happens here takes place against the gloomy background of a mounting famine (v. 1): there is the father's request, Judah's definitive demand, reference to the death that threatens the little ones, the brothers' fear of the potentate before whom want forces them to appear. The whole chapter is really concerned with departure and arrival. This ordinary, everyday event becomes a tense drama because of the famine on the one hand, and the threat and unpredictability of ''the man'' on the other. However, the drama takes place in the simple events that are part of departure and arrival.

The tension reaches its climax in the greeting of peace with which the steward answers the brothers' fearful explanation. It is the representative of the dread potentate who takes away their fear: ''Do not be afraid, your God has. . .!'' This extraordinary change is confirmed by the man's greeting when the word *peace* sounds three times in the dialog. The steward's answer, commissioned by higher authority, corresponds in wording (form and content) to the later assurance of well-being which has an important place in Israel's worship, and which Deutero-Isaiah takes up in his preaching to the exiles. Without the experience narrated here neither this liturgical assurance of well-being nor its resumption by Deutero-Isaiah would be possible. Here it is experienced by simple people in small groups in early times without any institutional framework. God's action and talk about God began in the simple forms of secular events.

What is peculiar to ch. 43 is that the assurance ''Do not be afraid—God has acted'' bridges a wide gulf and is heard beyond it. It comes from the foreign potentate, in a foreign land, and in the territory of another religion. Such is the context of the reference to God here.

The Goblet

Literature

Genesis 44:1-8: J. Hunger, *Becherwahrsagung bei den Babyloniern* (1903). A. van Hoonacker, "Expository Notes (Gen IV 7; XLIV 5; 1 Sam X 12)," Expo. 10 (1915) 452-459; "Was Josef's Beker (Gen 44) een Tooverbeker?" *I. Teirlinck Album* (1931) 239ff. J. Pedersen, *Seelenleben und Gemeinschaftsleben* (1934). G. R. Driver, *Studies of OT Prophecy* (1950) esp. 69. F. Horst, "Recht und Religion im Bereich des AT," EvTh 16 (1956) 49-75. H. Gese, *Lehre und Wirklichkeit in der alten Weisheit* (1958). W. Preiser, "Vergeltung und Sühne im altisraelitischen Strafrecht," Fests. E. Schmid (1961) 7-38. J. Scharbert, "*šlm* im AT," Fests. H. Junker (1961) 209-229. J. de Fraine, *Adam and the Family of Man* (1962; Eng. 1965). A. S. van der Woude, "De *mal'ak* Jahweh: Een Godsbode," NedThT 18 (1963/64) 1-13. W. Eisenbeis, *Die Wurzel* šlm *im AT*, BZAW 113 (1969). T. H. Gaster, *Myth. . .* (1969) 218-222. M. R. Lehmann, "Biblical Oaths," ZAW 81 (1969) 74-92.

Genesis 44:9-17: J. J. Glueck, "Nagid—Shepherd," VT 13 (1963) 144-150. H. G. Jefferson, "Psalm LXXVII," VT 13 (1963) 87-91. A. Laurentin, "*We'attāh-Kai nun*. Formule caractéristique des Textes juridiques et liturgiques," Bib 45 (1964) 168-197, 413-432. D. R. Hillers, "*Berît 'am*: 'Emancipation of the People,' " JBL 97 (1978) 176-182. G. Gerleman, "Der Sinnbereich 'fest-los(e)' im Hebräischen," ZAW 92 (1980) 404-415.

Genesis 44:18-24: Z. W. Falk, "Hebrew Legal Terms. I," JSS 5 (1960) 350-354. L. Jacobs, "The Qal Vaḥomer Argument in the Old Testament," BSOAS 35 (1972) 221-227. E. M. Borobio, "El Midrás de Neofiti, Gen 44,18. Dos versiones diferentes de una Hagadá," EstB 35 (1976) 79-86. I. Riesener, *Der Stamm* עבד *im AT: Eine Wortuntersuchung unter Berücksichtigung neuerer sprachwissenschaftlicher Methoden*, BZAW 149 (1979).

Genesis 44:25-34: N. H. Snaith, "The Meaning of the Hebrew אָף," VT 14 (1964) 221-225. H. A. Brongers, "Bemerkungen zum Gebrauch des adverbialen *we'attāh* im AT," VT 15 (1965) 289-299 esp. 294.

Text

44:1   Then Joseph gave orders to his steward: Fill the men's sacks with grain, as much as they can carry[a] [and put each one's silver in the top of his sack].[b]

2   And my goblet, the silver goblet,[a] put in the top of the sack of the youngest [together with his money for the grain].[b] And he did as Joseph told him.

3   In the morning, at first light,[a] the men were sent on their way with their asses.

4   They set out from the city and had not gone far[a] when Joseph said to his steward, Up and after them! And when you have caught up with them say to them, Why have you returned evil for good?

5   Why have you stolen my silver goblet?[a] Is it not the one from which my lord drinks[b] and in which he practises divination? You have done wrong in doing this.

6   When he caught up with them, he repeated all this to them.

7   But they said to him, How can my lord say anything like this? Far be it from your servants to do anything like this!

8   See, 'the'[a] silver that we found in the top of our sacks we brought back to you from the land of Canaan! How could we have stolen silver or gold from your master's house!

9   With whichever of your servants it is found, he shall die,[a] and we, we shall be your master's slaves.

10 He said, Well then, be it as you say; whichever of you had it shall be my slave, but the rest of you will be free.

11 Each quickly lifted his sack to the ground and opened it.

12 He searched them, beginning with the eldest down to the youngest.[a] And the goblet was found in Benjamin's sack.

13 Then they tore their garments, and each loaded his ass and they returned to the city.

14 When Judah and his brothers arrived at Joseph's house, he was still there; they prostrated to the ground before him.

15 And Joseph said to them, What is this that you have done? Did you not know that a man such as I practices divination?

16 And Judah said, What can we say to my lord? What reply can we make? How do we justify ourselves?[a] God has discovered the wickedness of your servants; we, we are my lord's slaves, both we and the one who was found to have the goblet.

17 But he said, Far be it from me to do this; the one who was found with the goblet shall be my slave; but you can return to your father in peace.

18 Then Judah approached him[a] and said, Please, my lord, may your servant have a word in your ear,[b] and let not your anger flare against your servant, for you are as the Pharaoh.[c]

19 My lord asked your servants, Have you a father and brother?

20 We answered my lord, We have a father who is old and a younger brother who was born to him in his old age.[a] His brother is dead; he is his mother's only surviving child, and his father loves him.[b]

21 You asked your servants, Bring him down here to me that I may set my eyes on him.[a]

22 We said to my lord, The boy cannot leave his father; if he leaves him, his father will die.[a]

23 You said to your servants, If your youngest brother does not come down with you, you shall not come into my presence.

24 When we returned to your servant, my father, we recounted to him the words of my lord.

25 When our father said, Go back again and buy us some food,

26 we said, We cannot go back; only if our youngest brother is with us can we go back. We cannot enter the man's presence unless our youngest brother comes with us.

27 Then your servant, my father, said to us, You know that my wife bore me two sons.

28 One left me, and I said, He must[a] have been torn to pieces! And I have never seen him again.

29 And now you will take this one from me as well; if any misfortune happens to him, you will bring my grey hair in sorrow to Sheol.[a]

30 Now[a] were I to come to your servant, my father, and the boy, with whom his life is bound up, were not with me,

31 he would die when he saw that the boy were not 'with us',[a] and your servants would bring the grey hair of your servant, our father, in sorrow to Sheol.

32 Your servant has made surety for the boy before my[a] father; I said, If I do not bring him back, I shall bear the guilt before my father all my life.

33 So now let your servant remain[a] as your slave in the place of the boy, and let the boy return with his brothers.

34 How can I go back to my father if the boy is not with me! I could not bear to look[a] on the distress that would come upon my father.

1a Construction, BrSynt §151.   **b** Subsequent addition.

2a Construction, Ges-K §135n.   **b** Subsequent addition.

3a Construction, Ges-K §§144c, 142e; BrSynt §35a; J. Blau, VT 9 (1959) 134.

4a Construction, Ges-K §§156f, 164b; BrSynt §138a; D. B. Redford, VT.S 20 (1970) 38.

5a To be supplied with Gk (H. Holzinger, J. Skinner).   **b** Construction, BrSynt §151; Ges-K §119m; on inf. abs. D. B. Redford VT.S 20 (1970) 44f.

8a Read הכסף with Sam, Gk (as in Gen. 43:21, 22).

9a Construction, Ges-K §§112ii, 138f; BrSynt §157. ומת as in Gen. 31:32, legal language.

12a Construction, Ges-K §156d; D. B. Redford, VT.S 20 (1970) 38; יחפש as in Gen. 31:35, see H. G. Jefferson, VT 13 (1963) 87-91; on גדל R. Mosis, ThW I, 934, 937.

16a צדק hithp. only here in this sense.

18a As in Gen. 43:19, see Z. W. Falk, JSS 5 (1960) 350-354. **b** ''In the sense of submissive courtesy,'' L. Rost.   **c** Construction, Ges-K §161e; BrSynt §8a, 15d, 105b.

20a Child of old age as in Gen. 21:2, 7; 37:3   **b** Construction, BrSynt §12.

21a Construction, Ges-K §106m; BrSynt §135c.

22a Construction, Ges-K §159g; BrSynt §135b.

28a אך ''to be sure,'' N. H. Snaith, VT 14 (1964) 221-245.

29a Construction, Ges-K §112kk.

30a On ועתה, H. Brongers, VT 15 (1965) 294, in sense of ''and so.''

31a Add אתנן (as in v. 30) with Sam, Gk, Vg, Syr (H. Holzinger).

32a Sam אביו.

33a Form, Ges-K §69p; form of the request, Ges-K §109h.

34a פן without governing verb; construction, Ges-K §152w.

Form

Ch. 44 is a part of the account of the second journey of Joseph's brothers to Egypt which begins in 43:1 and ends with 45:28. Within this account ch. 44 (together with 45:1-9) deals almost exclusively with an interruption of the return journey (apart from vv. 3, 4a), caused by the false accusation of stealing the goblet. Within the interruption only 44:1-17 is concerned with dramatic action; all is centered on Judah's address to Joseph, vv. 18-34, and the latter's reaction, 45:1-9, which leads to the resolution. The structure demonstrates the narrator's intention to bring the narrative to its climax here. The sudden dramatic reversal of fortune follows Judah's address. The narrative span, begun in ch. 37, reaches its resolution here. The construction of ch. 44 corresponds to that of ch. 43: 43:16-17 / 44:1-2, 4-6 Joseph's commission to the steward; 43:18-23 / 44:7-13 the brothers before the steward; 43:26-30(34) / 44:14-17(18-34) the brothers before Joseph.

The literary device of doubling appears in clear relief here. The mounting tension from the first to the second meeting leads to resolution and deliverance; two journeys and two meetings with Joseph on the second journey prepare it.

Commentary

[**44:1-17**] The first part of ch. 44, vv. 1-17, is divided into two scenes: the brothers before the steward (vv. 1-13) and the brothers before Joseph (vv. 14-17). The first scene is joined with the brothers' departure from Egypt. This is preceded by Joseph's first instruction to the steward (vv. 1-2a); Joseph's second instruction and its execution follows (vv. 4b-6). Then comes the encounter with the brothers (vv. 7-13).

[**44:1-2**] Joseph gives instructions to his steward, just as he had done on the occasion of the first departure from Egypt (42:25). But there is a difference; in the first, all the brothers fell under the suspicion of theft; here it is only Benjamin. There is a mounting tension; in the first case it was a question of the silver; here it is a very valuable, personal possession of Joseph's (on גביע cf. comm. on vv. 4b-5). The subsequent additions in vv. 1 and 2, mentioning the silver as well as the goblet, markedly disturb the planned tension and mounting crisis. The words are clearly an insertion inasmuch as they have no function in the context; there is no mention of the silver when the sacks are opened (vv. 11-12). Joseph's intention in giving the instructions is to bring about a situation close to that which was the point of departure of the story in ch. 37; the aim is to bring about the resolution. Joseph's instructions consist of two parts: first he instructs the steward to fill the sacks of all the brothers—"as much as they can carry." This is in accord with the underlying theme that runs through the whole narrative. The resolution is about healing the breach, but about preservation from famine as well. At the first meeting the concern of this powerful foreigner for the hungry families was a cause of surprise (42:19, "take grain for your hungry households"). The concern is still there.

[**44:3-4a**] The language of the itinerary is the background of vv. 3-4a; the whole passage has the form of a travel account. Joseph's second set of instructions follows immediately: "they had not gone far when. . . ." These instructions extend to the end of vv. 4b-5; v. 6 gives a brief report on their execution (instructions v. 4b וחשׂגתם, execution v. 6 וישׂגם). A form of speech characteristic of Hebrew is manifest here: "Up, after them. . .catch up. . .say to them. . ."; he puts on the steward's lips what he is to say to the brothers. It is a form which says that the messenger faces the addressees with the words of the one who instructed him. They are listening to the words of the sender (A. S. van der Woude, NedThT 18 [1963/64] 1-13).

[**44:4b-5**] There are three parts to the accusation that the steward is to level at the brothers. The first and third are of a general kind, "Why have you returned evil for good?'' The brothers had been received as guests, they had shared a meal with the master of the house, and now they had shown outrageous disdain for their host! And, not least, their action amounted to a crime. What they had done is not only morally wrong, but is also a crime which must be punished. One expects to find the specific accusation between these two general ones. It is missing in the MT; but the Gk (cf. Syr and Vg) adds, ''And why have you stolen my silver goblet?'' The MT mentions the specific purpose for which it is used. The omission in the MT can be explained inasmuch as v. 5 is concerned with the instruction, not with the accusation proper; Joseph leaves out the accusation of stealing the goblet when giving the instructions, because it was taken for granted. More likely, it is a case of a scribal error because grammatically the beginning of v. 5, הלא זה, demands an antecedent.

V. 5 says that the silver goblet is Joseph's personal drinking vessel and that he uses it for divination.

גביע is a goblet (KBL) in 44:2,12,16 and Jer. 35:5, perhaps calix-shaped (cf. Ex. 25:31-34; 37:17-20). Joseph uses it not only for drinking but also for divination (KBL, ''divination from the cup''). Divination is forbidden later in Israel as a pagan custom (Lev. 19:26; Deut. 18:10); it is mentioned in a proclamation of judgment over Egypt in Is. 19:3. It was enough for the author of the Joseph story to know that divination was practiced in Egypt; and the form mentioned here, using a drinking vessel, is attested elsewhere in antiquity (T. H. Gaster, *Myth, Legend.* . . [1969] 218-222; H. Ringgren, ''Gottesspruch,'' ''Orakel,'' BHH I [1962] 598-600). The view of J. Vergote, *Joseph en Egypte.* . . (1959) 172-176 (taken up by H. C. Schmitt, following Cunen, *La lécanomancie* [diss. Lüttich, 1956-57]), that cup-divination is first attested in Egypt in the Hellenistic period, and so Mesopotamian influence must be seen here, is unnecessary. Also the translation of ב ''in regard to the goblet'' is to be rejected (J. Vergote, following A. van Hoonacker [1931], L. Ruppert [1965], H. C. Schmitt [1980]). The question whether Joseph actually practised divination with the cup is not appropriate to the text; the purpose of the sentence here is merely to give force to the accusation. Nor is it to the point to speak of the ''theft of a holy object'' (G. von Rad). Divination is not a matter of cult. Nothing is said about the precise source of the omen; one can only guess: E. A. Speiser: ''Omens were based on the appearance of the liquids inside the container''; T. H. Gaster: ''. . .from figures which appeared in the water.'' In any case there were many sorts of divination of this type—right up to the present-day cup readings from coffee grounds and tea leaves.

[44:7-9] The brothers are shocked and indignant before the steward and insist on their innocence (v. 7). They are deeply offended, ''How can you say anything like this of us?'' (as in 39:19). They reject the charge: ''Far be it from us!'' (cf. Gen. 18:25). As confirmation they refer to their conduct so far. On the previous occasion they had said to Joseph, ''we are honest people'' (42:11). They have already demonstrated their honesty by bringing back the money found in their sacks. V. 8b corresponds to v. 7b. They would never perpetrate such a theft. An exclamation follows which is meant to show the steward that they are just as upset about the theft as he is. If any one of them is the thief, then he should meet with the severest punishment (cf. Gen. 31:32); and the others too would be prepared to go into slavery. H. Gunkel: ''Ancient Israel was used to common satisfaction from a whole group.'' The brothers say this in the utter certainty of their innocence.

[**44:10**] The steward agrees with the brothers' proposal and takes them at their word, v. 10; גַּם־עַתָּה means here "very well then." At the same time he modifies the punishment to reasonable proportions; the guilty one will become a slave, the rest will go free. On the use of נָקִי here, cf. D. R. Hillers, JBL 97 (1978) 179. Just as עָוֹן can mean guilt and punishment, so can נָקִי mean blameless, not guilty.

[**44:11-13**] Search and discovery of the goblet: a similar scene is described in Gen. 31:30-35. The description here is masterly in the little that it says and in the much that it does not say. The excitement expressed in the brothers' reply (vv. 7-9) is continued in their haste (יְמַהֲרוּ) to prove their innocence. The steward searches the baggage (חִפֵּשׂ, likewise Gen. 31:35; cf. H. G. Jefferson, VT 13 [1963] 87-91) from the eldest to the youngest (cf. 43:33). These simple words capture the tension as they wait.

[**44:13**] The brothers' horror and shock are expressed simply in their gesture of tearing their garments (v. 13; cf. 37:34). The gesture says at the same time that all the brothers are affected. Their reaction to this blow, Benjamin's feelings, and much more the narrator compresses into the sparse words which report what they must now do; they load their donkeys again (on עָמַס, D. B. Redford, p. 62; H. C. Schmitt, p. 132) and return together to the city, to "the man."

[**44:14-17**] This scene takes place in the house of the Egyptian minister of state. It is introduced in v. 14 and includes Joseph's accusation (v. 15), Judah's answer (v. 16), and Joseph's judgment (v. 17); Judah's address follows (vv. 18-34).

[**44:14**] The introduction prepares us for Judah's role as spokesman for his brothers ("Judah and his brothers"). Joseph is still at home and the brothers prostrate themselves before him. In contrast to 43:26 the stronger verb נָפַל is used to express complete submission. There is a subtle touch here; in Joseph's dreams the brothers bowed before him; as the dreams are fulfilled, the act of bowing is varied; it has a different nuance on each occasion.

[**44:15**] Joseph's accusation (v. 15) is no more than an appendage to that already made by the steward. It consists of a question expressing amazement that they had ever attempted such an outrage. The reason is given in the second sentence: It was to no purpose, I'd have discovered it in any case. This resumes the motif from v. 5; "the man" is no ordinary man; he can see what lies hidden. From the brothers' standpoint, this is the strongest expression of how powerless they feel and are as they stand exposed to the potentate; they are not guilty. If the foreigner can divine, then he should know that they are not guilty. Their position is hopeless; an impartial inquiry would vindicate them. But it makes no sense to ask for one. The tension has now reached its climax.

[**44:16**] The situation of the brothers is hopeless and Judah lets the foreign potentate know it: What could we now say to justify ourselves? It makes no sense, we know. But Judah does not let it rest at this. He preserves the dignity of the men deceived by the potentate and caught in a trap; he in no way admits guilt; nevertheless, he accepts manfully and submissively what has befallen them as a punishment from God, the retribution of a guilt whose enormity they have only now admitted (cf. 42:21), and under which they stand. "God has discovered the guilt of your servants." Judah's confession that God has discovered their guilt is more important than that someone has discovered the goblet. Judah cannot admit a theft. But while admitting a long-standing guilt he sets it in a broader context in which it is not the powerful man at the Egyptian court, but God who acts and directs. The brothers have withstood the test to which Joseph submitted them. He can now make himself known.

In the last sentence (v. 16c) Judah freely takes the punishment upon himself, thereby sacrificing the freedom of them all. He stands by his statement that all are to bear the punishment together with the guilty one (v. 9). Judah does not admit theft; he says, "the one who was found to have the goblet." The punishment which he accepts together with his brothers has now taken on another meaning.

[**44:17**] The Egyptian minister of state does not accept Judah's explanation. The "guilty one" alone is to bear the punishment of servitude. Joseph has thus achieved what he had intended from the beginning, to restore the original grouping. In ch. 37 the event that brought about the breach took place between the father, the brothers, and the youngest son. It is so again. What will the brothers do? Judah gives the answer in his address.

[**44:18-34**] Judah's speech is the longest in the Joseph story and in the whole of Genesis. The tension had reached its climax in v. 17 with Joseph's pronouncement of sentence; the turning point begins with Judah's speech and Joseph's reaction. It is divided into the introductory request for a hearing, (v. 18), the argumentation (vv. 19-32), and Judah's request. The argumentation of the request follows the sequence of events which have led to the present situation: it begins with the first encounter with Joseph (vv. 19-23) and the report to the father (v. 24); then comes the conversation with the father before the second journey (vv. 25-29) which is not possible unless they return with Benjamin; Judah has provided surety for him (v. 32). The meaning and intent of Judah's reasoned request becomes clear only when the sequence of events from the first encounter with Joseph down to the present undergoes two expansions; one looks to the past, to the loss of Joseph (vv. 27-29), the other to the future, the probable death of the father if Benjamin is not there (vv. 30-31).

A presupposition to the understanding of vv. 18-34 is that the form and style are "narrative speech" (M. Weiss, VT 13 [1963] 456-475; Bib 46 [1965] 181-206). It is by its very nature different from formal reproduction; it is a new and independent presentation of what has happened, arising out of a new situation which itself of necessity gives rise to alterations (B. Jacob speaks of the "stylistic law that has to bring variations into the presentation of the same event according to the different circumstances in which it is recounted"). From the very outset then it is unlikely that such variations are to be traced back to different literary sources.

[**44:18**] Solemnly and circumspectly, Judah requests a hearing; the introduction indicates that he is going to say something decisive. Judah approaches (נגשׁ as in Gen. 18:23; 43:19; בי אדני as in 43:20) because he is the one responsible; he it is whom the father will question. The last sentence, "for you are as the Pharaoh," is no *captatio benevolentiae* (attempt to curry favor; F. Delitzsch, and others). It gives the reason for "let not your anger flare. . .," which explicates the request for a hearing; the meaning is, "I know that there can be no gainsaying the king" (B. Jacob). The introductory words give some indication of the hopeless position of the speaker; he is conscious that what he is going to say must be said.

[**44:19-23**] Judah begins with the first conversation between the minister of state and the brothers (42:7-20). The lord knows it all; he needs only to be reminded. But in doing so Judah lays a basis for his argumentation to which the lord must assent. The text of the narrative refers back to the conversation in 42:12-16 (plus 18-20), but the repetition diverges notably from it. Judah uses it only insofar as it serves as the basis for his request in v. 33. This determines the division here: vv. 19-23 comprise Joseph's inquiry about the father and the brother (v. 19) and the brothers' reply (v. 20, similar to the conversation between the brothers and the father in 43:7); then comes Joseph's demand to bring the younger brother (v. 21, with further insistence in v. 23), and the brothers' defensive reply in v. 22. Judah is careful to leave out anything that could be unpleasant for the lord. The accusation of spying and Simeon's arrest are of no importance as grounds for the request; they can be omitted. Judah is taking the same line when he describes Joseph's demand to bring the boy down with them as a demonstration of goodwill; this is the meaning of the expression שִׂים עֵינִי עַל (Jer. 24:6; 39:12; 40:4). There is another modification which is an addition to 42:7: in answer to Joseph's inquiry (cf. 42:13) Judah adds that the youngest son is particularly dear to the father (v. 20); and further, by way of defense (v. 22), that if they cannot bring him with them it could be the cause of the father's death. The motive behind the modification is obvious. Judah is appealing to Joseph's human sensitivity (so E. I. Lowenthal, *The Joseph Narrative in Genesis* [1973]); this is the culmination of his address (vv. 31-33). It is a misunderstanding of this modification of ch. 42 to postulate that these words presuppose a lost fragment of J (as A. Dillmann and others).

[**44:24-29**] The second part of Judah's address repeats the conversation between the brothers and their father before their second journey down to Egypt (43:2-10). Here too there is a notable difference; Judah says only what can give substance to his request which is to follow. On their return from their first journey they had given a report to their father (v. 24; cf. 42:29-38). When their father asked them to go back again and buy grain (v. 25), they explained that they could only return to Egypt if Benjamin went with them (v. 26; cf. 43:3-5); then comes their father's answer (vv. 27-29; cf. 42:36, 38).

[**44:25-26**] It should be clear to the lord from the father's request and the brothers' refusal to return without Benjamin that they have adhered strictly to his demand. These verses repeat 42:29 and 43:3, 5 almost word for word.

[**44:27-29**] The repetition should introduce only the father's answer on which Judah lays the whole weight. According to the previous account the father had spoken these words (42:36, 38) when the brothers returned from their first journey. Now he begins by reminding them, "You know that. . .!" Judah wants to explain to the Egyptian lord whom he is now addressing what the loss of Benjamin would mean to the father. This is why he has to mention the wife who bore him only two sons (v. 27b) and why he must speak of Joseph, the lost son (v. 28). The foreigner to whom he is speaking cannot of course understand what is being suggested; but he can grasp what the loss of Benjamin would mean. This is all that Judah is concerned with.

This recollection of what happened at the beginning of the story has yet further significance for both narrator and listeners. Joseph now hears for the first time what happened at home when the brothers came back without him. He hears of his father's lament and grief which still persists; he hears the father's cry "torn to pieces, torn to pieces!" which still echoes in the brothers' ears; he hears too that the brothers now speak differently of the preferential love for the children of this particular wife. Judah's rehearsal of the events, with its interplay of foreground and background, shows a highly refined narrative art such as is unique to the narrator of the Joseph story in the whole of Genesis. It differs here from the equally valuable, but very different, narrative style of J.

[**44:30-32**] The ועתה at the beginning of v. 30 introduces a consequence of what has just been said (stated specifically only in v. 33). It looks to the future and makes the foreigner aware of what will happen if the brothers return to their father without Benjamin. Judah deliberately says, "Were I to come. . .," so as to make known beforehand that he will take responsibility. He synthesizes in v. 30 what he has explained in vv. 27-29 with the parenthesis ונפשו קשורה בנפשו "to whose heart his heart is bound," on whom his whole life (soul) hangs (cf. 1 Sam. 18:1). With these words Judah now (ועתה) passes from his explanatory account on to his appeal to the foreign potentate; given the situation, he wants to move him to a humane decision. It is this that he underscores in v. 31; the father is so attached to the youth that he would die if he saw that Benjamin was not with them on their return. He expresses his concern for the aged father by making the old man's lament his own (42:38). There has been a change.

[**44:32**] Judah adds, as it were by way of appendage, that he has made surety for Benjamin (cf. 43:9). He does not want this to play a conspicuous part; it is not to be the real reason for his request. Further, he alleges it so as to explain that it is he among the brothers who is making the request in v. 33.

[**44:33-34**] These verses are introduced by ועתה, the same word as in v. 30. Judah makes his proposal in a brief, sober sentence—he is to remain as Joseph's slave in Benjamin's place. He has explained the reason for his request from the whole course of events, from the first journey right up to the present moment. It is to this that he appeals to guarantee the request.

[**44:34**] Judah underscores his appeal in the concluding sentence in which he resumes vv. 30-31: "I could not look on my father's distress." The narrator uses a particularly delicate touch here to express Judah's profound emotion; he leaves out the courteous formula "your servant." It is a matter here simply of son and brother.

Purpose and Thrust

In vv. 1-13 of ch. 44 Joseph pushes the testing of the brothers to a climax which allows no further tension; resolution must follow immediately on the false accusation. It does, but in a surprising way; the last and most serious accusation brings the brothers to a confession of guilt (vv. 14-17); Joseph withdraws the charge only when he makes himself known (ch. 45). Ch. 44 is stamped by Judah's confession of guilt (v. 16) and his readiness to take upon himself the punishment threatening Benjamin (vv. 18-34). Judah's address presupposes what he said in v. 16 in face of the accusation. There he sets Joseph's accusation, in this case addressed to an innocent party, in the broader context of God's action toward the family of Jacob. It is here that it acquires meaning; the way had already been prepared in 42:21, "we are certainly guilty in regard to our brother," with the realization of the more profound implications of the cycle of crime and punishment. The brothers wanted to conceal their crime, but God has now exposed it. During the long interval, God was not only with Joseph (ch. 39), but also with the brothers, though in a very different way. He pursued them as they tried to hide their guilt (cf. Gen. 3:9). As the brothers accept what is happening to them now as a punishment of their former guilt, they recognize that God has been caring for them all along. This has brought about the change in them.

Some exegetes contest that there has been any change in the brothers. But the mere fact that the narrator reconstitutes the initial situation of ch. 37 in ch. 44 shows that it is his intention to make clear in this way that something has changed in the brothers. One can describe it as a change of heart, repentance (שׁוּב; μετάνοια). But what is peculiar to the present situation is that the change of heart is the result of the brothers' experience. Searching reflection in the real sense of the word is a necessary consequence. The presupposition is that the hour for such a change of heart must come. When it does come it needs neither a call to repentance nor an institution. The Joseph story shows here that acknowledgment of one's own guilt and the resulting change of heart acquire their meaning and integrity from the journey through life as a whole, and that often that journey is long. But what alone is decisive is the recognition that it was God who led the brothers—as well as Joseph—this long journey to the hour that Judah speaks of in v. 16.

Here, at the climax and turning point of the Joseph story, the Bible speaks for the first time of vicarious suffering (vv. 18-34). All exegetes regard and evaluate this passage as the high point of the story. Attention should be given to the literary and theological aspects alike. Many describe the verses as a masterpiece of rhetorical art; the narrator has thus succeeded in bringing his story of Joseph and his brothers to an artistic climax. But this does not suffice to say what is the real significance of the address in the narrative as a whole. The narrator has achieved something that apparently is but seldom achieved in the literature of the world; at the climax he presents the whole story in a nutshell in the argumentation underlying Judah's request. Judah's address links what has happened since the first journey with what has preceded, right back to the beginning (vv. 27-29), and with what is to be expected in the future (vv. 30-31)—Jacob's death—so as to form a self-contained sequence. The listeners thus have the opportunity to reflect on the narrative as a whole from this short summary.

The theological aspect of Judah's address is not immediately evident; there is not a single sentence about God. However, it is a necessary consequence of what Judah had already said in v. 16. God has discovered the brothers' guilt; hence, one of them offers himself as a slave in a foreign land in place of the youngest. He prefers to take the punishment upon himself rather than cause his father distress yet again. It is indeed vicarious suffering, but in a very different sense than that of the servant of the Lord at the end of the era of judgment prophecy or in the New Testament in the case of Christ. There is a path that leads from the Joseph story right up to the very threshold of community; the healing of a breach is possible only when there is one who is ready to take the suffering upon oneself. A readiness to do this as an extreme resort so as to serve the peace and well-being of a community is always incumbent on God's people on the way, even on the small unit of the family.

Joseph Makes Himself Known
to His Brothers

Literature

Genesis 45: W. Bousset, *Wiedererkennungsmärchen und Placidas-Legende: Neue Texte zur Geschichte eines Wiedererkennungsmärchens und zum Text der Placidas-Legende*, ed. W. Lüdtke (1917). A. Murtonen, "The Use and Meaning of the Words *leḇārēk* and *berākāh* in the OT," VT 9 (1959) 158-177.

Genesis 45:1-8: W. E. Müller, *Die Vorstellung vom Rest im AT* (diss. Leipzig, 1939) = with H. D. Preuss (1973) esp. 117. H. Kruse, "Die 'dialektische Negation' als semitisches Idiom," VT 4 (1954) 385-400.. E. Schild, "On Exodus III 14, 'I am that I am,' " VT 4 (1954) 296-302. G. F. Hasel, *The Remnant: The History and Theology of the Remnant from Genesis to Isaiah*, AUM 5 (1972) esp. 135-159; "Semantic Values of Derivatives of the Hebrew Root *šʾr*," AUSS 11 (1973) 152-169.

Genesis 45:9-15: F. Nötscher, "Heisst *Kābōd* auch 'Seele'?" VT 2 (1952) 358-362. J. Simons, *The Geographical and Topographical Texts of the OT* (1959), "Egypt" 244-246. J. L'Hour, "L'alliance de Sichem," RB 69 (1962) 161-184. R. Rendtorff, "Botenformel und Botenspruch," ZAW 74 (1962) 165-177. A. J. Bjørndalen, "Zu den Zeitstufen der Zitatformel. . . כה אמר im Botenverkehr," ZAW 86 (1974) 393-403. J. P. Meier, "Two Disputed Questions in Matt 28:16-20," JBL 96 (1977) 407-424. A. M. Vater, "Narrative Patterns for the Story of Commissioned Communication in the OT," JBL 99 (1980) 365-382.

Genesis 45:16-24: M. H. Gottstein, "נשׂי אלהים (Gen XXIII,6)," VT 3 (1953) 298-299. M. Mannati, "Ṭûb-Y. en Psaume XXVII 13: La bonté de Y., ou les biens de Y.?" VT 19 (1969) 488-493. J. Heller, "Die Symbolik des Fettes im AT," VT 20 (1970) 106-108. M. Delcor, "Quelques cas de survivances du vocabulaire nomade en Hébreu Biblique," VT 25 (1975) 307-322.

Genesis 45:25-28: E. Pfeiffer, "Glaube im Alten Testament," ZAW 71 (1959) 151-164. K. Rupprecht, "עלה מן הארץ (Ex 1,10; Hos 2,2): 'sich des Landes bemächtigen'?" ZAW 82 (1970) 442-447. D. Marcus, "The Verb 'to Live' in Ugaritic," JSS 17 (1972) 76-82.

Text

45:1 Joseph could now no longer control himself[a] in the presence of all his attendants[b] and cried, Let everyone leave my presence. So there was no one with Joseph when he made himself known[c] to his brothers.

2 But he wept so loudly that all the Egyptians[a] and the house of the Pharaoh heard him.[b]

3   Then Joseph said to his brothers, I am Joseph! Is my father still alive? But his brothers were not able to reply, so stunned were they as they faced him.[a]

4   Then Joseph said to his brothers, Come closer to me! And they did so. He said, I am Joseph your brother whom you sold[a] into Egypt.

5   Now then, do not be distressed[a] or reproach yourselves that you sold me here, because God sent me ahead of you to save lives.

6   There has now been a famine in the land for two years, and there are five more years to go in which there will be neither ploughing nor harvest.

7   But God sent me ahead of you [to preserve you a remnant in the land and to keep you alive, a great host of survivors].[a]

8b He had made me a father to the Pharaoh and master over all his household and ruler over the whole of Egypt.

8a So then it was not you who sent me down here, but God.

9   Hurry, go back to my father and say to him, Your son Joseph says, God has made me ruler over the whole of Egypt; come down to me; do not delay.

10 You are to dwell in the land of Goshen[a] and be near me,[b] you, your sons, your grandsons, your sheep and your cattle and all that you have.

11 I will take care of you there,[a] for there are still five years of famine to come, and see that you and your household and all that you have are not reduced to poverty.[b]

12 You see now with your own eyes, and your brother Benjamin sees, that it is my mouth that speaks to you.

13 And tell my father of the dignity[a] that is mine in Egypt and of all that you have seen here; hurry, bring my father down here.

14 Then he threw his arms around Benjamin's neck and wept, and Benjamin wept on his neck.

15 Then he kissed his brothers as well and wept and embraced them. Only then did his brothers speak to him.

16 The news spread to the Pharaoh's house, Joseph's brothers have arrived. And the Pharaoh and all his courtiers were pleased.

17 Then the Pharaoh told Joseph to say to his brothers, Do this:[a] load[b] your donkeys and go to the land of Canaan.

18 Bring your father and your households and come to me! I will give you the produce[a] of Egypt and you shall eat of the fat of the land.[b]

19 Now you are to instruct them:[a] This is what you are to do. Take wagons[b] from Egypt for your little ones and wives and bring[c] your father and come down!

20 Have no regrets over your household possessions[a] because the produce of the whole of Egypt will be yours.

21 The sons of Israel did so;[a] in accordance with the Pharaoh's instructions Joseph gave them wagons and provisions for the journey.

22 To each of them he gave a festal robe, but to Benjamin he gave three hundred pieces of silver and five festal robes.

23 He likewise[a] sent to his father ten donkeys loaded with the produce of Egypt, ten she-asses loaded with grain, bread, and provisions[b] for his journey.

24 As he farewelled his brothers on their departure he said to them, Do not quarrel[a] on the way!

25 So they went up from Egypt to the land of Canaan to their father Jacob.

26 They told him, Joseph is still alive and is ruler over the whole of the land of Egypt! But his heart remained cold, for he did not believe them.

27 But when they had told him everything that Joseph had said to them, and he had seen the wagons that Joseph had sent to bring him down, then the spirit of their father Jacob revived.

28 And Israel said, Enough;[a] Joseph my son is alive. I will go down and see him before I die.

1a אפק hithp., likewise Gen. 43:31; cf. 1 Sam. 13:12, always in the absolute. **b** Construction, Ges-K §138d.   **c** Num. 12:6.
2a Read with Gk כל־הַמִּצְרִים.   **b** Gk and Syr niph., but MT is possible.
3a In vv. 3 and 4 Gk differs from MT.
4a On the relative clause, Ges-K §138d; BrSynt §153a; E. Schild, VT 4 (1954) 297ff.; T. C. Vriezen, RechBibl 8 (1963) 44.
5a עצב niph., "be distressed," "grieve"; in hithp. Gen. 6:6; 34:7.
7a On the difficulty of the construction in v. 7, to which H. Gunkel and J. Skinner drew attention, and on the interchange in the following verse, see comm.
10a Instead of Goshen Gk reads Γέσεμ Ἀραβίας (as in Neh. 6:1). Cf. J. Skinner in detail ad loc. and J. Vergote, *Joseph en Egypte. . .* (1959) 183-187.   **b** אל can designate the state of rest at the goal achieved; BrSynt §108.
11a The same verb as in 47:12; 50:21.   **b** ירש niph. as in Prov. 20:13; others derive it from רוש.
13a On כבוד with this meaning, F. Nötscher, VT 2 (1952) 358-362.
17a On the construction, BrSynt §133a.   **b** The verb only here; see M. Delcor, VT 25 (1975) 310.
18a Also in vv. 20, 23; cf. Gen. 24:10; 2 Kings 8:9; M. Mannati, VT 19 (1969) 488-493.   **b** The expression is found only here; cf. J. Heller, VT 20 (1970) 106-108.
19a Really "the command is over to you," "you are empowered," A. Dillmann. Others read piel with Gk and Vg.   **b** עגלה is a carriage or freight wagon (Egypt. *'agolt*, loanword), cf. BRL^2 1977, 366 with picture.   **c** For this meaning, M. H. Gottstein, VT 3 (1953) 298-299.
20a Cf. Deut. 7:16; Is. 13:18.
21a Many regard the first sentence as a gloss; perhaps it is deliberate, meant to balance the imperatives in v. 19.
23a On the form, Ges-K §102g; "so pointed only here," J. Skinner.   **b** The word occurs elsewhere only in 2 Chron. 11:23; Ps. 144:13.
24a Sam has hithp., perhaps correctly; cf. Is. 37:28f.
28a לי to be supplied with Gk, Targ, Syr. On the exclamation, BrSynt §11a; cf. Ex. 9:28; Num. 16:3; Deut. 1:6; 2:3; 2 Sam. 24:16.

Form

Ch. 45 is the immediate continuation of ch. 44. The scene in which Joseph makes himself known to his brothers, vv. 1-8, takes the place of an answer to Judah's request, 44:(18), 33-34. Then follow the instructions about the father (vv. 9-13), the greeting of the brothers (vv. 14-15), the confirmation of the invitation to the father by the Pharaoh (vv. 16-21), presents and farewell (vv. 22-24).

The source division of ch. 45 reached its high point with H. Gunkel and O. Procksch; each proposes something very complicated and very different. H. Gunkel acknowledges that it is uncertain. Hence J. Skinner concludes that a complete separation into sources is not possible; likewise E. A. Speiser. H. Donner has studied the division into sources in ch. 45 and concludes that it rests merely on "external formalities of literary style" which show no signs of serious contradiction or tension (*Die literarische Gestalt.* . . [1976] 20-24). He maintains that it is a unity and resumes many of the arguments of W. Rudolf (BZAW 63 [1933] 145-184). An argument against source division, according to Donner, is that the attempts of H. Gunkel, O. Procksch, O. Eissfeldt, M. Noth, L. Ruppert (one can add H. C. Schmitt) diverge so markedly from each other. A particularly weighty argument is the apparent doublet in vv. 3 and 4. H. Gunkel writes, "Joseph reveals himself twice—3a/4b." But they are two different sentences, the second a necessary expansion of the first (so W. Rudolf, G. von Rad, E. A. Speiser, G. W. Coats, H. Donner, and others). D. B. Redford comments that the separation of v. 3 from v. 4 into two sources "rends asunder a passage as delicate in feeling as any in the Joseph-story. . .. That Joseph should repeat his words under these circumstances would be the most natural thing in the world! And why should a redactor preserve variants virtually identical?" (VT.S 20 [1970] 109). Other repetitions are of a literary kind. One must agree with H. Donner that there is nowhere a manifest contradiction. Ch. 45 is a particularly obvious example where only a preconception can have led to source division. It is significant too that H. C. Schmitt (BZAW 154 [1980]), while maintaining the separation into Reuben and Judah layers, assigns the main part to the Reuben layer; there are only fragments of the Judah layer. He rejects any source division of vv. 5b-8.

Commentary

[**45:1-8**] Joseph's speech, introduced in vv. 1-2, is divided into an address to the brothers (vv. 3-8) and instructions relating to the father (vv. 9-13). The address to the brothers is a self-contained unity; vv. 5-8 cannot be separated from vv. 3-4.

[**45:1-2**] The introduction, vv. 1-2, has the important function in the Joseph story as a whole of making the transition from political back to family history; what happens, what is said, now takes place within the family circle of Jacob. The last sentence of v. 1 says this expressly; with the withdrawal of the attendants and courtiers the scene changes from an event in the Pharaoh's court to an event in the family of Jacob. Joseph is so moved that he is on the verge of tears (v. 1a); with the change of scene he can let them flow (v. 2a). The Egyptians can certainly hear him, but they take no part in what now happens between the brothers, v. 1bβ.

[**45:3-8**] Joseph's address to his brothers is introduced, "And Joseph said to his brothers." Joseph has once more become their brother and as such he speaks to them. His deep emotion is shown by the two abrupt sentences, "I am Joseph! Is my father still alive?" But he had long since known this (e.g., H. Gunkel); it does not square with the context (G. W. Coats). Nevertheless, he puts the burning question as the son inquiring about his father; it is not the same question as that of the official beforehand. Joseph so surprises his brothers with the two questions that they are, as it were, struck dumb.

[**45:4**] After the first emotional outburst Joseph has to bridge the gap. He does this with both word and gesture (v. 4), corresponding to the first step in the rapprochement (vv. 1-3). But for the brothers the scene has not yet changed; they remain as it were outside the pale, at a distance, as the custom of the court demanded. Joseph asks them to come closer to him; they do so (v. 4a). Once more he makes himself known as their brother, but now recalling their common history,

". . .your brother whom you sold into Egypt" (v. 4b). Anyone could say, "I am Joseph"; only he could say, "I am Joseph your brother whom. . . ." The situation requires this extension of the first sentence. The narrator intends this progressive heightening; it gives the scene its character. This is confirmed by the structure, two three-part divisions: word for word the same introduction vv. 3aα-4aα, the gesture vv. 1-4aβ, the words to the brothers vv. 3aβ-4b. This is typical of the narrator of the Joseph story; his doublings always have a narrative purpose.

[**45:5-8**] Context and structure of vv. 5-8. These verses play a leading role in all explanations of the Joseph story. They are almost always regarded, with 50:19-21, as its central theological statement. G. von Rad writes, "Here in the scene of recognition the narrator indicates clearly for the first time what is of paramount importance to him in the entire Joseph story: God's hand, which directs all the confusion of human guilt ultimately toward a gracious goal." And W. Brueggemann: "the center and focus of the Joseph narrative" (JAAR 40 [1972] 96-109). The central significance given to 45:5-8 has often led to the text being isolated from its context as if it were an independent sentence or teaching; so H. P. Müller: "the teaching to be derived from the course of the action" ("Die weisheitliche Lehrerzählung im AT und seiner Umwelt," WO 9 [1977] 77-98). The narrator's intent is discovered only when these words are explained out of the context of vv. 1-8 and their broader context as well. The context requires no explanation. Joseph had to recall the past so as to identify himself beyond doubt. But he had also to touch on the brothers' guilt (vv. 1-4). He does everything to calm them, to remove the fear that must have been welling up within them. He calms them in vv. 5-8.

Joseph calms his brothers; the sentence is in two parts; the part introduced by כִּי, vv. 6-8, explains what he means. The words of v. 5 have the structure of an assurance that all will be well: Do not be distressed (so literally 50:20), God has acted (G. W. Coats has seen this correctly, CBQMS 4 [1976] 90f.). But it is an assurance given in a noncultic or precultic form (cf. comm. on 43:23). What Joseph wants to say to his brothers in v. 5 is said with a verb in the perfect: God has acted (as 44:16). The narrator's intention is not to be found in a sapiential saying or teaching, but only in the sentence which alleges God's action as the reason why the brothers are not to be distressed: God has sent me ahead of you. Joseph wants to turn the eyes of the brothers to this action of God and thus remove their fear. It is explained further in vv. 6-8.

Almost all explanations of the passage speak of God's providence (H. Gunkel, G. von Rad, D. B. Redford). But one must be quite clear that this is not what the text is talking about. The Joseph story knows nothing of a concept of this kind. Had the narrator wanted to say something like this, he would have had to express himself differently. To explain the verse as the working of God's providence does not fit the structure of v. 5, which sentence is in the perfect; the explanation could only be described as a reflective conclusion from what has been said.

The explanation of v. 5 that Joseph gives in vv. 6-8 raises considerable difficulties to which the commentators have given attention. The main difficulty is that v. 7b does not fit the context comfortably:

> to preserve you [as] a remnant in the land,
> to keep you alive,
> [as] a great host of survivors.

How can Jacob's family be described as a "remnant"? A remnant of
what? (The word שארית occurs only here in the Pentateuch.) The parallelism in
form indicates poetic language which has a strange effect in a sentence of explanation. Two words, "remnant" and "the saved" (or survivors) occur predominantly only in prophecy (for list of places, L. Ruppert, *Die Josepherzählung der Genesis. . .* [1965]; H. Wildberger, E. Ruprecht, THAT II, 844-855 and 420-427,
with bibliog.). Those few passages where both words stand in parallelism are decisive for the understanding of v. 7b. They belong to the context of the late
prophetic expectation of salvation; see particularly Is. 37:32 = 2 Kings 19:31 (cf.
H. Wildberger, *Jesaja 28–39*, comm. on 37:32): For out of Jerusalem shall go
forth a remnant, and out of Mount Zion a band of survivors; cf. Is. 10:20; 15:9;
Ezra 9:14. H. C. Schmitt also puts the sentence in the late prophetic period because of the parallelism remnant/survivors (the designation "a remnant in the
land" also points in this direction). V. 7b then is a late expansion like the late expansions in the patriarchal promises. It is easier to understand the insertion when
the words להחיות לכם, taken by the interpolator from the Joseph story (cf. v. 5),
are bracketed out; the parallelism thereby becomes clearer.

A further difficulty, closely linked with this, is that the sequence of the
sentences after v. 6, i.e., in vv. 7-8, are difficult to follow; several exegetes have
drawn attention to this. The difficulty can be met if it is presupposed that it arose
only with the insertion of v. 7b.

In v. 5 Joseph bases the statement "God sent me ahead of you" on God's
intention "to save lives." The verb is deliberately without an object; God's purpose does not concern the family of Jacob alone. It is explained further in vv. 6-8:
God "sent him ahead" (a circumlocution pardoning the brothers) so as to avert by
his administration the famine in Egypt and beyond. V. 6 follows directly on this;
there have already been two years of famine and five more still remain. The explanation now must tell how God (through Joseph) intervened against the famine. V.
7a begins, "But God sent me ahead. . . ." Originally v. 8b followed: God raised
Joseph to high office in Egypt which enabled him to take practical measures. The
sequence of the sentences has been disturbed by the subsequent insertion of v. 7b;
v. 8b follows on v. 7a; it explains to the brothers why they can be at ease. By way
of conclusion Joseph repeats once more, and so with emphasis, what this means
for the brothers: "So then it was not you who sent me down here, but God." This
closes the explanation. Only now does its self-contained structure become clear,
underscored by the device of *inclusio*: the first sentence begins (v. 5a) and the last
ends (v. 8a) with ועתה. The restored text is as in the translation above.

[**45:5**] The ועתה in v. 5 stands out in contrast to the relative clause in v. 5b,
"then—but now!" The fear that could seize them because of what they had once
done he averts in two sentences (cf. 50:19). The verb עצב niph. means "be distressed," "grieve," as, e.g., in 1 Sam. 20:3, 34. The second verb is literally,
"let there not blaze up in your eyes," the anger that is directed at a single person
(cf. Gen. 31:35). Joseph does not want to diminish in any way the brothers' guilt,
much less deny it; rather it remains heavy on them, as 44:16 has shown. Joseph
puts all that was set in motion in Jacob's family by the brothers' crime into a
broader context, that of God who protects and sustains life; he thus lets his brothers know that he has forgiven them. The narrator shows his human understanding
by allowing Joseph to let his brothers know that they have been forgiven (similarly

in ch. 32) without saying as much. The brothers are thus spared being put to shame. The narrator's intent is at the same time to make a theological link between the both cycles of the Joseph story. The same God who protects life (מחיה) in the kingdom of the Pharaoh heals the breach in Jacob's family; both together form a harmony.

[**45:6**] V. 6 carries the למחיה of v. 5 further. God's purpose was to preserve life in face of the extraordinary length and severity of the famine. The famine is described in v. 6b as אין־חריש וקציר (both together in the Sabbath command in Ex. 34:21). The rhythm of sowing and harvest (Gen. 8:22), which sustains life, is disturbed for a long period.

[**45:7a,8b**] But God can preserve life even where its rhythm is interrupted: This is why he brought me here (v. 7a); this is why he raised me to high office (v. 8b). The office is described in different terms than in ch. 41, conditioned by the address to the brothers; Joseph wants to make his position comprehensible to them (D. B. Redford: they have a Hebraic ring). He describes it under three aspects. He is "father to the Pharaoh," inasmuch as he counsels him like a father; there is no exact equivalent in Egypt. He is "master over all his household," as in 41:40 insofar as the house or court of the Pharaoh is the center of the whole kingdom. He is "ruler of the whole of Egypt" and so can carry out the practical measures which the land needs. It is precisely Joseph's high status in Egypt, seen under these aspects, that enabled him to execute the economic measures he had proposed.

[**45:8a**] Joseph has thereby explained to his brothers what he means by asking them to be calm. Once more (ועתה, as in v. 5) he comes back to the operative sentence, deliberately introducing a variation by referring to them, "So then it was not you who sent me down here, but God." Joseph tells his brothers in the first (v. 5) and last sentences (v. 8a) that God has been at work. At the same time God has "saved lives" and brought together again those who have been separated; his action comprises the crisis in the great kingdom of Egypt and the endangerment to the family of Jacob.

[**45:7b**] This later expansion expresses the point of view of a period when the existence of Israel was constantly under threat; it is an insertion promising that a remnant will remain from those who have survived the contemporary catastrophe. The person who inserted it found a point of contact between God's action, as Joseph describes it here, in face of a catastrophe, and God's intervention on behalf of his people under threat in the postexilic period. It is particularly valuable for the exegesis of vv. 5-8 because whoever inserted it did not understand Joseph's explanation to his brothers as some sort of abstract belief in providence, but as trust in God who acts to save and preserve.

[**45:9-13**] After Joseph's explanation with the forgiveness implied in it, one expects now what happens only in vv. 14-15, namely, the appropriate gesture of greeting. But the instructions concerning the father take precedence (vv. 9-13); this is due to Joseph's urgent longing to see his father again, as already indicated in his first question, "Is my father still alive?" The formal message is conveyed in vv. 9-12, followed by the more general commission to give a full report to the father (v. 13).

[**45:9-12**] These verses are divided into the commission (v. 9a) and the message (vv. 9b-12). The narrator uses here the official form for commissioning a messenger as well as the messenger formula (cf. *Genesis 12–36*, comm. on 32:4-6), not only because Joseph sets such store on his very words reaching his father ("hurry, go back. . ."), but also because the form allows the sender to speak to the addressee immediately by means of the messenger's voice. As is often the case the message contains an indicative (v. 9b) and an imperative part (vv. 10-12). The indicative part tells that he has become ruler of Egypt; he reports this in the form "God has made me. . ." so as to point out the connection between the paternal house and the kingdom of the Pharaoh; it is God who has made the impossible possible. The invitation to his father to come down to Egypt constitutes the imperative part (vv. 9bβ, 10-12; it is expressed in the last four words of v. 9 as a pressing invitation to come quickly, and is developed in vv. 10-11. In v. 10a he tells Jacob where he is to live, and in v. 10b includes the whole of Jacob's family, his stock, and his possessions. The land of Goshen is "an area on the eastern edge of the delta near the desert" (J. Simons), "Wadi Tumilat, a narrow valley between the Nile and the Bitter Lake" (H. Gunkel); it is "most likely" chosen as a settlement (O. Procksch) because it was "on the border region where immigrants of this kind used to wait for notice concerning their story" (J. Simons). This being so, then this piece of information does not anticipate the Pharaoh's decision, nor can one suppose that v. 10a is a subsequent addition (W. Rudolf, after 47:6). The additional note "and you shall be near me" is not intended as an exact indication of place; it is meant to contrast with the present long distance between them. The assurance that he will take care of them there (v. 11) does not contradict v. 10 nor is it superfluous, because it has regard to the situation caused by the prevalent famine. The verb "take care" (pilp. of כול) is used in the same sense in 47:12; 50:21; ירשׁ niph. "that you. . . are not reduced to poverty," KBL; cf. Prov. 20:13; 23:21; 30:9.

[**45:12**] Joseph's message to his father is now concluded. It is reliable and confirmed by the fact that the brothers and Benjamin, who had not shared the previous experience, are eyewitnesses. It was really Joseph who said this (v. 12).

[**45:13**] Moreover, they are to tell their father about Joseph's highly regarded position at the Egyptian court (כבוד in this sense, THAT I, 794-811; F. Nötscher, VT 2 [1952] 358-362) and above all what they have seen of his work there.

[**45:14-15**] Joseph was so taken up with the message to his father that only now does he greet and embrace his brothers (cf. Gen. 24:33, comm.); once again they are truly his brothers. He first throws his arms around Benjamin, and then the others. Only then is the ban really lifted, only now can they speak to Joseph as to their brother. The breach is now really healed.

[**45:16-21**] Immediately after the greeting and reconciliation Joseph gives his brothers lavish presents and takes leave of them (vv. 22-24). In the meantime, however, Joseph's invitation to Jacob's family must be confirmed by the Pharaoh (vv. 16-21). Joseph belongs to the court, and the court must give its consent if he wants to bring his family to Egypt.

[**45:16**] V. 16 resumes the scene of vv. 1-2. The attendants and courtiers had withdrawn (v. 1), but they had noticed what was going on (v. 2). The news of it was passed on to the Pharaoh (v. 16a). Just as at the beginning the Pharaoh and his court had given their approval to the advice of the unknown Hebrew slave (41:37, the same expression), so too they now give their approval and are glad that Joseph is united again with his family.

[45:17-20] The Pharaoh confirms Joseph's invitation to his father by sanctioning it as his own command. One certainly cannot say that the Pharaoh's command in vv. 17-20 stands opposed to Joseph's invitation (vv. 9-13). The narrative as a whole tells us much more; the Pharaoh has occasion here to do a service for his minister of state who had saved his kingdom from famine, and he does it joyfully. What follows is a statement of the Pharaoh to his minister (v. 17aα) who is to pass it on to the brothers (vv. 17aβ); it is thus the Pharaoh's command that the brothers carry out: זאת עשׂו. When they fetch their father, they do so under the Pharaoh's instructions (v. 21aα).

[45:17b-20] Hence the Pharaoh's command to the brothers through Joseph agrees with the instructions that Joseph has given (vv. 9-13): load the animals. . . return to Canaan. . . bring your father down (vv. 17b-18a), together with a generous offer to take care of them in Egypt (v. 18b). Joseph named a particular strip of land, Goshen; the Pharaoh speaks in more general and generous terms of "the produce of Egypt," "that you may eat of the fat of the land" (particularly fertile land, an expression used only here; cf. J. Heller [1970]; M. Mannati [1969], bibliog. above). The Pharaoh then adds specific instructions for the return journey: the brothers are to take wagons with them from Egypt for the children, wives, and Joseph's aged father. In choosing the wagons they are not to consider the household goods; they can obtain these in plenty in Egypt. The Pharaoh has thereby granted them permission to cross the border into Egypt on their return.

Repetitions and contradictions have been found in the text of vv. 9-13. But there are no real contradictions; the repetition is intentional; the generous royal instructions of vv. 17-20 differ clearly from the sober and more modest instructions of Joseph.

[45:21] It is expressly reported that the Pharaoh's instructions are carried out (v. 21a; cf. v. 17); it is a necessary complement to v. 17; it is not a gloss, as W. Rudolf thinks. The brothers are once more united with Joseph as בני־ישׂראל. Joseph procures for them the wagons "in accordance with the Pharaoh's instructions." He also gives them supplies for the journey, indicating that they are to depart immediately.

[45:22-24] Joseph gives them presents and takes leave of them. These verses could follow immediately on vv. 14-15. The presents are part of the reconciliation, as it were a ברכה (cf. *Genesis 12–36*, comm. on 32:1ff.; 33:11). When Joseph presents the brothers with festal robes (actually changes of clothes, for special occasions), there may be a thought of Joseph's tunic with its sleeves. But it is significant that the narrator does not need to make any such reference. When Benjamin receives five festal robes and 300 silver pieces in addition, Joseph trusts that the other brothers will perceive this predilection. He also sends presents for his father to testify to his love for him as well as a sign of his joy that he is now in a position to bestow largess on the old man. And so he takes leave of his brothers. He gives them an admonition for the journey, "Do not quarrel. . .!" (v. 24). The narrator is saying with subtle sensitivity that despite the change, they know that they are not angels.

[**45:25-28**] The return of the brothers to the father: These verses bring to a close the section that began in 43:1 with the father's request to the brothers to go to Egypt a second time. The return journey, interrupted in 44:6, now continues; but everything has changed. Only v. 25 speaks of the return, corresponding to an itinerary (cf. 42:29). Attention is entirely on the meeting with the father (vv. 26-28). Again the parallel is unobtrusive; it is the broader context that makes itself heard. Just as the brothers were unable at first to grasp that Joseph was "the man" (v. 3), so too the father cannot believe it as the brothers make their report. The language is stronger here: "his heart remained cold, for he did not believe them"(v. 26). The narrator wants to allude to 37:31-36 and for a moment it seems that the old estrangement might return. But the brothers now deliver Joseph's formal message (vv. 9-13). "They told him all that Joseph had said to them." At the words "God has made me. . ." he recognizes his son again. He can now acknowledge the wagons as witness and believe the story behind it all; his spirit revives (cf. Pss. 22:27; 69:33).

[**45:28**] This verse follows immediately on what precedes and is shown by the context to be the transition to ch. 46. The change of name from Jacob in v. 27 to Israel in v. 28 does not postulate a different source for v. 28 (as do many exegetes). As we have already seen (Excursus on "Israel," ch. 43), the change of name is no conclusive criterion for source division. One cannot be certain of the reason for the change here (see the suggestions of F. Delitzsch and B. Jacob). In any case it is a storyteller who puts v. 28 after v. 27. It is the same storyteller who at the beginning, ch. 37, repeated Jacob's lament, "Joseph is torn to pieces, torn to pieces," and who now brings to its conclusion the span arching from that moment to the present with the words, "Enough. Joseph my son is alive!" He is now confident that he will see him again and this gives him the strength to undertake the long journey. He will then be able to die in peace.

Purpose and Thrust

The title of ch. 45 is "Joseph makes himself known to his brothers." He can do this only by reminding them of their guilt. "I am Joseph your brother whom you sold into Egypt." By making himself known to them he has at the same time forgiven them. He can do this because the brothers have passed the test set for them and because Judah had already said, "God has discovered the wickedness of your servants." Joseph, however, hides his forgiveness in the sentence in which he brings together what has happened in Jacob's family and what has happened through his instrumentality in the kingdom of Egypt. God has preserved the family in a time of famine and brought it together again while preparing the occasion for it in Joseph's activity at the court. The two cycles that make up the Joseph story come together in God's action which both forgives and preserves, an action embracing Jacob's family and the kingdom of Egypt. When the brothers entered Joseph's house to face their last and most severe test, the steward received them with the same words that Joseph uses at the end to describe all that has happened: ''Fear not! God has. . ..'' The two lines of the Joseph story come together in God's marvellous action; it is this that gives the narrative its cohesion and purpose.

Genesis 46:1-30

Jacob's Journey to Egypt:
His Reunion with Joseph

Literature

Genesis 46:1-4: E. Norden, *Agnostos Theos: Untersuchungen zur Formgeschichte religiöser Rede* (1913; 1971[5]) esp. 177-239. A. Poebel, "Das appositionell bestimmte Pronomen der 1. Pers. Sing. in den westsemitischen Inschriften und im AT," AS 3 (1932) 60-72. W. Zimmerli, *Geschichte und Tradition von Beerseba im AT* (diss. Göttingen, 1932). S. H. Hooke, *In the Beginnings* (1947; 1950[2]). S. Yeivin, "Beersheba, City of the Patriarchs," *Zion* 20 (1953) 117-127. W. Zimmerli, "Ich bin Jahwe," BHTh 16 (1953) 179-222 = ThB 19 (1963) 11-40. N. Glueck, "The Age of Abraham," BA 18 (1955) 1-9. K. T. Andersen, "Der Gott meines Vaters," StTh 16 (1962) 170-188. F. M. Cross, "Yahweh and the God of the Patriarchs," HThR 55 (1962) 225-259. S. Plath, "Furcht Gottes: Der Begriff ירא im AT," AzTh II,4 (1963) esp. 114-122. A. Cody, "When Is the Chosen People Called a *Gôy*," VT 14 (1964) 1-6. J. P. Hyatt, "The Origin of Mosaic Yahwism," *Mem. of H. Trantham II* (1964) 85-93. A. Besters, " 'Israël' et 'fils d'Israël' dans les livres historiques (Genèse—II Rois)," RB 74 (1967) 5-23. H. M. Dion, "The Patriarchal Traditions and the Literary Form of the 'Oracle of Salvation,' " CBQ 29 (1967) 198-206. J. G. Heintz, "Oracles prophétiques et 'Guerre Sainte' selon les Archives Royales de Mari et l'Ancien Testament," VT.S 17 (1969) 112-138. A. Ohler, *Mythologische Elemente im AT: Eine motivgeschichtliche Untersuchung* (1969). G. W. Coats, "The Wilderness Itinerary," CBQ 34 (1972) 135-152. G. I. Davies, "The Wilderness Itineraries: A Comparative Study," TynB 25 (1974) 46-81. F. Langlamet, "Rezension K. Jaroš, *Die Stellung des Elohisten zur kanaanäischen Religion,*" RB 83 (1976) 105-108. R. Rendtorff, *Das überlieferungsgeschichtliche Problem des Pentateuch* (1976; 1977[2]). C. Westermann, *The Promises to the Fathers* (1976; Eng. 1980). G. Hentschel, "Jakobs Kampf am Jabbok (Gen. 32,23-33)—eine genuin israelitische Tradition?" *Fests. z. 25 jähr. Bestehen d. phil.-theol. Studiums im Priesterseminar Erfurt* (1977) 13-37. J. Van Seters, "The Yahwist as Theologian? A Response," JSOT (1977) 15-19.

Genesis 46:5-7: S. de Vries, "The Hexateuchal Criticism of Abraham Kuenen," JBL 82 (1963) 31-57.

Genesis 46:8-30: M. Noth, *Die israelitischen Personennamen im Rahmen der gemeinsemitischen Namengebung*, BWANT 3, 10 (1928; 1966[2]); *Das System der zwölf Stämme Israels*, BWANT 4,1 (1930; 1966[2]). F. M. Abel, *Géographie de la Palestine II* (1938) esp. 255. H. Eising, *Formgeschichtliche Untersuchung zur Josepherzählung der Genesis* (diss. Münster, 1940). P. Dhorme, "Abraham dans le cadre de l'histoire," *Recueil E. Dhorme* (1951) 191-272. W. Helck, *Die Beziehungen Ägyptens zu Vorderasien im 3. und 2. Jt. v. Chr.*, ÄA 43 (1962). L. Ramlot, "Les généalogies bibliques: Un genre littéraire oriental," BVC 60 (1964) 53-70. A. Wieder, "Ugaritic-Hebrew Lexicographical

Notes,'' JBL 84 (1965) 160-164. N. P. Bratsiotis, ''נֶפֶשׁ—ΨYXH. Ein Beitrag zur Erforschung der Sprache und der Theologie der Septuaginta,'' VT.S 15 (1966) 58-89. D. Lys, ''The Israelite Soul according to the LXX,'' VT 16 (1966) 181-228. A. Ahuvyah, '' 'Alle, die nach Ägypten kamen' (Gen. 46, 8-27),'' BetM 3 (1966/67) 119-122. D. A. McKenzie, ''The Judge of Israel,'' VT 17 (1967) 118-121. T. C. Vriezen, ''Exodusstudien: Exodus I,'' VT 17 (1967) 334-353. W. Wifall, ''Asshur and Eber, or Asher and Heber? A Commentary on the Last Balaam Oracle, Num. 24,21-24,'' ZAW 82 (1970) 110-114. H. Donner, ''Die Palästinabeschreibung des Epiphanius Monachus Hagiopolita,'' ZDPV 87 (1971) 42-91. G. W. Coats, ''A Structural Transition in Exodus,'' VT 22 (1972) 129-142. H. Weippert, ''Das geographische System der Stämme Israels,'' VT 23 (1973) 76-89. H. G. M. Williamson, ''A Note on 1 Chronicles VII 12,'' VT 23 (1973) 375-379. W. Speyer, ''Genealogie,'' RAC (1976) 1145-1268. R. R. Wilson, *Genealogy and History in the Biblical World*, YNES 7 (1977). J. M. Sasson, ''A Genealogical 'Convention' in Biblical Chronography?'' ZAW 90 (1978) 171-185.

Text

46:1   So Israel set out with all that he had. Now when he came to Beersheba he offered sacrifice[a] to the God of his father Isaac.

2   Then God spoke to Israel in a vision[a] by night. He said, Jacob, Jacob! And he said, Here I am!

3   And he said, I am God, the God of your father. Do not be afraid to go down[a] to Egypt, for I will make you a great nation there.

4   I will go down to Egypt with you, and I myself will bring you back again,[a] and Joseph shall close your eyes.

5a   Then Jacob set out from[a] Beersheba.

5b   So the sons of Israel carried Jacob, their father, and their little ones and their wives on the wagons that Pharaoh had sent to fetch them.

6   And they took their cattle[a] and their possessions which they had acquired in the land of Canaan and came to Egypt, Jacob and all his descendants with him,[b]

7   his sons and his grandsons, his daughters and his granddaughters;[a] he brought all his descendants down to Egypt with him.

8   These are the names[a] of the sons of Israel who came to Egypt, Jacob and his sons: Reuben was Jacob's firstborn;[b]

9   the sons of Reuben were: Hanoch,[a] Pallu,[b] Hezron,[c] and Carmi.[d]

10   The sons of Simeon: Jemuel,[a] Jamin,[b] Ohad,[c] Jachin,[d] Zohar,[e] and Shaul,[f] the son of a Canaanite woman.

11   The sons of Levi: Gershon,[a] Kohath,[b] and Merari.[c]

12   The sons of Judah: Er,[a] Onan, Shelah, Perez, and Zerah; now Er and Onan died in the land of Canaan; and the sons of Perez were Hezron[b] and Hamul.[c]

13   The sons of Issachar: Tola,[a] Puvah,[b] Iob [Yashub],[c] and Shimron.[d]

14   The sons of Zebulun: Sered,[a] Elon,[b] and Jahleel.[c]

15   These are the sons of Leah, whom she bore to Jacob in Paddan-aram, with his daughter Dinah;[a] his sons and daughters numbered thirty-three in all.

16   The sons of Gad: Ziphion,[a] Haggi,[b] Shuni,[c] Ezbon,[d] Eri,[e] Arodi,[f] and Areli.[g]

17   The sons of Asher: Imnah,[a] Ishvah,[b] Ishvi,[c] Beriah,[d] and Serah[e] their sister.
And the sons of Beriah were Heber[f] and Malchiel.[g]

18   These are the sons of Zilpah, whom Laban gave to Leah his daughter, and these she bore to Jacob, sixteen persons in all.

19   The sons of Rachel, Jacob's wife: Joseph and Benjamin.

20   Manasseh and Ephraim[a] were born to Joseph in the land of Egypt from Asenath, the daughter of Potiphera the priest of On.
21   The sons of Benjamin: Bela,[a] Becher,[b] Ashbel,[c] Gera,[d] Naaman,[e] Ehi,[f] Rosh, Muppim,[g] Huppim,[h] and Ard.[i]
22   These are the sons of Rachel, whom she 'bore'[a] to Jacob—fourteen persons in all.
23   The sons of Dan: Hushim.[a]
24   The sons of Naphtali: Jahzeel,[a] Guni,[b] Jezer,[c] and Shillem.[d]
25   These are the sons of Bilhah, whom Laban gave to Rachel his daughter, and these she bore to Jacob—seven persons in all.
26   All the persons belonging to Jacob who came to Egypt, bodily descendants, not including the wives of Jacob's sons, were sixty-six in all.
27   The sons of Joseph, born to him in Egypt, were two. The persons of Jacob's family who came to Egypt were seventy[a] in all.
28   Now he sent Judah ahead of him to Joseph; 'would he come to meet him?'[a] And they came to the land of Goshen.[b]
29   Then Joseph had his chariot made ready and went up to Goshen to meet his father. 'And when he saw him',[a] he threw his arms around his neck and wept and embraced him for a long time.
30   Then Israel said to Joseph, Now I am ready to die,[a] now that I have seen your face and know that you are alive.[b]

1a On the paronomasia, BrSynt §91.
2a Plur. with sing. meaning, see comm.
3a Form, Ges-K §69m.
4a Inf. abs., Ges-K §113w; BrSynt §93c; cf. Gen. 27:33; 31:15.
5a The phrase קום מן is typical of the itinerary; all passages in B. Jacob, comm. ad loc.
6a Vv. 6-7, P; cf. Gen. 12:5; 31:18; 36:6.   b Cf. Gen. 17:7, 9f.; 35:12.
7a The sons' daughters are mentioned only here.
8a אלה שמות as in Gen. 25:13; 36:10.   b בכר as in Gen. 27:32; 35:23; 49:3; cf. 25:13.
9a (1) Son of Cain, Gen. 4:17; (2) Son of ירד, Gen. 5:18f., 21-24; 1 Chron. 1:3; (3) Son of Midian, Gen. 25:4; 1 Chron. 1:33; (4) Son of Reuben, Gen. 46:9; Ex. 6:14; Num. 26:5; 1 Chron. 5:5. Explanation of name, *Genesis 1–11*, comm. on 4:17.   b Also Ex. 6:14; Num. 26:5, 8; 1 Chron. 5:3. According to M. Noth, from פלא "to act miraculously," BWANT 3, 10 (1928, 1966²); cf. פליה, Neh. 8:7; 10:11.   c Ex. 6:14; Num. 26:6; 1 Chron. 3:3; second son of Perez, 46:12; Num. 26:21; 1 Chron. 2:5, 9, 15, 21, 24f.; 4:1; Ruth 4:18f.   d Ex. 6:14; Num. 26:6 (the parallels from Ex. 6; Num. 26; and 1 Chron. 2–8 will not be given in detail in what follows); the father of Achan, Josh. 7:1, 18; perhaps derived from כרם.
10a In this form also in Ex. 6:15f; Num. 26:12; 1 Chron. 4:24 נמואל.   b Meaning "good fortune," to be understood as a good omen, M. Noth, BWANT 3,10 (1928, 1966²) 224; cf. בנימין.   c Missing in Num. and 1 Chron., also in Gk; uncertain, some suggest a link with אהוד.   d Meaning, "he is [let him be] firm," or "may God make firm," M. Noth 222; in 1 Kings 7:21, name of a pillar in the temple.   e In Num. 26:13, זרח; Gen. 23:8; 25:9, father of the Hittite Ephron; meaning "pink" perhaps, M. Noth 225.   f In Gen. 36:37f., an Edomite king.
11a A son of Moses, Ex. 2:22;18:3; variant גרשם Ezra 8:2; meaning "(hand)bell" (?), M. Noth 223.   b Meaning, following the Ug. 'qht = "hero"? According to Ex. 6:18 Moses and Aaron are from the line of Kohath.   c Also in Ezra 8:19 as a Levitical family; meaning "physical strength" (?), M. Noth 225.
12a On the sons of Judah, cf. comm. on 38:1-19.   b See v. 9.   c Pass. part of חמל = "spared"? M. Noth 181; Sam., as 1 Chron. 4:26, חמואל.
13a Judg. 10:1, as a judge from the tribe Issachar and son of פואה as Sam, Syr; meaning

"mollusk''? Cf. D. A. McKenzie, VT 17 (1967) 118-121.   **b** Judg. 10:1 פּוּאָה.   **c** Read יָשׁוּב with Gk, Sam, Num., 1 Chron.; abbreviated theophoric name, "May God attend."   **d** Cf. Judg. 10:1 שָׁמִיר on the mountains of Ephraim, Tola's native town; cf. the masc. name שֶׁמֶר (Shemer = "rich harvest''?), 1 Kings 16:24.

14a *bu-srd* (KBL) occurs in Ug.   **b** Cf. Judg. 12:11 the judge אֵילוֹן from Zebulun (meaning "tree," M. Noth 230).   **c** Probably from יָחֶל לָאֵל, "let him wait for God''; differently M. Noth 204.

15a Cf. *Genesis 12–36*, comm. on 29:31-35; 30:17-21.

16a Sam, Gk, Num read צָפוֹן; in Josh. 19:27; Judg. 12:1 a city to the east of the Jordan.   **b** Meaning "born on a feast day''; others suggest that it is a shortened form.   **c** So far unexplained.   **d** Perhaps with Sam, Syr, אֶצְבְּעוֹן; Num. 26:16 אָזְנִי.   **e** Meaning "watchful'' (from עוּר)?   **f** Meaning "hunchbacked''? M. Noth 227.   **g** Unexplained.

17a Perhaps the same meaning as יָמִין, v. 10.   **b** Missing in Num. 26:14; cf. A. Wieder, JBL 84 (1965) 160-164.   **c** Could be a variant of b.   **d** Son of Asher, Gen. 46:17; from Ephraim, 1 Chron. 1:23; from Benjamin, 1 Chron. 8:13; from Levi, 1 Chron. 23:10f.; according to M. Noth 224, following Arab., "outstanding.''   **e** Cf. Akk. *surḥu*, KBL, M. Noth 180; short for "may God grant success''(?).   **f** Also the Kenite חֶבֶר, Judg. 4:11, 17, 21, meaning "the companion,'' cf. W. Wifall, ZAW 82 (1970) 110-114.   **g** "God is king''; cf. אֱלִי מֶלֶךְ, also Num. 26:45; M. Noth 36,118,140.

20a Cf. text and comm. on 41:52a.

21a Gen. 36:32f., king of Edom; according to the Arab. means "eloquent.'' **b** Missing in 1 Chron. 8, but present in Num. 26:35 among the sons of Ephraim; according to M. Noth 230 (cf. KBL) means "young male camel.''   **c** According to M. Noth, "with long upper lip.'' With Gk and 1 Chron. 8:3 add וַיִּהְיוּ בְנֵי בֶלַע.   **d** In Judg. 3:15 the father of Ehud; in 2 Sam. 16:5 the father of Shimei; a name expressing trust, M. Noth 148.   **e** Syrian army commander in 2 Kings 5; Ug. *n'mn*; נַעַם = "gracious'' + ān.   **f** From אֵחִי to וְחֻפִּים read with Num. 26:38f. וַאֲחִירָם וּשְׁפוּפָם וְחוּפָם.   **g** Cf. H. G. M. Williamson, VT 23 (1973) 375-379.   **h** For the previous four names one should probably read with Num. 26:28f., "and Ahiram and Shephupham and Hupham.''   **i** In Num. 26:40 he is a son of בֶּלַע; 1 Chron. 8:3 אַדָּר; meaning, according to KBL, M. Noth "hunchbacked.''

22a Read יַלְדָה with a number of Mss, Sam, and Symm.

23a Gk Ἀσομ; perhaps read שׁוּחָם with Num. 26:42, or חֻשִׁי with 2 Sam. 15:32.

24a יַצָּה = "to distribute,'' plus אֵל KBL; M. Noth 204, "may God give a share.''   **b** Name of a bird, *pterocles senegallus*, M. Noth 230.   **c** Shortened form, probably "formed by God,'' following Gen. 2:7.   **d** Sam and 1 Chron. 7:13 have וְשִׁלֵּם; Bab. *šilimmu*; M. Noth, surrogate name in the sense: God has replaced the dead child.

27a In Gk the total is 75, likewise in Acts 7:14; Manasseh and Ephraim have five sons more here.

28a Read with Gk לְהַקְרוֹת, cf. comm. on v. 28.   **b** Gk has another place-name.

29a Read וַיֵּרָא אֵתוֹ.

30a On the cohortative, Ges-K §108b; BrSynt §60; הַפַּעַם as in Gen. 29:34; 30:20.   **b** Cf. Gen. 43:28; 45:28.

Form and Setting

The Joseph narrative has reached its climax in ch. 45. Joseph has been reconciled with his brothers and has requested them to bring his father down to Egypt. Still to be narrated is the father's arrival in Egypt, the meeting, the provision made for him and his family there during the famine, and finally his death. The journey begins in v. 5b which follows immediately on 45:25-28. The sons of Israel put their father, the children, and the women on the wagons that the Pharaoh had sent; it is continued in vv. 28-30 with Jacob's arrival and the meeting with Joseph. The provision for the family begins in vv. 31-34 and is continued in 47:1-12. The remaining parts of ch. 46 do not belong to the Joseph narrative but are a continuation of the patriarchal story of Gen. 25–36. Vv. 1-5a are a promise, fitted into an itinerary, corresponding to the promises elsewhere in Gen. 12–36; they are foreign to the Joseph story. Vv. 6-7 are an itinerary in the language of P which has been expanded by a list of names in vv. 8-27. All these parts, the itinerary, the revelation to the patriarch with the travel instructions and the promise, together with the genealogical list, belong in form and content to the patriarchal story. Just as the beginning of the Joseph story in ch. 37 is an insertion (cf. above on ch. 37, Form), so too is the conclusion, chs. 46–50. P appears again in these chapters, just as in ch. 37; there is no sign of his hand in between (apart from single sentences added later).

J and P, therefore, contained a closing section following on chs. 25–36, which told how Jacob came down to Egypt after his son Joseph. It formed the link between the patriarchal story and the book of Exodus.

Commentary

[46:1-5a] The text of vv. 1-5a is a literary unity, even though a synthesis of a variety of elements. The unity is demonstrated by the fixed form of the itinerary: Jacob (or Israel) set out, v. 1aα; he came to Beersheba, v. 1aβ; he offered sacrifice there, v. 1b, and received a divine oracle, vv. 2-4; he set out from Beersheba, v. 5a. This is a fixed sequence often attested (cf. *Genesis 12–36*, comm. on 12:1-5). It is this combination of itinerary, a divine oracle given to the patriarch, and an act of worship that shows that 46:1-5a is part of the patriarchal story. None of these elements occurs in the Joseph story.

It is significant that exegetes who concentrate on source division have not noted or given attention to this difference in form and content in vv. 1-5a (O. Procksch has noted it but has not drawn the consequences); but those who understand the Joseph story as a unity, as a self-contained narrative, had to note it (W. Rudolf, D. B. Redford, G. W. Coats, H. Donner). I refer in particular to D. B. Redford, pp. 18-20, where he gives a convincing presentation of the difference. H. Donner follows him.

[46:1a, 5a] The Itinerary: departure. . . arrival with detail of the place. . . stop. . . departure (with same detail of the place). See the general remarks on itineraries in *Genesis 12–36*, pp. 54-58 and the individual itineraries in Gen. 12–36. The basic plan is always the same, but it admits of variants. The place from which Jacob sets out in v. 1a is not mentioned because it is obvious from the context in which it originally stood in the Jacob story. According to 37:14 Jacob was previously in Hebron; but the link with a previous itinerary is not retained.

[46:1b] Part of the patriarchal itinerary is the act of worship during a stop, as in Gen. 12:8-9 or 28:18. The present passage is the only place where there is mention of a sacrificial meal; cf. Gen. 31:54. Jacob presents the offering to "the God of his father Isaac." God is described here as the God of his physical father, thus stating that Jacob through him, even in foreign parts, remains bound to his father (B. Jacob). On the God of the Fathers, cf. *Genesis 12–36*, pp. 105-112, "The Religion of the Patriarchs."

[46:2-4] This is a divine oracle addressed to Jacob. There is never in the Joseph story a divine oracle addressed directly to a person, never anything like a revelation; but these are an essential part of the patriarchal story. There is here a deliberate counterpart to the patriarchal story as a whole, as we see from the instruction joined to the promise at the beginning of Abraham's migration in 12:1-5; and there is the same combination as Jacob prepares to enter a foreign land. The oracle addressed to Jacob consists of the introduction (v. 2), the instruction (v. 3a), and the promise (vv. 3b-4).

[46:2] The introduction consists of three sentences, each beginning with ויאמר. The first says that God spoke to Jacob in a vision by night, מראת הלילה. It should be noted that the description "vision by night" is not apposite here. The present passage differs from Gen. 28 in that here Jacob sees nothing. What is introduced is merely something that Jacob hears. But even more striking is the plural (visions) which likewise is not apposite. Most exegetes alter it to the singular without any textual basis or explanation of how the alteration to the plural took place.

מראת meaning "vision" occurs elsewhere in Ezek. 1:1; 8:3; 40:2; 43:3, and "vision by night" (with חזיון) only in Job 4:13. When one examines the Ezekiel passages one finds a plural with a singular meaning in 8:3 and 40:2 (". . .brought me in visions of God. . ."), and a variation of singular and plural in the same sentence in 43:3. In Ezek. 1:1 the word can have a singular meaning (cf. נפלאות = something marvellous; the plural does not mean a number of visions but plurality in what is seen). It is not necessary, therefore, to understand it with Ges-K §124 as a "plural of intensity" (H. Donner considers this quite improbable). The fact that the word in the plural carries this meaning elsewhere only in Ezekiel shows the sentence in v. 2 is speaking a late language, at least that of the exile. This is supported further by the less vivid use of "vision" in the sense of revelation; there is no question of a vision here.

V. 2b is a call and the reaction to it, as is often the case in the patriarchal story but never in the Joseph narrative. It should be compared with Gen. 22:11 where the double call with the reaction הנני takes its meaning from the situation, whereas in 46:2b it is stylized, as in Gen. 31:11 (see *Genesis 12–36*, comm. on 22:11b; 31:11). Further, v. 2b, like Gen. 22:11, is in fact not appropriate to a vision by night. The whole of v. 2 is a highly stylized introduction in later language which can only characterize the promise that follows as a divine revelation. This late stylized speech can use "Israel" and "Jacob" as synonyms without offense.

[46:3-4] The promise with the instruction in v. 3a has an obviously synthetic stamp. Its background is the assurance of well-being; but it has been modified and expanded notably (on the assurance of well-being, cf. *Genesis 12–36*, comm. on 15:1a, 1b). Belonging to the fixed form of the assurance of well-being, both in and outside of what is attested, are v. 3a "I am. . .," v. 3bα "Do not be afraid. . .." and v. 3bβ (the reason with the introductory כי which, however, is notably expanded here in vv. 3bβ-4).

God reveals himself to Jacob as האל אלהי אביך; אל is a very general and widespread Semitic designation for God (the mention of the name at the beginning of a promise as in Gen. 17:1), whereas "the God of your father" is very specific, the designation of the God of the patriarchs. The juxtaposition of the two, however, is entirely in accord with the patriarchal stories, as the revelation at Bethel, Gen. 28, and the names composed with El in Gen. 12–36 make abundantly clear.

[**46:3b**] The reassurance "Do not be afraid. . .!" can refer to the state of fear caused by the appearance or to the situation in which the addressee finds himself. The latter is obviously intended here: ". . .to go down to Egypt." Jacob would be seized with fear at the great risk of even a temporary settlement in Egypt with his whole family and the consequent grave potential dangers (it was different with Abraham in Gen. 12). This is countered by the promise in v. 3bβ, "for I will make you a great nation there." This is part of the tradition of the promises to the patriarchs and a variant of the promise of increase which occurs in Gen. 12:2; 17:20; 18:18; 21:13, 18; 46:3; cf. Ex. 32:10; Num. 14:12 (C. Westermann, *The Promises to the Fathers* [1976; Eng. 1980] 149-155; R. Rendtorff, *Das überlieferungsgeschichtliche. . .* [1977²] 47). It is a late promise related to the extent of Israel in the period of the monarchy. The idea of extent appears first with that of the people. The orientation here is toward the future, beyond the patriarchal story (*Genesis 12–36*, comm. on 12:2). Gen. 46:3 differs from the passages just noted by the further specification "there," in Egypt. The growth of Jacob's family to a people is to take place in Egypt. And Ex. 1:7 says that this is precisely what happened. There is an obvious connection here. The formulation of this promise to Jacob is looking at the growth of the Israelites (= the sons of Israel-Jacob) in Egypt which leads to the exodus and their becoming a people, as v. 4 expressly says. The promise to Abraham stands at the turning point from remote antiquity to the patriarchal period, "I will make you a great nation" (12:1-3); so too the promise to Jacob stands at the turning point from the patriarchal period to the period of the exodus, "I will make you a great nation there" (46:2-4). The promise, therefore, has been formed by a late transmitter who already presupposes the link between the patriarchal story and the story of the people in the Pentateuch.

[**46:4a**] The transmitter has adjusted the promise of support (or the promise of aid, e.g., Gen. 31:3; 35:3) to this changed situation, just as he had the promise of increase. Instead of the simple "I will be with you" (e.g., Gen. 26:3) there is a sentence in two parts promising God's aid on the way down into Egypt and on the way back, thus linking the patriarchal period with the exodus. The context shows with certainty that ". . .I myself will bring you back again" looks to the exodus and not to Jacob's burial procession (so too H. Gunkel). The consequence of this link is that there is a change in the object of the sentence. "I will go down with you" refers to Jacob the father and his family; "I will bring you back again" refers to "Jacob," the people that has grown from the family, to the group from which the people of Israel takes its origin. It must be clearly grasped that in v. 4a the transmitter intends to fashion a firm link between Jacob's journey down into Egypt, which concludes the patriarchal story, and the exodus from Egypt, which begins the history of the people. It is the same God at work in both movements (cf. Ex. 3). The patriarchal stories as a whole and the exodus story as a whole were both at hand to the transmitter who formulated this verse; he joined them into a continuous unit (cf. Gen. 50:24).

[**46:4b**] The concluding sentence of the promise is most unusual and moving, "and Joseph will lay his hand on your eyes," i.e., he will close your eyes in death; he will be there when you die. It is unusual because it stands in marked contrast to the preceding sentence in v. 4a which embraced historical perspectives on a broad scale; it is a personal matter. It has no connection whatever with the tradition of the promises to the patriarchs. The intention of the transmitter is clearly to join the promise he has shaped, and which corresponds to the promises to the patriarchs in Gen. 12–36, with the Joseph narrative with which it has nothing to do apart from this sentence. He takes the motif of 45:28; and 46:30 and joins it with the promise. It is precisely in this link that the passage shows a striking parallel to Gen. 15:13-16; there too we have a preview of the sojourn in Egypt and the exodus (vv. 13-14) joined with a personal oracle to Abraham announcing to him that he will die in peace. Both passages are late expansions; both link the patriarchal period with the exodus, and both have a personal oracle. The two texts are remarkably close to each other; it could be the same transmitter speaking in both cases.

[**46:5a**] This sentence belongs to the itinerary and follows immediately on v. 1. V. 1aβ reports the arrival at Beersheba; then follows the account of what happened during the stop (vv. 1b-4), and the departure (v. 5a). The itinerary in vv. 1 and 5a is retained without alteration; the modifications made by the late transmitter affect only vv. 2-4. It is to be presumed that in the older form a simple promise of aid together with an instruction stood in place of vv. 2-4; this is characteristic of the Jacob narratives (Gen. 28:15(20); 31:3; 32:10). After the report of the departure from Beersheba (v. 5a) one would expect the arrival in Egypt, which occurs only in v. 28b.

[**46:5b**] The transmitter has skillfully attached this sentence here from the conclusion of the Joseph story which likewise deals with the departure of Jacob's family from Canaan to Egypt. Jacob's departure (vv. 1a, 5a), like all similar itineraries in the patriarchal story, is that of the nomad; but it takes place in a different way in v. 5b which does not correspond with the patriarchal movements; the journey is made on wagons. There is a contradiction, therefore, between vv. 5a and 5b, though the text does not indicate it directly. The account in v. 5b is linked immediately with the return of the brothers to their father in 45:25-28; it is possible that one or more sentences have fallen out. In other words, v. 5a belongs to the conclusion of the Jacob story, v. 5b to the conclusion of the Joseph story. The transmitter has succeeded in making an apparently seamless transition from the one to the other.

   A scene such as that described in v. 5b would be unthinkable in the patriarchal story. The brothers who had returned from Egypt lift their father Jacob and their wives and children on to the wagons that Joseph, their youngest brother, now a high official in Egypt, had put at their disposal (together with provisions for its journey) for this purpose, at the instruction of the Pharaoh. The journey to Egypt, which is to preserve them against the ever-present threat of famine, can now take place. In the Joseph story vv. 28-30 follow on v. 5b.

[**46:6-27**] The P account of Jacob's emigration with his whole family is inserted here, vv. 6-7. The list in vv. 8-27 is to be regarded as a secondary expansion of this on the part of P. One perceives the continuity of the narrative better when one for the moment brackets out the list.

[**46:6-7**] The exegetes are in broad agreement that P is speaking here. The verses follow smoothly on v. 5 because they too belong to the itinerary form and carry it further. The smooth transition is skillfully enhanced by the simple omission of the verb "to depart" (cf. v. 5a) and by retaining only the expansion "they took. . . ."

157

The next verb follows in v. 6b, ". . .and came to Egypt," the immediate continuation of the itinerary of v. 5. All further details show clearly the language of P; cf. Gen. 12:5; 31:18; 36:6; כל זרעו אתו Gen. 17:2, 9f.; 35:12. The detailed enumeration of what was taken down in vv. 6f. is independent of the Joseph narrative; this is shown by the fact that it does not conform with the instruction of the Pharaoh not to bring their possessions with them.

B. Jacob has rightly pointed out that v. 7 (P) is the only passage where the daughters of the sons of Jacob are mentioned with the daughters of Jacob; "there were a lot of them." P also emphasizes in vv. 6f. that "all his seed" (descendants; the repetition in vv. 6b and 7b underscores this) joins the caravan down to Egypt and mentions all who belong to this group: sons and grandsons, daughters and granddaughters; he thus gives expression to the change to a new epoch, the transition from the story of the family to the story of the people. Both with Abraham and Israel it was necessary to make a separation between the sons of each; the main line was continued only in Isaac and Jacob. But now, as they make the journey down to Egypt, all belong there; "all his offspring remained together" (E. I. Lowenthal, *The Joseph Narrative in Genesis* [1973]).

[**46:8-27**] The narrative thread is interrupted by a list which spells out in detail those mentioned in general in v. 7. It is clearly an expansion by P which does not square entirely with the brief information in vv. 6-7. It is not a genealogy in the strict sense, but a list (for the difference cf. *Genesis 1–11*, 14f.); hence שמות (as in Gen. 25:13; 36:10), not תלדות (against D. B. Redford, p. 22). It has a clearly synthetic character which is further apparent in the two conclusions, vv. 26 and 27. A list of the descendants of Jacob covering three generations (probably still without numbers) has been reworked for the present context into a list of the sons of Jacob who at that time went down from Canaan to Egypt. This explains to a great extent the unevenness and contradictions in vv. 8-27.

The list is arranged in accordance with the mothers of the sons of Jacob (as in chs. 29–30; 35:23-26; 36:9-14): vv. 8b-15 the sons of Leah (numbering 33); vv. 16-18 the sons of Zilpah (numbering 16); vv. 19-22 the sons of Rachel (numbering 14); vv. 23-25 the sons of Bilhah (numbering 7). Each part carries an introductory and a concluding formula showing that the text is an independent tradition; one can presume that the individual pieces are abbreviations of what were originally genealogies. From different points of view the resumptive formulas give a sum total of 66 in v. 26 and 70 in v. 27. What is significant in this arrangement is the great importance that it gives to women as mothers in this early period. The arrangement preserves an element that goes far back into early times, whereas the numbers are a very late element. It is certain that the number 70 was at hand to the author of vv. 8-27 (Ex. 1:5; Deut. 10:22; Ex. 24:1-9); it was originally a round number giving the approximate number of the members of a family now grown to a tribe (cf. Judg. 8:30; 12:14, the 70 sons of Gideon). The difference in number, 66 in v. 26 (without Jacob and Joseph and his sons) and 70 in v. 27, shows that 70 is a round number here. But the synthesis is also contrived; the sons of Leah (numbering 33) comprise half of the grand total; each of the maids has half as many sons as her mistress, even the sums of the digits agree; Benjamin has the most sons. This construction can have arisen only in a later period.

The origin and growth of this list is to be seen in the context of a number of parallels even if it is no longer possible to plot its course in detail. The frame finds a parallel in Ex. 1:1-7 (Ex. 1:1a is word for word the same as Gen. 46:8a); T. C. Vriezen deals with both texts in detail (VT 17 [1967] 347-352; cf. W. H. Schmidt, *Exodus* II/1, 26-30). The comparison shows that Gen. 48:8-27, just as Ex. 1:1-7, forms a transition from the patriarchal story to the exodus, thus presupposing the exodus tradition (cf. G. W. Coats, VT 22 [1972] 129-142). The census of the Israelites "who came forth out of the land of Egypt" in Num. 26 presents a parallel; it took place at the Jordan opposite Jericho (Num. 26:1-4); it is the counterpart to Ex. 1:1-7, as is shown by the large numbers of those registered at the end of each section. The sons have now become "families" (in the broad sense) מִשְׁפָּחֹת, Num. 26:5ff. The names are in such broad agreement that there must be a connection. The differences are relatively few. There is a further parallel in Ex. 6:14-16, but only to the sons of Reuben, Simeon, and Levi. An additional parallel for all names is found in 1 Chron. 2–8. The parallels show that we are dealing with an independent tradition. It arose independently of the Joseph story (four sons of Reuben in Gen. 46, two in Gen. 42; Benjamin's many sons are not congruent with so young a man) and independently of the P narrative (v. 7, daughters and granddaughters; vv. 8-27, only one daughter and one granddaughter). That it followed an independent path of tradition is also evident from the two different lists which are the basis of 46:8-27. Er and Onan (not Dinah) appear in the register of Jacob's male descendants, but not in the exodus register; nor do Joseph and his two sons appear, because they were already in Egypt. It was originally a list of the sons and grandsons of Joseph as individuals and not, as J. Skinner writes, "a list of the leading clans"; this it became only in Num. 26; the names themselves, almost exclusively personal names, show this (there are only two regional or place-names). The individual sections are probably abbreviations of genealogies of the sons of Jacob. The absence of names with יהוה as a constituent part shows that they go back to the presedentary period. The many striking parallels to the names in the book of Judges also argues for this.

[46:8] The heading in v. 8 is word for word the same as Ex. 1:1a where there is a simple enumeration of the names of the 12 sons of Jacob; here we find "Jacob and his sons." The last sentence, "Reuben was Jacob's firstborn" (as in Gen. 49:3; cf. 29:32), could be a fragment of such an enumeration.

[46:9-15] The six sons of Leah are listed and the sum total of 33 is given at the end (v. 15). That it is a mere list is shown by the simple enumeration of the names: "the sons of Reuben: A, B, C, D"; interruption is rare, as at the end of v. 10, "Shaul, the son of a Canaanite woman," a reference to a well-known figure or narrative. A note is added to the sons of Judah, "Er and Onan died in the land of Canaan" (v. 12). This is the only place in vv. 9-15 where two grandsons, sons of Perez, are named; the reason is probably that the names Er and Onan had previously fallen out; chronologically they do not fit into the account of the exodus. V. 12 presupposes a knowledge of ch. 38, although Perez and Zerah are described, by simplification, as sons of Judah. The words וְאֵת דִּינָה are incongruous and are an addition; only sons were named in the list of Jacob's descendants. The sum total of the sons of Leah was 33; her maid Zilpah had 16, just under half that number.

[46:16-18] The 16 grandsons of Zilpah, stemming from Gad and Asher, are listed without interruption or additions; here also two grandchildren are named, two sons of Beriah (v. 17b). The note "whom Laban gave to Leah his daughter" presupposes a knowledge of the Jacob-Esau story. The designation of a person or an individual by נפש probably first came about in the context of the late enumeration; it is not found in the patriarchal stories (cf. N. P. Bratsiotis, D. Lys [1966], bibliog. above).

[46:19-22] The formulation of v. 19 falls outside the pattern; Rachel is described expressly as Jacob's wife who bore him Joseph and Benjamin. This emphasis on Rachel also presupposes a knowledge of the Jacob story. One can see again in v. 20 that two lists have been worked together. Joseph and his sons do not belong to the list of those who came down from Canaan to Egypt with Jacob; the appendix in v. 27 states this expressly. The relative sentence with אשר in v. 20a has been inserted mechanically from Gen. 41:50, thus disturbing the relationship between subject and object there. The list of the sons of Benjamin in v. 21 also presents difficulties. The MT counts 10 sons, which is striking when compared with the other lists and is not at all congruous with the young Benjamin of the Joseph story. The Gk and Num. 26:38-40 give Benjamin only five sons; the others are grandsons, which is even less congruous chronologically. The names themselves are up to a point questionable and patient of different readings. In the closing sentence, v. 22, ילדה is to be read for ילד; the generations are felt to be so closely knit that the list can say that Rachel bore Jacob his grandchildren; no contradiction is seen between vv. 22 and 19.

[46:23-25] There is a plural "the sons" in v. 23 although only one name follows; this can be regarded as an example of the pattern imposing itself, as in Gen. 36:25. But it is also possible that names have fallen out. The concluding formula does not seem to be struck from the same die.

[46:26-27] This conclusion of the list is very complicated. At first glance it appears as a synthesis, but it is much more complicated than a mere putting together of vv. 26 and 27. The original conclusion is v. 27b: "The persons of Jacob's family who came to Egypt were seventy in all." All else is appendage either by way of correction or expansion. The transmitters thought this necessary because the interweaving of two lists had to be explained. But this has not really succeeded in vv. 26, 27. What is intended is clear enough, but only this, namely, that Joseph and his two sons (v. 27a) were not among those who came down; v. 27a, therefore, is a corrective explanation of v. 26; there can only have been 67. Vv. 26, 27a do not say, or say only indirectly, that Jacob's *sons* numbered 70, and hence could not include Jacob. This is how the number 66 for the caravan down to Egypt came about. What has been said holds. The two numbers, 66 in v. 26 and 70 in v. 27, are thus clearly explained. Everything else is an attempt to even out, and each detail cannot be pinned down.

The formation of v. 26 can be explained as follows. At the basis of the verse lies a sentence, "The persons ('souls') of Jacob's family, his bodily descendants [who came to Egypt], were sixty-six in all." Without the addition "who came to Egypt" this is the superscription of the list of Jacob's physical sons. This is demonstrated by the expression יצאי ירכו, "who came from his loins," which occurs only here and in Judg. 8:30 and in both cases designates "70 physical sons.'' This superscription is linked with that of the list of the exodus from Egypt by the addition הבאה מצרימה (words later separated by ליעקב) and by the alteration of the number 70 to 66. A transmitter then added ''not including the wives of Jacob's sons,'' because it struck him that Jacob's wives had been mentioned, but not the wives of his sons. This lengthened the sentence to such an extent that the כל־נפש at the beginning was repeated at the end before the predicate.

The necessary explanations of the individual names have been given above in the notes on the text. Reference should be made to the variants found in BHK and BHS and to the occurrence of the names in other places in KBL; see too BHH and M. Noth, *Die israelitischen Personennamen. . .* (1928; 1966²). The following remarks are by way of summary: (1) The deviations in the parallels are relatively few; there is certainly an older tradition behind the list. They increase with the sons of Benjamin; there has been subsequent alteration here. (2) Names which occur often in other places are rather rare here, such as חנן (v. 9), שאול or תולע; this allows the conclusion that the list was by origin a unity and old. (3) The names show that the list is one of personal names, not one of tribes or clans, as many exegetes suppose; it is a list belonging to the social structure of the family. It arose within the family embracing three generations of the family of Jacob: Jacob and his wives, their sons, and their sons (and by way of addition some sons of the next generation). The names with few exceptions are personal names (two regional names in vv. 13 and 16). The gentilic name is usually distinguished linguistically from the personal name, e.g., ימני from ימין (Num. 26:12); only in a few cases has the personal name subsequently become a gentilic name, as כרמי (v. 9), קהתי (v. 11). (4) The following types of personal names occur: (a) *Names of animals:* תולע (v. 13), בכר (v. 21), גוני (v. 24); names of plants, אלון (v. 14); cf. *Genesis 12–36*, comm. on 36:1-43. (b) *Parts of the body:* צחר (v. 10), מררי (v. 11), אשבל (v. 21), ארד (v. 21); personal attributes ערי (v. 16), בלע (v. 21); a name expressing the joy or wish of the parents גרשון (v. 11), חמול (v. 12), ימין (v. 10). (c) *Theophoric names:* ימואל (v. 10), מלכיאל (v. 17), יחצאל (v. 24); shortened names פלוא (v. 9), יכין (v. 10); ישוב (v. 13, cj.), שרח (v. 17), גרא (v. 21), יצר (v. 24), שלם (v. 24). These three groups prove that the names have been given to children on the occasion of their birth. (5) The period in which the list arose cannot be determined precisely; there are, however, two pointers to an early period: (a) the theophoric names are formed with אל, never with יהוה; (b) parallels to the names occur with striking frequency in the period of the judges, כרמי (v. 9), the father of Achan, אהד (v. 10?), שאול (v. 10), תולע (v. 13), אלון (v. 14)—all judges, גרא (v. 21), the father of Ehud; add חבר (v. 17; Judg. 4:11) and צפון (v. 16).

[46:28-30] It is not P's detailed passage, vv. 6-7, but the long list, vv. 8-27, that effectively disturbs the flow of the narrative. One must keep the conclusion in view so as to enter into the stream again. At the end of ch. 45 Jacob cries out, ''. . .Joseph my son is still alive! I will go and see him before I die!'' (45:28). Thereupon the brothers set out at once with their father; vv. 28-30 follow immediately on this with the account of the arrival in the land of Goshen and the reunion of father and son there.

V. 28 speaks of the preparation for the arrival and the arrival itself; Joseph comes to meet his father in Goshen (v. 29a); the reunion takes place in v. 29b; Jacob's words to Joseph in v. 30 resume what he said before the departure (45:28).

[**46:28a**] V. 28 presents formidable difficulties; the text has not been preserved in its original form; the divergencies among the versions attest to this. The position of the object (Judah) at the beginning of v. 28 shows that a sentence has been lost between vv. 5b and 28 which postulated such a position. Jacob sends Judah before him to Joseph. The purpose can only be to notify Joseph that he is on the way (so H. Holzinger, following E. Kautzsch, J. Skinner). But the MT literally would run, "so as to point the way before him to Goshen." The text is questionable; the hiph. of ירה is found only here with this concrete meaning; one would expect an object (O. Procksch); גשן and לפניו both follow twice in quick succession (according to D. B. Redford the first גשנה is a gloss). The versions diverge; Sam and Syr have the niph. of ירה, Gk has συναντῆσαι αὐτῷ which presupposes להקרות לו. The Gk is to be preferred because of the difficulty in the MT; it corresponds to the meaning one expects from the context (so too O. Procksch).

[**46:28b**] V. 28b is also difficult because it seems to have no connection with v. 28a; so, for example, J. Wellhausen who for this reason wants to put it with v. 29. But this is unlikely because of the change of subject. Rather, v. 28b is to be understood as constituting part of an itinerary. Sentences of this sort are often inserted loosely into the context because they were originally independent. V. 28b follows on the itinerary sentences vv. 1a and 5a.

[**46:29**] The continuation of v. 29 confirms the explanation of v. 28a which follows the reading of the Gk: "Then Joseph had his chariot made ready," that is, when Judah brought him the news of Jacob's arrival. The לקראת in v. 29 corresponds likewise with the להקרות (Gk) in v. 28. Joseph "goes up"; "this is the usual expression for the journey from Egypt to Palestine" (H. Holzinger), even though this was only part of that way. The meeting, the reunion of father and son, follows. The Joseph story has two climactic points. There is the reunion with the brothers preceded by the forgiveness (ch. 45); then comes the reunion with the father as a distinctly separate event characterized by joy and emotion after long separation. Expression is thus given to mature experience; each alike is part of human experience—separation through guilt and separation through grief. The abolition of the one and the other are always independent experiences. The reunion of father and son is described by gesture alone, the embrace and the kiss. The intensity is underscored by the עוד (long, continual, as in Ruth 1:14; "again and again"). The meeting is introduced by the words וירא אליו "and he appeared to him." Some exegetes note that this expression is used elsewhere only of appearances of God (Gen. 12:7; 18:1); but it causes no offense. It is variously explained: "This exalted expression serves to emphasize the solemnity of the moment" (O. Procksch) or "he meets him primarily as the high state official" (H. Holzinger). I would question both explanations. Joseph certainly does not meet his father "as the high state official" but as a son. And further, the expression used elsewhere only to describe an appearance of God, "and he appeared to him," seems to me to be impossible here; this would destroy the correlation between the two verbs ויפל—וירא. This verbal sequence, of which the first is וירא, occurs so frequently in both the patriarchal story and the Joseph story and is so significant for them (cf., e.g., Gen. 18:2b) that it must also be present here; the event that sets the narrative in motion is the act of seeing. Further, the expression in Gen. 12:7 and 18:1 is stylized due to the later development of the promises; it is not therefore part of the patriarchal stories themselves. The special emphasis, and O. Procksch has rightly seen this, can only be a later, supplementary underscoring of the meeting. The narrator of the Joseph story had said: וירא אתו, just as, e.g., Gen. 33:1-4; but see further 46:30.

[46:30] Jacob now gives expression to what this reunion means to him. The verse brings the high point of the Joseph story to its close; it is spoken in retrospect over the narrative as a whole. The first word speaks of death, the last of life. Jacob can now die in peace; the lament of the father for his beloved son which runs through the whole narrative (37:33-34; 43:14; 44:28) is at an end. The verse at the same time anticipates the concluding account of Jacob's death. Jacob can now say, ". . .I have seen your face and know that you are alive." With these words the "political narrative" merges back definitively into the "family narrative." At this moment the son's high office and all that he has achieved in it is of no importance to the father. He can die in peace because his son lives, and when he dies the stream of life will continue in the life of his son and his descendants.

Purpose and Thrust

The result of the exegesis is that we distinguish in ch. 46 the conclusion of the Joseph narrative (vv. 5b, 28-30), the conclusion of the patriarchal story or the Joseph story (vv. 1-5a, 6-7, 8-27), and the drawing together of both into the block which has been handed down in ch. 46: (1) The conclusion of the Joseph narrative requires, in harmony with ch. 37, that both the reconciliation with the brothers (ch. 45) and the reunion with the father (ch. 46) be told. The reunion means for Joseph that he has found once more the link with his father's house. What the names of his sons had already hinted at is now a reality: the high Egyptian official remains a link in his ancestral chain, as the development of the Joseph story and its assumption into the traditions of Israel shows. Jacob can die in peace because Joseph is again one of the family and his history continues in him. (2) That Joseph belongs there is made clear by the insertion of his story into the Jacob story. Jacob's journey down into Egypt is consciously described as a counterpart to this. On the one hand, there is the response to the invitation of Joseph and the Pharaoh in v. 5b and the journey on the wagons that the Pharaoh has provided; on the other, there is the quite different journey in patriarchal fashion, and emigration into a foreign land. This journey had begun with the command to Abraham to set out for Canaan in Gen. 12:1-5 and concludes with the encouragement to go down to Egypt; both are linked with promises. But the present promise looks beyond into the history of the people, described in miniature in the list of 70 and by the announcement of the later exodus from Egypt. The transition from family to people described here is due to the action of God. The God of the fathers who was with them, who was guiding and protecting them, will make them into a great people in Egypt (cf. Ex. 1:7); he will then lead them out of Egypt again (46:3), into the land in which their fathers had wandered as immigrants. (3) The synthesis of the two in the text that lies before us looks not only to the link between the patriarchal and exodus stories, but also to that between the patriarchal story and the history of the Israelite kingship. It was the God of the fathers who preserved his family from famine by means of Joseph's royal office. All that remains to narrate is the provision made for Jacob and his household in Egypt during the prolonged famine and, finally, his death.

163

Joseph Provides for His Family
Jacob Blesses the Pharaoh
Appendage (47:13-26)

Literature

Genesis 46:31-34: A. Alt, "Die Herkunft der Hyksos in neuer Sicht" (1954) = KS 3 (1959) 72-98. S. Shibayama, "Notes on *Yārad* and *'Alāh*: Hints on Translating," JBR 34 (1966) 358-362.

Genesis 47:1-12: R. Smend, *Die Erzählung des Hexateuch auf ihre Quellen untersucht* (1912). J. Pedersen, *Israel, Its Life and Culture I-II* (1926-40) 132-202. E. Wiesenberg, "A Note on מזה in Psalm LXXV 9," VT 4 (1954) 434-439. G. R. Driver, "Two Problems in the OT Examined in the Light of Assyriology," Syr. 33 (1956) 69-87. S. Talmon, "Divergences in Calendar-Reckoning in Ephraim and Judah," VT 8 (1958) 48-74. A. Jirku, "Zu einigen Orts- und Eigennamen Palästina-Syriens," ZAW 75 (1963) 86-88. D. B. Redford, "Exodus I11," VT 13 (1963) 401-418. W. F. Albright, *Yahweh and the Gods of Canaan: A Historical Analysis of Two Contrasting Faiths* (1968) ch. 2D, 79. W. Helck, "Die Bedrohung Palästinas durch einwandernde Gruppen am Ende der 18. und am Anfang der 19. Dynastie," VT 18 (1968) 472-480 esp. 480. G. Gerleman, "Nutzrecht und Wohnrecht. Zur Bedeutung von אחזה und נחלה," ZAW 89 (1977) 313-325.

Genesis 47:13-26: A. H. Godbey, *The Lost Tribes, a Myth: Suggestions towards Rewriting Hebrew History* (1930). A. H. Gardiner, *The Wilbour Papyrus* (1948). J. M. P. van der Ploeg, "Studies in Hebrew Law I," CBQ 12 (1950) 248-259. H. S. Gehman, "Some Types of Errors of Transmission in the LXX," VT 3 (1953) 397-400. F. K. Kienitz, *Die politische Geschichte Ägyptens vom 7. bis zum 3. Jh. vor der Zeitwende* (1953). J. Blau, "Zum angeblichen Gebrauch von את vor dem Nominativ," VT 4 (1954) 7-19. F. Steiner, "Enslavement and the Early Hebrew Lineage System: An Explanation of Gen. 47,19-31; 48,1-16," Man. (1954) 73-75. H. J. Stoebe, "Anmerkungen zu 1 Sam VIII 16 und XVI 20," VT 4 (1954) 177-184. O. Eissfeldt, *Die Genesis der Genesis: Vom Werdegang des ersten Buches der Bibel* (1958; 1961²) esp. 41, 46. K. Baer, "The Low Price of Land in Ancient Egypt," JARCE 1 (1962) 25-42 esp. 33. B. S. Childs, "A Study of the Formula 'Until this Day,' " JBL 82 (1963) 279-292. M. C. Doubles, "Toward the Publication of the Extant Texts of the Palestinian Targum(s)," VT 15 (1965) 16-26. P. Victor, "A Note on חק in the OT," VT 16 (1966) 358-361. H. P. Müller, "Die phönizische Grabinschrift aus dem Zypern-Museum KAI 30 und die Formgeschichte des nordwestsemitischen Epitaphs," ZA 65 (1975) 104-132.

Genesis 47:27-28: W. Brueggemann, "The Kerygma of the Priestly Writers," ZAW 84 (1972) 397-414 esp. 405, 407. S. Gevirtz, "The Life Spans of Joseph and Enoch and the Parallelism: *šib 'ātayim—šib 'îm wešib 'āh*," JBL 96 (1977) 570-571.

Text

46:31   Then Joseph said to his brothers [and to his father's household],[a] I will go up and inform the Pharaoh; I will say to him, My brothers and my father's household who were in the land of Canaan have come to me.

32   These men are shepherds; [they breed cattle].[a] They have their own flocks and herds and have brought all their possessions.

33   When the Pharaoh summons you and asks, What is your occupation?

34   You are to say, Your servants have been cattle breeders from our youth and still are, both we and our fathers; and so you[a] will be able to remain in the land of Goshen, because all shepherds[b] are an abomination in Egypt.

47:1   So Joseph went and told the Pharaoh. He said, My father and my brothers have come from the land of Canaan with their sheep and cattle and all their possessions and are now in the land of Goshen.

2   He then took five of[a] his brothers[b] and presented them to the Pharaoh.[c]

3   When the Pharaoh asked his[a] brothers, What is your occupation? they answered the Pharaoh, Your servants are shepherds,[b] we and our fathers.

4   And they said further to the Pharaoh, We have come to sojourn in the land; your servants have no feed for their sheep because the famine is severe in the land of Canaan. So please allow your servants to settle in the land of Goshen.

5   Then the Pharaoh said to Joseph,[a] So your father and your brothers have come to you.

6   The land of Egypt lies open to you. Settle your father and your brothers in the best part of the land;[a] let them settle in the land of Goshen; and if you know that[b] there are competent men[c] among them, put them as overseers over my own herds.

7   Then Joseph brought in his father Jacob and presented him to the Pharaoh. And Jacob blessed[a] the Pharaoh.

8   And the Pharaoh asked Jacob, How many are the years of your life?

9   And Jacob answered the Pharaoh, The years of my sojourning are one hundred and thirty. Few and hard have been the years of my life and they have not reached the years of the life of my fathers[a] in the time of their sojourning.

10   And Jacob blessed the Pharaoh. Then he left the Pharaoh's presence.

11   And Joseph settled his father and his brothers in the best part of the land. . .as the Pharaoh had commanded, and he gave them land in Egypt, in the land of Rameses.

12   And Joseph provided his father and his brothers and the whole of his father's family with food according to the number of the children.[a]

27a So Israel dwelt in the land of Egypt, in the land of Goshen,

27b and they acquired land in it and were fruitful and became very numerous.

28   And Jacob lived another seventeen years in the land of Egypt, so that his life-span covered[a] one hundred and forty-seven years.

13   Now there was no food in the land because the famine was very severe so that the land of Egypt and the land of Canaan languished.[a]

14   So Joseph collected[a] all the silver that was in the land of Egypt and the land of Canaan in return for the grain that the people bought and deposited it in the Pharaoh's palace.

15   When the silver in the land of Egypt and the land of Canaan had run out, all the Egyptians came to Joseph and said, Give us bread! Why

should we die before you? 'The'[a] silver has all[b] run out.

16   And Joseph said, Give your cattle, and I will give you 'bread'[a] in exchange for your cattle if your silver has run out.

17   So they brought their cattle to Joseph, and Joseph gave them bread in
exchange for their horses, sheep, herds and donkeys. In that year he
provided[a] them with bread in exchange for all their cattle.

18   But when the year was ended, they came to him again in the second
year and said, My lord, we cannot hide[a] from you that the silver has run
out. Our herds too belong to our lord.[b] We have nothing left for our lord
but our bodies[c] and our land.[d]

19   Why should we die[a] before your eyes, we and our land as well? Buy us
and our land for bread, and we and our land will be in bondage to the
Pharaoh. Give us seed so that we may live and not die and our land not
become[b] a desert.

20   So Joseph bought up all the land of the Egyptians for the Pharaoh. The
Egyptians sold all their fields because the famine lay heavy upon
them. The land became the Pharaoh's.

21   And the people 'he put in servitude to him'[a] from one end of Egypt to
the other.[b]

22   But he did not buy the land of the priests. They had a fixed income[a]
from the Pharaoh and they lived[b] from this. So they had no need to sell
their lands.

23   Joseph said to the people, Listen, I have bought you and your land for
the Pharaoh; here is seed for you[a] that you may sow the land.

24   However, you must hand over a fifth 'of' the produce[a] to the Pharaoh.
Four-fifths are to be yours to sow your fields and to 'provide food for
you'[b] and for those in your households and for your children.[c]

25   And they said, You have saved our lives! May we find favor in the eyes
of our lord; we will be slaves to the Pharaoh.

26   So Joseph made it a statute over the land of Egypt which holds to this
day that they must[a] hand over a fifth to the Pharaoh. Only the land of
the priests did not become the Pharaoh's property.[b]

46:31a Missing Gk, probably an addition from v. 31b.

32a The כי-clause is rightly regarded as an addition (e.g., H. Gunkel).

34a On the construction, BrSynt §145bδ.   **b** Some Mss read the plural; cf. BrSynt §72b.

47:2a Cf. 1 Kings 12:31; Ex. 33:2; see E. Wiesenberg (1954) 437, S. Talmon (1958) 50,
bibliog. above.   **b** Sam expands with עמו.   **c** Cf. Gen. 43:9.

3a Sam, Gk, and others: "the brothers of Joseph."   **b** Probably a misspelling for רעי
Ges-K §145r; BrSynt §72b.

5a The text is not to be altered following the Gk as is done in BHK and proposed by a number of exegetes.

6a Only vv. 6, 11; Ex. 22:4 speaks of fields.   **b** On the construction, Ges-K §120e; on
the conditional sentence with the double perfect, Ges-K §159gho.   **c** BrSynt §76d; 135b.

7a On ברך cf. article in THAT with lit; cf. especially Ps. 129:8.

9a On the construction, Ges-K §128a; BrSynt §24c.

12a BrSynt §1071δ.

13a ותלה from להה (Sam ותלא) only here, one of the many rare expressions occurring in
vv. 13-26.

14a לקט piel, used only here of money.

15a Read הכסף with Sam, likewise in v. 16.   **b** אפס only here and in v. 16 in Pentateuch.

16a לחם to be inserted with Sam, Gk, and others.

17a נהל only here with this meaning.

18a The אם כי is elliptical.   **b** אל expressing the rest at the goal achieved.   **c** גוית in this sense elsewhere only in Ezek. 1:11, 23; Dan. 10:6; Neh. 9:37; otherwise means "corpse."   **d** On the Gk version of v. 18, cf. H. S. Gehman (1953), bibliog. above.

19a Gk breaks up what appears to it to be an impossible zeugma.   **b** On the form, Ges-K §67p; cf. Ezek. 12:19; 19:7.

21a Read העביד אתו לעבדים with Sam, Gk, (Vg); likewise the Pal. Talmud, M. C. Doubles (1965), bibliog. above.   **b** Ges-K §139e, n. 3.

22a חק as in Prov. 30:8; 31:15; Ezek. 16:27; Lev. 10:13f.; J. P. M. van der Ploeg, CBQ 12 (1950) 252.   **b** On אכל M. Ottosson, ThWAT I 256-259; on construction, Ges-K §1121.

23a On הן—הא, BrSynt §4; 5b; הא Aram. interjection; elsewhere only Ezek. 16:43; Dan. 2:43.

24a That which comes in, produce; the ב at the beginning is either "at the harvesting" (so TargO, F. Delitzsch, A. Dillmann), or מה or ה (following Gk) is to be read for ב; cf. BHS.   **b** Separate thus.   **c** The two last words are probably an addition; they are missing in Gk.

26a Read לחמש לפרעה with Gk.   **b** Vv. 27-28 follow v. 12.

28a Read יהיו with Sam and others.

Form and Setting

As in ch. 46, so too in ch. 47, the Joseph narrative is wedged into the Jacob story. One must distinguish three constituent parts of different origin: (1) Belonging to the Joseph story are 46:31—47:6, 11, 12, 27a. This comprises the audience with the Pharaoh (46:31-34; 47:1-6) and Joseph's provision for his brothers (47:11*, 12) along with the closing remark in v. 27a: Israel remains in Egypt. (2) Belonging to the conclusion of the Jacob story, continuing ch. 46, are 47:7-10, 11*, 27b, 28: Jacob blesses the Pharaoh, he settles in Egypt, his life span. These are P texts; in ch. 47 a part of the conclusion of the Joseph story is joined with a part of the conclusion of P's Jacob story. (3) The third part is the appendage, 47:13-26, the institution of the tax of the one-fifth in Egypt.

Regarding the first part: After the reconciliation with the brothers and the reunion with the father it remains to narrate Joseph's provision for Jacob's family in Egypt. All that was really needed was the short note in 47:11f.; however, detailed preparation is made by an audience with the Pharaoh 47:1-6 for which Joseph gives his brothers instructions (46:31-34). The reason for the detail is the narrator's concern to base the settlement of Jacob's family and the provision made during the famine expressly on the Pharaoh's guarantee.

In part two the arrangement makes the audience of the father with the Pharaoh follow that of the brothers; the point of contact is that Joseph presents both. This is to be explained from the way in which the priestly patriarchal story is arranged.

The appendage, the third part, is an individual narrative which the author relates to Joseph and adapts to the Joseph narrative.

Commentary

[46:31-34] Joseph tells his brothers that he will notify the Pharaoh of the arrival of his family with their father. At the same time he counsels them how to answer when they are summoned before the Pharaoh. The advice concerns their being allowed to remain in Goshen (46:33-34).

[46:31] The preceding narrative, especially 45:16-20, requires that Joseph must now notify the Pharaoh of the arrival of his family. This presupposes that the Pharaoh has previously approved their coming (45:16-20); otherwise Joseph's words to him would have to take a different turn. That this is the first that the Pharaoh hears of their coming (a view of many exegetes who accept another source here) is out of the question. It is in accordance with courtly style when Joseph, as often in direct speech, repeats details of which the Pharaoh is already well aware.

[46:32] Joseph stresses that his brothers are shepherds. There are two parts to the sentence: they are small-cattle herdsmen—they have brought their cattle with them. This emphasis is heard all the more clearly when צאן and צאנם follow each other immediately in the middle of the sentence. The words in between כי־אנשי מקנה היו yield no good sense; this is not a real reason. They are to be regarded (as H. Gunkel) as a gloss and doubling from v. 34. By mentioning that they have brought their herds, Joseph wants to suggest to the Pharaoh that they want to continue with their present occupation.

[46:33-34] The brothers are to answer in the same way when the Pharaoh questions them. They are to emphasize further that their fathers exercised the same occupation from their youth (vv. 33-34). The wish that the Pharaoh allow them to settle in Goshen does not explain adequately this firm insistence. Pharaoh's answer shows that there is no difficulty here. But the wisdom of Joseph the statesman goes much further. The Pharaoh is to be assured that his brothers entertain no ambitions to rise higher under the aegis of their brother, the Pharaoh's highest minister. In relation to his brothers and the Pharaoh Joseph is concerned to preserve the lines of division between the court to which his office binds him and the provision made for his family. He is indeed a wise statesman.

Many exegetes say that the last reason given in v. 34b, ''because all shepherds are an abomination in Egypt,'' cannot be demonstrated from Egyptian sources and is too general to apply to shepherds as such (e.g., E. A. Speiser). One must agree with A. Dillmann and others who for this reason take the remark as applying only to non-Egyptian nomads (cf. 43:32). It is possible that Joseph is thus giving his brothers a warning.

[47:1-6] The audience with the Pharaoh: The structure of the text is difficult because it is at the same time an audience for Joseph, the minister, and Joseph's brothers. But this becomes understandable on reflection. The introduction (v. 1a) is followed by Joseph notifying the Pharaoh of the arrival of his family (v. 1b). Then comes a parenthesis (v. 2); Joseph presents five of his brothers to the Pharaoh. The Pharaoh puts a question to the brothers (v. 3a); they answer (v. 3b); and immediately on this comes their request and the reason for it. Only in vv. 5-6 comes the Pharaoh's answer to Joseph's notification, which takes up v. 1 again because of the long gap between the two (v. 5b). In the first part (v. 6a) he offers Joseph's family ''the best part of the land''; in the second he gives permission allowing them to settle in the land of Goshen. The Pharaoh thus gives an indirect answer to the brothers' request in v. 4.

When one understands vv. 1-6 as an artificial, but notably abbreviated fusion of two separate audiences into one, then every sentence therein has its own proper place and meaning.

If one does not note that there are two different parties to the audience, then v. 5 must appear as an inappropriate answer to the brothers' request in v. 4. This is probably the reason for the text of the Gk which has v. 6b, "let them settle in the land of Goshen," follow on v. 5a, and inserts a preparatory sentence as v. 5, "Now Jacob and his sons came to Joseph in Egypt; and when the Pharaoh, the king of Egypt, heard of it. . .''; vv. 5 and 6a then follow. J. Wellhausen maintained that the text of the Gk was the original; he was followed by A. Dillmann, H. Gunkel, O. Procksch, J. Skinner, G. von Rad, and others. But against this W. Rudolf has rightly recognized that the Gk took offense at v. 5 as an answer to v. 4 and hence went on to expand and transpose. D. B. Redford and H. C. Schmitt have followed him because this explanation is in accord with the practice of the Gk. What is decisive against the Gk as the original text is that it has misunderstood the composition of the audience; its insertion interrupts and disturbs the account of it.

[**47:1**] Joseph has communicated his intent to his brothers in 46:31f. and now carries it out; there is word-for-word agreement (cf. D. B. Redford, pp. 84f.). The account is restricted to what is necessary and the ceremonial introduction is omitted. The remark that his family is now in Goshen prepares what follows.

[**47:2**] A parenthesis is now added telling that Joseph brought five of his brothers with him. He presents them to the Pharaoh; again the court ritual is omitted.

[**47:3**] The Pharaoh addresses the brothers with a question about their occupation. They answer as Joseph had instructed them (46:33f.) and confirm to the Pharaoh that they are shepherds.

[**47:4**] There is good reason why what follows is introduced once more with, "and they said further to Pharaoh." Their answer to the Pharaoh's question concludes with v. 3. They now say something further of their own initiative, namely, why they have come and what they request of the Pharaoh. They explain to him that they have come because of a severe famine (43:1) that has threatened the lives of their families and their herds. At the same time they explain that they want temporary residence only, as גרים, and so without the full rights of land owners, until the famine is over. It is only then that they put forward their request, introduced by ועתה, that they be allowed to settle in Goshen.

It is here that the purpose of the audience becomes clear. Joseph had not instructed his brothers to say this; it was due to their own initiative. The Pharaoh is to hear from the brothers themselves that they have no desire to rise above their present occupation and that they want to settle where they can exercise it.

[**47:5-6**] The Pharaoh's answer in vv. 5-6 is directed to Joseph as the official answer of the Pharaoh to his minister who is responsible for carrying out his instructions. The Pharaoh has not yet responded to Joseph's communication in v. 1. He now takes it up, but with a conscious nuance (B. Jacob): "So your father and your brothers have come *to you*." He is happy that his minister, to whom he owes so much, is united again with his father and his brothers. With royal generosity he leaves it open to his minister to choose a place for his family to live: "The land of Egypt lies open to you" (cf. 45:18). So far the Pharaoh has spoken expressly to his minister; he now gives an answer to the particular request made by the brothers: they may settle in the land of Goshen. But he goes beyond what is asked; he offers those who are competent and suited (אנשי-חיל = competent, capable men, as in Ex. 18:21) the possibility of rising to overseers in the royal domains. According to A. Erman such an office is entitled: "Supervisor of the horns, paws, and toes."

[47:7-10] A further audience follows immediately in vv. 7-10. Joseph presents his father to the Pharaoh. The audience is not connected with vv. 1-6, but belongs to the priestly writing (so most exegetes) and has been appended to the preceding by a redactor. Within the priestly writing it is part of the conclusion of the story of Jacob and so of the conclusion of the patriarchal story. It is not, therefore, part of the Joseph story even though the beginning of v. 7a gives this impression. It is neither a narrative nor even an expanded genealogical note. One might describe it as an account of a blessing. The middle part of this short scene comprises a question by the Pharaoh (v. 8) and Jacob's reply (v. 9). Jacob blesses the Pharaoh both at the beginning and the end.

[47:7] An audience with the Pharaoh demands a special occasion; but in the priestly context we no longer know what this was; for the redactor it was the Pharaoh's generous reception of Jacob's family into his land. A sufficient reason would be the desire of the Pharaoh's highest minister to present his father who had come to see him. The appropriate greeting would be a prostration or some equivalent form of obeisance. Instead it is simply said, "And Jacob blessed the Pharaoh." Exegetes are divided as to whether a "mere" greeting or an act of blessing is meant. But the word ברך does not admit of this alternative. It can, to be sure, mean a simple greeting (e.g., 1 Sam. 13:10; 2 Kings 4:29); but the meaning "bless" always resonates. In certain circumstances, determined on each occasion by the context, the meaning "blessing" prevails. This is the case especially on the occasion of a farewell when the one who remains blesses the one who is departing (before a journey) or vice versa (before death). The meaning of the blessing must emerge from the context. As part of the audience it is of course also a greeting; but in this particular situation it has the force of a blessing. Jacob enters the Pharaoh's presence as a foreigner, a shepherd from the steppes who, through the mediation of his sons, has to beg the Pharaoh's minister for bread. He goes through the procedure of blessing the great potentate before whom he stands. It is this incongruity that gives this blessing its peculiar character and dignity. And just because the creator has given his blessing to all creatures (Gen. 1:28), so too the humblest has something to give or bestow by blessing (Job 29:13; 31:20). This is the case with Jacob, even though meeting the Pharaoh for the first time; it is his farewell. He is face to face with death. Even the Pharaoh of Egypt has a share in the blessing that the one departing this life has to pass on. It is this that is expressed in the brief exchange in vv. 8-9.

[47:8-9] The Pharaoh asks Jacob about his age. This is not a matter of mere curiosity (so G. W. Coats); it is an act of sharing. It binds together momentarily the Pharaoh as a person with this foreign person. It is a question of what they have in common. Jacob answers the king by giving the number of the "days of his years." But he does not want to glory in the number; they have been "few and hard." The words are spoken from a position of lofty perspective; they are the mature fruit of a life of experience. The one blessed also has his share of human suffering. The word "few" (brief) is not subject to measurement; it refers to the long periods of suffering which have shortened his life (37:35; 45:27). Jacob calls his years "the years of his sojourning." This phrase does not occur elsewhere in P who speaks only of "the land of sojourning" (Gen. 17:8; 28:4; 36:7; 37:1; Ex. 6:4). It is possible that this points to a later level within P (so L. Ruppert following R. Smend, who also considers that the number 130 is calculated from 47:28 (P). But a general use of this sort would also be possible in a text belonging to the conclusion of the patriarchal story.

[47:10] The meeting ends with Jacob blessing the Pharaoh again (*inclusio*); he then leaves the presence (cf. 2 Sam. 14:17, where a blessing also closes an address to a king; J. Hoftijzer, VT 20 [1970] 442; J. Pedersen, *Israel. . .* [1926] 182-202).

      Jacob now goes to meet his death. He wants to bless his children and their children before he dies. But the king of Egypt is also included in the dying man's blessing. There is a remote point of contact here with the promise of blessing made to Abraham which extends to "all the families of the earth" (Gen. 12:1-3; cf. *Genesis 12–36*, comm. ad loc.). Not only in the Yahwist's patriarchal story, but also in the priestly account, the blessing given to each of the successive patriarchs is not restricted to the ancestors of Israel and the people of Israel which took its origin from them. It reaches far beyond the patriarchs and is directed to the whole of the human race.

[47:11-12] These verses follow, at least in part, on 46:28—47:6. The Pharaoh's approval, given in v. 6, is spelled out in detail; the הושב of v. 6 corresponds to ויושב (v. 11a); this is as "the Pharaoh had commanded" (v. 11b); likewise the Pharaoh's במיטב הארץ from v. 6 recurs in v. 11. But v. 11 is a synthesis; a note about the place should follow immediately on "and Joseph settled his father and his brothers. . ." (v. 11a, corresponding again to v. 6); instead, a new sentence is inserted, "and he gave them property in Egypt. . .in the land of Rameses." There are two peculiarities here. "The land of Rameses" occurs only in this passage (and in a secondary insertion in the Gk in 46:28); it is a city in Ex. 1:11; 12:37; Num. 33:3, 5, one of the storage cities which the Israelites had to build in Egypt, and then the city from which they began their exodus. "The land of Rameses" is an anachronism here (cf. W. F. Albright, *Yahweh and the Gods of Canaan* [1968] 79; D. B. Redford, VT 13 [1963] 401-418). The second peculiarity is the use of אחזה, a word characteristic of P (Gen. 17:8; 23:4, 9, 20; 36:43; 47:11; 48:4; 49:30; 50:13; cf. G. Gerleman, ZAW 89 [1977] 317). The sentence "and he gave them property in the land of Egypt" contradicts the request of the brothers in v. 4, לגור בארץ; if they possess land they are no longer גרים. One can conclude then with certainty that the sentence inserted is taken from or belongs to P; it was probably part of P, along with vv. 7-10. The continuation of 46:28—47:6 then is: "And Joseph settled his father and his brothers in the best part of the land (in the land of Goshen), as the Pharaoh had commanded."

[47:12] V. 12 is not a doublet of v. 11, as many exegetes think, but its necessary expansion; it is written in face of the famine which is still prevailing in Egypt. The family would not be helped merely by being allowed to settle; it must also be provided with food (the same word in 45:11). They receive sufficient to satisfy them, according to the number of "children's mouths."

[**47:27-28**] The conclusion, vv. 27-28, is separated from 48:28—47:1-12 by the insertion of the appendage, vv. 13-26. In the Joseph narrative 46:28—47:1-6, 11-12 concludes with v. 27a, "So Israel dwelt in the land of Egypt, in the land of Goshen." The P insertion, vv. 7-10, 11*, concludes with vv. 27b-28.

[**47:27a**] The proposal that Joseph sent to his father through his brothers is now a reality, "You shall dwell in the land of Goshen" (45:10). The Joseph narrative could now close. However, the death of Jacob belongs here also; this had been anticipated in 45:28 when the brothers brought their news.

[**47:27b-28**] It is the general opinion that vv. 27bf. belong to P. In accordance with 47:11b the members of Jacob's family acquire property in Egypt (the same form as in Gen. 34:10). They multiply there; the phrase points forward to Ex. 1:7 where Gen. 47:27 is resumed immediately; it occurred previously in the promise of Gen. 35:11. Then comes the information about Jacob's age, of equal importance for P; he lived another 17 years in Egypt and the sum total of his life span was 147 years (cf. 47:7-10).

Purpose and Thrust [46:31-34; 47:1-12, 27-28]

There are still echoes of the famine motif in the request of the brothers as they stand before the Pharaoh (v. 4); it binds the two cycles of the Joseph narrative together (chs. 37:42-45f. and 39–41; cf. Intro., II); the motif of reunion resonates in the Pharaoh's answer in v. 5. The narrator thus closes his narrative cycle; it is no mere chance that the final words are spoken in an audience with the Pharaoh. Joseph had been rejected by his brothers and had come to the court of the Egyptian king; as the king's minister he had brought about the reconciliation with his brothers and had enabled the family to survive the famine; all this presupposes the institution of the monarchy. The narrator recalls Joseph's dreams in ch. 37. The closing audience is a silent witness to the positive value of the monarchy. Joseph's words about the hidden action of God on the occasion of the reconciliation includes the Pharaoh's throne as well. At the same time, however, the audience makes clear that Joseph's brothers are not to make a career for themselves at the Pharaoh's court under the auspices of their brother, the minister. They are to remain what they were; they stay on the borderland as shepherds of their flocks; they remain "aliens." A time will come when they will depart so as to become "Israel" (47:27a).

In P's final synthesis with the conclusion of the Jacob story, the audience of the patriarch Joseph with the Pharaoh follows that of the brothers; though it is such an entirely different audience it is nevertheless meaningful and harmonious in the overall context of the patriarchal story. The old man from foreign parts blesses the Pharaoh in all the splendor of his throne. He is able to bless him because in the greeting-blessing God's blessing is communicated, and before God both the Pharaoh and the old man are as one—human. The blessing which the patriarchs have received and pass on in their family extends further (Gen. 12:3) because it is the blessing of the creator.

Commentary

[47:13-26] An appendage: the introduction of the one-fifth tax in Egypt. This text as an individual narrative is given its stamp by the etiological conclusion in v. 26. The phrase "to this day" determines the text as an etiological narrative (cf. *Genesis 12–36*, pp. 51-52). A current practice is to be explained from an event in the past (so too H. Gunkel). The text arose as an independent unit and has been attached to the Joseph story as a later appendage; it interrupts the continuity between vv. 11-12 and 27f. The content confirms this. What is narrated here has no function in the narrative span of the Joseph story (so too J. Wellhausen, J. Skinner). It is to be explained from its etiological conclusion. It arose from awareness of an amazing situation in the area of property ownership in Egypt, an awareness given concrete form long after Joseph's time. The phrase "to this day" always indicates a long period of time. Looking back over this period the current situation is explained by Joseph's action as known to the author through the Joseph narrative. He presupposes it, and attaches the present story to it, however loosely.

The division of the text is difficult and raises a number of questions. There are three parts: the situation (introduction) (vv. 13-14), the first year (vv. 15-17), the second year (vv. 18-26). The device of heightening is used here. Under the pressure of the famine Joseph collects all the Egyptian farmers' money (vv. 13-14), all their cattle (vv. 15-17), and land and reduces the people to servitude (vv. 18-21). This is obviously an intellectual construction because none of these stages is in reality feasible. The division is striking in that the second part (the second year, vv. 18-26) is much longer than the first (vv. 15-17); the outcome is mentioned twice (vv. 20-22 and 26) and this disturbs the overall structure. Joseph's answer to the Egyptians' plea in vv. 18-29 follows only in vv. 23-24; in between comes the first outcome (vv. 20-22), which differs from the second (v. 26). This gives rise to further incongruities. The two most striking are (1) that the measures taken by Joseph in vv. 13-15a affect Egypt and Canaan and from there on to the end only Egypt; and (2) that the measures taken in vv. 13-22 are to alleviate the famine (first outcome), and in vv. 23-24 to provide seed for sowing (second outcome).

The style has drawn only negative comments from the exegetes. H. Holzinger speaks of an "unpalatable style" which is to be attributed neither to J nor to E. G. von Rad observes: "The narrative is somewhat schematic and betrays a theoretical interest"; "Joseph's partner, the starving people, is rather anonymous and colorless." The awkward style is seen in various details. It is striking that many words which occur elsewhere only seldom or not at all are late (proof for this in D. B. Redford). The question is continually raised of the relationship of what is narrated here to the actual situation in Egypt, of which we otherwise know nothing. In any case we are poorly informed about the economic history of Egypt (J. Vergote, *Joseph en Egypte* [1959]). Vergote is of the opinion that the Egyptian sources known to us present a much more complicated picture than does the present narrative (D. B. Redford; H. C. Schmitt). In any case one can say that generally from the first dynasty to the Ptolemaic period the king was regarded theoretically as the sole owner of land in Egypt (D. B. Redford; R. de Vaux; H. Holzinger had already said this, as had Herodotus and Diodorus). It squares poorly with this that somewhere in the middle of this history a minister bought all the land for the Pharaoh. But "so far we have no domestic information about this from Egypt" (A. Dillmann; likewise R. de Vaux and others). Many exegetes point to the rise of the New Kingdom after the expulsion of the Hyksos as a possible historical setting when the crown appropriated a great deal of land belonging to the nobility. D. B. Redford on the contrary favors the Saitic period (H. C. Schmitt opposes it). If a historical setting were established one would have to say at the same time that the causes of such an appropriation were other than those described in Gen. 47.

If one takes as starting point that it is a matter of an etiological narrative, then one must admit that the background is not precise and detailed information but rather vague and general knowledge of Egyptian affairs. This applies too to the information provided by Herodotus and Diodorus which has a similar ring; both also mention that the priests are exempt from tax. This is in accord with Gen. 47 where no distinction is made between the sovereign right of the Pharaoh over the whole of the land of Egypt and the fact of certain royal domains, as presupposed in 47:6. Only from a distance could the life of the Egyptian farmers as a whole appear as bondage; D. B. Redford points out that in all periods there was free landed property. The special rights of the temple lands are appreciated correctly.

[47:13-14] By way of introduction the first two verses expound the situation which the author obviously uses as his point of contact with the Joseph story, in particular with 41:53-57, the famine in Egypt. He derives from this text that the famine prevailed also in Canaan (41:57; 42:1-4). But he mentions Canaan together with Egypt only in vv. 13, 14, 15a, and not afterwards. The author thereby wants to make a bridge from the Joseph story (so too H. C. Schmitt, BZAW 154 [1980] 66). In v. 14 he mentions only briefly the first measures taken by Joseph; this is more by way of exposition, because he found it in the Joseph narrative at hand to him (41:57), where, however, the buyers were only those coming from other lands. He draws the consequence that Joseph collected "all the money" from Egypt and Canaan and delivered it over to the Pharaoh.

[47:15-17] After the money had run out (v. 15a), Joseph takes the Egyptian farmers' cattle in exchange for the bread he gives them (vv. 15-17). The introduction (v. 15a) is followed by the negotiation: the Egyptians ask Joseph for bread (v. 15b); Joseph requires their cattle in exchange (v. 16). The transaction follows in v. 17; the Egyptians bring their cattle (v. 17a) and Joseph gives them bread (v. 17b).

[47:15-16] The introduction (v. 15a) resumes the situation (v. 14); and so once again "Egypt and Canaan" appear. Only Egyptians take part in the subsequent negotiations (vv. 15b, 16). The request of the Egyptians for bread (v. 15b) is formed on the pattern of 41:55 ("the people cried to the Pharaoh for bread," and he referred them to Joseph); it is divided into lament and request, the lament following the request. The reason is an unnecessary and clumsy addition; likewise in v. 16b, which merely repeats the introduction (v. 15a). Joseph's answer is quite cool and businesslike: Bring your cattle (הבו—הבו), and I will exchange them. This is not a true reflection of reality; how could it be carried out practically? Hence B. Jacob is of the opinion that what is meant is only a legal agreement. But, as G. von Rad notes, this fits poorly with "they brought their cattle to Joseph" (v. 17a).

[47:17] The carrying out of the agreement follows in v. 17 with an enumeration of the cattle that the Egyptians (the Canaanites are missing) brought to Joseph (cf. H. J. Stoebe, VT 4 [1954] 177-184). The execution closes with a resumé: Joseph provided for the Egyptians in return for their cattle (the verb נהל in this sense is found only here). The determination in time, ''in that year'' echoes on here without any further precision.

[47:18-26] This second part diverges markedly from the first (vv. 15-17). It too begins with a petition, vv. 18-19, which at the same time contains an offer. Joseph's answer follows only in vv. 23-24 with the agreement of the Egyptians in v. 25. The outcome is different in vv. 20-22 and v. 26.

[47:18-19] The second petition begins with a chronological note; after the year has ended the Egyptians approach Joseph again in the second year. It is difficult to make a link between this and the seven years of famine in the Joseph story, as some exegetes attempt (H. Gunkel, B. Jacob, E. I. Lowenthal), because there is no chronological note in vv. 13f. The chronology that determines vv. 18-26 is expressed rather in the request and offer of the Egyptians in vv. 18b, 19. Joseph has received all their money and likewise all their cattle; all that remains to them is their own persons and their land. They offer Joseph both in return for bread so that they and their land may not perish. They want to put themselves with their land in servitude to the Pharaoh. There is an incongruity here inasmuch as the request of the Egyptians is concerned with bread (v. 19a, just as in vv. 15-17), whereas their offer is concerned with seed (v. 19b). The explanation derives from the different outcome in vv. 20-22 and v. 26. The bread belongs to the three stages of the famine, v. 18b, the seed to the tax of one-fifth. They are joined together clumsily in a passage of awkward style (vv. 18-19).

[47:20-22] One expects now Joseph's answer to the request and offer, following the sequence of v. 16 and v. 15b in the first part. Instead the outcome is described in vv. 20-22, corresponding to v. 17b; Joseph's answer is given clumsily in vv. 23-24. The outcome, vv. 20-22, is divided into the sale of the land (v. 20), the enslavement of the people (v. 21), and the exemption of the priests (v. 22). The two verses 20 and 21 (bracketing out the exemption in v. 22) form an obvious conclusion. Joseph buys all the arable land of the Egyptians for the Pharaoh and puts the whole people in servitude ''from one end of Egypt to the other'' (see above for the emendation of the text). This then is the outcome of the measures taken by Joseph in the three stages of the famine. The author of vv. 13-16 knew two traditions; this is the outcome in one of them.

[47:22] The priests are exempt. Joseph did not acquire their land (v. 22a); they did not need to sell it because they had an income from the Pharaoh from which they were able to live (חק with the meaning ''income'' in P, Ex. 29:28; Lev. 10:13f., and in late writings Ezek. 16:27; Prov. 30:8; 31:15; cf. J. P. M. van der Ploeg, CBQ 12 [1950] 252; P. Victor, VT 16 [1966] 359). The privileges of the priesthood accord with the historical reality, but the situation is even more complicated and variable than it appears here (cf. R. de Vaux, *Ancient Israel* [1958; Eng. 1962] 379ff., 403ff.; D. B. Redford, VT.S 20 [1970] 238f.).

[**47:23-24**] Only after all this is concluded do we have in vv. 23-24 Joseph's answer to the request and offer of the Egyptians in vv. 18-19 (O. Procksch: v. 23 follows on v. 19); however, it is adapted in anticipation of the other outcome in v. 26. In the two parts of v. 23 Joseph guarantees the request made to him (v. 23a) and accepts the offer of the Egyptians. The two parts are introduced by הֵן and הֵא (both are intended as demonstrative interjections; הֵא is found elsewhere only in Ezek. 16:43; and Dan. 2:43). It now becomes clear why the talk here is no longer of bread but of seed. The Egyptians must hand over to the Pharaoh one-fifth of the produce that comes from the seed: "Four-fifths [of the seed given to you] is to be yours; you can dispose of it as seed and to provide food for yourselves, your families and your children. You have an abundance for all this."

[**47:25**] In this way v. 25 becomes comprehensible. It can only refer to the assurance given by Joseph in vv. 23b, 24 with the emphasis on the guarantee (v. 24b). Pointing to the seed given them, they can say, "you have saved our lives"; and in the second part they can give expression to their gratitude with "may we find favor in the eyes of our lord." The last sentence could be an addition, harmonizing with v. 19b. It is also possible that "we will be slaves" is meant in the general sense of courtly language. Were v. 25 to refer to the outcome in vv. 20-22, then this would be so macabre or even so hypocritical a reaction that it could not even be attributed to the most inept of authors.

[**47:26**] The concluding v. 26a belongs to a different tradition from the conclusion in vv. 20-22. In it the introduction of the tax of one-fifth of the produce had been explained by means of a generous gift of seed to the people in a year when the harvest failed; it meant the saving of the lives of the farmers. The conclusion, vv. 20-22, refers only to the three successive and intensifying stages; it says nothing of the one-fifth tax. In fact a tax of one-fifth would be meaningless because in vv. 20-22 the Egyptian farmers lose all—their money, their cattle, their land, and their freedom; in giving over one-fifth in vv. 24, 26 they lose far less. The last sentence, v. 26b, is an addition by the author in which he balances v. 26 and vv. 20-22. It is not at all appropriate; what should be said here is that the priests do not have to pay the one-fifth tax. It is only a briefer repetition of v. 22.

Closing Remarks on 47:13-26

It emerges from the exegesis that 47:13-26 is a later addition to the Joseph story. It has been added by an author who had been impressed by the way in which land ownership was distributed in Egypt and wanted to derive it from Joseph and the measures he introduced. He knew the Joseph story and attached the addition loosely to it. But it has no perceptible function there. One can certainly not say that what is narrated here "brings Joseph's influential activity in Egypt to its peak" (F. Delitzsch). The mind of the author was that it was Joseph who carried through the measures which deprived the Egyptians of all their money, cattle, land, and freedom and thus substantially increased the power and property of the Pharaoh (so the majority of authors). Some have seen here a later stage in the process of idealizing the patriarchs (e.g., E. A. Speiser). But is such the case? Some have also thought that behind the narrative one can discern attitudes at the court at about the period of Solomon which wanted to legitimize the taxing of the people by means of the patriarchs (F. Crüsemann, WMANT 49 [1978]); this too is perhaps possible. But such attitudes are not necessary to explain 47:13-26; the etiological conclusion suffices to explain its origin. And this goes for the two motifs which are so clumsily united here, one with its outcome in vv. 20-22, and the other with its outcome in v. 26.

Jacob's Testimony

Literature

Genesis 47:29-31: C. Bruston, "Les trois récits de la mort de Jacob," RThQR 4 (1906) 359-366. B. Alfrink, "L'expression שָׁכַב עִם אֲבוֹתָיו," OTS 2 (1943) 106-118. R. C. Dentan, "The Literary Affinities of Ex XXXIV 6f.," VT 13 (1963) 34-51. J. Barr, "St. Jerome and the Sounds of Hebrew," JSS 12 (1967) 1-36. O. Böcher, "Der Judeneid," EvTh 30 (1970) 671-681. J. G. Heintz, "Aux origines d'une expression biblique: *ūmūšū qerbū*, in A.R.M., X/6,8?" VT 21 (1971) 528-540.

Genesis 48: A. F. Rainey, "Family Relationship in Ugarit," Or 34 (1965) 10-22. J. C. H. Lebram, "Jakob segnet Josephs Söhne. Darstellungen von Gen. XLVIII in der Überlieferung und bei Rembrandt," OTS 15 (1969) 145-169. E. Cortese, *La terra di Canaan nella storia sacerdotale del Pentateuco* (PaideiaSuppl alla RivBibl 5 [1972]). J. Van Seters, *Abraham in History and Tradition* (1975) esp. 88f. W. Kornfeld, "Nicht publizierte hebräische Bibelfragmente aus der Papyrussammlung der oesterreichischen Nationalbibliothek," AAWW.PH 117 (1980) 1-8.

Genesis 48:1-7: K. Budde, "Genesis 48:1-7 und die benachbarten Abschnitte," ZAW 3 (1883) 56f. F. Delitzsch, *Prolegomena eines neuen hebr.-aram. Wörterbuches zum AT* (1886) 95f. R. Franckh, "Zur Bedeutung von עוֹלָם," ZAW 34 (1914) 232f. E. Dhorme, *L'évolution religieuse d'Israel I* (1937) esp. 342-344. F. Willesen, "The אפרתי of the Shibboleth Incident," VT 8 (1958) 97f. I. Mendelsohn, "A Ugaritic Parallel to the Adoption of Ephraim and Manasseh," IEJ 9 (1959) 180-183. E. J. Bickerman, "Bénédiction et Prière," RB 69 (1962) 524-532. M. Tsevat, "Studies in the Book of Samuel," HUCA 33 (1962) 107-118. N. A. von Echelen, "Abraham als Felsen (Jes 51,1)," ZAW 80 (1968) 183-191. J. Blenkinsopp, "Kiriath-Jearim and the Ark," JBL 88 (1969) 143-156. H. Donner, "Adoption oder Legitimation? Erwägungen zur Adoption im AT auf dem Hintergrund der altorientalischen Rechte," OrAnt 8 (1969) 87-119. M. Haran, "*Zebah hayya mîm*," VT 19 (1969) 11-22. A. Verger, "Il problema dell'adozione nella Benesi," *Studi in onore di E. Volterra VI* (1969) 483-490. W. L. Holladay, "The Covenant with the Patriarchs Overturned," JBL 91 (1972) 305-320. W. Vogels, "Invitation à revenir à l'alliance et universalisme en Amos IX 7," VT 22 (1972) 223-239. H. J. Boecker, "Anmerkungen zur Adoption im AT," ZAW 86 (1974) 86-89. W. J. Dumbrell, "The Role of Bethel in the Biblical Narratives from Jacob to Jerobeam I," AJBA 2.3 (1974/75) 65-75. A. G. Auld, "Judges I and History: A Reconsideration," VT 25 (1975) 261-285. P. D. Miller, "The Blessing of God. An Interpretation of Numbers 6:22-27," *Interp.* 29 (1975) 240-251. E. Vogt, "Benjamin geboren 'eine Meile von Ephrata,'" Bib 56 (1975) 30-36. G. Garbini, "La tomba di Rachele es ebr. *bērâ* 'ora doppia cammino,'" Bi e Or 19 (1977) 45-48.

Genesis 48:8-14: M. D. Goldman, "The Root פלל and its Connotation with Prayer," ABR 3 (1953) 1-6. D. R. Ap-Thomas, "Notes on Some Terms Relating to Prayer," VT 6 (1956) 225-241. J. Ziegler, "Zur Septuaginta-Vorlage im Deuteronomium," ZAW 72 (1960) 237-262. P. Humbert, " 'Etendre la main,' " VT 12 (1962) 383-395. E. A. Speiser, "The Stem *pll* in Hebrew," JBL 82 (1963) 301-306. H. Mowvley, "The Concept and Content of 'Blessing' in the OT," BiTr 16 (1965) 74-80. D. J. Wiseman, "Syria: Alalakh," *Archaeology. . .*, ed. D. W. Thomas (1967) 127f. A. de Wilde, "Eine alte Crux Interpretum. Hiob XXIII2," VT 22 (1972) 368-374. C. Houtman, "Zu I Samuel 2,24," ZAW 89 (1977) 412-417.

Genesis 48:15-22: C. Bruston, "La mort et la sépulture de Jacob," ZAW 7 (1887) 202-210. B. Stade, "Die Dreizahl im AT," ZAW 26 (1906) 124-141. A. Bentzen, *Introduction to the OT I-II* (1948/49; 1952²), "Poetry: Patriarchal Words." A. R. Johnson, "The Primary Meaning of the Root גאל," VT.S 1 (1953) 67-77. O. Eissfeldt, "Zwei verkannte Militär-technische Termini im AT," VT 5 (1955) 232-238. A. Jepsen, "Die Begriffe des 'Erlösens' im AT," *Fests. R. Hermann* (1957) 153-163. I. Mendelsohn, "On the Preferential Status of the Eldest Son," BASOR 156 (1959) 38-40. M. Dahood, "Ugaritic-Hebrew Philology," Bi e Or 17 (1965). W. Janzen, "'*Ašrē* in the OT," HThR 58 (1965) 215-226. E. C. Kingsbury, " 'He Set Ephraim before Manasseh,' " HUCA 38 (1967) 129-136. G. Wehmeier, "The Theme 'Blessing for the Nations' in the Promise to the Patriarchs and in Prophetical Literature," *Bangalore TheolForum* 6 (1974) 1-13. V. Hirth, *Gottes Boten im AT. Die alttestamentliche Mal'ak-Vorstellung unter besonderer Berücksichtigung des Mal'ak-Jahwe-Problems*, ThA 32 (1975). K. Jaroš, *Sichem II* (1976) 67-98. O. Keel, "Der Bogen als Herrschaftssymbol," ZDPV 93 (1977) 141-177.

Text

47:29 When the time drew near that Israel was to[a] die, he summoned his son Joseph and said to him, If I have found favor in your eyes, put your hand under my thigh and be loyal and true[b] to me; do not bury me in Egypt.

30 When I lie[a] with my fathers, bring me out of Egypt and bury me in their grave. He answered, I will do as you have said.

31 And he said, Swear to me. And he swore to him. Then Israel inclined towards the head of the bed.[a]

48:1 Now after this Joseph was told,[a] See, your father is ill. So he took his two sons Manasseh and Ephraim with him 'and went to Jacob'.[b]

2 And Jacob was informed,[a] See, your son Joseph is coming to you. Then he summoned up his strength and sat up in bed.

3 And Jacob said to Joseph, God Almighty appeared to me in Luz[a] in the land of Canaan and blessed[b] me.

4 And he said to me, See, I will make you fruitful and multiply you so that you become a gathering of nations.[a] I will give this land to your descendants after you as a permanent possession.[b]

5 Now your two sons, who were born to you in the land of Egypt before I came down, belong to me. Ephraim and Manasseh are mine, like Reuben and Simeon.

6 But the children born to you after them, they belong to you. They shall be called after the name of their brothers in the matter of their inheritance.

7 When I was coming from Paddan,[a] I[b] lost Rachel;[c] she died on the way in the land of Canaan when there was still some distance to go to Ephrath; and I buried her on the way to Ephrath, that is, Bethlehem.

8 When Israel saw Joseph's sons he asked, Who are these?[a]

9 Joseph said to his father, These are the sons whom God has given me here. And he said,[a] Bring them here to me[b] and I will bless[c] them.

10   Israel's eyes were dim[a] with age and he could not see. But when he
     brought them to him, he kissed and embraced them.

11   And Israel said to Joseph, I had not expected[a] to see you again;[b] and
     now God has allowed me to see your sons as well!

12   Then Joseph lifted them from his knees and bowed[a] towards[b] the
     ground.

13   Then Joseph took the two of them and put Ephraim on his right, Isra-
     el's left, and Manasseh on his left, Israel's right, and brought them to
     him.

14   And Israel stretched out his right hand and laid it on Ephraim's
     head—he was the younger[a]—and his left hand on Manasseh's head,
     crossing[b] his arms—for Manasseh was the firstborn.[c]

15   He blessed Joseph[a] and said,
         The God before whom my fathers Abraham and Isaac walked,
         the God who was my shepherd[b] my whole life long[c] to this very day,

16   the angel,[a] who ransomed me from all distress, may he bless these
     boys so that my name may live on[b] in them,
         and the name of my fathers Abraham and Isaac, so that they may
         grow and become many[c] in the land.

17   When Joseph saw that his father had laid his right hand on Ephraim's
     head, he was displeased, and he grasped his father's hand so as to
     lift it from Ephraim's head to Manasseh's,

18   saying to his father, No, my father, this is the firstborn; put your hand
     on his head.

19   But his father refused and said, I know, my son, I know well.[a] He too
     shall become a people, he too shall be great. Nevertheless, his
     younger brother shall be greater than he, and his descendants shall
     be a company of peoples.[b]

20   That day he blessed them, saying, In 'you'[a] will Israel bless 'itself'[b]
     with these words, May God make you like Ephraim and Manasseh.
     Thus he gave Ephraim precedence over Manasseh.

21   And Israel said to Joseph, See, I am about to die. But God will be with
     you and will bring you back to the land of your fathers.

22   And I, I present to you[a] one[b] ridge of land in preference to your broth-
     ers; I took it from the Amorites with my sword and bow.

47:29a Likewise 1 Kings 2:1; cf. J. G. Heintz, VT 21 (1971) 528-540.   **b** As in Gen.
24:49; 32:11; cf. R. C. Dentan, VT 13 (1963) 34-51.
30a Protasis; cf. Deut. 31:16; B. J. Alfrink, OTS 2 (1943) 106-118.
31a Gk τῆς ῥάβδου αὐτοῦ, presupposing הַמַּטֶּה; Jacob bowed over the head (top?) of the
staff; cited thus in Heb. 11:21. J. Barr has given a convincing explanation why the Gk understood the word in this way (JSSt 12 [1967] 31f.).
48:1a The indefinite personal subject, Ges-K §144d n. 2; BrSynt §36d; the plural is more
usual. Better to point וַיֹּאמֶר; so the versions; cf. Is. 2:2.   **b** Add with Gk.
2a Read with Gk לֵאמֹר. . . וַיֻּגַּד.
3a On the equating of Bethel and Luz, cf. A. G. Auld VT 25 (1975) 271.   **b** "Blessed
me" in the sense of "promised me."
4a קְהַל עַמִּים, as in Gen. 28:3, with which the whole verse is to be compared; also
35:11.   **b** As Gen. 17:8.
7a In all other passages Paddan-aram, which Sam and Gk add by way of
harmonization.   **b** עָלַי in the sense of "to my loss"; J. Skinner, "to my
sorrow."   **c** Sam and Gk add "your mother"; read MT.
8a Sam and Gk add לְךָ.
9a Gk adds "Jacob."   **b** On the form, Ges-K 58g; 61g; B. Jacob "Take them (by the

hand and bring them) to me.''   **c** On the form, Ges-K §29q; 60d.
10a ''To be heavy,'' used of an organic malfunction; A. de Wilde VT 22 (1972) 368-374;
an explanatory note as Gen. 27:23; 37:21.
11a פלל only here meaning ''expect'' ''suppose''; cf. E. A. Speiser, JBL 82 (1963)
301-306; D. R. Ap-Thomas, VT 6 (1956) 225-241; C. Houtman, ZAW 89 (1977)
412-417.   **b** On the form, Ges-K §75n; 115b; cf. Gen. 31:28; 50:20.
12a Sam, Gk, Syr read the plural.   **b** On the ל, really ''on his countenance,'' BrSynt
§107a; Gk and Syr read לו אפים.
14a ''Although he. . .,'' Ges-K §141e.   **b** Circumstantial verbal clause Ges-K
§156d; usually means ''cross'' (also KBL), following an Arabic verb šakala; likewise Gk
and Vg; on the other hand some follow I שׂכל ''understand''; B. Jacob ''he reflected on his
hands.''   **c** The last three words are missing in the Gk.
15a By way of harmonizing Gk reads אתם.   **b** On the construction, BrSynt
§99a.   **c** As Num. 22:30; Gk, Syr, Vg ''from my youth.''
16a Sam has המלך.   **b** Compare Gen. 21:12.   **c** On the construction, BrSynt
§107id; the verb דגה occurs only here, perhaps related to דג (the spawning of fish) and
דגן(?).
19a On the asyndetic repetition, BrSynt §134e.   **b** Deut. 33:17.
20ab The text before us reads, ''in you Israel is to bless.'' One cannot exclude this as the
original text; what is meant becomes clearer when one reads, instead of the qal, the niph. or
the hith. meaning, ''to use someone's name as a proverbial blessing formula'' (H.
Holzinger).
22a ''I hereby grant to you,'' Ges-K §106i.   **b** On the form אחד, Ges-K §130g.

Form

After the reconciliation (ch. 45) and the reunion of father and son (ch. 46) there
follow in 46:31—47:28 the provision for the family and its settlement in Egypt
(with expansions). Something else begins in 47:29-31—the death and burial of Jacob, introduced in 47:29 by ''When the time drew near when Israel was to die.''
With this begins the account of the death of the patriarch Jacob. The prelude (Jacob's last words and legacy) and likewise the interment are part of this. Joseph
promises his father to inter him in Canaan (47:29-31), and fulfills the promise,
mentioned expressly in 50:5, in 50:1-14. The whole complex 47:29—50:14 is
thus clamped together.

There is constant anticipation of Jacob's death throughout the Joseph narrative (37:35; 42:38; 43:27f.; 44:22, 29, 31; 45:9, 13, 28; 46:30); it is to be expected, therefore, that it will conclude with an account of his death (so too H.
Gunkel; differently, D. B. Redford). The drama between Joseph and his brothers
also concerns the father; must he ''go down mourning into the realm of the dead''
(37:35 and elsewhere; especially at the climax in 44:29) or can he die in peace (so
in 45:25)? The movement of the narrative therefore demands an account of Jacob's death at the end. The death of Jacob the patriarch belongs at the same time to
another context of which it is likewise an essential constituent, namely, the conclusion of the story of Jacob as a part of the patriarchal story. The account of Jacob's death in 49:29-33, found only in P, is conclusive proof of this. The whole is
in essence not narrative but account, a genealogical report of Jacob's last will,
death, and burial, even though with narrative adornments and adaptations.

Gen. 47:29-31; 48; 49:1-28 form a part of the entire complex
47:29—50:14; they are texts of the last dispositions of Jacob before his death.
These texts are independent of each other and of different origin. This holds at
first glance for 49:1-28, the ''blessing of Jacob,'' which has its form of a last will

and testament of Jacob only through stylization and has been positioned here for that reason. J. Wellhausen, M. Noth, and W. Rudolf have recognized that the synthetic structure of ch. 48 is not to be explained by mere literary critical methods (in agreement D. B. Redford, G. W. Coats, and others); on the other hand, many exegetes from A. Dillmann to H. C. Schmitt adhere to source division. H. C. Schmitt, for example, divides the text into the minutest literary parts which he assigns to a whole series of layers. In order to explain the structure one must begin by asking whether it is possible to discern in it self-contained units. A first unit is the self-contained scene, 47:29-31, together with the fulfillment of the promise made there in 50:1-14. The first verse of ch. 48 is obviously a new beginning. A new scene narrates a visit of Joseph to his ailing father (48:1-12). Joseph brings his two sons with him so that he may bless them. The scene reaches an obvious conclusion in v. 12. It is interrupted by a P text in vv. 3-6(7) in which Jacob adopts Ephraim and Manasseh and gives them the rank of fathers of independent tribes. This too is an independent, self-contained unit; v. 7 is an appendage to it.

A new unit begins in v. 13. It gives an account of a blessing given to Joseph's sons by Jacob in which Jacob gives Ephraim precedence over Manasseh. It concludes with v. 20b. But the scene lacks a real beginning. A blessing of Joseph's sons by Jacob is already narrated in vv. 1-12; vv. 13-20 are appended as a continuation, giving the impression of a blessing completed in two parts. After Joseph had brought his sons to Jacob in v. 10b (this act concludes in v. 12), he brings them to him again in v. 13. Nevertheless, it is still easy to recognize the two units as of independent origin. Only vv. 13-20 are concerned with the precedence of Ephraim over Manasseh (so the conclusion, v. 20b); vv. 1-12 deal only with the blessing of Joseph's sons which closes in v. 12 as they are taken away. Vv. 13-20 have undergone subsequent expansion, just as vv. 1-12. The promise (vv. 15-16) sharply interrupts the continuity between vv. 13-14 and vv. 17-19 and shows by its language that it is a foreign body in the context. V. 20a is also a subsequent addition. The unit vv. 13-20b is followed by two further appendages in v. 21 and v. 22 which are connected with what precedes only by the situation, namely, the imminent death of Jacob. All these parts of ch. 48 are of independent origins. (On the relation of these parts to each other and on their literary connection, see below, "Genesis 46–50: Survey").

Commentary

[**47:29-31**] Jacob's request and Joseph's promise: The introduction, v. 29aα, is the introduction to the whole section that follows, right down to ch. 50. It is followed by Jacob's request that Joseph not bury him in Egypt. Joseph promises (v. 30b); Jacob demands that he swear it. After Joseph has sworn, Jacob inclines his head.

[**47:29**] It is not only in the patriarchal stories that the last dispositions or wishes of a dying person are of great significance (see the exegesis of Gen. 27 in *Genesis 12–36*). They are often part of the account of a death introduced by the phrase "When the time drew near. . ." (cf. J. G. Heintz, VT 21 [1971] 422f.). So Jacob summons his son Joseph. The submissive formulation in the request that he lays upon him is striking, "If I have found favor in your eyes. . ." (cf. Gen. 19:19; 30:27; 32:6; 33:8, 10, 15, etc.) ". . .be loyal and true to me" (really a hendiadys; cf. Gen. 24:49; THAT, and R. C. Dentan, VT 13 [1963] 34-51). It is possible to explain this from Joseph's high office (O. Procksch). However, it is better seen in the context of a pressing request expressed in the threefold נא and the assurance given by the oath. Jacob is an old man and feels a stranger in Egypt, and the strangeness weighs upon him and makes him anxious. He does not belong to Egypt; and so whatever of life remains to him is taken up with the wish to be buried where he belongs, that is, with his fathers (cf. the wish of Barzillai in 2 Sam 19:37; Ruth 1:17). He knows that Joseph alone has the power and the means to brings his body to the land of his fathers; hence he petitions him so submissively and guarantees the petition by requiring an oath (it is different in 49:29 where the request is directed to all the sons). It is possible that the narrator wants by this means to give expression to the dying man's anticipation of the future; the future of his family, of the sons of Israel, will be in Canaan, not in Egypt.

The demand for the gesture that accompanies the oath comes at the beginning (v. 29), not in v. 31, thus showing that Joseph intended right from the start to make Joseph confirm his promise with an oath.

[**47:30**] The first sentence in v. 30 is the antecedent of a condition, ''When I lie with my fathers. . .'' (on the phrase see Deut. 31:16; 1 Kings 2:10; Gen. 25:8; cf. *Genesis 12–36*, comm. on 25:8; B. J. Alfrink, OTS 2 [1943] 106-118). The next sentence, which is a positive statement of the last sentence of v. 29, echoes the repressed urgency, ''Bring me out of Egypt!'' Only then comes the positive request, ''Bury me in their grave!'' This seems to stand in direct contradiction to 50:5. When Joseph asks leave of the Pharaoh he says that his father's request was, ''Bury me in the tomb which I hewed out for myself.'' This must refer to Jacob's request in 47:30; hence many exegetes (J. Wellhausen, H. Gunkel, J. Skinner, G. von Rad, and others) have concluded that the words ''in their grave'' (47:30) are an accommodation to P (ch. 23, Machpelah) and that the original of 47:30 also read ''in my grave''; they emend the text accordingly (cf. BHK apparatus). This is possible, but not at all certain. There are often variants when speeches are repeated in other situations. Jacob's request to his son is deeply emotional and ''in their grave'' obviously refers to the beginning of v. 30: ''When I lie with my fathers. . . bury me in *their* grave!'' This can also have the broader meaning: in a grave near them, where they are. This then does not exclude the formulation that Joseph deliberately uses in the Pharaoh's presence.

[**47:31**] Joseph makes the promise and Jacob asks him to confirm it with an oath (v. 31; cf. comm. on v. 29). The gesture is the same as in Gen. 24:2, 9 and Tob. 14:12f. (cf. T. C. Vriezen, ''Eid,'' BHH, I, 374-376 with bibliog.; O. Böcher, EvTh 30 [1970] 671-681). The closing sentence, v. 31b, is comprehensible only from the anxiety and apprehension in the face of death that colors Jacob's request in vv. 29-31a. Joseph's promise, sealed by an oath, removes this concern, as v. 31b shows. Jacob is conceived as sitting on the bed during his conversation with Joseph (cf. Gen. 27:19; 48:2). He now inclines ''toward the head(s) of the bed'' (or, with B. Jacob, ''toward the head-end of the bed''). We no longer know the meaning of the phrase על־ראש המטה. The parallel in 1 Kings 1:47 is clear; here too an old man, David, bows himself upon the bed and the action is accompanied by an exclamation of praise to God. The verb השתחוה is also clear. At this moment the old man can only express what he wants to say by this gesture; it describes "the reverent act of thanksgiving of the patriarch" (F. Delitzsch; similarly almost all exegetes). His last wish is fulfilled.

[48:1-12] Joseph's visit to his ailing father is introduced in vv. 1-2 and closed in vv. 11-12; in the middle stands the blessing of Joseph's sons by Jacob, vv. 8-11; there is an interruption with vv. 3-6(7), P.

[48:1-2] This is a new beginning over against 47:29; it is the distinctive introduction of a narrative scene. The visit presupposes that something has happened beforehand. Jacob has fallen ill; as the scene is a visit to the deathbed, Jacob's death will follow. It comes meaningfully after 47:29-31; both have their setting before Jacob's death. The scene is introduced; Joseph learns that his father is ill and makes ready to go to him with his two sons; the father learns of his coming and prepares for it. This introduction expresses nicely the meaning of a visit in the life of the patriarchs. There is an occasion for each visit which renders it necessary (cf. other visit narratives, Gen. 18; 19; 24). Accordingly, something happens during the visit which is significant for both parties. It is an essential constituent part of the history that binds the two. The father, though ill and with death imminent, prepares for the visit; he, the infirm one, will be the giver.

[48:1] The function of the sentence, "And it happened after these things" (v. 1), is to insert an individual event into a broader context (cf. Gen. 15:1; 22:1, 20; 39:7; 40:1; Josh. 24:29, *Genesis 12–36*, comm. on 22:1). As here, so in Gen. 22:20 it introduces information concerning Abraham. The ויאמר requires an impersonal subject, "one said to Joseph"; the passive would be better here, as in v. 2, and that is what the versions, Gk, Syr, Vg, read, corresponding to Gen. 22:20. Following the Gk, "and went to Jacob" is to be added. This is required by the preceding verb, "so he took. . . with him," and the rhythm of the sentence.

[48:2] Joseph brings his sons with him (v. 1) and Jacob makes preparations (v. 2); both actions have the same goal, the conferring of the blessing. So the patriarch summons up his strength and sits upright (cf. ch. 27, strengthening before the act of blessing). The preparations on both sides underscore without further ado the importance attached to this blessing.

[48:3-6] The verses that follow clearly interrupt an already existing continuity; v. 8 follows on v. 2. The language is that of P; all exegetes agree on this. The text has been inserted subsequently by P; it belongs to the context of the Jacob story of the priestly writing.

The text consists of a calling to mind for Joseph's benefit of the promise that Jacob received at Luz (Bethel), and a disposition about Joseph's sons (vv. 5-6). It deals neither with a blessing given to Joseph's sons (vv. 1-12 minus vv. 3-7), nor with the precedence which the younger acquires over the elder (vv. 13-19, 20b).

[48:3-4] The introduction, "and Jacob said to Joseph," is a redactional link between vv. 3-6 and vv. 1-2. The immediate sequence to vv. 1-2 follows only in vv. 8ff. What Jacob says in vv. 3-6 has no motivation in vv. 1-2 and follows only very superficially on them. The recollection of the revelation and promise in Bethel,

vv. 3-4 (= 35:[6], 9, 11, 12), alone serves as the reason for vv. 5-6. There is no other passage where P makes the one who has received a promise repeat it almost word for word. The differences are not important (cf. *Genesis 12–36*, comm. on 35:9-12).

On this matter, see W. Brueggemann, ZAW 84 (1972) 406; R. Rendtorff, *Das überlieferungsgeschichtliche. . .* (1976; 1977²) 136-141; A. S. Kapelrud, "Fruchtbarkeit," BHH I, 530f.; P. D. Miller, *Interp.* 29 (1975) 240-251. On פרא and רבה, A. von Uchelen, ZAW 80 (1968) 183-191. G. W. Coats notes that אל שדי stands in a number of places in the context of the promise of increase; cf. D. B. Redford, p. 129, n. 1.

This recollection presupposes the long separation between Jacob and Joseph. Two important consequences follow: (1) The text 48:3-6 demonstrates with certainty that P contained its own conclusion to the Jacob story independent of the Joseph narrative. (2) This conclusion of P presupposes a rather long separation between Jacob and Joseph. Joseph came down to Egypt before Jacob; this tradition, therefore, existed independently of the Joseph narrative.

[48:5-6] The ועתה at the beginning of vv. 5-6 is very striking (it always introduces a consequence from what has preceded), for there is no thought of any such consequence in the same text in Gen. 35:9-12; it would be impossible there. How then is this consequence in 48:5-6 after vv. 3-4 to be explained? It can be understood only in the sense of a legitimation. One should recall the list of the 70 descendants of Jacob in ch. 46. P still lacks a legitimation of the two sons of Joseph, born in Egypt of an Egyptian mother, as later tribal fathers. It is this legitimation that is here. And in P's view this is possible only through Jacob, the father. This is the only way that the following of vv. 5-6 (ועתה) on vv. 3-4 becomes comprehensible. Jacob, one of the three founding fathers, has received a direct revelation from God (v. 3); this is nowhere said of Joseph. Hence Jacob alone is justified in legitimating the two sons of Joseph as fathers of tribes of Israel by declaring them to be his own sons; לי־הם (on the formula, W. Vogels, VT 22 [1972] 231) is a declaration with legal force; it is further underscored when he puts them on the same footing as Reuben and Simeon, his two eldest sons. Jacob thus gives Joseph's two sons the status of his own sons. This can be called "adoption" in a rather broad sense (cf. H. Donner [1969]; H. J. Boecker [1974], bibliog. above; A. Phillips, VT 23 [1973] 349-361); in fact it is meant as legitimation, because the sons remain with their parents; and it is a subsequent legitimation which refers only to their future as fathers of tribes. This text then is an example of the way in which P determines sacral law; the special status of the tribes of Ephraim and Manasseh is based on their legitimation by Jacob, the background to which is the revelation and promise made to him (for details, A. Dillmann; cf. H. Gunkel). P does not intend to portray here a scene that actually took place in this way; he wants only to legitimate the autonomy of the two tribes. P presents this legitimation as an event instead of an etiology, to which it is very similar; one can also regard it as a late adaptation of the etiology inasmuch as it is not a real narrative.

[48:6] V. 6 can be understood only from what has preceded. There is no mention elsewhere of additional sons of Joseph, not even by P. And they are spoken of here only hypothetically; v. 6 serves only to specify v. 5 more precisely. The legitimation is thus restricted to these two; it does not hold for any sons born later.

[48:7] The legitimation concludes with v. 6; v. 7 has no function in it. It is a literal, though partly adapted, repetition of 35:16 and 19 (v. 7b, cf. 35:16, 19; v. 7a, cf. 35:19; change from 3rd to 1st person). Jacob continues his account of the reception of the revelation in Bethel (vv. 3-4) with the death of Rachel which, in Gen. 35, immediately follows the former. Whereas vv. 3-4 repeat a P text, 35:15-21 belong to J (see *Genesis 12–36* ad loc.).

There have been many attempts to explain this account of Rachel's death in the context of vv. 3-6 or from the broader context of ch. 48. F. Delitzsch: "In the presence of Joseph the memory of the unforgettable flashes through Jacob's mind"; similarly, J. Skinner and W. Rudolf; Ch. Bruston, ZAW 7 (1887) 207f., considers that Jacob's request originally concluded in v. 7 with the wish to be buried in Rachel's grave. H. Gunkel takes this up, and O. Procksch modifies it somewhat. According to A. Dillmann P wants, by means of v. 7, to create a transition to 49:29ff., before which it originally stood (but v. 7 cannot be P). W. Rudolf wants to transpose v. 7 after v. 11, so as to follow the introductory words; but he must alter notably the text that follows. Further attempts to explain the text are to be found in W. Rudolf and B. Jacob. Several exegetes, e.g., J. Skinner and G. von Rad, see no possibility of solving the problem.

All these attempts at a solution do not pay sufficient attention to the fact that v. 7 repeats 35:16, 19 with scarcely an alteration; the latter belonged to a different literary layer from 35:11, 12 (= 48:3-6); moreover, in ch. 35 the pericope vv. 16-21 follows immediately on the pericope vv. 3-15. The simplest and clearest explanation, as K. Budde (ZAW 3 [1883] 56f.) and, following him, H. Holzinger, had seen, is that a later transmitter wanted to expand vv. 3-6 or vv. 3-4 from ch. 35, where vv. 16-21 follow immediately on the divine revelation. He must have had at hand ch. 35 in its present form. This subsequent expansion presupposes an understanding of Genesis as a coherent story in which the transmitter saw the revelation at Bethel and the death of Rachel as belonging together. And so he added it. It can be that the situation—Jacob in the face of death speaking to Joseph—called for it.

[48:8-12] Vv. 8-12 follow on vv. 1-2, which form the introduction; Vv. 1-2, 8-12, form a self-contained narrative scene, Joseph's visit with his sons to his father who is dangerously ill.

[48:8-9] Jacob sees Joseph's sons coming in (vv. 1-2) and asks about them; Joseph responds. Jacob's question, "Who are these?" and Joseph's answer presuppose that Jacob has not yet seen them. This is possible only shortly after Jacob's arrival in Egypt (so too G. von Rad). As the scene takes place shortly before Jacob's death, then Jacob died soon after his arrival, not 17 years later, as P says in 47:28. Further, according to the description in 48:1-2, 8-12, Joseph's sons are still boys; according to P they would be at least 20 years old at the time of Jacob's death. There is here an obvious contradiction between 48:1-2, 8-12 and P's conclusion of the Joseph story, showing that they are of different origin. The action in the Joseph narrative runs its course from beginning to end in a tightly bound sequence. The laws of narrative would exclude a priori a period of 17 years in which nothing happens.

Joseph replies, "These are the sons whom God has given me here." This answer corresponds with the report of the birth and naming of the sons in 41:50-52. There is a similar question and answer in 33:5.

[48:9b] Jacob then asks Joseph to bring the boys to him so that he can bless them. Underlying this is the blessing ritual which was developed in Gen. 27 (cf. *Genesis 12–36*, ch. 27, Form). Of the five parts mentioned there, the following occur here: 1. the demand of the father (v. 9b); 2. the identification of the one to be blessed (vv. 8-9a); 4. presentation and touch (kiss) (v. 10b). Missing are 3. offering of food and drink, strengthening of the one who blesses (though this is hinted at by ויתחזק in v. 2) and 5. pronouncement of the blessing.

[48:10a] A parenthesis follows in v. 10a. Jacob could no longer see well (this is not in contradiction to vv. 8a, 11). Like the corresponding sentence in Gen. 27:1, also in the context of a blessing, the purpose of the parenthesis is to explain something in the course of the narrative. Though it has no function in vv. 1-2, 8-12, it does in vv. 13-20. The reference to the dimming of the eyes has the same function here as in ch. 27. V. 10a thus belongs to vv. 13-20 and has been inserted here because vv. 13-20 are not a complete scene but were appended to vv. 1-2, 8-12 as their continuation. The transmitter who put vv. 1-2, 8-12 and 13-20 together so as to form a single scene was of the opinion that the appropriate place for this remark was at v. 10a, before the act of blessing.

[48:10b, 11] Joseph brings his two sons to their grandfather who kisses and embraces them (v. 10b). Physical touch belongs to the action of blessing even when in the present description the personal emotion, the joy aroused in the grandfather (to which he gives expression in v. 11), is in the foreground. There is a heightening of emotion as Jacob addresses his son, "you. . .your sons." This is so clearly a reference back to a motif in the Joseph narrative (cf. especially 45:26-28) as to demonstrate that this scene also belongs there; v. 9b also supports this. Further, Jacob understands his seeing of Joseph's sons as an action of God, just as Joseph understands the gift of sons in a foreign land in the same way (v. 3b). The narrator thus points silently to God's "assistance" which spans so broad a gap (cf. chs. 45 and 50).

[48:12] V. 12 clearly closes the narrative scene. Both sentences in v. 12 presuppose that Jacob has blessed Joseph's two sons. The procedure of blessing is over and so Joseph takes his sons away.

מעם ברכיו need not mean that the boys were sitting on Jacob's knees; this is unlikely in the case of an old man, ailing and sitting on the bed. It probably means that they were standing at or leaning upon his knees, as in Rembrandt's well-known painting of this scene (cf. J. C. H. Lebram, OTS 15 [1969] 145-169). It is an appropriate conclusion when Joseph, on taking leave of his father, bows before him. The gesture speaks for itself and needs no justification. It links the farewell with the thanks for the blessing that the grandfather has dispensed to the boys, as well as with the answer to the father's exclamation in v. 11. The bow is also to God who has dealt so wondrously with his father and himself. But the pronouncement of the blessing with its introduction, "And Israel blessed the two, saying. . .," is missing. One would expect it here after v. 11 because word and action are both part of the procedure (cf. ch. 27). The absence can be explained only by the insertion of vv. 15-16, words of blessing, into the scene expanded by vv. 13-20. The blessing in vv. 15-16 would have displaced the pronouncement expected between vv. 11 and 12 (see also the excursus at the end of the commentary on this chapter).

[48:13-20] The scene in 48:13-20 concerns the precedence of Ephraim over Manasseh (cf. H. C. Schmitt, BZAW 154 [1980] 152-156). The scene lacks an introduction; it has been appended subsequently to vv. 1-2, 8-12; it is attached to v. 9b, Jacob's request to Joseph. The parenthesis (v. 10a), which has no function in the scene vv. 1-2, 8-12, belongs to vv. 13-20 where it is in its correct place. It explains the positioning of the boys in v. 13, which is the direct continuation of v. 10a. וַיַּגֵּשׁ at the end of v. 13, following the וַיִּקַּח at the beginning, is an express doublet of the יָגֶשׁ in v. 10b. In other words, the scene vv. 13-20, which has no introduction of its own, was appended to the scene vv. 1-2, 8-12 after v. 9. V. 10a is already part of vv. 13-20; the two scenes overlap with the וַיַּגֵּשׁ of v. 10b (= v. 13b); the quite different scene of vv. 13-20 begins with v. 13a. The difficulty has arisen because the conclusion of the first scene (vv. 10b-12) has been left standing in between. This second scene is self-contained. Its subject is the content of the closing sentence (v. 20b): ''Thus he gave Ephraim precedence over Manasseh.'' The sequence of events is: the boys are brought forward (v. 13), the laying on of hands (v. 14) and the blessing (vv. 15-16), Joseph's attempt to correct the laying on of hands (vv. 17-18) and the father's refusal (v. 19), and the conclusion (v. 20b).

[48:13-14] The doubling with respect to the previous scene is not limited to the presentation of Joseph's sons. Presupposing the five elements of blessing noted above (comm. on v. 9b), a closer examination reveals three of them in this scene as well: the presentation in v. 13 (4) is linked with Joseph's concern about identification (2), which is also the subject of vv. 14, 17-19. The touching consists here in the laying on of hands (4). If one takes into consideration the conferring of the blessing (5) in v. 13, then the second scene as a whole forms a doublet to the first. A blessing is conferred in both, though in very different ways; Jacob is the one who blesses in both cases and the two sons of Joseph are the recipients.

Joseph takes his two sons by the hand, putting Ephraim on his right and Manasseh on his left so that Manasseh would be on Jacob's right and Ephraim on his left. He does this out of consideration for Jacob and his failing sight (v. 10a belongs here). But Jacob does what is utterly unexpected, crossing his hands (שָׂכַל, piel, really ''to weave'') so that his right hand rests on Ephraim's head. This is the first occasion on which a blessing is given by the laying on of hands; it is probably a later form which became common in the liturgy (cf. J. Coppens, ''Handauflegung,'' BHH, II, 632-636; P. Humbert VT 12 [1962] 383-395). The description in vv. 13-14 is extremely detailed; there is no justification for striking out single sentences such as ''he was the younger.'' The passage is concerned solely with the question, Who will be the privileged one? Here lies the basic difference from the scene in vv. 1-2, 8-12, in which this question does not arise.

[48:14] V. 14 too is entirely determined by the question of precedence. Joseph's careful preparations are thwarted by Jacob as he crosses his hands, laying his right on Ephraim's head. Jacob, who confers the blessing, has decided beforehand that the younger must take precedence.

[48:15-16] One would expect the pronouncement of the blessing to follow the gesture; but from Joseph's point of view the blessing, which determines the destiny of the one blessed, may not be pronounced before Jacob's gesture has been corrected. Hence the words of v. 17, ''When Joseph saw. . .,'' must have followed

188

originally on v. 14; it would have made no sense to have corrected the gesture after the blessing had been pronounced. The blessing (vv. 15-16), therefore, is certainly a later insertion; this is frequent in the patriarchal story because the formulas of blessing and promise have an independent tradition history. The language of vv. 15-16 confirms this.

One can only speculate about the origin of the blessing pronouncement in vv. 15-16. The introductory words, "He blessed Joseph and said," cannot mean that "Joseph is blessed in his children" (H. Gunkel and others). Any understanding of the patriarchal stories excludes this. The Gk has correctly perceived this and consequently altered את־יוסף to אתם. This is harmonization, as is the case so often in the Gk, but does not explain the MT. It is unlikely that את־יוסף can be due either to carelessness or to a scribal error. One must presume then that an older text contained a blessing upon Joseph which was followed by another over his sons. But the text as preserved contains only a blessing over Joseph's sons. It has been put together out of two parts, a promise of increase and a declaration about God. It is only the simple promise of increase in the form of a benediction that is appropriate to the context. It can be reconstructed as follows:

> May the God of my father(s) bless the boys,
> so that they may grow and become many in the land.

An older promise of increase, in which God was the one who promised, has been changed here into a benediction. The underlying promise was in rhythmic form 2:2::2:2. The contrary opinion (O. Procksch and others) that the present text of vv. 15-16 is rhythmic is incorrect; it is clearly prose. The attempt to print it in rhythmic form in BHK and, unfortunately, in BHS is an error. It has been later expanded first by the threefold declaration about God in language like that of the psalms, and then by the addition of the wish that the name of the fathers may live on in them. It is this wish, to which the twofold naming of Abraham and Isaac corresponds (nowhere else in the Joseph narrative), that best shows the meaning of the narrative. Its liturgical language is very obvious also in the naming of God three times; as has often been noted, this corresponds to the Aaronic blessing in Num. 6:24-26 (cf. also Pss. 80:2; 50:1f.). But the correspondence goes much further. "May he bless these boys" is the equivalent of "May Yahweh bless you. . .," "may he keep you" (cf. vv. 15b and 16a); and there are echoes of "may he make his face shine on you" in "before whose face" in v. 15bα. The purpose of this expansion is clear from its obvious parallel to the blessing of Aaron: a place in the liturgy of Israel is given to the tradition of the fathers by joining it to the deathbed blessing of the last of the three patriarchs. This is the clearest and most important passage in the Old Testament where one can recognize the link between patriarchal tradition and the liturgy of Israel.

[**48:15**] "May God bless the boys!" is expanded by repeating the subject three times, thus giving expression to a threefold action of this God. The structure of the benediction is the same as that in Num. 6:24-26. These three statements synthesize God's action toward the patriarchs Abraham, Isaac, and Jacob (as in Ex. 3:6); in v. 15bα Abraham and Isaac are mentioned, in vv. 15bβ and 16a Jacob speaks of God's action toward himself. V. 15bα is an obvious recollection of Gen. 17:1(P) where God addresses Abraham in the imperative (cf. also Gen. 24:40; 5:22; 6:9 for "walk before"). The perfective form "before whom my fathers. . .walked" has here a broader meaning; the whole life of Abraham and Isaac is described as a path before God, as a path vis-à-vis God. This includes every conceivable relationship to God, every event mutually affecting the patriarchs and God. In the two following statements about God Jacob synthesizes in a confession, as it were, what God has meant for him: he is God in act who blesses and rescues. Jacob summarizes God's constant blessing (". . .my whole life long to this very day," as in Num. 22:30) in the image of the shepherd. This is its first occurrence in the Old Testament. It corresponds to the blessing given to Jacob in Gen. 28:15(20), "I am with you and will keep you wherever you go." The image of God as shepherd was first used with reference to Israel as a people (Ps. 80:2; Gen. 49:24?), and only later to the individual (Ps. 23:1). Later linguistic usage is also evident in the present passage.

[**48:16a**] God's saving action is expressed in the words: ". . .the angel, who ransomed me from all distress." גאל with God as subject occurs here for the first time. מלאך is used as an alternative for God (cf. *Genesis 12–36*, comm. on 16:7a, Excursus; V. Hirth, ThA 32 [1975]); the author is thinking of those passages in the patriarchal story where the *mal'āk* is the one who rescues from distress, e.g., Gen. 21:17 or 22:11. Later usage is particularly evident with גאל (cf. J. J. Stamm, *g'l*, THAT I 383-94, with bibliog.). God's action as גאל of the individual is found only in Ps. 19:15; Job 19:25, and of the people in Ex. 6:6 (P) and 15:13, and particularly in Deutero-Isaiah, often parallel to a verb of rescuing. The verb occurs with מן only in a few late passages where it has a derived meaning. Indicative of late usage is the close parallel in Jer. 31:10f. (L. Rupert) where God also appears as shepherd together with מן. H. Donner summarizes: "The hymn-like proclamations point to a predominantly exilic or postexilic mentality."

[**48:16b**] To the wish expressed in the blessing is joined the wish that his name and the name of his fathers (once again the sequence Abraham, Isaac, and Jacob) may live on in his grandchildren; cf. Gen. 21:12. Following on what has preceded, this can only be a wish that the history of the patriarchs, which was a history with God, may continue in them. It does not at all mean, as misinterpreted in Sirach, that the praise ("name" = "praise") of the fathers may never grow silent in generations to come. The fact that the sentence has been inserted into an ancient blessing helps in the understanding of it. Blessing is the power of fertility, of growth to the full (v. 16aβ and 16bβ). The late theologian makes his addition under the influence of tradition, that the history of the patriarchs and their experience with God may continue in the grandchildren. Understood in this way the benediction in vv. 15-16 provides valuable evidence for a late period, exilic or early postexilic, which links the patriarchal period with the history of Israel; it is a theological explanation that gives the patriarchal period meaning for the time for which he was writing.

[**48:17-20**] Vv. 17-20 are a continuation of vv. 13-14. The beginning of v. 17, which follows directly on v. 14, shows that the blessing in vv. 15-16 is a later insertion.

[**48:17**] V. 17 confirms that the remark in v. 10a belongs to this scene. Joseph thinks that Jacob has confused the two boys because his sight is not good and wants to correct the mistake. It is presupposed that the right hand confers the more powerful blessing. Throughout the world the right hand is the stronger or better, but not because it is the hand by which the oath is taken (H. Gunkel). The procedure here in ch. 48 differs from that in ch. 27, though both deal with the privilege of the firstborn; this is expressed in ch. 27 in the difference in the blessings pronounced, in ch. 48 in the gesture of blessing. There are not in ch. 48 two blessings, one for Manasseh and one for Ephraim, each formulated differently; the reason is that there was no such tradition. This is also an indication of the purely etiological character of the scene; the gesture is sufficient to express mere precedence.

[**48:19**] But Jacob does not go along with Joseph's attempt to correct his gesture. His refusal reflects a calm self-assurance throughout, "I know, my son, I know well." Expression is thus given to the conviction that in Israel, especially in the early period, as well as among many other peoples, a breadth of view and an insight into the future was attributed to the dying which gave great importance to what they said before death (cf. T. H. Gaster, *Myth, Legend. . .* [1969] 214f.). Jacob's further explanation in v. 19b is a brief reproduction of the words of benediction. This explains why the blessing which one would expect after v. 14 is missing. The author of this scene is not concerned, as in ch. 27, with the concrete promise made to each, but solely with the precedence of the younger over the elder; he was able to express this better by the gesture of blessing. Accordingly, the blessing given the one in v. 19b differs only quantitatively from that given the other. The brief reproduction allows one to conclude that it is a matter of the traditional promise of increase in two parts. The late text does not distinguish between blessing and promise. The elder is to become a people and is to become great; but the younger will become greater and his descendants will grow into a company of peoples. All these expressions have been taken over from the well-known formulations of the promise of increase, only that more is held in prospect for the younger than for the elder.

[**48:20**] This is just what the closing sentence (v. 20b) says: "Thus he gave Ephraim precedence over Manasseh." The appendix (48:13-20) has been created so as to anchor the precedence in an ancestral, foundational pronouncement so as to legitimate it. It is an etiological appendix of which there are many in the patriarchal stories. The exegesis has demonstrated that it is an appendix or an appendage to an existing narrative. As in many etiological expansions elsewhere in the patriarchal narratives, Manasseh and Ephraim are here meant to be representatives of tribes. The episode presupposes the historical process, often clearly attested in the Old Testament, of Ephraim's rise to be the leading tribe of "the house of Joseph" (cf. E. C. Kingsbury, HUCA 38 [1967] 129-136; R. de Vaux, *The Early History. . .* 2 [1971; Eng. 1978] 642-653). The appendage then has no roots in the patriarchal period; rather it arose in the period when the rise of Ephraim needed such a legitimation. However, it should not be regarded as invention or fiction; it is the expression of a "prehistorical" conception of history; in the period of transition from family to political structures in society, historical events were explained by the family structures underlying them.

[**48:20a**] A blessing pronouncement (v. 20a) has been prefixed to the conclusion (v. 20b); again it interrupts the continuity between vv. 19 and 20b; it is therefore

an addition. The introductory sentence, ''And that day he blessed them saying. . .,'' demonstrates this; it is inappropriate after v. 19b and serves only the insertion of v. 20aβ. The same probably holds as well for the words that follow,
''with [or in] you may Israel bless,'' if one does not read with the versions, ''in
'you' [pl.] will Israel 'bless itself' with these words. . .'' (''Israel'' here is the
people; never so in the Joseph story). These words, namely, ''may God make you
like Ephraim and Manasseh,'' are to be understood in accordance with Gen.
12:3b; 18:18; 22:18; 26:4; 28:14; Ps. 72:17 (cf. *Genesis 12–36*, comm. on 12:3b).
This sentence is part of a promise in all other parallel passages in Genesis, generally the conclusion, where it stands in the context of the promise of increase. As it
has the effect of a clumsy addition in 48:20, one must reckon it as a subsequent expansion of the promise of increase implied in v. 19b. The saying itself can be an
old tradition which has been passed on and can go back to the period of the tribes.

[**48:21-22**] Two appendages follow which have no connection with each other or
with what has gone before. The accumulation of such appendages and additions in
ch. 48 is due to its position at the end of the Jacob story. Apart from the fact that
the Joseph narrative and the Jacob story are dovetailed in these concluding chapters 46–50, ch. 48 (with 47:29-31) deals with Jacob's last words before his death;
and so it is the obvious place to preserve and attach single, independent sayings of
Jacob that have been handed down.

[**48:21**] The saying in v. 21 is a promise of the dying Jacob to his son Joseph in
which he announces the return from Egypt to the land of the patriarchs. It is to be
understood as a theological clamp which is meant to bind the leading out of Egypt
in Exodus–Numbers more firmly with the story of the patriarchs (so too H.
Gunkel). The exodus from Egypt has already been promised to the fathers (C.
Westermann, *The Promises to the Fathers* [1976; Eng. 1980] 21ff., 140-149).
One can only understand v. 21 together with 50:24. The relationship of the two to
each other is most easily explained in this way: Joseph's announcement of the exodus from Egypt at the end of the Joseph story carries greater weight when, in
48:21, it is traced back to Jacob, one of the three founding fathers.

[**48:22**] This second appendage is an isolated tradition, quite foreign to the context. ''The verse comes from a different context unknown to us'' (H. Gunkel). It
has been inserted here because it is a legacy to the son before death, ''And so I
present to you,'' נתתי in the same sense as in Gen. 23:11. The peculiar construction is to be understood as follows, ''שכם (a shoulder? H. Gunkel) as an additional
share over and above your brothers'' (so I. Mendelsohn, BASOR 156 [1959] 39,
n. 9). It is clear that Jacob is here presenting to his beloved son Joseph שכם as a
plot of land over and above the share given to his brothers. This cannot be
Shechem but must mean a smaller piece of land which can be described as ''a
shoulder.'' Even though the word does not occur elsewhere in the Old Testament
in the metaphorical sense of ''ridge,'' it can have this meaning here. The word has
perhaps been chosen as an allusion to the city of Shechem (lit. on Shechem, *Genesis 12–36*, pp. 98-99, 143, 522). Jacob adds that he himself took the territory from
the Amorites ''with sword and bow.'' Jacob is presented here as the leader of an
armed band, a portrayal that appears elsewhere in the patriarchal story only in
Gen. 14 and 34 and accords with the period of the judges. The saying is conceivable only as spoken in Canaan (H. Gunkel, H. C. Schmitt, and others); the division

of Jacob's heritage makes sense only there. On the expression "with sword and bow" cf. O. Eissfeldt (VT 5 [1955] 232-238) and O. Keel (ZDPV 93 [1977] 141-147). Eissfeldt, who deals with all passages where the expression occurs, understands sword and bow as weapons for close combat and combat at a distance, i.e., as the equivalent of all weapons. Jacob wants to say that he acquired it with his own strength. The present passage has nothing to do with Gen. 34, nor with the purchase of a piece of land in Gen. 33:19 (cf. Josh. 24:32). R. de Vaux treats the matter in detail with further literature (*The Early History. . .* 2 [1971; Eng. 1978] 637-640).

Excursus: The Blessings in Genesis 48

Blessing pronouncements and promises have an independent tradition history; this is the reason why they undergo many variations and why later forms take the place of older. The case of ch. 48 is particularly complicated and it is extremely difficult to determine the relationship of the blessing pronouncements to each other and their meaning in the context.

The blessing procedure is narrated in vv. 1-12 (minus vv. 3-7) and 13-20. But there is no pronouncement in vv. 1-12; it must have had its place between vv. 11 and 12. Its absence is probably to be explained by the appending of vv. 13-20 to vv. 1-12. The appendage joins two originally independent texts so as to form one act of blessing; it became necessary then to displace the pronouncement and/or substitute something else for it. Vv. 13-20 contain or imply three different blessing pronouncements. The context requires that Jacob pronounce a blessing over Ephraim and one over Manasseh. Both are implied in v. 19b, but they are reproduced only in their abbreviated (prosaic) form in the answer that Jacob gives to Joseph's attempt to correct him. But there is no blessing pronounced over each of the two grandchildren themselves. The reason for this is the structure of vv. 13-20. One would expect the two pronouncements in the course of the blessing procedure after v. 14, where in fact the pronouncement vv. 15-16 has been secondarily inserted. But Joseph's attempt to correct Jacob (vv. 17-18) would be meaningless had the pronouncement already been made.

Ch. 48 thus contains the following blessing pronouncements:

1a.	vv. 15-16	a late, liturgically adapted blessing;
1b.	vv. 15-16	a rhythmic blessing to be reconstructed from it;
2.	v. 19b	the indirect reproduction of a blessing;
3.	v. 20a	"may God make you";
4.	vv. 3-4	Jacob gives an account of the promise made to him.

Apart from the liturgical reworking in vv. 15-16, all three texts 1b, 2, 3 are variants of the promise of increase. Behind all three texts, therefore, lies the tradition of a promise of increase made to one of the sons of Joseph by Jacob. The rhythmic form of the pronouncement derived from v. 16 is closest to the underlying tradition. This is underscored by the fact that Jacob, in the introduction to the blessing of Joseph's sons (vv. 3-4, P), recalls the promise of increase (and the promise of the land) made to him in Bethel.

Purpose and Thrust

What unites these texts is the situation before the death of the last of Israel's founding fathers and the importance given to it in all of them. See *Genesis 12–36*, ch. 27, Purpose and Thrust, for reflections on the relationship between patriarchal blessing and tradition. The blessing of the patriarch extends from one generation to the next and creates continuity· between them. It acquires an increased importance in the transition from one epoch to the other. The patriarchal period ends with the death of Jacob; the sojourn in Egypt introduces the period of the exodus and the settlement in Canaan.

All texts in 47:29—48:22 are directed to this transition and all are concerned with the continuity, though in very different ways. The chapter has made a synthesis out of parts of different origin; it thus shows the fact of the continuity and how it was preserved by means of that transition from the conclusion of the patriarchal period, across the different epochs of the history of the people of Israel, right down into the late period. This extends from the simple act of the blessing of the sons by their grandfather (vv. 1-12), in which the children who had grown up in a foreign land are taken up into the family of the patriarchs, down to P's sacral act of legal sanction (vv. 3-6); it then moves to the late theological explanation (vv. 15-16), which anchors the link between the history of the patriarchs and the history of the people in God's action. The promise of increase runs through all these stages and acquires a particular importance in the transition from the patriarchal period to the period of the exodus from Egypt (v. 21).

Jacob's Death and Burial

Literature

Genesis 49:28b-33: T. C. Vriezen, "'*Ehje 'ašer 'ehje*," *Fests. A. Bertholet* (1950) 498-512. S. Talmon, "The Sectarian יחד—A Biblical Noun," VT 3 (1953) 133-140. K. J. Illman, *Old Testament Formulas about Death* (1979).

Genesis 50:1-14: F. L. Griffith, *Stories of the High Priests of Memphis* (1900) esp. 29f. P. Dornstetter, *Abraham: Studien über die Anfänge des hebräischen Volkes* (1902) esp. 90f. M. J. Lagrange, *Études sur les religions sémitiques* (1905²). W. Spiegelberg, "Die Beisetzung des Patriarchen Jakob (Gen. 50,2ff.) im Lichte der ägyptischen Quellen," OLZ 9 (1923) 421-424. P. Heinisch, "Die Trauerbräuche bei den Israeliten," BZfr 13,7-8 (1931); "Die Totenklage im AT," BZfr 13,9-10 (1931). R. Gordis, "Studies in Hebrew Roots of Contrasted Meanings," JQR 27 (1936/37) 55f. C. Virolleaud, "Les Rephaïms dans les poèmes de Ras Shamra," CRAIBL (1929) 638-640, und RES (1940) 77-83; Syria 22 (1941) 1-30. A. Lucas, *Ancient Egyptian Materials and Industries* (1948³) esp. 337. A. R. Johnson, *Studies in OT Prophecy* (1950) esp. 86f. N. H. Tur-Sinai, "The Ark of God at Beit Shemesh (1. Sam VI) and Pereṣ 'Uzza (2. Sam VI; 1. Chron XIII)," VT 1 (1951) 275-286. B. Gemser, "*Be'ēber hajjardēn*: In Jordan's Borderland," VT 2 (1952) 349-355. A. F. Shore and H. S. Smith, *A Demotic Embalmer's Agreement (Pap. Dem. B.M. 10561)*, AcOrK 25 (1960) esp. 290. S-ShRin, "Ugaritic—OT Affinities II," BZ 11 (1967) 174-192. L. Wächter, "Der Tod im AT," AzTh 2,8 (1967). G. Fohrer, *Studien zur alttestamentlichen Theologie und Geschichte*, BZAW 115 (1969). S. McEvenue, "A Source-Critical Problem in Nu 14,26-38," Bib 50 (1969) 453-465. H. W. Wolff, *Anthropology of the Old Testament* (1973; 1977³; Eng. 1974). H. Y. Priebatsch, "Jerusalem und die Brunnenstrasse Merneptahs," ZDPV 91 (1975) 18-29. J. C. de Moor, "*Rāpi'ūma*—Rephaim," ZAW 88 (1976) 323-345.

Text

49:1a Jacob summoned his sons.

28b Then he blessed them, 'each one of them,'[a] with a special blessing for each.

29 He gave them[a] his orders and said, I am to be gathered to 'my kindred';[b] bury me with my fathers in the cave on the plot of land of Ephron the Hittite,

30 in the cave on the plot of land at Machpelah east of Mamre in the land of Canaan, '   ,'[a] which Abraham bought as a burial place from Ephron the Hittite.

31 There Abraham was buried and his wife Sarah; there Isaac was buried
and his wife Rebekah; and there I buried Leah—

32 the plot of land and the cave on it were bought from the Hittites.[a]

33 When Jacob had finished giving this charge to his sons, he drew his
feet up onto the bed. Then he breathed his last and was gathered to his
kindred.

50:1 Then Joseph bent over[a] his father's face and wept over him and kissed
him.

2 Joseph then ordered the physicians[a] who were at his service to embalm[b] his father. The physicians embalmed Israel.

3 They completed their work in forty[a] days, the usual time for embalming.[b] The Egyptians mourned for him for seventy days.

4 When the period of mourning[a] was over, Joseph spoke to the Pharaoh's court, If I have found favor in your eyes, speak 'on my behalf'[b] to
the Pharaoh and say to him,

5 My father made me take an oath and said, I am dying;[a] in the grave
that I hewed[b] for myself in the land of Canaan, there you are to bury
me. And now I would like to go up and bury my father;[c] then I will return.

6 The Pharaoh answered, Go up and bury your father as he made you
swear to do.

7 So Joseph went up to bury his father and there went up with him all the
Pharaoh's courtiers, the elders of his household and all the elders of
the land of Egypt,

8 together with Joseph's household, his brothers and the household of
his father. Only their children,[a] sheep, and cattle were left behind in the
land of Goshen.

9 Chariots and horsemen also went up with them; it was a very large
company.

10 When they came to the threshing floor of Atad,[a] which is on the far side
of the Jordan, they raised a loud and sad lament. He mourned his father for seven days.

11 When the inhabitants of the land, the Canaanites, saw the lamentation
at the threshing floor of Atad, they said, How sadly the Egyptians are
mourning![a] So the place was called Abel-mizraim; it is on the far side of
the Jordan.

12 So his sons[a] did as he had commanded them.

13 His sons brought him[a] to the land of Canaan and buried him in the cave
on the plot of land at Machpelah, east of Mamre, which Abraham had
bought as a burial place '   '[b] from Ephron the Hittite.

14 Then Joseph returned to Egypt, he and his brothers and all who had
gone up with him to bury his father, after they had buried[a] his father.

49:28ba The אשר is missing in three Mss, Gk, and Syr; with F. Delitzsch, H. Gunkel, J.
Skinner, and others read איש אשר.

29a Missing in Gk.   **b** Read עַמִּי, corresponding to v. 33; so H. Gunkel, J. Skinner,
and others.

30a The second את־השׂדה is an addition, likewise in 50:13; Gk is shorter.

32a The whole of v. 32 could be an addition; syntactically it does not follow on what precedes, is clumsily constructed, and is mere repetition.

50:1a This is the only passage where someone falls on the face of another; hence the appropriate translation is "he inclined."

2a Here for the first time; elsewhere Ex. 15:26; Jer. 8:22; 2 Chron. 16:12; Sir. 10:10; 38:1.
See H. Wolff (1973), bibliog. above.   **b** Only here in vv. 2, 3, 26.

3a On the number 40, cf. S. McEvenue (1969), bibliog. above.   **b** Abstract plural
here only.

4a בכית only here; suffix is objective gen.   **b** With Gk add עלי.
5a Asyndetic conditional sentence, BrSynt §4.   **b** Syr "which I bought for myself."
c Sam adds כאשר השבעני.
8a On the absence of את, BrSynt §96.
10a גרן, "threshing floor," "barn floor"; often in combination; אטד, "bramble,"
"thorny bush," KBL, elsewhere only in Judg. 9:14f.; Ps. 58:10.
11a On construction, BrSynt §134d.
12a The antecedent lacks the suffix, an indication that vv. 12-13 are an insertion from P.
In P the suffix can refer to 49:33.
13a Syr inserts ויביאוהו.   **b** The second את־השדה is to be omitted, as 49:30.
14a The last four words are missing in Gk and are regarded by many as a gloss; but they
could have been put at the end deliberately for emphasis.

Form and Setting

The concluding part of chs. 46–50, which deals with the death and burial of Jacob,
takes its special character from the redactional joining of the two independent
works, the Joseph narrative and the Jacob story; both end with Jacob's death and
burial. The redactor has stamped the synthesis by means of a deliberate doublet;
Jacob's commission to bury him in Canaan is given to Joseph in 47:29-31 and to
all the brothers in 49:29-32. The structure shows that the doublet is deliberate.
The two texts 47:29-31 and 49:28b-33 frame the section that begins with the announcement of Jacob's death in 47:29 and ends with the death itself in 49:33. In
contrast, the death and burial of Jacob, 49:33 and 50:12-13, are given once only in
the text of P, as previously in the case of the deaths of Abraham (25:9) and Isaac
(35:29). The text of P, 49:28b-33 and 50:12-13, has been amalgamated with the
report in the Joseph narrative in such a way that it cannot be detached from it. Joseph's grief over his father's death in 50:1 (Joseph narrative) is the reaction to the
report of Jacob's death in P (49:33), and the burial, 50:12-13 (P), is the goal of the
account of the journey up to Canaan 50:4-11 (Joseph narrative). As on a number
of occasions in the patriarchal story, two threads are woven together at the close of
a narrative.

The units 49:1a, 28b-33 and 50:12-13 form the conclusion of the Joseph
story in the priestly writing. The so-called "blessings of Jacob" (49:1b-28a) has
been subsequently added. In 49:28b Jacob blesses his sons; this is introduced by
49:1a; in vv. 29-33 he charges them to bury him in the cave at Machpelah; v. 33
reports his death.

Gen. 50:1-14 is divided into the lament for the dead (vv. 1-3) and the procession to Canaan for the burial (vv. 4-14). It is a report shaped into narrative form
which follows step by step the procedures proper to the death of a family member.
In vv. 1-3 is the weeping, the official mourning, and the preparation for burial; the
procession to Canaan precedes the burial; in vv. 4-6 is the request for leave to go
to Canaan and its granting; then comes the procession with further mourning (vv.
7b-11); vv. 10b-11 are an etiological appendage, vv. 12-13 the burial, and v. 14
the return.

Commentary

[49:1a, 28b-33] This text consists of three parts: the blessing (v. 28b), introduced by v. 1a, the charge (vv. 29-32), and the death (v. 33); the sequence of the
three verbs is the same in Gen. 28:1(P).

[49:28b] V. 28a is the conclusion of the blessing of Jacob (48:1-27); v. 28b is the beginning of the text of P. The verb ויברך in P requires an introduction which can be found in 49:1a, "Jacob summoned his sons"; this corresponds to the introduction in 47:29b (so too T. C. Vriezen [1950], bibliog. above). He has a special blessing for each of his sons (on the word order see T. C. Vriezen, who understands the sentence as a paronomastic relative). The subsequent insertion of the blessings of Jacob fits it well.

[49:29-32] Jacob's charge to his sons (vv. 29-32) is divided into his anticipation of his death (v. 29a; cf. 47:29a and the two last words of 49:33), the precise determination of the place (vv. 29b, 30a, 32), and something of his history (vv. 30b, 31).

[49:29-30] Jacob announces his death to his sons in vv. 29-30 in the phrase, "I am to be gathered to my kindred," as in Gen. 25:8 (cf. *Genesis 12–36*, comm. ad loc.); S. Talmon, "from the community to the community of the dead" (1953, 137, bibliog. above). The determination of the place is involved (vv. 29b, 30a, 32) and contains several repetitions, making it difficult to determine whether the repetition is deliberate or the text has undergone subsequent glossing. The description and the words agree with Gen. 23, the grave in the cave of Machpelah on the plot of land of Ephron the Hittite that Abraham bought from him (*Genesis 12–36*, comm. on ch. 23). It is particularly important for P that the property has been acquired legally, as ch. 23 shows.

[49:31] The last sentence v. 31 that, according to P, Jacob spoke before his death, shows in an impressive way one aspect of his understanding of history. The heavily accentuated rhythm of the three sentences— שׁמה קברו. . . שׁמה. קברו. . . ושׁמה קברתי—brings together the three generations of the patriarchal story. The journey of the three patriarchs Abraham, Isaac, and Jacob comes to its conclusion in their common burial place. It was a wandering in the "land of sojourning"; it ends in a grave that belongs to them in the land promised to their descendants. Ch. 23 speaks of Sarah's death and burial, 25:8f. of Abraham's death, 35:29 of Isaac's burial. There is no account of the burial of Rebekah and Leah; this is a small but important indication that tradition in Israel contained more than what was reduced to writing.

Thus v. 31, Jacob's last words, forms an impressive conclusion to the patriarchal story in its three generations.

[49:32] V. 32 is only a repetition, incorrectly inserted; it is meant to bridge v. 31 and link with v. 30 (A. Dillmann). It gives the impression of a later addition.

[49:33] Jacob's death is reported soberly and in a few words. The first sentence, "When Jacob had finished giving this charge to his sons," cannot refer only to the instruction in v. 29; it is rather the formulation of the redactor who thereby closes the section begun in 47:29-31 (see below, chs. 46–50, Survey). The scene begins in 48:2 with Jacob sitting up on the bed; as it now closes, "he drew his feet up onto the bed" (so too A. Dillmann). Those authors who do not attribute this sentence to P command assent here (A. Dillmann, H. Gunkel, H. C. Schmitt with bibliog.). The verb גוע also describes dying in Gen. 6:17; 25:8; 35:29(P).

[50:1-14] The account of the burial is determined entirely by Jacob's charge in 47:29-31 and 49:29-32. The procession to Canaan and the burial there link the Joseph narrative with the history of Israel and anticipate it.

[50:1] Joseph's immediate reaction to Jacob's death (49:33P) is a spontaneous expression of grief and love. This is entirely in the spirit of the Joseph narrative. One recalls his first question to his brothers after making himself known to them, ''Is my father still alive?'' 45:3 (or 46:4).

[50:2-3] But the death rites require a definite procedure. Joseph commands the physicians who are at his service (this is the first time that there is talk of a physician) to embalm his father. This they do. It is only here and in the case of Joseph himself in 50:26 that the Old Testament speaks of the mummification of a person. After he has expressed his grief, his first concern is to fulfill his father's last will (47:29-31). The mummification of the corpse is necessary for the journey to Canaan. It is at the same time the rite of the land, where there is a long period of mourning and special reverence is paid to the dead.

The physicians in Egypt, as in many other places, were originally priests. There they became a special guild in which there were further divisions of labor. One group were embalmers. This art was nowhere cultivated as it was in Egypt; it is one of those Egyptian characteristics of which the Joseph narrative is full. On embalming, cf. J. Vergote, pp. 197-200; D. B. Redford, pp. 240f.; H. C. Schmitt, pp. 132, 144; R. de Vaux, *Ancient Israel*, 56. Herodotus describes embalming in detail (cf. B. Jacob); he gives 70 days as the time required (so too *EBrit*. 15 [1971] 987f.). The period of mourning generally depends on it, thus giving 70 days between death and burial. The period of 40 days for embalming is not attested (J. Vergote; H. C. Schmitt); on the number 40 see S. McEvenue (Bib 50 [1969] 454). The author of the Joseph story puts the official mourning at 70 days; there may be echoes here of Diodorus who says that the period of mourning for a king lasted 72 days (so too H. Holzinger and H. Gunkel). Both figures reflect but an approximate knowledge of the length of time required for embalming and of the period of official mourning. It is important for the narrator that great respect was thereby shown to the father of Joseph. Israel mourned Aaron and Moses for 30 days (Num. 20:29; Deut. 34:8); the usual period of mourning in Israel was 7 days (1 Sam. 31:13). For further literature on embalming, see bibliog. above, and the *EBrit*. 15 (1971) 987f.

[50:4-14] The burial must now follow; but it must take place in Canaan, following Jacob's wish (47:29-31; 49:29-32).

[50:4] After the period of mourning, Joseph does not direct his request for leave of absence directly to the Pharaoh; he communicates it through ''the house of the Pharaoh,'' that is, through other high officials at court. Different reasons are suggested for this (B. Jacob has brought them together). It is most likely that he could not appear before the Pharaoh because of the mourning rites (hair, beard, clothing).

[50:5] The request to the Pharaoh reproduces Joseph's own words. It is characteristic of the style of the Joseph narrative that the request is not presented in an abstract concatenation of subordinated sentences, but as a short history, as something that has happened. It reproduces in narrative form the request of the father, from which follows Joseph's own request to the Pharaoh in three parts.

199

[50:5a] Joseph lets the episode narrated in 47:29-31 unfold before the Pharaoh. His father, face to face with death (הנה אנכי מת), makes him swear, "Bury me in. . .." The episode in three parts in 50:5 is the same as in 47:29-31, but the wording is very different. Prominent in 47:29-31 is the contrast, "Do not bury me in. . ., but in. . ."; this is entirely missing in v. 5. The reason for the difference is that the addresses are different. Joseph reproduces the request of his father with the words "in the grave that I hewed for myself in the land of Canaan," so that the Pharaoh may better understand in his own terms what Jacob meant: "in my own grave, with my own people." It would be wrong to conclude from this to a contradiction between 50:5 and 47:29-31. Perhaps it presupposes the Egyptian custom of providing for the construction of a grave before death (so A. Erman). E. I. Lowenthal writes, "he paraphrases prudently his father's words in keeping with Egyptian mores" (p. 149). There is no justification, therefore, for inferring from these words an older tradition about a grave of Jacob in west Jordan (so M. Noth, D. B. Redford, H. C. Schmitt).

[50:5b] The ועתה (a consequence of what has just been described) in v. 5b introduces Joseph's request. I would like to go up (vv. 7-11) and bury my father (vv. 12-13); then I will return (v. 14). The request in three parts anticipates the three parts that follow; the structure is repeated in announcement and execution.

[50:6] The Pharaoh grants him his request. The last words of his answer, כאשר השביעך, point back to the first sentence of Joseph's request in v. 5a, אבי השביעני and so clamps together the dialog in vv. 5-6; at the same time it forms a broader clamp around chs. 48–50; all that follows in vv. 7-14 is but the execution of v. 5b. Such unobtrusive links as these with their echoes, extending across short and long spans in the narrative, give it the structure of an organic and carefully articulated whole.

[50:7-11] The procession to Canaan and the place of burial: vv. 7-9 describe the departure of the procession and the participants, v. 10a the arrival and the mourning; vv. 10b-11 form an etiological appendage.

[50:7-9] The Pharaoh's assent means that the funeral procession befits the dignity of the highest minister of state. Not only the members of the family (v. 8a) but also Egyptian dignitaries are there (v. 7b). The twofold "all" is deliberate exaggeration. The distinguished representatives come from both the Pharaoh's household and the land of Egypt (v. 7b); it is the same distinction as in 45:8. There is also a military escort (v. 9), adding pomp to the solemn occasion (cf. G. von Rad). This description of the funeral procession from Egypt to Canaan serves also to allow something of the splendor of the monarchy to shine through once more. In chs. 39–41 the Pharaoh's court was the focal point of the action; in chs. 42–45 there was the marked contrast between the royal court and the family; from ch. 45 on the action took place within the family. Now, after Jacob's death, the splendor of the royal court, in which Joseph is the highest official, comes once again to the foreground. But there is a touch of irony here. There is not a word about splendor or honor, such as belongs to Joseph's exalted position, from the moment of his elevation in ch. 41 right down to the present passage, 50:7-9; now it is not he but his father who is honored by the grand funeral procession. There are many representatives of funeral processions in Egyptian burial chambers, particularly at the sanctuary of Abydos.

[50:10-11] Vv. 10-11 stand in relation to vv. 7-9 as arrival to departure. The original intention was arrival at the place where Jacob was to be buried. But the burial is reported in vv. 12-13, following P; hence vv. 10-11 now appear as a stopover where a solemn mourning was held.

[50:10a] Following the pattern of the itinerary, an account is now given of the arrival at Goren-Atad (i.e., a threshing floor or barn floor enclosed by brambles which served to winnow the grain; it occurs only here as a place-name). It is described both here and in v. 11 as lying "on the far side of the Jordan." Here "a loud and solemn lament for the dead" was held. The solemnity is underscored here as in vv. 7-9. This can only mean the lament for the dead which was the goal of the procession in vv. 7-9, i.e., the solemn event linked with or following on the burial. V. 10a then originally ran, "And they came to. . . ." "There they buried Jacob and held. . . ."

[50:10b] V. 10b sounds like a fresh beginning; the subject is "he," Joseph, in contrast to the plural in v. 10a. The mourning is called אבל here, whereas in v. 10a it is מספד. Then there is reference to the period of seven days which corresponds to the usual period of mourning in Israel (1 Sam. 31:13). One concludes from this that vv. 10aβ and 10b are doublets (so too H. Holzinger).

[50:11] V. 10b goes with v. 11 because this etiological appendage requires the word אבל for the mourning (vv. 10b and 11). The language of v. 10a shows clearly that it belongs to the Joseph narrative and is a continuation of vv. 7-9, whereas the etiological appendage does not accord with its style at all, though it does with that of the patriarchal stories. It is a typical etiology: a place acquires its name or a new name through an event that took place there in ancient times. It could have its origins in J's conclusion to the Jacob story which has not been preserved.

   V. 11 is a short narrative or narrative scene in itself in three parts. The inhabitants become aware of what is going on, and they confirm that it is a rite of mourning. The narrator concludes from what took place to an explanation of the place-name Abel-mizraim.

   The local details in v. 11aβ are difficult. The "inhabitants of the land" are described as Canaanites, but the place where it all happened, Goren-Atad, lies "on the far side of the Jordan" (vv. 11b, 10a). This would be the only passage in the Old Testament where the inhabitants of the land east of the Jordan are called Canaanites. This is not impossible, but very improbable. Further, a place east of the Jordan apparently presupposes that the funeral procession made a detour around the Dead Sea; it would be difficult to under-·stand why (J. Skinner); the description of the inhabitants as Canaanites in v. 11, however, very likely presupposes a place in Canaan west of the Jordan. Both place-names occur only here and are unknown. None of the suggestions made so far about their location has sufficient basis. As vv. 7-10a and 10b-11 belong to two different literary layers, they probably presuppose two different traditions about the location of Jacob's grave; one sets it east of the Jordan, the other in Canaan, west of the Jordan. More than this one cannot say. One must reckon with the possibility that the two traditions have been assimilated to each other in the text before us (M. Noth, *A History of Pentateuchal Traditions* [1948; 1966³; Eng. 1972] 88; J. Simons, *The Geographical and Topographical Texts of the OT* [1959]; R. de

Vaux, *The Early History of Israel* [1971; Eng. 1978] 129, 172, 175; H. C. Schmitt, BZAW, 154 [1980] 128).

[**50:11b**] The naming of the place after the solemn celebration of the mourning by the Egyptians is a contrived explanation, as is generally the case. The name אבל מצרים belongs to a group of place-names formed with אבל; e.g., Abel-shittim (Num. 33:49; see Judg. 11:33; 2 Sam. 20:15; 2 Chron. 16:4), in which אבל describes something that happened at the place; earlier it was rendered by "pasture" or some such; according to KBL it carries the meaning "watercourse," "stream." The narrator explains it as "the mourning of Egypt [or the Egyptians]." This sort of wordplay and reinterpretation, oral in origin, is very much in accord with the ancient traditions of the patriarchal story, e.g., Gen. 32:31; it does not fit the author of the Joseph story.

[**50:12-13**] This is P's account of the burial. In P 50:12-13 follows immediately on 49:29-33; the suffix of בניו refers to יעקב, the subject in 49:33. ". . .As he had commanded them" refers to 49:29-30 and 50:13b, and uses the same words as 49:29f. in giving precise details about the burial place. The conclusion drawn from the immediate succession of vv. 12-13 on 49:29-32 is that P's description of the death and burial knew nothing of the participation of the Egyptian court, vv. 7-9, or of a stopover. For P it is all the sons together who bury their father in the place determined by him after they brought him directly from Egypt to Mamre. Only this can be the meaning of v. 13a. Finally, the style too shows that different voices are speaking in vv. 12-13 and in vv. 7-9. Departure (v. 7) and arrival (v. 10) would have required a continuation, with departure from Goren-Atad and arrival at Mamre. But P is determined by the simple structure of charge (49:29-32) and execution (50:12-13). The insertion of P's vv. 12-13 shows the great importance that the P tradition of the death and burial of Jacob had for the redactor. This becomes clear from 49:31 because it assured for him the continuity and completeness of the patriarchal story.

[**50:14**] In the Joseph narrative (otherwise than in P's vv. 12-13) it is Joseph who conducts and leads Jacob's funeral procession, as v. 7 also shows. Joseph then returns to Egypt (v. 14), as he had promised the Pharaoh (v. 5), and his brothers and the retinue go with him (v. 7). The words "after they had buried his father," missing in the Gk, are not to be deleted. Though grammatically clumsy, they may have been deliberately put at the end so as to conclude the whole section which had begun with the announcement of Jacob's death (47:29), or to underscore that Joseph had kept his promise (47:31).

(Purpose and Thrust will be found at the end of the section on 50:22-26.)

Confirmation of the Reconciliation

Literature

Genesis 50:15-21: H. J. Stoebe, "Gut und Böse in der jahwistischen Quelle des Penta-teuch," ZAW 65 (1953) 188-204. J. Scharbert, "Vergebung," HThG II (1963) 740-748. T. C. Vriezen, "Geloof, openbaring en geschiedenis in de Oud-testamentische Theologie I," KeTh 16 (1966) 97-113. T. L. Fenton, "Ugaritica-Biblica," UF 1 (1969) 65-70. W. Brueggemann, "On Trust and Freedom. A Study of Faith in the Succession Narrative," *Interp.* 26 (1972) 3-19. K. Seybold, "Zwei Bemerkungen zu גמל/גמול," VT 22 (1972) 112-117. J. Schüpphaus, "Volk Gottes und Gesetz beim Elohisten," ThZ 31 (1975) 193-210. J. Krecher and H. P. Müller, "Vergangenheitsinteresse in Mesopotamien und Is-rael," *Saec.* 26 (1975) 13-44. I. Willi-Plein, "Hiobs Widerruf? Eine Untersuchung der Wurzel und ihrer erzähltechnischen Funktion im Hiobbuch," *Fests. I. L. Seeligmann* (1980).

Text

50:15 When Joseph's brothers saw that their father was dead, they said, Suppose[a] Joseph should hate us and pay us back for all the evil which we did[b] to him.

16 So they sent to Joseph saying,[a] Your father gave a command before[b] his death; he said,

17 Speak thus to Joseph, I pray you,[a] Forgive now the crime, the sin of your brothers; they indeed did you wrong!
So now we beg you, forgive the crime of the servants of the God of your father. And Joseph wept over their words to him.

18 Then the brothers themselves went in and prostrated before him and said, See, we[a] are your slaves!

19 Then Joseph said to them, Do not be afraid! Am I in the place of God?

20 You planned evil for me, but[a] God planned it for good so as to bring about[b] what is today, (that is) to preserve the lives of many people.

21 Well now, do not fear; I will provide for you and your little ones.
So he comforted them and reassured them.

15a לו with the apodosis suppressed, Ges-K §159y; BrSynt §170a.　　**b** Double accusa-tive Ges-K, §117ff.
16a Gk probably read ויגשו; MT is to stand; cf. Ex. 6:13; Jer. 27:4.　　**b** לפני temporal, BrSynt §1071.

17a אָנָּא is a particle specially used to strengthen a request; in the Hexateuch again in Ex. 32:31 where it is addressed to God, as in Ps. 118:25.
18a On the form, Ges-K §58k.
20a Sam, Gk, Syr, Vg with copula.   **b** On the infin. abs., Ges-K §75n.

Form and Setting

The repetition of the reconciliation of Joseph with his brothers has no necessary function in the course of the narrative. It would have a function had there been some previous motive for the brothers' concern in v. 15 and this had been indicated. But there is no cause for the new beginning in 50:15 and it is really beyond comprehension (D. B. Redford rightly points this out, pp. 163f.). The function of this text at the end of chs. 46–50, and so at the conclusion of the Joseph narrative, can be explained only from its amalgamation with the conclusion of the Jacob story. Thus the end, Jacob's death, which according to the plan of the Joseph narrative followed closely on the reunion of father and son, has been separated from the climax, the reconciliation with the brothers; they now stand so far apart that it seemed necessary to resume the reconciliation motif so as to restore the connection once more. One concludes then that this scene goes back to the person who reworked the material and amalgamated the end of the Joseph narrative with the end of the Jacob story.

The text, 50:15-21, forms a self-contained scene which is joined with what precedes by Jacob's legacy and death. It begins with the brothers' apprehension in v. 15 and ends with Joseph comforting and reassuring them, v. 21b. The brothers first send a message to Joseph (vv. 16-17); then follows a dialog face to face (vv. 18-21). The key words which are the grounds for comfort are in the middle of Joseph's answer, vv. 19-20.

Commentary

[**50:15**] The brothers now became aware of what Jacob's death meant for them (so B. Jacob renders וַיִּרְאוּ; J. Skinner, "they realized"). Joseph could take vengeance on them now that the father was dead. There is no basis at all for their fear in what has gone before. The reconciliation narrated in ch. 45 implies a forgiveness that is definitive. There can only be a literary purpose in repeating at the end the climax of the reconciliation with Joseph's explanation.

[**50:16-17**] The brothers are so afraid that they first send a message to Joseph (vv. 16-17; cf. ch. 32). By means of the messenger they inform him of a charge given by their father before his death: he should forgive the brothers the evil they have done (vv. 16b, 17a). It was held earlier (G. Hoberg) and still is today (G. W. Coats) that this charge is a creation of the brothers' anxiety; the majority, however, are of the opinion that it is a literary reworking (H. Gunkel); this holds also when the brothers simply reproduce their father's intention. What is important is that the brothers are even now still conscious of the evil they have done Joseph. So they add, Joseph should be so good as to forgive them because they are "servants of the God of your father." It is their relationship to the same God, the God of their family, that binds them; so they refer once more to their father. It is to be noted that the notion of the forgiveness of sin is used twice in vv. 16-17; it is deliberately avoided in ch. 45. Moreover, the father's words in v. 17a sound like a fixed prayer formula which indicates an editor at work. The message causes Joseph to weep, clearly because the brothers' mistrust in him has been reawakened; perhaps too he is moved by remembrance of the events that had led to the reconciliation.

[50:18] The brothers now approach him themselves (vv. 18-20). They have no need to repeat their request; as often, a gesture is enough; they prostrate themselves before him (v. 18a). But they give further strength to their request with the offer, "We will be your slaves"; they speak conscious of their guilt aroused once more (v. 18b).

[50:19-21a] Joseph's answer now follows; it is with this in view that the scene in vv. 15-21 takes up again the scene of reconciliation in ch. 45. It is framed by the formula of assurance, "Do not fear" (vv. 19a, 21a). V. 19b is a parenthesis; then Joseph explains why the brothers need not fear (v. 20) and promises to provide for them (v. 21a).

[50:19] The first reason is negative and rejects any cause for fear with the rhetorical question, "Am I in the place of God?"; this prepares the way for the positive part in v. 20 (F. Delitzsch, "Am I authorized to intervene in God's action?").

[50:20] The real reason, formulated positively in v. 20, repeats more briefly and in different terms that given in 45:5-8. The explanation shows what God has done and his purpose in doing it; and this is the reason for the "Do not fear," as in ch. 45; cf. 43:23. This gives clear expression to the brothers' guilt, "Yes, you planned evil for me" (the word חשׁב includes execution of the intent); but God's action is set over against this with the same verb חשׁב, "God planned it for good" (execution again included). This "for good" includes God's action in bringing guilt to forgiveness; for only then can the brothers' fear be removed. It is only in this context that Joseph's rhetorical question, "Am I in the place of God?" can be understood. It is not enough to say with O. Procksch and the majority of exegetes, "Even the evil design is included in God's plan"; God's plan is rather to bring the evil devised by the brothers to good in such a way that there can be forgiveness. Only thus does God's hidden purpose become clear, "to preserve the lives of many people." In Joseph's explanation, God's forgiveness, which leads to reconciliation, is joined to his action which saves the lives of many; it is directed, therefore, not only to the family of Jacob, but also to the Egyptians. Joseph's explanation, concentrated into a single sentence, embraces God's action in the two circles of the Joseph narrative; it joins simultaneously God's universal, life-preserving action with his forgiving action within a small group of people, the family of Jacob. This heavily weighted key sentence brings out the meaning of the Joseph story so clearly that one can understand this concluding appendage, vv. 15-21.

[50:21a] The "Do not fear!" is repeated (v. 19; in v. 21 with the introductory ועתה = "this being the case"); Joseph then assures his brothers that he will look after them, as he had promised (the same verb) his father when he invited him to come down to Egypt. The assurance presupposes that the famine is not yet at an end; P's chronology is different. He will provide for "you and your little ones"; the Joseph narrative shows continual concern for the children.

[50:21b] V. 21a concludes Joseph's answer to his brothers; v. 21b is the narrator's conclusion to vv. 15-21a. This concluding section began with the revival of the brothers' fear; but Joseph's answer has removed this; he has reassured them. The two verbs "comfort" and "speak to the heart" occur together also in Is. 40:1-2; cf. Gen. 34:3. The comforting here, as in the other passages, does not consist in mere words; they now have Joseph's promise that he will provide for them. Cf. the key verses in chs. 45 and 50.

(Purpose and Thrust will be found at the end of the section on 50:22-26.)

Epilog: Joseph's Old Age and Death

Literature

Genesis 50:22-26: L. W. King, *Legends of Babylon and Egypt in Relation to Hebrew Tradition*, Schweich Lectures 1916 (1918). A. Schulz, "Drei Anmerkungen zur Genesis (8,7-12; 23,3ss; 50,26)," ZAW 59 (1943) 184-188. J. B. van Hooser, *The Meaning of the Hebrew Root* PQD *in the OT* (diss. Harvard, 1962). F. V. Winnett and W. L. Reed, "The Excavation at Dibon (Dhībán) in Moab," AASOR 36/37 (1964). H. Fürst, *Die göttliche Heimsuchung* (1965). G. W. Coats, "An Exposition for the Wilderness Traditions," VT 22 (1972) 288-295. H. S. Gehman, Ἐπισκέπτομαι, ἐπίσκεψις, ἐπίσκοπος, and ἐπισκοπή in the Septuagint in Relation to פקד and Other Hebrew Roots: A Case of Semantic Development Similar to that of Hebrew," VT 22 (1972) 197-207. H. H. Schmid, *Der sogenannte Jahwist: Beobachtungen und Fragen zur Pentateuchforschung* (1976). H. F. Richter, " 'Auf den Knien eines anderen gebären'? (Zur Deutung von Gen. 30,3 und 50,23)," ZAW 91 (1979) 436-437. J. G. Williams, "Number Symbolism and Joseph as Symbol of Completion," JBL 98 (1979) 86f.

Text

50:22 Joseph remained in Egypt, he[a] and his father's household. And Joseph lived one hundred and ten years.

23 And Joseph saw Ephraim's sons[a] to the third generation.[b] And the sons of Machir, Manasseh's son, were recognized as Joseph's children.

24 And Joseph said to his brothers, I am dying. But God will certainly come to your aid, and bring you up from this land to the land which he swore to Abraham, to Isaac, and to Jacob.

25 Then Joseph made the sons of Israel take an oath saying, When God does indeed visit you, you are to take my bones 'with you'[a] from here.

26 So Joseph died at the age of one hundred and ten. They embalmed him and put[a] him in a coffin in Egypt.

22a Gk adds "and his brothers."
23a Instead of בני read בנים with Gk, Sam, TargOJ, Syr.　　**b** Really great-great-grandchildren; what is meant is great-grandchildren.
25a Add at end אתכם with some Hebr. mss., Sam, Gk, Syr, Vg.
26a According to Ges-K §73g a passive Qal of שים may be seen in וַיִּישֶׂם; perhaps better to read וַיּוּשַׂם with BHS.

Form

The Joseph narrative originally ended with the death and burial of Jacob. This accords with the narrative span of the Joseph narrative as well as with its link with the end of the Jacob story. It closes with the words "after he had buried his father" (50:14); 50:15-21 was added to round off the whole, while looking back again to the climax, the reconciliation. Then two further and entirely different concluding passages were added, joined together in vv. 22-26 to form an epilog. The one gives an account of the evening of Joseph's life (vv. 22-23), the other adds Joseph's last words to his brothers (vv. 24-25), and reports his age and death. His age is mentioned twice, a sign that two different concluding passages have been tacked together.

Commentary

[**50:22-23**] These verses could well follow on v. 14. In v. 14 Joseph returned; in v. 22 Joseph remained. His father's family remains with him in Egypt. This is specified more precisely in v. 22b with the note about his age. One hundred and ten years were regarded in ancient Egypt as the ideal life span (J. Skinner, J. Vergote). One must agree with R. Rendtorff (BZAW 147 [1976;1977[2]] 135) when he points out that the attribution of v. 22 to J or E is highly questionable because a life span of this length (also v. 26) occurs nowhere else in these sources. And no one attributes v. 22 to P. It is scarcely ever possible to establish an author of passages like this, or even so much as guess.

[**50:23**] Good old age is a sign that Joseph has been blessed; so too is it when he experiences his descendants increasing into the third generation (v. 23, likewise Job 42:16; J. Skinner, "A life crowned with blessings"). בני שלשים means great-grandchildren. One would expect something after v. 23a mentioning Manasseh's descendants. Instead the new subject in v. 23b is "the sons of Machir," that is, the sons of Joseph's grandson, of whom nothing had been said previously. The predicate of this sentence also deals with a different matter: "They were born on Joseph's knees." Following Gen. 30:3, this can only mean that they were adopted by Joseph (cf. H. F. Richter [1979], bibliog. above). But this refers to tribal history (as 48:13-20). In Judg. 5:14 Machir is numbered among the tribes of Israel. V. 23b, then, is an etiological appendage or insertion, obviously modeled on 48:13-20.

[**50:24-26**] One expects after v. 23 "and Joseph died. . .." This sentence follows in v. 26 in a notably expanded form. Vv. 24-26 repeat almost sentence by sentence what has already been said; these are for the most part imitations which expand the account of Joseph's death following that of Jacob. As with Jacob's death in ch. 48, so too Joseph's is preceded by an address to the brothers; there is a promise (v. 24) and a charge (v. 25). Then follows the report of Joseph's death (v. 26a) and of the preservation of his corpse (v. 26b).

[**50:24**] Joseph's words have no introduction corresponding to 47:29-31; there is only a hint of it in the אנכי מת taken over from 48:21. This is an indication that the one who made the addition did not intend it as an event from Joseph's life, but wanted to create by means of this promise a link between the patriarchal story and the story of the exodus. The promise is found in a shorter form in 48:21; its original place is here, at the end of Genesis. The beautiful rhythmic language of v. 24 shows it to be the original form. The words announce the leading forth from Egypt in a sentence divided into two parts; both make use of the language of the psalms to express God's attention and intervention. The promise uses the word פָּקַד for God's attention; it occurs again in the same context in Ex. 3:16; 4:31; 13:19. This verb alone shows that the purpose of 50:24 is to throw a bridge across to the exodus event—"I will visit you" (50:24); "I have visited you" (Ex. 3:16; 4:31; on the verb, J. B. van Hooser [1962], bibliog. above). The second sentence announces God's intervention: "He will bring you up from this land"; it is a fixed phrase used 42 times to describe the rescue from Egypt (all passages cited by G. Wehmeier, "עלה," THAT II, 287-289). The land of promise is described as "the land which he swore to Abraham, Isaac, and Jacob." The three names occur together here for the first time after the death of Jacob. They sum up the patriarchal period and story at its very end, making a transition to the beginning of the story of the people. The promise is described as an oath sworn by God to the patriarchs; so in Gen. 22:16; 26:3; 24:7; cf. also the enactment of the oath in 15:7-21; these are all late passages. This oath is always concerned with the promise of the land; so too in the passages in Ex. 13:5, 11; 32:13; 33:1; the wording of the last passage is very close to 50:24. But the real emphasis lies in Deuteronomy where the expression occurs 22 times, e.g., Deut. 7:8, 12, 13; 8:1. This is in accord with Deuteronomic language (cf. *Genesis 12–36*, lit. to ch. 15; R. Rendtorff, BZAW 147, 75-79; H. H. Schmid, *Der sogenannte Jahwist* [1976] 119f.; C. A. Keller, "שבע," THAT II, 855-863).

[**50:25**] A charge is here added to the promise. It is the same as that which the dying Jacob laid on his sons or son Joseph, namely, to bury him in Canaan. It is the work of the one who supplied the supplements, imitating Jacob's charge, but adapting it to the different situation. V. 24 was introduced by "Joseph said to his brothers"; in v. 25 he has the "sons of Israel" take an oath. This can only mean that he has his brothers take the oath as representatives of the later generation of the Israelites of the exodus (which of them were still alive at the time of Joseph's death?). The verbs פָּקַד and עלה in v. 25b refer to the exodus, resuming and repeating the promise of v. 24. This makes it further clear that the charge is a later construction. The same tradition occurs in Ex. 13:19; Moses takes the remains of Joseph, referring to Joseph's charge in 50:25, which he cites word for word. Josh. 24:32 reports the burial of Joseph's remains; the place is, according to Gen. 33:19, the plot of land at Shechem which Jacob had bought and, according to Josh. 24:32, left to his son. Here too there is reference to Joseph's charge (cf. M. Noth, *A History of Pentateuchal Traditions* [1948; 1966³; 1972] 83).

[**50:26**] The epilog closes with Joseph's death (v. 26); his age, given in v. 22, is repeated. As in the account of Jacob's death, so too here, the embalming follows; but it is only a short note and no subject is given. The conclusion of the epilog, with the further note that his corpse was put in a coffin, thus anticipates once more the exodus from Egypt when Joseph's last charge can be carried out (coffin: really a box; the same word is used for the ark; see the citation from the *T. 12 Patr.*, Joseph 20, in L. Ruppert, *Die Josepherzählung der Genesis* [1965] 202; according to this an importance was attributed to Joseph's remains at the exodus almost like that given to the pillars of fire and smoke).

Purpose and Thrust

A further survey of the concluding texts, 49:28b-33; 50:1-26, confirms that the real conclusion of the Joseph narrative is the death and burial of Jacob (49:28b-33; 50:1-14). What follows is almost entirely repetition and imitation. In the middle of 50:15-21 is the key passage from 45:5b-8, altered only a little and set in a new situation. Moreover, vv. 16-17 resume the motif of the deathbed charge from what has preceded.

Most of the epilog, 50:22-26, is repetition: Joseph remained in Egypt (cf. 47:27); life span cf. 47:9; v. 23a, cf. 48:11; v. 23b, cf. 48:3-6; v. 24, cf. 48:21, here reversed; v. 25, cf. 47:29-31 and 49:29-32; v. 26a, cf. 49:33; v. 26b, cf. 50:2.

The accumulation of repetitions in 50:22-26 demonstrates clearly that this appendage was inserted by a transmitter who adhered as closely as possible to the Joseph narrative.

The intentions of these appendages and expansions are important. All are concerned, though in different ways, to bind the Joseph narrative firmly to the traditions of the people of Israel. This is done indirectly in 50:15-21 where the redactor, so to speak, fits and fixes the Joseph narrative into the Jacob story. The concern to throw a bridge from the Joseph narrative to the story of the exodus from Egypt is obvious in the promise of "bringing up" on the lips of Joseph (50:24, as 48:21); add too his request that those making the exodus take his remains with them (v. 25). Finally, the reference to the adoption of the sons of Machir (v. 23) indicates a link with the tribal history (as 48:3-6,13-20). Even if all these are but hints, the expansions are nonetheless evidence that the reproduction of the Joseph narrative is directed by the concern to bind it in a variety of ways to the story of the people. One can thus understand better why the Joseph narrative was preserved, taken up into the canon, and so continued to have its effects in the present.

The death and burial of Jacob, 49:28b-33 and 50:1-14, the conclusion of the Joseph narrative, are also worked into the story of the patriarchs, though in a quite different way; it is from this that the story of the people arises. The narrative began with the open breach in Jacob's family which would have sent Jacob to the grave in grief. As a result of the reconciliation of the brothers and the reunion of father and son, Jacob can die in peace. But this also means that he is to be buried with his fathers. The narrator describes the fulfillment of this wish in the solemn funeral procession from Egypt to Canaan, and thus at the end of the narrative points the direction in which the story of the descendants of Jacob and Joseph will continue.

Genesis 46–50: Survey

The Joseph narrative as far as ch. 45 runs its course in a continuous, coherent, and clearly arranged sequence of events; the conclusion, chs. 46–50, is complicated. It contains expansions, doublings, breaks in continuity, and much that does not seem to belong immediately to the Joseph narrative. The reason for this is that the conclusion of the Joseph narrative issues into the conclusion of the Jacob story. The diversity between chs. 46–50 and chs. 39–45 shows itself most clearly in the convergence of several streams in chs. 46–50. The text as a whole divides as follows:

1. 46:1-30 Jacob comes to Egypt, reunion of father and son.
2. 46:31-34; 47:1-28 provision for Jacob's family and its settlement in Egypt.
3a. 47:29-31; 48; 49:1-32 Jacob's legacy.
3b. 49:33—50:14 Jacob's death and burial.
4. 50:15-21 confirmation of the reconciliation.
5. 50:22-26 epilog: Joseph's old age and death.

The preceding parts of the Joseph narrative already anticipate Jacob's coming to Egypt and the reunion with the father, the settlement of and provision for the family in Egypt, and Jacob's death. It is certain, therefore, that these parts belong entirely or in part to the Joseph narrative.

The exegesis has shown the following to be the conclusion of the Joseph story in chs. 46–50.

1. 46:5b, 28-30	the reunion
5b	Jacob's departure (follows on 45:24-28)
28-30	arrival in Goshen
2. 46:31-34; 47	provision for family and settlement in Egypt
46:31-34	the brothers prepare for the audience
47:1-6	audience of Joseph and his brothers with the Pharaoh
47:11, 12, 27a	settlement in Egypt
3. 47:29-31; 48–50	Jacob's death
a) Jacob's legacy	
47:29-31	request to Joseph to be buried in Canaan
48:1-2, 8-12	Jacob blesses Joseph's sons

b) (48:28b-33 Jacob's death)

50:1	Joseph weeps over his father
50:2-3	embalming and 70 days mourning
50:4-14	(omit vv. 12-13) burial in Canaan
50:14	conclusion; Joseph returns to Egypt.

The Joseph narrative concludes with his return to his high office in Egypt (by which "the lives of many were preserved") after he has buried his father.

The remaining components of chs. 46–50 are not a unity. A part of the text demonstrably belongs to P; on this all scholars agree. In inquiring about the P component of chs. 46–50, regard must be had to the conclusion of the Jacob story according to P and its function in the present text, i.e., in the conclusion of the Joseph narrative. The P component can be divided into the same three parts as in the Joseph narrative; the differences are slight.

1. 46:6-7	emigration to Egypt; vv. 8-27, list of names
2. 47:7-10	Jacob blesses the Pharaoh
47:11*, 27b	settlement in Egypt (Rameses). They settle permanently in the land and multiply (transition in v. 28, Jacob's age).
3. Jacob's legacy, death, and burial	
a) Jacob's legacy	
48:3-6(7)	Jacob adopts (and blesses) Joseph's sons
49:1b, 28b	Jacob blesses (all) his sons
49:29-32	charge: burial in Machpelah
b) 49:33	Jacob's death
50:12-13	his sons bury Jacob in Machpelah

The P component considered in itself: The conclusion of the priestly account of the Jacob story is preserved here in its entirety, or almost so. It presents a self-contained piece which leads from Jacob's emigration to Egypt to his death. Only one text, 47:7-10 (Jacob blesses the Pharaoh), has no corresponding text in the Joseph narrative; this can only be explained from P's story of the patriarchs. The conclusion from this data is that the redactor, who inserted the Joseph narrative into the patriarchal story, joined it to the conclusion of P's Jacob story in such a way as to preserve the two.

The P component joined to the Joseph narrative: The overwhelming majority of P texts run parallel to the Joseph narrative. One can speak here with complete confidence of a doubling. Chs. 46–50 presuppose two originally separate accounts of the emigration of Jacob to Egypt until his death. The clearest and most striking proof of this is the parallelism of themes:

Jacob's request to bury him in Canaan (47:29-31/49:29-32)
The execution of this request (50:3-14/50:12-13)

The clearest and most striking proof of the work of a redactor is the fact that the death and burial of Jacob is reproduced only according to the formulation of P. It is precisely the same with the accounts of the deaths of Abraham and Isaac; the same redactor, therefore, was at work through the whole of the patriarchal story.

There is a series of texts which belong neither to the Joseph narrative nor to

P. One must distinguish between two groups in these expansions. First, there are the expansions to P; the tithe of one-fifth and 50:15-21, the confirmation of the reconciliation. The second group comprises 46:1-5a, at the beginning; with this the redactor of chs. 46–50 introduces the conclusion of the Jacob story. Then follow two self-contained blocks of expansions, one of which is inserted before the death of Jacob (48:13-22, add 49:1b-28a), the other after Jacob's burial (50:22-26). Two conclusions follow from this. First, the data show that with these two additions there can be no question of an independent and continuous layer as is the case of the P text; they are redactional expansions. The hand of a redactor working to a plan is evident when the expansions are found at the beginning and the end, before and after the death of Jacob. The hand of the redactor is even more obvious when, by means of these expansions, he links the patriarchal story with the story of the exodus. All three expansions contain the promise of the exodus from Egypt (46:4; 48:21; 50:24f.). Second, the expansions are to the Jacob story, not to the Joseph narrative. This holds also for the epilog, 50:22-26. The account of Joseph's last days is necessary for the patriarchal story, but not for the Joseph narrative.

This explains the remarkable diversity between chs. 46–50 and chs. 37–45. The amalgamation of the Joseph narrative and the Jacob story in chs. 46–50 did not merely mean the weaving together of two literary threads (Joseph narrative and P); it meant over and above this the resumption of a whole series of expansions which were inserted into the conclusion of the Jacob story, which is at the same time the conclusion of the patriarchal story.

Prescinding from the two expansions, 50:15-21 in the Joseph story and 46:8-27 in P, and from the blessings of Jacob in ch. 49, there are four groups of additions, all attesting *genera* characteristic of the patriarchal story:

1. Itinerary: 46:1-5a; the basis is an itinerary with stations and a promise;
   48:7 (P) Rachel's death and burial remain in their original place (35:16,19), in an itinerary context; likewise the etiology of Abel-mizraim (50:10b-11).
2. Etiological additions or expansions:
   a. related to tribal history:
      | 48:13-20 | Jacob gives Ephraim precedence over Manasseh; |
      | 48:3-6 | Jacob adopts Ephraim and Manasseh; |
      | 50:23b | Joseph adopts the sons of Machir; |
      | 48:22 | conveyance of the ''shoulder''—etiology of place? |
   b. 50:10b-11 etiology of Abel-mizraim;
   c. 47:13-26 reference to an Egyptian institution, the tithe of one-fifth.
3. Blessings and promises:
   a. 46:2-4 revelation and promises to Jacob;
   b. 48:15-16;
      48:20a blessings secondarily inserted;
   c. 46:4; 48:21;
      50:24-25 exodus promise.
4. Genealogy:
   50:22-26 Joseph's last days and death as redactional expansion.

The conclusion is that all these expansions have come from traditions about the patriarchal story. It is thus confirmed that each of these expansions has its own line of tradition and is not to be ascribed to a literary source; they form no literary continuity. But this says nothing about the age of the individual texts. They lie along the long road from the origins of the patriarchal traditions right up to the close of the Pentateuch. One cannot determine more precisely the period in which any of the texts originated; one can only indicate more or less the earliest and latest stage.

The earliest stage: one can still discern traces of a conclusion of the Jacob story older than P. Behind 46:1-5a lies an old prepriestly itinerary corresponding to those in the patriarchal story. Further, the redactor wanted to indicate by 46:1-5a the introduction of the close of the Jacob story; for this purpose he probably made use of an old itinerary available to him which he expanded. The note about Rachel's death and burial, 48:7, attached to a P text, 48:3-6, belongs originally to J (35:16,19); it has been adapted to the present context. The rhythmic blessing, derived from 48:15-16, could come from J. This would also be a possibility for the blessing in 48:20a. Of the etiological appendages and expansions one can only say that this form occurs neither in the Joseph narrative nor in P; nor does it belong to the early stage of the formation of the patriarchal story; but it does belong to that stage which extends from the beginning of the sedentary period to the beginning of the monarchy; nor can one exclude further activity later.

The latest stage of the expansions is evident in the redactional links which point the way from the patriarchal period over to the period of the exodus (46:4; 48:21; 50:24-25); they presuppose the Pentateuch already existing.

The Blessings of Jacob

Literature

Genesis 49:1-27: H. Zimmern, "Der Jakobsegen und der Tierkreis," ZA 7 (1892) 161-172. F. de Moor, *La bénédiction prophétique de Jacob* (1902). P. Riessler, "Zum Jakobsegen," ThQ 90 (1908) 489-503. C. H. Cornill, "Zum Segen Jakobs und zum jahwistischen Dekalog," BZAW 27 (1914) 101-113. F. Zorell, "Der Jakobsegen Gen. 49,1-27," BZ 13 (1915) 114-116. E. Sachsse, "Untersuchungen zur hebräischen Metrik (. . . Gn 49 . . .)," ZAW 43 (1925) 173-192. E. Dhorme, *La Poésie Biblique* (1931). F. M. T. Böhl, "Wortspiele im AT," JPOS 6 (1926) 196-212 = *Opera Minora* (1953) 11-56.475f. E. Burrows, *The Oracles of Jacob and Balaam* (1938/1939). W. F. Albright, "The Oracles of Balaam," JBL 63 (1944) 207-233. F. M. Cross and D. N. Freedman, "The Blessing of Moses," JBL 67 (1948) 191-210. J. M. Vosté, "La bénédiction de Jacob d'après Mar Išoʻdad de Merw (c. 850)," Bib 29 (1948) 1-30. W. Amerding, "The Last Words of Jacob Gen. 49," BibSacr 112 (1955) 320-329. B. Vawter, "The Canaanite Background of Genesis 49," CBQ 17 (1955) 1-17. J. Coppens, "La bénédiction de Jacob: Son cadre historique à la lumière des parallèles ougaritiques," VT.S 4 (1957) 97-115. H. J. Kittel, *Die Stammessprüche Israels, Genesis 49 und Deuteronomium 33 traditionsgeschichtlich untersucht* (diss. Berlin, 1959). S. Herrmann, "Das Werden Israels," ThLZ 87 (1962) 561-574. E. Osswald, "Zum Problem der Vaticinia ex eventu," ZAW 75 (1963) 27-44. J. R. Porter, "The Pentateuch and the Triennial Lectionary Cycle," *Essays Pres. to S. H. Hooke* (1963) 163-174. A. H. J. Gunneweg, "Über den Sitz im Leben der sogenannten Stammessprüche (Gen. 49; Dtn 33; Jdc 5)," ZAW 76 (1964) 245-255. H. J. Zobel, *Stammesspruch und Geschichte*, BZAW 95 (1965). G. Fohrer, " 'Creation' Motifs in Ancient Hebrew Poetry," CBQ 29 (1967) 393-406. C. M. Carmichael, "Some Sayings in Genesis 49," JBL 88 (1969) 435-444. T. H. Gaster, *Myth. . .* (1969), "Jacob's Last Words," 214f. M. Fishbane, "Jeremiah IV23-26 and Job III3-13: A Recovered Use of the Creation Pattern," VT 21 (1971) 151-167. R. Smend, "Zur Frage der altisraelitischen Amphiktyonie," EvTh 31 (1971) 623-630. C. Westermann, "Weisheit im Sprichwort," Fests. A. Jepsen (1971) 73-85 = ThB 55 (1974) 149-161. A. D. H. Mayes, "Israel in the Pre-Monarchy Period," VT 23 (1973) 151-170. M. Aberbach and B. Grossfeld, "Targum Onqelos on Genesis 49. Translation and Analytical Commentary," *Aramaic Studies I* (1976). E. Cortès, *Los discursos de adiós de Gn 49 a Jn 13-17. Pistas para la historia de un género literario en la antigua literatura judia* (1976). D. N. Freedman, "Divine Names and Titles in Early Poetry," Fests. G. E. Wright (1976) 55-107. M. Metzger, "Probleme der Frühgeschichte Israels," VF 22 (1977) 30-43. D. N. Freedman, "Pottery, Poetry, and Prophecy: An Essay in Biblical Poetry," JBL 96 (1977) 5-26. G. Brin, "The Birthright of the Sons of Jacob," Tarb. 48 (1978/79) 1-8.

Genesis 49:1-2: W. Staerk, "Der Begrauch der Wendung בְּאַחֲרִית הַיָּמִים im alttestamentlichen Kanon," ZAW 11 (1891) 247-253. H. Wildberger, "Die Völkerwallfahrt zum Zion Jes II 1-5," VT 7 (1957) 62-81. C. Roth, "The Subject Matter of Qumran Exegesis," VT 10 (1960) 51-68. B. Renaud, *Structure et attaches littéraires de Michée IV-V*, CRB 2 (1964) 89-90, review R. Tournay, RB 74 (1967) 119. E. Lipiński, "באחרית הימים dans les textes préexiliques," VT 20 (1970) 445-450.

Genesis 49:3-7: S. A. Cook, "Simeon and Levi," AJT 13 (1909) 370-388. J. Meinhold, "Textkonjekturen (Gen. 49:5.13; Num. 24:8.17)," ZAW 38 (1920) 169-171. H. H. Rowley, "Zadok and Nahushtan," JBL 58 (1939) 113-141. S. H. Blank, "The Curse, Blasphemy, the Spell and the Oath," HUCA 23 (1950/51) 73-95. O. Plöger, "Priester und Prophet," ZAW 63 (1951) 157-192. F. Nötscher, "Heisst *kābōd* auch 'Seele'?" VT 2 (1952) 358-362. J. Reider, "Etymological Studies in Biblical Hebrew," VT 4 (1954) 276-295. M. Dahood, "A New Translation of Gen. 49,6a," Bib 36 (1955) 229. M. S. Seale, "The Glosses in the Book of Genesis and the JE Theory," ET 67 (1955/56) 333-335. H. H. Rowley, "Mose und der Monotheismus," ZAW 69 (1957) 1-21. H. Cazelles, "Ras Schamra und der Pentateuch," ThQ 138 (1958) 26-39. S. Lehming, "Zur Überlieferungsgeschichte von Genesis 34," ZAW 70 (1958) 228-250. C. Westermann, *Basic Forms of Prophetic Speech* (1960; 1978⁵; Eng. 1967). M. J. Dahood, "*MKRTYHM* in Genesis 49,5," CBQ 23 (1961) 54-56. N. Walker, "The Renderings of *Rāṣôn*," JBL 81 (1962) 182-184. A. H. J. Gunneweg, *Leviten und Priester*, FRLANT 89 (1965). W. Krebs, " '. . .sie haben Stiere gelähmt.' (Gen. 49,6)," ZAW 78 (1966) 359-361. A. D. Crown, "Judges V 15b-16," VT 17 (1967) 240-242. J. R. Boston, "The Wisdom Influence upon the Song of Moses," JBL 87 (1968) 198-202. J. A. Emerton, "Some Difficult Words in Gen. 49," *Essays Pres. to D. W. Thomas* (1968) 81-92. M. Dahood, "Ugaritic-Hebrew Syntax and Style," UF 1 (1969) 15-36. P. D. Miller, "Animal Names as Designations in Ugaritic and Hebrew," UF 2 (1970) 177-186. S. Gevirtz, "The Reprimand of Reuben," JNES 30 (1971) 87-98. D. J. Kamhi, "The Root *ḥlq* in the Bible," VT 23 (1973) 235-239. J. Barr, "ἐρίζω and ἐρείδω in the Septuagint: A Note Principally on Gen. XLIX 6," JSS 19 (1974) 198-215; "After Five Years: A Retrospect on Two Major Translations of the Bible," HeyJ. 15 (1974) 381-405. D. N. Freedman, *Early Israelite History in the Light of Early Israelite Poetry* (1975). R. Péter, "פר et שׁור. Note de lexicographie hébraïque," VT 25 (1975) 486-496. R. P. Gordon, "Targum Onkelos to Gen. 49,4 and a Common Semitic Idiom," JQR 66 (1975/76) 224-226. C. H. J. de Geus, *The Tribes of Israel: An Investigation into the Presuppositions of Noth's Amphictyony Hypothesis*, SSN 18 (1976). B. Chiesa, "Contrasti ideologici del tempo degli Asmonei nella Aggādāh e nella versioni di Genesi 49,3," AION 37 (1977) 417-440. C. Westermann, *Praise and Lament in the Psalms* (1961; 1977⁵; Eng. 1981). W. G. E. Watson, "Gender-Matched Synonymous Parallelism in the OT," JBL 99 (1980) 321-341.

Genesis 49:8-12: F. Delitzsch, *Messianische Weissagungen in geschichtlicher Folge* (1890) ch. 2, §9,35-41. E. Sellin, "Die Schiloh-Weissagung Gen. 49,10," Fests. A. Zahn (1908) 369-390. G. C. Aalders, "De Silo-profetie," GThT 15 (1914) 341-355. R. Eisler, "Das akkadische *šilu* 'Gebieter,' " MGWJ 69 (1929) 444-446. H. Gressmann, *Der Messias*, FRLANT 29 (1929) esp. 220ff. S. Lönberg, "Die 'Silo'-Verse in Gen. 49," ARW 27 (1929) 369-384. F. Nötscher, "Gen. 49,10: שִׁילֹה = akkad. *šēlu*," ZAW 47 (1929) 323-325. B. S. Olivera, "Non auferetur sceptrum de Juda (Gen. 49,10)," VD 6 (1929) 16-19,52-57. A. Jirku, "Der Juda-Spruch Gen. 49,8ff. und die Texte von Ras šamra," JPOS 15 (1935) 12-13. P. Joüon, "Genèse 49,11," Bib 21 (1940) 58. E. Sellin, "Zu dem Judaspruch im Jaqobssegen Gen 49,8-12 und im Mosesegen Deut 33,7," ZAW 60 (1944) 57-67. K. Smyth, "The Prophecy concerning Juda," CBQ 7 (1945) 290-305. J. Lindblom, "The Political Background of the Shilo Oracle," VT.S 1 (1953) 78-87. T. H. Gaster, "Short Notes on Gen. XLIX 10.26," VT 4 (1954) 73-79. A. S. Kapelrud, "Genesis XLIX 12," VT 4 (1954) 426-428. S. Mowinckel, *He that Cometh: The Messianic Hope in the OT and in the Time of Jesus* (1956). O. Eissfeldt, "Silo und Jerusalem," VT.S 4 (1957) 138-147. W. L. Moran, "Genesis 49,10 and Its Use in Ez 21,32," Bib 39 (1958) 405-425. J. Blenkinsopp, "The Oracle of Judah and the Messianic Entry," JBL 80 (1961) 55-65. W. L. Moran, "The Hebrew Language in Its North-west Semitic Background," Fests. W. F. Albright (1961; 1965²) 54-72. J. S. Croatto, "El uso finito del infinitivo absoluto," RivBib 24 (1962) 113. E. M. Good, "The 'Blessing' on Judah, Gen. 49,8-12," JBL 82 (1963) 427-432. H. P. Müller, "Zur Frage nach dem Ursprung der biblischen Eschatologie,'' VT 14 (1964) 276-293. R. Criado, '' 'Hasta que venga Silo' (Gén 49,10). Ricientes explicaciones catolicas,'' EstB 24 (1965) 289-320; CuBi 23 (1966) 195-219. M. Treves, ''Shilo (Gen. 49,10),'' JBL 85 (1966) 353-356. H. D. Preuss, *Jahweglaube und Zukunftserwartung*, BWANT 5,7 (1968). B. Margulis, ''Gen. XLIX 10/Deut. XXXIII 2-3. A New Look at Old Problems,'' VT 19 (1969) 202-210. D. Robertson, ''The Morphemes -Y(-Ī) and -W(-Ō) in Biblical Hebrew,'' VT 19 (1969) 211-223. H. P. Rüger, ''Zu RŠ 24.258,'' UF 1 (1969) 203-206. F. I. Andersen, ''Orthography in Repetitive Parallelism,'' JBL 89 (1970) 343-344. *The Hebrew Verbless Clause in the Pentateuch* (1970). H. Cazelles, ''Shilo, the Customary Laws and the Return of the Ancient Kings,'' *OT Essays in Hon. of G. H. Davies* (1970) 238-351. L. Sabottka, ''Noch einmal Gen. 49,10,'' Bib 51 (1970) 225-229. A. Malamat, ''Mari,'' BA 34 (1971) 2-22. A. Demsky, '' 'Dark Wine' from Judah,'' IEJ 22 (1972) 233f. H. J. Zobel, ''Das Selbstverständnis Israels nach dem AT,'' ZAW 85 (1973) 281-294. C. Westermann, ''Der Web der Verheissung durch das AT,'' ThB 55 (1974) 230-249. F. Pili, ''Possibili casi di metatesi in Genesi 49,10 e Salmo 2,11-12a,'' Aug. 15 (1975) 457-471. A. Caquot, ''La parole sur Juda dans le Testament lyrique de Jacob (Gen. 49,8-12),'' Sem. 26 (1976) 5-32. C. Westermann, ''Das Schöne im AT,'' Fests. W. Zimmerli (1977) 479-487. S. A. Geller, *Parallelism in Early Biblical Poetry*, HSM 30 (1979). P. D. Miller, ''Synonymous-Sequential Parallelism in the Psalms,'' Bib 61 (1980) 256-260. L. Monsengwo-Pasinya, ''Deux textes messianiques de la Septante: Gen. 49,10 et Ez 21,32,'' Bib 61 (1980) 357-376. S. Gevirtz, ''Adumbrations of Dan in Jacob's Blessing on Judah,'' ZAW 93 (1981) 21-37. R. Martin-Achard, ''A propos de la bénédiction de Juda en Genèse 49,8-12(10),'' RB 89 (1982) 121-134.

Genesis 49:13-19: A. Alt, *Die Landnahme der Israeliten in Palästina: Reformations-programm* (1925) = KS I (1953; 1963³) 89-125. E. Täubler, ''Die Spruch-Verse über Sebulon,'' MGWJ 83 (1939) 1-37 = (1963). O. Eissfeldt, ''Gabelhürden im Ostjordanland'' (1949) = KS III, 61-66; (1954) = KS III, 67-70. A. Kuschke, ''Die Lagervorstellung der Priesterschriftlichen Erzählung. Eine überlieferungsgeschichtliche Studie,'' ZAW 63 (1951) 74-105. C. Westermann, ''Das Hoffen im AT,'' ThB 24 (1964) 219-265. P. A. H. de Boer, '' 'Vive le roi!' '' VT 5 (1955) 225-231. W. Beyerlin, ''Das Königscharisma bei Saul,'' ZAW 73 (1961) 186-201. J. Frankowski, ''Requies, Bonum Promissum Populi Dei in VT et in Judaismo (Hebr 3,7-4,11),'' VD 43 (1965) 124-149, 225-240. K. H. Bernhardt, ''Nomadentum und Ackerbaukultur in der frühstaatlichen Zeit Altisraels,'' Dtsch. Akad. d. Wiss. Berlin 69 (1968) 31-40. W. L. Holladay, ''Isa III 10-11: An Archaic Wisdom Passage,'' VT 18 (1968) 481-487. A. R. Hulst, ''De betekenis van het woord *menuhā*,'' *Schrift en Uitleg* (1970) 62-78. B. Margulis, ''A Ugaritic Psalm (RŠ 24.252),'' JBL 89 (1970) 292-304. A. F. Rainey, ''Compulsory Labour Gangs in Ancient Israel,'' IEJ 20 (1970) 191-203. S. Herrmann, *A History of Israel in OT Times* (1973; 1980²; Eng. 1975). S. Gevirtz, ''Gen. 49,14-15,'' ErIs 12 (1975) 111. A. Globe, ''The Muster of the Tribes in Judges 5,11e-18,'' ZAW 87 (1975) 169-184. H. Donner, *Einführung in die biblische Landes- und Altertumskunde* (1976) esp. 87f. A. Kuschke, ''Sidons Hinterland und der Pass von Ĝezzin,'' ZDPV 93 (1977) 178-197. H. M. Niemann, *Untersuchungen zur Herkunft und Geschichte des Stammes Dan* (diss. Rostock, 1979). J. L. Kugel, ''The Adverbial Use of *kî tôb*,'' JBL 99 (1980) 433-435. G. Robinson, ''The Idea of Rest in the OT and the Search for the Basic Character of Sabbath,'' ZAW 92 (1980) 32-42.

Genesis 49:20-28a: E. I. Fripp, ''Note on Genesis XLIX 24b-26,'' ZAW 11 (1891) 262-266. E. Zorell, ''Desiderium collium aeternorum (Gen. 49,26),'' ZKTh 33 (1910) 582-586. L. Gry, ''La bénédiction de Joseph (Gen. XLIX 22-27),'' RB 14 (1917) 508-520. N. H. Torczyner, ''אביר kein Stierbild,'' ZAW 39 (1921) 296-300. B. S. Olivera, ''Filius accrescens Joseph (Gen. 49,22-26),'' VD 6 (1926) 102-110. W. E. Barnes, ''A Taunt Song in Gen. 49,20-21,'' JThS 33 (1931/32) 354-359. E. Burrows, ''The Meaning of El Šaddai,'' JThS 41 (1940) 152-161. J. M. Allegro, ''A Possible Mesopotamian Background to the Joseph Blessing of Genesis XLIX,'' ZAW 64 (1952) 249-251. J. Muilenburg, ''A Study in Hebrew Rhetoric: Repetition and Style,'' VT.S 1 (1953) 97-111. O. Eissfeldt, ''Religionshistorie und Religionspolemik im AT,'' VT.S 3 (1955) 94-102. N. Walker, ''Concerning the Function of *'eth*,'' VT 5 (1955) 314-315. J. Blau, ''Gibt es ein emphatisches *'ēt* im Bibelhebräisch?'' VT 6 (1956) 211-212. F. Dumermuth, ''Zur deuteronomischen Kulttheologie und ihren Voraussetzungen,'' ZAW

70 (1958) 59-98. M. Dahood, "Ras Shamra-Ugarit et l'AT," CAB 12 (1960) esp. 68f. J. G. Thierry, "Remarks on Various Passages of the Psalms," OTS 13 (1963) 77-97. H. A. Brongers and A. S. van der Woude, "Wat is de betekenis van *'ABNAYIM* in Exodus 1,16?" NedThT 20 (1965/66) 241-254. J. P. Hyatt, "Was Yahweh Originally a Creator Deity?" JBL 86 (1967) 369-377. P. D. Miller, "El the Warrior," HThR 60 (1967) 411-431. L. R. Baily, "Israelite 'El Šadday an Amorite Bêl Šadê," JBL 87 (1968) 434-438. V. Salo, " ' Joseph, Sohn der Färse,' " BZ 12 (1968) 94-95. P. C. Craigie, "The Song of Deborah and the Epic of Tukulti-Ninurta," JBL 88 (1969) 253-265. T. L. Fenton, Fests. G. Friedrich (1973) 9-24. M. Girard, *Louange Cosmique: Bible et animisme* (1973) 19ff. Y. Avishur, "*Krkr* in Biblical Hebrew and in Ugaritic," VT 26 (1976) 257-261. M. Saebø, "Den ene Gud og Herre: Bemerkinger til det gammeltestamentlige Gudbegrep," TTK 4 (1977) 241-253. H. P. Müller, "Einige alttestamentliche Probleme zur aramäischen Inschrift von Dēr 'Allā," ZDPV 94 (1978) 56-67. M. Wyatt, "The Problem of the 'God of the Fathers,' " ZAW 90 (1978) 101-104. G. Rendsburg, "Janus Parallelism in Gen. 49,26," JBL 99 (1980) 291-293. B. Kedar-Kopfstein, "Die Stammbildung *qôṭel* als Übersetzungsproblem," ZAW 93 (1981) 254-281.

Text

49:1   Then Jacob summoned his sons and said, Gather round, and I will tell[a] you what will happen to you in the days[b] to come.

2   Come together and listen,[a] sons of Jacob, listen to Israel your father!

3   Reuben, my firstborn[a] are you, my strength, the fruit of my manly vigor,[b] preeminent in pride, preeminent in might;[c]

4   'you foamed over'[a] like water, you will be preeminent[b] no more, because you climbed into your father's bed,[c] then defiled my couch ' ,[d]

5   Simeon and Levi are brothers, tools of violence are their swords.[a]

6   [I will not dally in their council, I will not share in their assembly];[a] for in their anger they murdered men, and in their recklessness they hamstrung oxen.

7   Cursed be their anger for it was fierce, their wrath for it was cruel.[a] I will scatter them in Jacob, I will disperse them in Israel.

8   Judah are you;[a] your brothers praise you; your hand is on the neck[b] of your enemies; the sons of your father bow before you.

9   Judah is a lion's[a] cub, from the kill,[b] in the valley he comes up'.[c] He lay down, crouched[d] like a lion, like a lioness, who dares rouse him?[e]

10   The scepter shall not pass from Judah, nor the staff[a] from between his feet, until 'his ruler'[b] comes, and the nations are obedient[c] to him.

11   He tethers[a] his ass[b] to the vine, and his ass's colt to the grapevine;[c] he washes his cloak in wine, his garment[d] in the blood of grapes.[e]

12   His eyes are darker than wine,[ab] his teeth[c] whiter than milk.

13   Zebulun dwells[a] at the shore of the sea,[b] he shall be a haven for ships;[c] his flank is upon Sidon.

14   Issachar is a boney ass, between the cattle pens[a] he crouches.[b]

15   When he saw that the resting place was good,[a] the[b] land was pleasant, then he bent his back to the burden, and submitted to forced labor.[c]

16   Dan executes judgment[a] for his people as one of the tribes of Israel.

17   Dan [let him be like][a] a serpent on the way, [like] a viper[b] on the road, who bites the horse's fetlock,[c] so that its rider falls backwards.

18   [I hope for thy salvation, Yahweh.]

19   Gad, raiders raid him, but he raids on their heels.[a]

20   Asher, his food is rich,[a] he provides delicacies for the king.

21   Naphtali, a hind in flight,[a] who[b] bears comely[c] fawns.[d]

22   Joseph is a young and verdant tree,[a] a young and verdant tree by the spring; its branches climb over the wall.[b]

23   The archers[a] harrassed[b] and shot at[c] him, they pressed him hard;[d]

24a But his bow remained firm,[a] and flexible[b] his arms and hands.[c]

24b By[a] the hands of the Strong One of Jacob, by the 'name'[b] of the shepherd, the stone of Israel,

25   by the God of your father—may he help you, by 'God'[a] Almighty—may he bless you, with the blessings of heaven above, with the blessings of the deep that crouches[b] below, with the blessings of breast and womb.

26   The blessings of your father are richer than the blessings of the ancient 'mountains',[a] and the splendor of the eternal hills. May they come[b] upon the head of Joseph, and upon the crown[c] of the blessed[d] among his brothers.

27   Benjamin, a ravening wolf;[a] in the morning he devours his prey, in the evening he divides the booty.

28a These are all the twelve tribes of Israel. And this is what their father Jacob said to them.

1a The apodosis to an imperative is either in the jussive or cohortative, BrSynt §135c.   **b** The phrase occurs 14 times in the OT, cf. H. Wildberger, VT 7 (1957) 62-81.

2a Not to be deleted; repetitive style; cf. W. F. Albright, JBL 63 (1944) 207-233; J. Muilenburg, VT.S 1 (1953) 97-111.

3a With postpositive accent.   **b** Cf. Deut. 21:17; Job 40:16.   **c** Pausal עַז.

4a Read פחזת with Sam, Gk, TargO, and others; BHK apparatus.   **b** On the form, Ges-K §53n.   **c** Plural of local extension, Ges-K §124b.   **d** The incomprehensible עלה is to be omitted, BHK and others; the versions make the adaptation to the 2nd pers.

5a Hapax leg., not explained (KBL); all the versions understand it as a weapon; details in J. Skinner, comm. ad loc.

6a The fem. follows נפשי, BrSynt §16g.

7a The subjects are in parallelism also in Amos 1:11, the predicates in Song 8:6.

8a The separate pronoun is emphatic, Ges-K §135e; BrSynt §123b.   **b** On the possibility of expanding this half-verse, see comm. below.

9a גור also in Deut. 33:22.   **b** טרף is used only of animals of prey.   **c** MT reads "from preying, my son, you have come up"; see comm. below.   **d** Verbs of motion are often asyndetically juxtaposed, BrSynt §133a.   **e** Cf. Deut. 33:11; Num. 24:9.

10a שבט and מחקק as the leader's staff, cf. Deut. 33:21; Num. 21:18; Judg. 5:14; Ps. 60:9.   **b** MT שׁילה; for the versions, BHK, J. Skinner in detail; lit. below in comm. ad loc.; read מִשְׁלֹה.   **c** יקהת = "obedience" only here; the versions explain it as "hope" (BHK apparatus); cf. B. Margulis, VT 19 (1969) 203.

11a אסרי (as v. 12 חכלילי) with hireq compag. (or the old case ending), cf. W. L. Moran, Fests. W. F. Albright (1961) 60; J. S. Croatto, RivBib 24 (1962) 113; D. Robertson, VT 19 (1969) 211-223.   **b** On the two words for "ass," E. Lipiński, VT 20 (1970) 445-450; A. Malamat, BA 34 (1971) 2-22; riding on an ass, Judg. 10:4; 12:14; Zech. 9:9.   **c** Only here, "vine with pink grapes" KBL, especially precious wine.   **d** Only here.   **e** Ugaritic parallel, H. P. Rüger, UF 1 (1969) 206.

12ab Trans. following A. S. Kapelrud, VT 4 (1954) 426-428; the inscription יין כחל was found on a wine jar from the Hebron region, = "dark colored wine," A. Demsky, IEJ 22 (1972) 233f.   **c** On the expression, Ges-K §93dd; milk and wine, cf. Is. 7:15.

13a F. M. Cross and D. N. Freedman, JBL 67 (1948) 204.   **b** Cf. Judg. 5:17; Deut. 1:7; Josh. 9:1.   **c** The link between חוף and ships is found only here; attempts at emendation (BHK) are not convincing. On the location of Zebulon, A. Kuschke, ZDPV 93 (1977) 178-197; E. Täubler, MGWJ 83 (1939) 1-37.

14a O. Eissfeldt, FF 25 (1949) 8-10; differently A. D. Crown, VT 17 (1967) 240-242, "to squat on one's haunches."   **b** רבץ as in v. 9.

15a Sam fem.; the reason for the masc. could be the formal use of the phrase כי טוב; cf. W. L. Holladay, VT 18 (1968) 481-487; J. L. Kugel, JBL 99 (1980) 433-435.   **b** את with a coordinate object in Gen. 49, only here, cf. Ges-K §117b.   **c** Cf. Deut. 20:11; Josh. 16:10; 17:13; Judg. 1:28, 30, 33, and elsewhere; on the construction, Ges-K §111a.

16a Other derivations from a root דנן "to be strong," J. A. Emerton, *Essays Pres. to D. W. Thomas* (1968) 88-91.

17a "As later addition linking this verse with 16," H. J. Zobel, BZAW 95 (1965) 18.   **b** Horned viper, *cerastes cornutus*.   **c** The consonant with Šᵉwâ is strengthened by *Dageš forte dirimens*, Ges-K §20h.

19a עקבם (the מ at the beginning of v. 20) with Gk, Syr, Vg.

20a Literally, "fat (Sam שׁמן) is his food."

21a Cf. 2 Sam. 2:18, "swift of foot as a wild gazelle," and Job 39:5.   **b** The fem. would be better, J. Skinner, BHK; but MT is possible.   **c** שׁפר = "to be beautiful," "to please"; cf. Ps. 16:6.   **d** אמר = "lamb" is not Hebr., but it occurs in Assyr., Aram., Arab.

22a Not to be deleted with BHK, O. Procksch, H. J. Kittel, *Die Stammessprüche Israels*. . . (diss. Berlin, 1959), and others; deliberate repetitive style. The בֵּן is not to be shortened to בֶּן on rhythmic grounds. פרת is a rare fem. ending, Ges-K §96, here because of the wordplay on פרת = Ephrath; another form פריה "fruitful," Is. 17:6. J. A. Emerton makes another suggestion, "Joseph is a tamarisk of the Euphrates"; see under v. 16a.   **b** On the construction, BrSynt §50a.

23a בעל in combinations can express simple belonging, BrSynt §74b.   **b** This verb begins an independent saying; it is possible that some words have fallen out before it. The piel of מרר is a reaction to the preceding.   **c** וירבו would be better, so H. Gunkel; on the form, Ges-K §67m. On רבב = "shoot," Ps. 18:15.   **d** On שׁטם, T. L. Fenton, UF 1 (1961) 67-70.

24aa ישׁב meaning "to stay firm," Ps. 125:1; Lev. 12:4.   **b** פזז 2 Sam. 6:16; cf. Y. Avishur, VT 26 (1976) 257-261.   **c** Literally "arms of his hands."

24ba A new unit begins with v. 24b. The מן 24b, 25a forms a sequence related to v. 25b, ברכת.   **b** Read שֵׁם for שָׁם?; the parallel "by the hands"—"by the name" would be a distinct possibility in relation to blessing; the text of 24bβ is certainly disturbed; the half-verse is overloaded, and the two nouns, רעה and אבן, stand side by side without a connection. Reconstruction is not possible; one of the two predicates has been added later; cf. D. N. Freedman, *Fests. G. E. Wright* (1976) 63-66; he proposes "shepherd of the sons of Israel."

25a Read ואל with Sam, Gk, Syr; better still would be מאל. Because of the parallelism את would not be possible.   **b** רבצת is metrically superfluous, whereas it is necessary in Deut. 33:13 (J. Skinner); perhaps a harmonization.

26a Read הררי עד with Gk and probably על־ before תאות. The parallelism mountains/hills is common, Deut. 33:15; Num. 23:7; Hab. 3:6; cf. F. M. Cross and D. N. Freedman, JBL 67 (1948) 200, n. 52; G. Rendsburg, JBL 99 (1980) 291-293: it means at the same time ancestors and mountains.   **b** Deut. 33:16 has here תבואנה.   **c** Cf. Deut. 33:16, 20; Num. 24:17; Ps. 68:22.   **d** נזיר also Deut. 33:16.

27a Descriptive imperf.

Form

Gen. 49 is a collection of tribal sayings. There is general agreement on this, whatever the differences in the assessment of the chapter as a whole or in its details. A parallel to Gen. 49 is the "Blessing of Moses" (Deut. 33), which is likewise a collection of tribal sayings, 12 in all, mentioning the names of the tribes of Israel (or the sons of Jacob). Another parallel, though only approximate, is Judg. 5:14-18, a part of the Song of Deborah.

This text of Gen. 49 (with the parallels) brings us into another world. It is not an original part either of the patriarchal story or the Joseph narrative; the parallels in Deuteronomy and Judges show this. It concerns the tribes of Israel in the land of Canaan in the period of the judges. A thorough and comprehensive exegesis of the text would have to include the two parallels, Deut. 33 and Judg. 5, study the form of the tribal sayings as a whole, and take into account the historical, geographical, and linguistic background. The present exegesis is restricted to the 28 verses of ch. 49.

This collection of tribal sayings contains long (Judah, Joseph) and short texts. The Judah and Joseph texts are dealing with the two tribes dominant later; and so it is probable that vv. 8-11 and 22-26 are expanded texts. The first two texts, vv. 3-4 (Reuben) and vv. 5-7 (Simeon and Levi), diverge markedly from the others in form and content. The normal tribal saying is short, no longer than the average saying in Proverbs. It says something about one of the tribes in one or two lines. Like the individual epigrams in Proverbs, the tribal sayings arose as individual sayings or in small groups. The number 12 comes only at the stage when they are collected. It is an independent element in the tradition which has an independent and lively tradition (M. Noth, BWANT [1930; 1966^2], bibliog. above; the presentations of the history of Israel of G. Fohrer, A. H. J. Gunneweg, S. Herrmann, R. de Vaux, R. Smend). The individual sayings are independent of the number 12 which itself arose independently of them. In fact the number of tribal sayings in Gen. 49 does not amount to 12 because, for example, Dan contains two sayings and Judah three; neither in Deut. 33 is the number 12. The origin of the sayings and their collection are objects of separate studies. The short sayings each describe the quality of a particular tribe, mostly by comparison with an animal (vv. 9, 14, 15, 16-17, 21, 22, 26; Deut. 33:17, 20, 22) and/or by means of a word-play (vv. 3b, 4, 8, 13, 14, 16, 19, 20, 22); there is none in Deut. 33; H. J. Zobel proposes also vv. 7b, 12, 24 (BZAW 95 [1965]), but this is uncertain. A comparison of Gen. 49 and Deut. 33 shows that the original form of the tribal saying predominates in Gen. 49, developments and adaptations in Deut. 33. The most common development is into a wish, a request, or a blessing. This means that the tribal saying in Gen. 49 is secular (apart from the developments) and that the sayings in Deut. 33 are heavily theologized; this indicates that they are in a process of transition to a cultic function.

The function of the tribal sayings is obviously to praise or blame. A tribe (or two together in a few cases) is praised or blamed each time. There is no way of knowing who is the source of the praise or blame. It is here that the problem of the *Sitz im Leben* of the tribal sayings begins. A comparison of Gen. 49 and Deut. 33 with Judg. 5:14-18 helps to answer the question.

The verses in Judg. 5:14-18 are the first stage in the tribal sayings. They are not individual, self-contained, and independent sayings, but constituent parts of a context from which they cannot be loosed, the description of Deborah's battle. In the Song of Deborah there is the call to battle (v. 12); then follows the list of the tribes that answered it: Ephraim, Benjamin, Machir, Zebulun, Issachar, Naphtali (vv. 14-15). They are celebrated as heroes (v. 13) who followed Deborah and Barak (v. 15). But Reuben (vv. 15bβ,16), Gilead, Dan, and Asher are blamed (v. 17) because they did not take part in the battle. Then Zebulun and Naphtali are praised for their outstanding bravery (for detail, H. J. Zobel, BZAW 95 [1965] 44-52).

Setting

Vv. 8-14 of Judg. 5 indicate the original *Sitz im Leben* of the tribal sayings. It is not the battle as such (so H. J. Kittel), but a convention following it, a debriefing or a more accurate critique of the strategy. Something like this is part of all campaigns, even today, and the assessment of the performance of the various units has its definite place. The main emphasis in Judg. 5 is on participation or nonparticipation; this is to be understood from the situation at the time when there was no central authority; participation was voluntary. Judg. 5:14-18 is concerned with a particular situation at a particular time; the collected tribal sayings in Gen. 49 and Deut. 33 are general and not tied to a situation. Praise and blame have a lasting value there. This is shown by the animal comparisons, the significance of the names, and the fact that the enemies are not mentioned by name. The setting in which they arose and were handed down is no longer the briefing after the battle, but the various occasions when the representatives of a number of tribes came together. Such meetings are mentioned in Josh. 24 and Judg. 20:1; they could be held for a variety of purposes. Those present inquired about others and exchanged information; they discussed others; it is here that such sayings had their setting and origin and meaning. This whole background shows clearly that each individual saying arose independently, or together with a group of other sayings; this is a consequence of their function of laying praise or blame. A good comparison is the way in which simple epigrams arise and are handed down in village life, especially when the men gather in the evening (L. Köhler: סוֹד). The sayings in Gen. 49 have a secular character, like these. They were only later taken over into the cultic tradition, as the more theological character of the sayings in Deut. 33 shows. Three stages of tradition, therefore, stand out in the three texts of Judg. 5; Gen. 49; Deut. 33 with rare clarity.

The framework and its origin form a separate question. Several parts are to be distinguished in vv. 1-2, 28: (1) a redactor has inserted the collection into a P context (vv. 1a, 28b); he explains them as the "blessings of Jacob"; (2) the real introduction to the collection of sayings, v. 2, presents vv. 3-27 as the address of a father to his sons; (3) only v. 1b understands the words as prophecy.

Finally, the number 12 applied to the tribes is an independent element; it arose from the history of Israel's development into a unity and designates Israel as a whole, consisting of 12 tribes.

Commentary

[49:1-2] The frame: The collection in ch. 49 being independent and self-contained, belonging originally neither to the Joseph narrative nor to the Jacob story, had to be inserted into the context by means of an appropriate introduction. It has been, and into a P context; v. 1a belongs to P and is continued in v. 28b:

> Then Jacob summoned his sons. . .
> and blessed them, a special blessing for each.

(Cf. comm. on 49:28b.) The tribal sayings have come down to the redactor as an independent tradition; he wants to legitimate them as Jacob's address before his death; this he does by means of the frame which gives the chapter its title of the blessings of Jacob. The collection itself has two introductions; its proper one is v. 2. Its rhythmic form is 3:3, corresponding to the sayings:

> Come together and listen, sons of Jacob,
> listen to Israel your father (v. 2).

This has probably been prefixed to the collection by the redactor; hence it gives the collection a new interpretation because the majority of the sayings are not words addressed by a father to his sons, but only the first three. These are congenial to the redactor, because he can use them to create the impression of words spoken by the father to his sons. He wants the real tribal sayings (in the 3rd person) to be understood like the first three. So he gives them a new interpretation as the words of Jacob in order to confer on them validity and solemnity (cf. E. Cortès, *Los discursos de adiós de Gen. 49 a Jn 13-17. . .* [1976]).

A third and quite different introduction in prose is added in v. 1b:

> Gather round, and I will tell you what will
> happen to you in the days to come.

The summons to listen is used in a way similar to Deut. 32:1, and the summons "Gather round. . ." is in the same context in Deut. 31:28, where in v. 29 the phrase "in the days to come" follows. This striking parallel demonstrates that Gen. 49:1b is a later addition to the introduction (vv. 1-2). The expression באחרית הימים is described by H. Gunkel, O. Procksch, KBL, and others as "a term belonging to prophetic eschatology." E. Lipiński takes another view, maintaining that the expression in v. 1 as in Num. 24:14 is Yahwistic (VT 20 [1970] 445-450). Particularly important for the prophetic usage are Is. 2:2 and Mic. 4:1. Here, as in most places (also Jer. 48:47; 49:39), and including Gen. 49:1 and Num. 24:14, the phrase announces a change which is to take place in the distant future (so H. Wildberger, VT 7 [1957] 62-81 and his *Komm.* ad loc.). These are the only two passages in the Pentateuch where the phrase occurs. The proclamation in Num. 24:14 of what will happen in the days to come concerns the ruler of the last days; ". . .a star shall come forth out of Jacob. . ."; hence Gen. 49:1b will likewise refer to a proclamation, taken over in vv. 10-12, of the ruler of the last days. V. 1b is appropriate to this one passage only in ch. 49, and certainly not to vv. 3-4 and 5-7, because these are not concerned with the "end of the days." The redactor who added v. 1b to the introductory v. 2 understood 49:8-10 as a messianic prophecy; for him it was the really important thing in ch. 49. G. Hoberg: "A potiori fit denominatio" (cf. C. Roth, VT 10 [1970] 51-68).

[**49:3-7**] The Reuben saying and the Simeon-Levi saying differ in three ways from all that follow: (1) They are an address to a person, an address of the father to his sons, in accordance with v. 2. (2) Both pronounce punishment for a crime; both crimes occur in the patriarchal story. (3) The form corresponds to this: both are divided into two parts according to guilt and punishment, and thus show a distant resemblance to the prophetic pronouncements of judgment (so H. J. Kittel, op. cit.). The correspondence between the two sayings, and their difference from all that follow, suggests that they were added in this form by the collector who was responsible for the introduction in v. 2.

[**49:3-4**] The structure of the Reuben saying: V. 3 is an address of the father to his firstborn son in which he extols him. In v. 4 Jacob deposes Reuben from his status as firstborn with the allegation that he defiled his father's marriage bed. V. 4 then contains a sentence of punishment with the reason. The text has a number of problems, but the structure is certain.

[49:3] V. 3 is structured rhythmically, 3:3::2:2. The first stichos is an address of the father to Reuben, his firstborn (chs. 29–30); אתה is the predicate. The second stichos of v. 3a, as well as the two members of v. 3b, extol the firstborn in a series of predicates; he is the fruit of his father's youthful vigor. In the Baal cycle from Ugarit, Danel is likewise described as the strength of his father (H. Cazelles, ThQ 138 [1958] 26-39). V. 3b continues in the same vein.

יתר means "beyond measure," "surpassing," though with this meaning only in poetic texts like Is. 56:12 and Ps. 31:24. W. F. Albright alleges the double יתר as an example of "early Israelite repetitive style" and translates "excelling in pride, and excelling in might" (*Yahweh and the Gods of Canaan* [1968] 17). The meaning of the two nouns שאת and עז is contested according as they are considered belonging to v. 3a or v. 4. But the "repetitive style" of v. 3b shows that it is a continuation and development of "my firstborn"; were that not intended, then it must be demonstrated grammatically. On the other hand, v. 4 indicates clearly a fresh beginning with the pronouncement of the punishment, אל־תותר, which is contraposed as a play on יתר in v. 3a. This is confirmed by the constant contrast of crime and punishment by means of wordplay in the prophetic pronouncements of judgment. It is certain then that v. 3b belongs to v. 3a both in content and in form, and that the two nouns have a positive meaning. Hence H. Gunkel's conjecture to read שאת instead of שאת (cf. BHK), "first in turbulence, first in ferocity," is to be rejected, as are similar suggestions, as well as H. J. Kittel's translation, "a paragon of revolt, a paragon of defiance." שאת means "lifting up" (KBL); it is used of the grandeur of God in Job 13:11 and 31:23. It can be rendered here by grandeur, pride, excellence, dignity. The other noun עז can, to be sure, be rendered "defiance," derived from the verb עזז; but the verb can also have the neutral meaning of "superiority" (Judg. 3:10; Ps. 9:20). O. Procksch's explanation, that the two nouns take on different colors, is possible.

[49:4] V. 4 also raises formidable textual difficulties. What is certain is that Reuben was deposed from his preeminence as firstborn because of his crime: "you will be preeminent no more" (hiph. of יתר).

The words פחז כמים in the present text are uncertain. פחזת is to be read with Sam and Gk and the majority of exegetes: "you foamed over like water." This meaning of the verb, however, is not attested but only deduced from the כמים. The participle of פחז in Judg. 9:4 and Zeph. 3:4 means "fresh"; in the latter it is in a prophetic accusation. The word order in 49:4aα is striking; H. Gunkel and J. Skinner suspect an extensive corruption of the text.

The reason for the punishment is given in v. 4aβ, "because you climbed into your father's bed," reproducing the narrative fragment from Gen. 35:22. V. 4b says what this means: "then you defiled my couch." So far the parallel stichos is clear; the following עלה makes no sense; the alteration to the 2nd person with Gk, Sam, TargO does not help. It can only be left unexplained.*

The exegesis of vv. 3-4 remains uncertain in a number of points because of the textual difficulties. The predicates extoling Reuben as the firstborn in v. 3 are striking and very forceful. It is possible that there are echoes here of an older and quite different tribal saying praising Reuben; perhaps the word play on יתר be-

---

*But see M. Dahood, Bib 45 (1964) 282 (translator).

longs here. This old and genuine tribal saying was reshaped (by the collector or author of the collection vv. 2-28?) on the basis of the tradition in Gen. 35:22 when the tribe of Reuben no longer existed. The "Reuben saying" is therefore a secondary formation. Apart from the fact that at the author's time the tribe of Reuben no longer existed, nothing historical can be concluded from it.

[**49:5-7**] Simeon and Levi: The author of 49:2-28 was obliged to take up these two tribes, just as he was to take up the tribe of Reuben, because they belonged to the list of 12 at hand to him (cf. Gen. 29–30). This text too is a literary construction based on a tradition of a crime perpetrated by both; this was the reason for their later dispersion. The structure is similar to vv. 3-4; however, Simeon and Levi are spoken of in the third person.

The structure: first, Simeon and Levi are named (v. 5a); then an accusation is brought against them (v. 5b). The accusation is unfolded in v. 6b, and their deed of violence is named. Then follows in v. 7a a condemnation in the form of a curse, and in v. 7b a specification of the punishment. This structure is very close to that of the prophetic oracle of judgment, which alone explains the use of the first person in v. 7b. On the parenthesis, v. 6a, see comm. below.

[**49:5a**] The first half-verse is to be explained from the necessity of putting the names at the beginning. The predicate אחים is simply intended to state the fact, and perhaps to state that the two of them took part together in the enterprise in v. 6b, as in Gen. 34 (so A. Dillmann). H. Holzinger's explanation, "brothers indeed," is not necessary. The accusation in the prophetic oracles of judgment is often first general; then the unfolding follows in a verbal sentence (C. Westermann, *Basic Forms. . .* [1960; 1978[5]; Eng. 1967]). This precise agreement with the prophetic accusation against Israel makes it certain that vv. 5-7 are a literary invitation which presupposes the development of such a form from that directed against the individual to that against the people.

[**49:5b**] Simeon and Levi are accused of exercising violence חמס, "tools of violence are. . ." (v. 5b). The meaning of the word that follows is uncertain, though it must refer to the instruments with which they exercised the violence described in v. 6b.

The word מכרתיהם (hapax) has been explained in very different ways; see the synthesis in B. Jacob, particularly of Jewish and earlier interpreters (bibliog. above, J. Meinhold [1920], J. Barr [1974]). All attempts to find a solution have done nothing to alter the conclusion on מכרה in KBL, "unexplained." The context certainly makes clear that it is a question of "instruments of violence"; hence the rendering "swords" is still the most likely (so Gesenius in the earlier editions, F. Delitzsch, A. Dillmann; "curved knives" from כרר, J. Skinner, H. J. Zobel, H. J. Kittel, and many others). There may be a corruption in the orthography, or a particular expression in the background belonging to the tradition indicated in v. 6b; M. Dahood (CBQ 23 [1961] 55-56) suggests a circumcision knife. The many conjectures which would explain the word otherwise are for the most part questionable because they are not in accord with the context.*

[**49:6a**] The basis for or development of v. 5 follows only in v. 6b; the כי at the beginning of v. 6b refers not to v. 6a but to v. 5. A parenthesis, v. 6a, has been in-

---

*See D. W. Young, JBL 100 (1981) 335-342 and M. Cohen, VT 31 (1981) 472-482 (translator).

serted in between. Earlier it was generally accepted that Jacob spoke this verse (F. Delitzsch, with reference to Gen. 34:30). But one requires very little sensitivity to language to realize that such a sentence is impossible on the lips of Jacob; and the author of vv. 5-7 can never have made him speak thus (H. J. Zobel: ''כבוד never occurs on the lips of Jacob''). It is the language of the Psalms and of the pious sage.

A reader has distanced himself from the cursed tribes by using such language. It is the same spirit that turned away from the ''counsel of the wicked'' and the ''circle of the scoffers'' in Ps. 1:1 which are described here by סד and קהל; the parallelism has the same meaning in both cases. And the parallelism of נפש and כבוד meaning ''I'' is in complete accord with the language of the Psalms; compare Ps. 103:1 with the כבוד of Pss. 16:9; 30:13; 57:9; 108:2, in all cases with the suffix of the first person. Following H. Gunkel, KBL (differing from Gesenius-Buhl) and F. Nötscher, (VT 2 [1952] 358-362) the vocalization is kebēdi = ''my heart'' (actually ''liver''); different in J. Pedersen, *Israel. . .*, I-II (1926) 238f.: ''Honor is soul,'' thus retaining the meaning ''soul'' for kābōd. What is important is that in Gen. 49:6, as in the passages in the Psalms, the word is in parallelism with ''I,'' and that all parallels occur in the Psalms. This is conclusive proof that the marginal gloss in v. 6 belongs to the language of the Psalms. On the feminine use of כבוד see M. Dahood, UF 1 (1969) 23.

[**49:6b**] The כי in v. 6b gives the reason for v. 5, not for v. 6a. As in vv. 3-4 the author takes up a tradition. It has been almost universally accepted that the reference here is to the attack by Simeon and Levi reported in Gen. 34. Some recent exegetes note that there is no mention of laming oxen in Gen. 34 (S. Lehming [1958], A. de Pury, RB76 [1969] 5-49, D. N. Freedman [1975], see bibliog. above). This difference would disappear if שור were to be understood as ''men'' or ''princes,'' following Ugaritic (so B. Vawter [1959] and P. D. Miller [1970], bibliog. above); but C. M. Carmichael rightly opposes this. The verb עקר in the piel proves that bulls or oxen are meant; עקר piel = ''to sever an animal's fetlock,'' ''to lame''; in the three other passages in which the piel occurs, Josh. 11:6, 9; 2 Sam. 8:4 = 1 Chron. 18:4, it refers to animals (cf. W. Krebs [1966], bibliog. above). A second difference lies in the motif. In Gen. 34 Simeon and Levi perpetrate the deed to avenge their sister's honor, and so incur Jacob's rebuke (34:30). But especially Gen. 35:5, the conclusion to Gen. 34, where a fear from God protects the departure of Simeon and Levi, is not appropriate to 49:7. One can therefore not say with certainty that 49:5-7 reproduces exactly the event narrated in Gen. 34. There must be another tradition; it remains an open question whether or not it is a variant of Gen. 34. רצון has here the meaning of wantonness (cf. N. Walker [1962]; on שור, R. Péter [1975]; both in bibliog. above).

[**49:7**] The punishment for the outrage they committed consists in a peculiar mixture of curse (v. 7a) and proclamation of judgment (v. 7b); both are pronounced not over two persons (v. 5a, ''Simeon and Levi are brothers''), but over two tribes. The curse is toned down notably; Simeon and Levi are not damned, but only their anger (this differs from the curse on Meroz, Judg. 5:23; cf. Gen. 3). It is thus no longer a real curse; in fact, the sentence merely says that they must be punished because of the fierceness of their anger (i.e., of their violence). V. 7b has clearly the form of a proclamation of judgment; the one who punishes (''I will'') is God. The situation of the father speaking to his sons (vv. 1-2) is abandoned here.

The peculiar mixed form of v. 7a and b argues for a literary construction. The content favors this; both tribes stand under the same punishment (v. 7b). "That a common doom did not overtake Simeonites and Levites is a matter of history" (H. H. Rowley, JBL 58 [1939] 117). Simeon is absorbed into the tribe of Judah and in Deut. 33:8-11 Levi receives high praise as the priestly tribe. The concentration of the two in v. 7b is therefore an artificial formation resulting from a later situation (on חלק, D. J. Kamhi, VT 23 [1973] 235-239). The oft-discussed question, whether Levi in vv. 5-7 is presumed to be a secular tribe, can only be answered in the following way; from the tradition available to him the author knows a tribe of Levi that once conducted a campaign with Simeon, and he knows that in his own time there is no longer a tribe of Levi with tribal land.

[**49:8-12**] Vv. 8-12 do not form a continuous whole; the text cannot be described as the Judah saying. "Judah" is mentioned three times and accordingly there are three independent Judah sayings (H. J. Kittel; A. Caquot [1976], bibliog. above) which are to be interpreted independently of each other. Vv. 8 and 9 are tribal sayings in the proper sense; vv. 10-12 are promise and blessing.

[**49:8**] When the series of tribal sayings (after vv. 3-4, 5-7) begins with Judah (v. 8), this is but following the ancient muster order in which Judah stands at the head (Num. 2:3; 10:14; cf. also Josh. 15:1).

    V. 8 is a tribal saying in three parts; the first and third sentences are in parallelism, the middle sentence gives the reason. The rhythm of the sayings presents difficulties.

    Without the אתה v. 8a forms a distinct 3:3 rhythm; with אתה it would read 2:2:3, which is decidedly poorer. Further, the wordplay is more effective without it. Some want for this reason to delete it (O. Procksch and others). The collector could have added it, intending thereby to underscore the saying as an address by the father in conformity with the frame. It can not be an intensification of the suffix of יודוך, as a number of exegetes, following Ges-K §135e, think, because it belongs in any case to יהודה, of which it is the predicate.

    Whether an addition or not, the meaning is "Judah are you!" i.e., you are what your name means, namely, "your brothers shall praise you." This is not an etymology, i.e., the purpose of the saying is not to explain the name Judah (as in Gen. 29:35); it is a pure wordplay that wants to say: he has shown himself as יהודה in a particular situation, such that his brothers praise him because of his heroic deed and acknowledge him as a hero. There is only a hint of the deed: "your hand is on the neck of your enemies," i.e., he seizes them in flight.

    The lone half-verse 8bα is very striking amid the strongly rhythmic structure of the tribal sayings. S. Gevirtz makes a proposal that commands attention (ZAW 93 [1981] 27). In the War Scroll, I QM, there is the pertinent expansion, col. XII, 10:
    Put out your hand on the neck of your enemy,
    and your foot upon the back of (the) slain.
This could correspond to the original text of 48:9, which would be reconstructed as follows:
    (You have put?) your hand on the neck of your enemies
    and your foot on the backs of (the) slain.
V. 8 would then be reconstructed:

> Judah, your brothers praise you,
> your father's sons bow before you.
> Your hand seizes your enemies by the neck,
> you put your foot on the neck of the slain.

The third stichos (v. 8b) is parallel to the first and is to be understood from it. "The sons of your father bow before you"; like v. 8aα, it is a reaction to Judah's heroic deed. The sentence certainly does not mean that Judah "claims the kingship for the tribe" (H. Holzinger), nor that "the tribes of Israel acknowledge him as lord" (H. Gunkel, J. Skinner), nor that "Judah is now to rise to the place of the firstborn" (H. J. Kittel). It has been concluded from explanations of this kind that the saying in v. 8 can only be from the period of David, because it was only then that Judah gained hegemony over all the other tribes. But this is unlikely because the period that gave rise to the tribal sayings ended with the beginning of the monarchy. The meaning is rather this: the brothers bow before Judah because they recognize him as a hero and a leader in battle on the grounds of his heroic deed in this present, particular situation of which we know no more. The word ידה (hiph. = "praise") also argues for the antiquity of the saying, that is, for its origin in the period of the judges; it is but rarely used with a person as object, and this points to early usage (for the passages, THAT I 674). But above all, 49:8 is close to the language used of the tribes in Judg. 5, where a tribe is praised for its bravery in battle with the common enemy (cf. Judg. 5:18). The whole verse then (not merely v. 8aβ, H. Holzinger, H. J. Zobel) is to be understood in the present; it is neither jussive nor a wish.

[49:9] V. 9 is a self-contained tribal saying, independent of v. 8 and vv. 10-12. It agrees, however, with v. 8 inasmuch as the tribe of Judah is praised and its competence is on the field of battle. But both sayings arose independently of each other.
  The saying consists first of the nominal sentence (v. 9aα) in which Judah is compared with a young lion. The comparison is then developed in a series of verbal sentences vv. 9aβ, 9bα, 9bβ in which the lion metaphor is continued with the two synonyms אריה and לביא. This rigid and obvious structure is notably disturbed by the change to the second person in v. 9aβ with the address "my son," and again with the third person in v. 9b. Moreover, the address "my son" does not conform to the style of the tribal saying. Hence H. J. Zobel, with many others, has said, "Originally it will have been preserved throughout in the form of a statement in the third person." The purpose was clearly to adapt the saying in v. 9 to that in v. 8 and thus to the frame by means of the alteration in v. 9aβ (address of the father to the sons, v. 2); the change goes back to the collector.

Attempts at reconstruction: "who has come up from preying in the meadow" (H. J. Zobel); "who tears to pieces the young animals" (H. J. Kittel, following KBL). Preserving by and large the traditional text one can conjecture: "he comes up from preying in the valley (בגי)." On the peculiar form of the synonymous parallelism, cf. P. D. Miller (1980); S. A. Geller (1979), bibliog. above. The threefold variation of the animal name as a stylistic device is popular in poetic language; e.g., the lion (Num. 23:24; 24:9; Is. 5:29; 30:6; and especially Ezek. 19:1-7). "Lion's cub" in v. 9a is, therefore, a synonym for the two designations of the lion in v. 9b (against H. J. Zobel). B. Vawter alleges a Canaanite lion-goddess by way of comparison (CBQ 17 [1955] 1-17); but in animal similes/metaphors it is a question of real animals; otherwise the comparison would lose its point.

The lion metaphor in v. 9aα is developed in three statements; he has seized prey; he brings it up with him, perhaps into his lair; there he lies down (v. 9bα; רבץ generally of animals), he crouches, and no one dares to rouse him, such fear he inspires (an exact parallel in Num. 24:9). All three statements therefore develop the animal metaphor; they do not go into explanations. The animal metaphor as such and its development adequately express the praise of the tribe of Judah; no explanation is necessary. The lion is seen as the most powerful, the strongest, and the most daring beast of prey; this is developed in three acts—and this is Judah!

The metaphor is everywhere comprehensible and everywhere used where lions are known. Even in countries where lions do not exist, a hero can be called ''Richard the Lionhearted'' (cf. 2 Sam. 17:10). Even more impressive, the lion has become the most used animal in heraldry; this goes back to the animal metaphor in tribal sayings. It occurs in two other tribal sayings, of Gad in Deut. 33:20 and of Dan in 33:22. Israel is compared to a lion in two of Balaam's oracles; the comparison has the same function, to praise its strength. ''Behold, a people! As a lioness it rises up and as a lion it lifts itself. . .'' (Num. 23:24); ''He crouched, he lay down like a lion, and like a lioness; who will rouse him up?'' (Num. 24:9). These passages are so close to the Judah sayings that one can take it that they have a common origin in one tribal saying; the application to Israel as a whole is secondary and took place in the course of the tradition. These parallels show the importance of the tribal sayings, which clearly continued to live on. An exciting reversal of the lion metaphor appears in Jer. 4:7, where the enemy threatening Judah from the north is compared to a lion: ''A lion has gone up from his thicket. . ..'' Judah is now a prey to the lion.

By way of conclusion to v. 9 mention must be made again of the study of S. Gevirtz (ZAW 93 [1981] 21-37); he tries to demonstrate that this saying originally concerned Dan and was secondarily applied to Judah, because the Danite territory in the south came into the possession of Judah.

[49:10-12] The text of vv. 10-12 is a self-contained unit. What it has in common with v. 8 and v. 9 is only that it is concerned with Judah and positive in its praise. It is not a tribal saying in the proper sense, but a promise to Judah, something like the oracles of Balaam with which it has points of contact, particularly in the description of the blessing (vv. 11-12). The passage is divided into a proclamation in v. 10 and a description of future blessing in vv. 11-12 (both go together in Deutero-Isaiah). The proclamation refers to an event in the future; vv. 11-12 describe a situation. Both go together in that the situation preserved in vv. 11-12 will come about after the event announced in v. 10.

[49:10] The proclamation in v. 10 is structured in two parts. It says that (a sort of) dominion will remain with Judah until one comes who wins the obedience of the nations. In order to understand this disputed verse it is important to take as the starting point this structure, which is certain and acknowledged by most scholars. Two chapters in the future history of Judah are to be distinguished. In the first, the situation as it now is, is to persist; i.e., Judah is to retain a sort of dominion which it now has. When vv. 10-12 are attached to the two tribal sayings in vv. 8 and 9, this suggests that supremacy over (the) other tribes is meant. This is also in agreement with the content of v. 8. If this is the case, then the second chapter in the history of Judah, which begins with v. 10bα, can only be the monarchy. This is also clearly the meaning of the proclamation in v. 10bβ. The submission of the nations (the surrounding Canaanite peoples) presupposes the centralized power of the monarchy. The description in vv. 11-12 confirms that this is the meaning, because the one of whom vv. 11f. speak can only be the king; beauty belongs to the monarchy (cf. Ps. 45).

The conclusion so far is as follows: vv. 10-12 are a promise to Judah. V. 10a promises that Judah will retain the dominion that at present belongs to it until it acquires the kingship. I emphasize that I have come to this conclusion without even raising the question of the meaning of the word שׁילה.

[49:10a] The two half-verses of v. 10a are in synonymous parallelism. The verb governs both parts; what is said of Judah in v. 10aα holds also for the words "from between his feet" in 10aβ; שׁבט and מחקק are intended synonymously. The statement of v. 10a is that of a single sentence; accordingly the tribe of Judah, v. 10a, is represented by the current leader of the tribe (v. 10aβ, "between his feet").

The two synonymous nouns שׁבט and מחקק are understood by many exegetes as the king's scepter; שׁבט can mean this, e.g., Ps. 45:7, but it is nowhere obvious that מחקק has this meaning. The basic meaning of both words is staff, stick, or club (cf. "Keule," BHH II 946; G. Liedke, WMANT 39 [1971] 159-161). It is used as "commander's staff" (KBL) and "marshal's staff" but as such it has no connection with the office of the king (for שׁבט cf. Is. 9:3; 14:5; Amos 1:5-8; for מחקק cf. Num. 21:18; Pss. 60:9; 108:9).

The closest parallel to the tribal sayings is Judg. 5:14-18 where in v. 14 the same words are in parallelism; it is certain, therefore, that the meaning in Gen. 49:10 must be the marshal's or commander's staff (so too W. F. Albright, JBL 63 [1944] 207-233; H. J. Zobel, op.cit., 13; H. J. Kittel, op.cit., 14); here it means sovereignty among a group of tribes. The use of these words for dominion also favors the view that the sovereignty of Judah among a group of tribes in v. 10a was in the period of the judges, even though we cannot determine it historically.

[49:10b] The עד־כי of v. 10b indicates the point in time when a broader form of dominion will take the place of the present. On this understanding of עד־כי, see J. Lindblom (VT.S 1 [1953] 83), O. Eissfeldt (VT.S 4 [1957] 138-147), G. von Rad (comm.), H. J. Zobel: "not to be understood exclusively but inclusively" (BZAW 95 [1965] 13). Only the monarchy can be meant; in v. 10bβ it is defined as dominion over the "nations." The word יקהת = "obedience" occurs only here (if Prov. 30:17 is to be emended, KBL); its meaning is adequately assured through Akk. and other Semitic equivalents. The versions Gk, Syr, Vg read תְּקְוַת; this is either a deliberate alteration or the word was unknown to them; "hope" suits neither the grammar nor the context, and such a translation presupposes the messianic interpretation. That the ruler to come wins the obedience of the nations, corresponds exactly to the historical reality under David and Solomon. To interpret עמים as all the nations of the earth would fall outside the context (this is against the messianic interpretation of J. Wellhausen and H. Gunkel, which many have followed). The ולו at the beginning of v. 10bβ refers to the preceding noun, שׁילה, subject of the "until. . .comes." שׁילה, therefore, is the one who wins the obedience of the nations. This can only mean a ruler (so, among others, E. Sellin, *Fests. A. Zahn* [1908] 369-390).

"The וְלוֹ shows that the antecedent. . .was a person" (H. Gunkel); hence it is unlikely, if not impossible, that the שִׁילֹה in the MT is a reference to a place, even if the ending is understood as an accusative of place (or direction). The many attempts at explanation show that שִׁילֹה is unsatisfactory as an indication of place. The context requires a personal subject for יָבֹא. V. 10bβ specifies this person as a ruler. The most obvious course is to accept a corruption in the text; מ has fallen out at the beginning, and מֹשְׁלֹה is to be read (either as a substantive or a participle; so F. Giesebrecht, E. Sellin, K. Marti, H. Gressmann, G. von Rad). This is confirmed by the close parallel in Mic. 5:1 in which the coming of a ruler (over Israel) from a particular place is also promised. There too it is a king coming out of Judah, and the place is further specified as Bethlehem. The reading given by the versions שֶׁלֹּה (or שֶׁלּוֹ), see BHK, is not excluded; however, it is unlikely, because v. 10b wants to distinguish the rule of the one to come from preceding tribal rule (the שֵׁלֹּה would refer to this). Nor can we exclude F. Nötscher's explanation of שִׁילֹה as an Akkadian loanword, *šēlu* = "ruler" (ZAW 47 [1929] 323-325; G. R. Driver, VT.S 16 [1967] 50ff.; S. Mowinckel, *He that Cometh* [1956]; further, J. Coppens, VT.S 4 [1957] 172). These three explanations can be seen as variants of one and the same; they all want to have "a ruler" as the subject of "comes." I leave aside the abundance of other explanations. It is no praiseworthy page in the history of O.T. exegesis that so many studies have been preoccupied with this one word. If authors have not first tried to explain this disputed word from its immediate and broader context, then they have brought nothing to the discussion. I refer instead to some syntheses of the discussion so far. The more recent are to be found in the commentaries of A. Dillmann 456-458, J. Skinner 521-524, B. Jacob 903-907 (especially for the Jewish explanations); add the further studies of J. Coppens, VT.S 4 (1957) 97-115; H. J. Kittel (1965), H. P. Müller (1964), B. Margulis (1969); J. A. Emerton (1968) reviews critically on pp. 93-98 the three studies of W. L. Moran (1961), E. M. Good (1963), and J. Lindblom (1953, accus. of place), deciding in favor of E. M. Good (all in bibliog. above). H. P. Müller (1964) classifies the attempted explanations as follows, with a bibliog. for each (likewise J. Skinner and H. J. Kittel): 1. a ruler: *(a)* emend text, *(b)* Akk. loanword *šēlu/šīlu*, *(c)* with the versions שֶׁלֹּה ("until he comes to whom it belongs); 2. accus. of direction: "to Shiloh," e.g., J. Lindblom; 3. שַׁילֹה "until tribute is brought to him," e.g., W. L. Moran. The whole discussion has not yet reached even a limited consensus.

[49:11-12] The coming of the ruler (v. 10bα) is followed by victory (v. 10bβ) and the state of prosperity and plenty (vv. 11-12). These verses, like vv. 25-26 in the Joseph saying and the oracles of Balaam, are a typical description of blessedness. Where the blessing is at work, there is plenty. The verses divide into the fertility brought about by the blessing (v. 11), and the blessedness of the ruler manifested in his beauty (v. 12).

[49:11] The participle in v. 11a, continued in v. 11b, has the ruler to come as subject; the blessing of fertility comes with him, he himself is the blessed one (v. 12). The promise of blessing is stamped throughout by parallelism. Blessing is promised to the king (v. 12) and to his land (v. 11). Fertility is described under the imagery of the noble vine. The image is continued with the wine (v. 11a) and the grape (v. 11b). The portrayal of plenty in vv. 11a and 11b serves to link the wine and the grape to the person of the king (the donkey is the king's mount in Zech. 9:9). The meaning is: "There is so much wine there that one could. . . ." Were one to detach the two images in vv. 11a and b from the parallelism and take each of them literally, then one would misunderstand the purpose of this dithyrambic verse. The parallelism remains determinative; in each half-verse two synonyms interact with each other to produce a nicely rounded piece.

[49:12] The closest parallel to the promise of blessing in v. 12 is the text of Num. 24:5-7; there too the image of the fertility of the land in vv. 5-7a is followed by the exaltation of the king. In Numbers the greatness of the king is extolled; here it is his beauty, and in particular the beauty of his countenance (presented in two parts); eyes and teeth are described under the similes of milk and wine; wine makes the eyes sparkle (Prov. 23:29f.; on the beauty of the king see C. Westermann, *Fests. W. Zimmerli* [1977] 230-249). Ps. 45 also speaks of and praises the beauty of the king (v. 3); here too the effect of the blessing is manifest. Part of the portrayal of David is that he is a handsome man (1 Sam. 16:18). There is here an important change from the period of the judges to that of the kings. The former is characterized by God's saving action where it is a matter of survival, the latter in addition by blessing, and so fullness and plenty. The king is the mediator of the blessing, and so is blessed himself. This shows out in his handsome appearance.

Closing remarks on vv. 10-12: These verses are not a tribal saying like vv. 8 and 9, but a promise of blessing for Judah joined with the promise of a king coming forth out of Judah; it is closely related to the Balaam oracles. The promise of blessing and the oracle of the seer are close to each other (C. Westermann, ThB 55 [1974] 236). It is not a messianic prophecy in the sense that it promises a king of salvation at the end-time (against J. Wellhausen, H. Gunkel). And the word *eschatological* is misleading here (so H. P. Müller, VT 14 [1964] 276-293). The promise binds two chapters in history together; in the time of the judges, when the tribes became sedentary, the period of the kings is promised. Vv. 10-12 do not describe a "paradise" but rather a state resulting from blessing, as is also found in Num. 22–24 and Deuteronomy. It is quite comprehensible why vv. 10-12 were attached to the two tribal sayings about Judah in vv. 8 and 9; the tribe of Judah has been praised for its success in war in vv. 8 and 9; in vv. 10-12 the promise is made to it that a king will arise from it, that it will become the royal tribe.

Period of origin: it is possible that vv. 10-12 originated in the time of David or Solomon (?); hence they could be a *vaticinium ex eventu*, as is generally said (E. Osswald, ZAW 75 [1963] 27-44). But that is not necessary. They can well be from the period of the judges, expressing the striving of a tribe for supremacy and at the same time for kingship (cf. Num. 22–24). For another explanation of vv. 8-12, cf. C. M. Carmichael, JBL 88 (1969) 435-444.

[49:13] The saying about Zebulun is in three parts, a verbal and two nominal sentences; the rhythm is uncertain. All three parts describe Zebulun's geographical situation. At first glance the saying consists solely of this three-part geographical note. It is very vague, ל indicating direction towards and על the place at which. The first stichos, "Zebulun—toward the shore of the sea it dwells," gives its direction as toward the Mediterranean Sea, and leaves open the question whether or not the territory touches it; some scholars think that it does (H. Holzinger, referring to Deut. 33:18, O. Procksch, H. Gunkel), others do not (R. de Vaux, E. Taubler, F. Delitzsch). The territory of Zebulun is described in Josh. 19:10-16. As the information there is deliberately imprecise, one must leave it so. The verb ישכן with ל is striking, but quite possible. Some exegetes find a hint of a wordplay in it, some others alter it to יזבל to get the wordplay (cf. BHK). However, it cannot be demonstrated that זבל means "dwell."

The second stichos, ''and shall be a haven for ships'' (A. Kuschke, ZDVP 93 [1977] 178-197), is made difficult by the repetition of לְחוֹף, because it does not accord with the poetic style of the tribal sayings. Hence many exegetes want to delete this stichos as a gloss. The third stichos, ''and his flank rests on Sidon,'' is also only an approximation; Sidon here means probably not the city but the territory of Phoenicia. Some exegetes regard the third stichos as a gloss; G. von Rad is of the opinion that the saying is incomplete.

But what does the saying mean? Some exegetes regard it simply as geographical information about Zebulun; but that would not be an adequate motive for the origin and transmission of a tribal saying. The majority see in it a word of praise of the tribe of Zebulun (J. Skinner, H. J. Zobel, among others), whereas H. J. Kittel hears it uttering a word of blame, particularly with reference to Judg. 5:17b (Dan and Asher). This parallel is pertinent above all because the same words, חוֹף and אֳנִיּוֹת, occur: ''and Dan, why did he abide with the ships? And Asher sat still at the coast of the sea, settling down by his landings.'' In Judg. 5:17 these sentences are clearly meant as a reproach. One supposes, therefore, a somewhat muted reproach in the Zebulun saying, because of Zebulun's aspiration for the sea and the opportunities for commerce (ships; see also Deut. 33:19b), and its leaning (''flank'') on Sidon.

Zebulun is praised in Judg. 5:18; but this does not exclude blame at another, probably later, period. The blame may be related to the lack of interest in the tribes as a whole, as in Judg. 5:17b; but one cannot conclude this with certainty from the indications given. Further, the similarity between 49:13 and Judg. 5:17b shows that the difficulties in the text of v. 13 may have been caused by insertions from Judg. 5:17b. It is also possible that the same or similar sayings were pronounced, now about one tribe and now about another, all the more so when they stand close to each other, as Asher and Zebulun.

[49:14-15] The saying about Issachar is a tribal saying based on an animal metaphor. The comparison, v. 14a, is first expanded in v. 14b by a participle, thus giving it further precision—an animal taking its ease. This expansion is then developed in a short narrative recounting two events (vv. 15a and 15b) which tell how the situation portrayed in v. 15a was arrived at; it is like a parable narrative. The resolution of the parable comes only in the last word.

[49:14] ''Issachar is a boney ass''; גֶּרֶם = ''bone,'' e.g., Prov. 17:22. The meaning is ''a strong ass.'' The further precision in v. 14b means strong but lazy: ''between the cattle pens he crouches.'' מִשְׁפְּתָיִם was explained by O. Eissfeldt (FF 25 [1949] 8-10) as forked pens, which accounts for the dual; the word occurs only here and in Judg. 5:16 in the same sense and context; KBL renders by ''saddlebags'' (so too E. A. Speiser and others). However, the verb (cf. 49:9) favors the meaning ''sheepfolds.''

[49:15a] A peculiar subtlety of these four half-verses is that their subject can be understood as the ass as well as the tribe of Issachar; this same subtlety is found also in the comparative sayings in Proverbs. Like the ass, so too the tribe, has sought out (וַיַּרְא) a peaceful, pleasant place in which to lie down (v. 14b). The last word מַס־עֹבֵד is used only of people, even though it can be applied easily to an ass. The phrase וַיַּרְא כִּי טוֹב is the same as in Gen. 1:4, 6, etc.

On the phrase, see W. C. Holladay (1968) and J. L. Kugel (1980) who wants to translate it, "He was very pleased with. . .." On מנחה A. R. Hulst (1970): "Quiet in the sense of security," p. 69; also J. Frankowski (1965), G. Robinson (1980), B. Margulis (1970). All references in bibliog. to Gen. 49:1-28a. The word alludes to the fertile plain of Esdraelon.

[**49:15b**] "He bent his back to the burden [infin.]." One thinks here of an ass as a beast of burden in contrast to the freely roaming wild ass (Job 39:5, 7). He has now found a peaceful livelihood; but it costs him his freedom. The last stichos says this, passing from the comparison to the thing compared: "he became a forced laborer"; the same phrase occurs in Josh. 16:10 where "the Canaanites. . .have become slaves to do forced labor." In 1 Kings 9:21 ". . .these Solomon made a forced levy of slaves. . .." On forced labor, see A. F. Rainey (IEJ 20 [1970] 191-203). The same word for forced labor, מס, occurs in a letter from the archive of Amenophis IV: "I alone bring men for the corvée from the town of Yapu. They come from Shu[nama]. . .." Sunem lies in the territory of the tribe of Issachar, and it is quite possible that those here brought into forced labor belong to this tribe. A. Alt sees it this way (KS 1 1953 [1925] 89-125). In this case, what is said of the tribe of Issachar in Gen. 49:15, would be confirmed by an attestation from outside Israel (so H. J. Kittel, 26; S. Herrmann [1973] 127f.; A. Globe [1975]; cf. bibliog. above).

Concluding remarks on vv. 14-15: This saying brings together an extremely expressive animal metaphor and a wordplay on the name "hireling"(?). It pronounces a harsh reproach over the tribe of Issachar. It was the goal of the immigrating tribes to reduce the Canaanites to forced labor (Judg. 1:28, 30, 33; Josh. 16:10); but Issacher accepts forced labor at the hands of the Canaanites, albeit reduced thereto by its situation in the middle of a ring of Canaanite forts. Some of these cities were still Canaanite at the time of David. This same tribe of Issachar is praised for its participation in the battle under Deborah (Judg. 5:15), but this concerns another, probably earlier, period.

[**49:16-17**] Vv. 16-17 contain two sayings about Dan. Vv. 16 and 17 are independent of each other and each has its own separate origin and transmission; one builds on a wordplay on the name (as Gen. 30:6), the other on an animal metaphor. What is common to them is that both speak of Dan in terms of praise.

[**49:16**] The saying consists of only one sentence, but divided into two parts. "The sentence says that Dan himself upholds justice, he holds his own in his struggles" (H. Holzinger). דין means here "to execute judgment," and עם are the people of his own tribe. He executes judgment just as well as any other tribe; this is what v. 16a says and the presupposition is that he does this even though he is only a small tribe. The words "tribes of Israel" are striking; they can only be uttered when Israel exists as a whole. One presumes then that the saying in its present form is a later construction which at the same time preserves the original form of the tribal saying.

[**49:17**] Once more, as in vv. 9, 14, 15, there is an animal metaphor; once more the language is vivid and imaginative and the structure clear and precise. Dan is compared to a serpent lurking by the way (v. 17a) that strikes a passing horse in the fetlock (v. 17bα) so that the rider is thrown backwards from the horse (v.

17bβ). The present metaphor differs perceptibly from the Judah metaphor of the lion (v. 9); the lion is conscious of his own power ("who dares rouse him?"); Dan is a small, though dangerous, serpent, referring to the smallness of the tribe; it has at its disposal all too few warriors to be able to engage its Canaanite enemies in open battle. Now and again it can risk a surprise attack, an ambush, as the metaphor describes it; the weaker resorts to a stratagem against the stronger, as did Jacob against Laban in different circumstances (Gen. 30). The יהי at the beginning of v. 17 is either a jussive form with an indicative meaning (W. Beyerlin, ZAW 73 [1961] 194) or a redactional link between the two Dan sayings (H. J. Zobel); it certainly does not indicate that the saying is a wish or looks to the future (P. A. H. de Boer, VT 5 [1955] 231); this does not fit the text of the saying, which is purely a description of what Dan does, as in v. 9.

As is often the case in parallelism, the general term "serpent" is made more specific in the second half of the verse, "horned viper"; it is "a small but very dangerous type of serpent" (H. Gunkel); the word is found only here. According to H. J. Zobel, the reference in v. 17b is to the horse and driver of a war chariot. This is possible, but the description makes one think more of a rider; so too S. Mowinckel (VT 12 [1962] 278-299), who is of the opinion that at that period the horse was used as a riding animal.

Concluding remarks on vv. 16-17: Dan is praised in both sayings; in both cases the praise conforms to the particular situation of the tribe of Dan as we know it from the book of Judges, especially ch. 18; the sayings are very close to the events they reflect. This, together with the pure form of the tribal saying in characteristic poetry, favors an origin in the period of the judges; cf. H. M. Niemann (diss. Rostock, 1979), who is of the opinion that vv. 16-17 catch that stage of development when the clan of Dan, not yet considered a tribe and possessing only one city, nevertheless was regarded as comparable with a tribe.

[**49:18**] "I hope for thy salvation, Yahweh!" This verse is immediately recognizable as a typical psalm exclamation; indeed, it belongs to a particular psalm form, the confession of trust (C. Westermann, *Fests. W. Zimmerli* [1977] 55; on קוה, ThB 55 [1974]). Ps. 119:166 is word for word the same, "I hope for thy salvation, Yahweh"; similarly Pss. 38:16; 39:8; 55:24b. The name Yahweh occurs only here in ch. 49. This verse makes sense only when it is recognized as a marginal note added to the whole collection of sayings (it stands right in the middle) by a reader in the exilic or postexilic period. He is expressing his shock at the spirit of the tribal sayings, and sets against it the piety of his own age which puts its trust and hope in God's help alone. It is a most impressive witness to critical biblical interpretation.

[**49:19**] The saying about Gad consists of a wordplay on the name; it is a sentence in two parts; four of the six words are from the root גדד. Marauding or robber bands oppress Gad; the name, the object of the sentence, is put at the beginning; but (ו adversive) Gad presses on their heels, he defends himself courageously against them. "Gad was constantly in danger from its southern and eastern neighbors" (BHH I 507). Again the very short saying sketches in extremely sharp lines the situation of a tribe which is clearly different from all others. One can understand how, according to Deut. 33:20f., it has apparently improved its position markedly. In both sayings the tribe of Gad is praised.

[49:20] The saying about Asher also consists of one sentence in two parts. Again the name stands at the beginning of a nominal sentence, v. 20a: "Asher, his food is rich" (literally, "fat is his food"). The sentence refers to the fertility of the stretch of land where Asher has settled, the coastal strip between Carmel and Phoenicia. Deut. 33:24 also speaks of its fertility. There is also a wordplay in the background here: אָשֵׁר = "good fortune" (the same meaning in Gen. 30:13, but explained differently). So far, what is said about Asher is positive. The second half of the verse reads, ". . .and he provides delicacies for the king"; this is usually understood as an extension or specification of the first half; he has so much that he can even deliver it, and has become renowned because of his "successful activity" (H. J. Zobel). This could be the meaning. Such export from Israel to Phoenicia is expressly mentioned in Ezek. 27:17. H. J. Kittel, on the contrary, understands the second half-verse as a reproach and translates, "but he provides delicacies for the king" (pp. 19f.). Asher is reproached because it provides for Canaanite courts. Judg. 1:32 (Asher lives in the midst of the Canaanites) favors this explanation; from this piece of information one "can suspect political dependence on the Phoenicians" ("Asser" in BHH I 141); see Judg. 5:17, where Asher is reproached for the same reason as Issachar in 49:19f. In any case the reproach in v. 20 is mitigated and reserved.

[49:21] The saying about Naphtali consists of one sentence in two parts. The first part is a comparative nominal sentence, the second part states something about the subject of the first; but the text is probably disturbed. The meaning depends on the pointing of the subject; אֵלָה = "terebinth" (the Gk understands it thus), or אַיָּלָה = "hind." So far there have been only animal metaphors; the qualifying word שְׁלֻחָה, "as swift of foot as a wild gazelle" (2 Sam. 2:18) and "who has let the wild ass go free?" (Job 39:5), is characteristic of an animal; the present passage is close to these two; hence we have here also an animal metaphor. This is confirmed by comparing it with Judg. 5:18, "Naphtali too on the heights of the field," and Ps. 18:34, "he made my feet like hinds' feet, and set me secure on the heights."

As is almost always the case, the second half-verse says something more specific about the way in which the animal mentioned in the first acts. The MT could be rendered, "who gives forth gracious speech"; but this is impossible as a concrete expansion of the first half-verse, even if one explains אילה as a terebinth. Instead of אמרי = "words," H. Gunkel reads אמירי = "lambs"; cf. Aram. Ezra 6:9, 17; 7:17, and אמר, a masculine noun meaning "lamb" (Ug., Akk; M. Noth, *Die israelitischen Personennamen*. . . [1928; 1966²] 230). The participle must therefore be read as feminine. Many accept this alteration.

Understood in this way, v. 21 praises the mobility and/or love of freedom of the tribe of Naphtali, which gains increase in the freedom of the mountains.

[49:22-26] Sayings about Joseph: Both the longer text as well as its content give preeminence to Judah (vv. 8-12) and Joseph (vv. 22-26). This preeminence is to be traced back to the collector of the sayings in ch. 49 who presupposes a predominance of Judah as well as a predominance of the Northern Kingdom. But this says nothing about the age of the individual sayings. Like vv. 8-12, vv. 22-26 are a collection. V. 22 is a metaphor, vv. 23-24a are spoken in praise of the tribe's military prowess, and vv. 24b-26 are a blessing or a promise of blessing on Joseph.

[49:22] V. 22 is an independent and self-contained metaphor. The text is difficult; the explanation can lay no claim to certainty. The rhythm is clear, 2:2:3, as is also the repetitive style, to which J. Muilenburg has drawn special attention (VT.S 1 [1953] 107f.). Both the style and the rhythm would be destroyed by deleting the second בן פרת. The repetition of פרת is obviously for the sake of emphasis, and because of this the name Joseph stands in second place; this must be saying something special; it must be an allusion to פרת = Ephraim; so the majority of exegetes. H. J. Zobel has rightly concluded from this that "the saying originally concerned the tribe of Ephraim"; C. H. J. de Geus writes: "The places in the OT which mention a Joseph tribe are all rather young." פֹּרָת is chosen for the sake of the allusion, fem. part. qal from פרה = "to be fruitful"; another form is פֹּרִיָּה = "fruit tree" (Is. 17:6).* This derivation acquires definite confirmation from Joseph's naming of Ephraim in 41:52, ". . .God has made me fruitful." One can say then that the usual translation, "a young fruit tree [or vine] is Joseph, a young fruit tree by the spring," is relatively certain. This suits well the third stichos, "its branches [tendrils] climb up over the wall." But this translation remains uncertain. בנות for branches or tendrils is possible, but unusual. The verb צעד means "to stride" and does not occur elsewhere in this context; the singular is grammatically possible (distributive); on צעד in detail, see H. J. Zobel, BZAW 95 (1965) 21, n. 110. The further detail עלי־שׁור corresponds well to עלי־עין at the end of the second stichos—the tree has irrigation and protection.

V. 22 diverges from the preceding metaphors in that it describes a tribe in terms of a plant; but there is no ground to object to this, all the more in view of Gen. 41:52 (cf. Ps. 80:9-16a; W. Beyerlin, *Fests. G. Friedrich* [1973] 9-24). With the metaphor, there is a wordplay on the name of the tribe; both occur also in vv. 14-15. It is clearly a pronouncement of praise. The tribe is praised because of its healthy growth, "the fertility rising up beyond the limits imposed" (W. Beyerlin, p. 14).

Other explanations: H. Gunkel supposes an animal metaphor and a parallelism, cow פרה and ox שׁור; likewise, E. A. Speiser: "a wild colt" פרא; so too V. Salo (BZ 12 [1968] 94-95): "Son of the heifer is Joseph; son of the heifer at the spring; a creature of her who walks at the side of the bull"; the translation follows the Ug. *prt* = "heifer." S. Gevirtz (HUCA 46 [1975] 33-54) supposes an allusion to the region indicated in Gen. 16:7, 14 in the parallelism of שׁור and עין: "at the spring of water on the way to Shur."

[49:23, 24a] The second saying speaks of hostile attacks on the tribe of Joseph and its courageous resistance. Some exegetes point to the abrupt change in speech from v. 22 to v. 23, although the verb at the beginning of v. 23 seems to continue what precedes in narrative fashion. But, given the form of the tribal sayings, this is not possible. The metaphor ends with v. 22. Another tribal saying of a different sort begins in v. 23. The name of the tribe is missing at the beginning of v. 23 (cf. vv. 16, 17, Dan). One assumes that the collector omitted the beginning so as to join v. 23 more firmly with v. 22. In the present text the suffix of the three verbs in v. 23a refers to the name Joseph in v. 22a. The cumulative effect of these three verbs is to throw into relief the oppression of Joseph by its enemies, who are described as archers. It is striking that the tribal sayings nowhere name the enemies

---

*See A. Caquot, Sem. 30 (1980) 43-56, *ben perat* = *populus euphratica*, "verdant [Euphrates] poplar" (trans.).

of the tribes. The reference can be to nomadic groups; but no conclusion can be drawn from this about their chronological position. The vivid description shows that it is a question of defensive measures. It can be presupposed then that the difficult v. 24a is speaking of the courageous defense of the tribe against its enemies (Gk is different; B. Vawter follows Gk, CBQ 17 [1955] 10f.). With studied art, the rhythm follows what the saying intends to express: v. 23 is a lively staccato 2:2 (three verbs), v. 24a is calmer 3:3 (two verbs). The two verbs, "he remained firm. . .and flexible," with the well-contrived parallelism, "his bow. . .his arms and hands," portray the courageous resistance: steadfastness and dexterity with weapon, arm, and hand. This attests to a highly developed artistic language at that early period.

The language of the first half-verse is uncertain; וַתֵּשֶׁב = "it remained" is questionable, likewise בְּאֵיתָן = "in firmness"; אֵיתָן is an adjective. But the meaning is clear. In the second half-verse, the verb פזז II (imperf. qal = "remained flexible") occurs elsewhere only in 2 Sam. 6:16 with the meaning "to hop, jump." The meaning of "the arms of his hands" is also difficult; one can only render it by "his arms and hands."

Closing remarks on vv. 23, 24a. This saying contains neither an animal metaphor nor a wordplay. But in common with the other tribal sayings it praises the tribe for its courageous resistance to threatening enemies. If, as assumed above, the collector has omitted the beginning of the saying, then it is possible that this saying contained an animal metaphor; but it is also possible that a detailed account has been abbreviated into the present saying.

[**49:24b-26**] It is difficult to determine the context of vv. 24b-26. It is certain that the tribal saying in vv. 23, 24a ends with v. 24a. Tribal sayings are entirely secular, in accordance with their setting in life. They do not speak of God's help; this occurs in other contexts. It is also certain that vv. 25-26 are not a tribal saying, but an invocation of blessing for the tribe (cf. vv. 10-12). Vv. 24b and 25a seem to be a formation of the collector as a transition from vv. 23, 24a to vv. 25-26.

[**49:24b**] Most exegetes regard v. 24b as the original continuation of v. 24a (all earlier exegetes, but also H. J. Zobel, H. J. Kittel).

A. Dillmann: ". . .enemies, against whom he has emerged victorious by the strength of the God of Jacob"; H. Holzinger: "the success is attributed to the helping hands of the Strong One of Jacob." To which one may remark that the names of the gods of the fathers belong to another tradition; they are foreign to the tribal sayings; moreover, v. 24b "presupposes the process of identification of Jacob and Israel already at work" (H. J. Zobel, p. 22). This points to a later period; it is not possible in the tribal sayings. Further, there is the cumulation of names for God which recalls 48:15-16; this is likewise a later construction. All this leads to the conclusion that vv. 24b, 25a are a formation of the collector who wanted thereby to link vv. 23-24a and vv. 25-26, perhaps with a deliberate theological purpose. The מִן at the beginning has no obvious point of reference; the sequence of hands (of God) and hands (of men) has a clumsy effect. V. 24bβ is corrupt and does not admit a restoration. MT reads literally: "From there the shepherd the stone of Israel." This much can be said: a description of God in v. 24bα is balanced by a parallel description of God in v. 24bβ; because of the correspondence, Jacob-Israel, this must be: "the stone of Israel" or "the shepherd of Israel." The מִשָּׁם = "from there" makes no sense here, though the מִן corresponds to the מִן at the beginning of v. 24bα. The correspondence would be complete if one were to accept: "From the hands of the Strong One of Jacob, from 'the arms of the shepherd' of Israel." In this case אבן would be a marginal gloss, difficult to explain. רעה would be better explained as a marginal gloss for the rarely occurring "stone" (but see אבן עזר) as a name for God. מִשֵּׁם = "from the name" is to be read for מִשָּׁם.

[**49:25a**] There are two further designations for God in v. 25a: "the God of your father" and אֵל־שַׁדִי; neither would be possible in a tribal saying. Both designations belong to the context of the patriarchal stories and their aftermath. The resemblance of the language to that of 48:15-16 is striking: "the God who. . ., the God who. . ., the angel who. . ., may he bless. . ."; in vv. 24b, 25: "(by) the Strong One of Jacob. . ., the shepherd (48:15) of Israel. . . (or, Stone of Israel). . ., the God of your father. . .and El Shaddai, may he bless you. . . ." The collector is speaking here in a late, liturgically colored language (see comm. on 48:15f.).

The conclusion regarding the four (or five) designations for God in vv. 24b, 25a is as follows: they are a secondary compilation from a later period; vv. 24b, 25a form a transition piece constructed by the collector and belong originally neither to the tribal saying in vv. 23, 24a, nor to the invocation of blessing in vv. 25-26; this is true too of v. 25a in its present form. Hence the opinion of the majority of scholars, beginning with A. Alt, that these names for God are attested in a very early text, is not correct.

Excursus on the Designations for God in 49:22-26

The context in which they stand contributes nothing to their understanding or explanation. They have been brought together by a later collector or redactor and taken from their original context. A discussion on their meaning, so far as they can still be explained, can take place only in the context of the religion of the patriarchs (cf. *Genesis 12–36*, pp. 105-122, 575-576). For a discussion of the designations for God in 49:24, 25, I draw attention to the following selection from the literature:

1. אביר יעקב: F. Dummermuth (1958); J. P. Hyatt (1967); P. D. Miller (1967); H. P. Müller (1978); M. Saebø (1977), all in bibliog. above; H. Gese, in *Die Religionen der Menscheit* 10, 2 (1970); R. de Vaux, *The Early History*. . . I [1971; Eng. 1978] 268-282.

2. רעה, רעה ישראל: *Genesis 12–36*, pp. 117–118; J. Skinner (1913-14); J. Dahse (1912); H. Gross (1960); W. Beyerlin (1973), bibliog. above.

3. אבן, אבן ישראל: H. A. Brongers and A. S. van der Woude (1965-66); M. Dahood (1959); O. Eissfeldt (1955), bibliog. above; H. Seebass, BZAW 98 (1966); O. Eissfeldt, Art, "Bethel," RGG[3] I.

4. אֵל־אביך: M. W. Wyatt (1978) bibliog. above; *Genesis 12–36*, 00;

5. אֵל־שַׁדִי: L. R. Bailey (1968) bibliog. above; K. Koch, VT 26 (1976) 299-332; F. M. Cross, *Canaanite Myth and Hebrew Epic*. . . (1973); HThR 55 (1962) 225-259; E. C. B. McLaurin, *Abr-Nahrain* 3 (1961-62) 99-118; H. Gese, *Die Religionen der Menscheit* 10, 2 (1970) 133.

6. The designations for God in the religion of the patriarchs: R. de Vaux, *The Early History*. . . I (1971; Eng. 1978) 268-282; M. Girard (1973) bibliog. above; works of F. M. Cross under 5; D. N. Freedman (1973); B. Vawter (1955), bibliog. above; N. C. Habel, JBL 91 (1972) 321-344.

[**49:25-26**] The invocation of blessing for Joseph in vv. 25-26 is simple and clearly divided. It begins with the subject (v. 25a): "El Shaddai, may he bless you"; it is the same beginning as in the blessing in Num. 6:24-26, except that there the verb is continued by verbs, here by nouns. V. 25 develops the content of the blessing in three stages. V. 26a is a parenthesis which stresses the value of the blessing. V. 26b brings v. 25 to a conclusion, naming those who receive the blessing.

It resembles the Joseph saying in Deut. 33:13-16 very closely in structure, form and content: Gen. 49: 25aβ/Deut. 33:13a, the subject of the blessing (passively expressed); 46:25b/33:13b-16aα, developments, what the blessing is to consist in; 49:26b/33:16b, the receiver of the blessing. The comparison in detail: in Gen. 49, אל-שׁדי, in Deut. 33 יהוה (passively expressed); agreement in "of heaven above," "of the deep"; "the ancient mountains"—"the eternal hills" (joined in Gen. 49 with a comparative). Peculiar to Gen. 49, fullness of blessings of breast and womb; Deut. 33 has מגד for ברכת in Gen. 49, and sets into relief sun and moon, and the finest produce of the land. An addition in Deut. 33 is v. 16aβ: "and the favor of him that dwelt in the bush." Both agree in 49:26b and 33:16b. These are two variants of the same invocation of blessing; the differences are minute and so permit the conclusion that there is a time gap in the traditions (similarly O. Procksch).

[**49:25a**] The collector has added the מן in v. 25a (missing in Syr) to form a sequence with מן in v. 24b. One can suppose that the parallelism which gives precedence to the salvation in v. 25aα over the blessing in v. 25aβ is also the work of the collector. The salvation can certainly refer to v. 24b, but not to vv. 25aβ-26. On the other hand, the invocation of blessing begins with v. 25aβ, a self-contained unit. This is confirmed by Deut. 33:13-16.

[**49:25b**] The blessing is developed in three stichoi in v. 25b. First there is the blessing of fertility on the land fed by the rain from the heavens above and from the streams and the springs that well up from the depths of the earth. Then there is the fertility of the body (of animals and humans), of breast and womb. Third there is the blessing dispensed by the mountains and hills; Deut. 33:15 has here the more ancient form. The sentences recall the promises of blessing in Deuteronomy which are very similar to the invocations here, e.g., Deut. 7:13; 28:3-6; the promise of blessing there is meant for Israel (on the promises of blessing in the patriarchal stories, cf. C. Westermann, *The Promises to the Fathers. . .* [1976; Eng. 1980] 155-159). The same sort of blessing invocation occurs, however, in the blessing that Isaac dispenses to Jacob (Gen. 27:28): "May God give you of the dew of heaven, and of the fatness of the earth, and plenty of grain and wheat" (see *Genesis 12–36*, comm.). The blessings in Gen. 27 are secondary and are related to the sedentary period; hence they stand close to those in Gen. 49; in both cases the language reflects the situation of Canaanite civilization.

[**49:26a**] The corresponding passage in Deut. 33:15 continues with the enumeration of the blessings: "with the finest produce of the ancient mountains, and the abundance of the everlasting hills." This is certainly the older form. It is deliberately adapted in v. 26. It is not the blessing of the mountains and hills that is invoked upon Joseph, but in its place the blessing of the patriarchs (this is really a *metabasis eis allo genos*): "The blessings of your father are richer than the blessings of the ancient mountains, of the eternal hills." When one takes into account that Deut. 33 adds further the blessings of the heavenly bodies (v. 14) and "of the earth and its fullness," one sees in the omission and adaptation in v. 26 a clear demarcation vis-à-vis any possible divinization of the forces of nature. Mountains and hills are often mentioned at Ugarit as dwelling places of the gods (J. Coppens, VT.S 4 [1957] 103f.). It is precisely this difference that makes it evident that such invocations were probably taken over from the surrounding Canaanite world; a series of linguistic equivalents makes this clear.

The incomprehensible הורי (perhaps a peculiar Canaanite form, G. J. Thierry, OTS 13 [1963] 77-97) is to be emended to הררי; the Gk and the parallel in Deut. 33:15 confirm this. The parallel also explains תאות in v. 26aβ; it is "what is desirable," corresponding to "the choicest gifts" מגד in Deut. 33:13-16 (cf. the "dew of Hermon," Ps. 133:3).

[**49:26b**] The closing sentence, in expansive parallelism, is word for word the same as Deut. 33:16b. The contrived structure follows the movement of the blessing: "From God. . .to the head of Joseph." The idea of the imposition of hands may lie in the background. "Of the blessed (anointed) among his brothers": נזיר cannot refer to the king; the word never designates the king, but rather the one who is consecrated to a special act "among his brothers."

Closing remarks on vv. 25-26: This passage is not a tribal saying, but an invocation of blessing on the tribe of Joseph, as vv. 10-12 are an invocation of blessing on Judah in descriptive form. The text further reveals, especially in v. 26b, that a blessing pronounced over a person (as in Gen. 27) has been transferred to a tribe. It agrees with the tribal sayings inasmuch as its function is the praise of the tribe, and comes close to them when at the end it describes Joseph as the "blessed among his brothers."

[**49:27**] The saying about Benjamin is a typical tribal saying with an animal metaphor as its base. It consists of a nominal sentence making the metaphor and two verbal sentences developing it in the rhythm 3:3:3. Benjamin is described as a ravening wolf. Nowhere else in the OT is the wolf spoken of so positively; later it is only the "angry wolf," especially in the prophetic proclamations of judgment (Jer. 5:6; Ezek. 22:27; Hab. 1:8; Zeph. 3:3). This argues for an early origin of the saying, certainly in the period of the judges. The metaphor praises Benjamin's prowess in war and/or lust for booty (cf. Judg. 5:14; 20). H. J. Kittel remarks on the striking difference in this saying between the person and the tribe. It is not appropriate to the Benjamin of the Joseph narrative. The metaphor is developed in two verbal sentences which, by means of parallelism, "in the morning. . .in the evening,"* describe the indefatigable preoccupation with booty and at the same time follow carefully its course: takes. . .divides. . .devours. A comparison of v. 27 with the Benjamin saying in Deut. 33:12 probably reveals two stages in the process of sedentarization of the tribes; v. 27 shows the earlier, when the existence of the tribe depended on plunder and struggle, Deut. 33:12 a later stage when it is said of Benjamin, "he dwells securely between his hillsides."

[**49:28a**] The collector draws the tribal sayings together in the first part of his closing sentence in v. 28a. He pointedly gives this description: "These are all the tribes of Israel, twelve in number"; in the second part he joins the sayings with the frame. They are accordingly something else, namely, words that the father addressed to his sons; this makes the transition to v. 28b possible. The redactional insertion of the tribal sayings becomes very clear in v. 28a. On the order of the 12 tribes in ch. 49, see H. Weippert, VT 23 (1973) 76-89.

---

*Better, "from *b*ᵉ. . .till *l*ᵉ" (trans.).

Purpose and Thrust

Overview of Genesis 49

vv. 1-2, 28a: Frame
      3-4:   Reuben: crime and punishment
      5-7:   Simeon and Levi: crime and punishment

			Wordplay	Animal Metaphor	Praise or Blame
v.	8	Judah	יד		Praise
	9	Judah		Lion	Praise
	13	Zebulun	זבל(?)		Light blame
	14-15	Issachar	איש שכר	Ass	Blame
	16	Dan	ידין		Praise
	17	Dan		Serpent	Praise
	19	Gad	גדד		Praise
	20	Asher	אשר		Light blame
	21	Naphtali		Hind	Praise
	22	Joseph	אפרת	Fruit tree (plant)	Praise
	23, 24a	Joseph			Praise
	27	Benjamin		Wolf	Praise

10-12 Judah: promise of blessing
25-26 Joseph: promise of blessing

    The meaning of ch. 49 in the broader context of Genesis, the Pentateuch, and the whole of the OT is to be determined first by the tribal sayings in their original sense; then by the several frames by which they have been appended or inserted; finally by the later explanations subsequently appended or inserted. The tribal sayings can be specified as a genre, clearly established by form and content, whose setting in life can be demonstrated with precision.
    The animal metaphors are to be seen in the broader context of the similes in proverbs. They are a particularly important group in the oldest layer of proverbs, and this is a further indication of their great antiquity. Practical knowledge and experience come together in the similes. The comparison of animals and humans belongs here. They are much more common in the pithy sayings of primitive peoples (C. Westermann, *Fests. A. Jepsen* [1971] 73-85 = ThB 55 [1974] 149-161, esp. n. 9). Understanding of one's own existence grows as one observes the animals (Gen. 2:19-20). Observation of animals and reflection on the relation-

ship between animals and humans form the context out of which the animal metaphors in the tribal sayings arose. One can conclude from the accuracy of the metaphors that the sayings arose in the period of the acquisition of the land, the period of the judges.

Typical of the wordplay is that one finds the type, the nature of the tribe, hinted at in its name. Name and nature are seen as coalescing into one. "Name" is understood here as that which it means for other people over against other things. The name has a good or bad echo (name = reputation). The significance of the name of a tribe for others or among others is a clear indication of the process of growth of a greater whole out of a number of clans or tribes. This process of common growth towards a whole presupposes a sense of belonging (common derivation) which is prepolitical and familial; it becomes steadily more important as the worth one has for the others and thus has a significance for the broader community. A good name means recognition by others ("Judah, your brothers praise you"). A bad name endangers or threatens the continuity with the greater whole. Hence this way of explaining names also points to an early origin of these sayings.

The two invocations or promises of blessing in the text before us, vv. 10-12 and 25-26, are joined with tribal sayings (vv. 10-12 with vv. 8 and 9; vv. 25-26 with vv. 22, 23, 24a); this indicates that both were already together in a preliterary stage. An original setting in life for the invocation of blessing is the farewell (Gen. 24:60). It is possible that at the meetings of the tribes or their representatives, at which the sayings arose and were handed on, a solemn farewell between the tribal representatives was part of the ritual; it was there that the invocations of blessing on a particular tribe can have had their setting in life. An authorized speaker and the presence of the other tribes would be part of such an event; invocations of blessing passing over into promise, speaking clearly of the preeminence of one tribe (vv. 8, 10-12, 26b) and anticipating the monarchy (vv. 10-12, 26b), would be more comprehensible. Further in favor of this is that in Deut. 33 invocation of blessing and prayer have increased remarkably over against Gen. 49; this is in accord with the change in the nature of these meetings, which are now moving in a sacral direction.

The meaning given to the tribal sayings (and the invocations of blessing for the tribes) by their setting is far removed both chronologically and in content from their original meaning and function. We do not know how the sayings were passed on from the time of their origin until they were brought together. A redactor fitted them into the P context by means of vv. 1a and 28b and thus proclaimed them to be pronouncements of blessings which Jacob dispensed to his sons ("blessing each with the blessing suitable to him"). That is, the tribal sayings which had their origin in the period when the tribes lived independently and were in the process of gradually coming together were backdated to the period of Jacob's death. The intention in doing this was twofold: the tribal sayings acquired a higher status by being proclaimed in the words of one of the primal fathers. The transmitter has thus succeeded in preserving these sayings which otherwise would certainly have been lost. Then there was the further intention of clamping firmly together the patriarchal period and the period of the judges by proclaiming them as words of Jacob. The traditions of these two eras had nothing in common; but here they are firmly stapled to each other. Both intentions are in our view "unhistorical," but both have indirectly acquired a high historical significance.

Vv. 2 and 28a probably originated when the collection was made, forming its frame. What was said of vv. 1a and 28b holds here as well. Here too the tribal sayings are given their authority as words of Jacob. In addition, the "twelve tribes of Israel" are being set in relation to each other, i.e., the intent is directed to the coming into being of the unity, Israel, from the tribes and tribal groups. The whole emphasis in these frame-verses is on the unity of the state of Israel at which the collection of the tribal sayings is aimed. The concern is to describe a basis in ancient times for this unity, Israel, which is continually exposed to threat and danger. The motivation here is expressly political.

It is only the supplement (v. 1b) that understands the sayings as a prophecy about the days to come, and it refers only to vv. 10-12 and perhaps 26b. It is not the intent of these texts to make a prophecy about the ruler of the end-time; the supplement (v. 1b) shows that they were understood later in this way. The sayings about Reuben (vv. 3-4) and Simeon and Levi (vv. 5-7) bear the mark of the language of the prophetic proclamation of judgment. They are not ancient tribal sayings, but literary formations demanded by the number 12. They show traces of an understanding of history stemming from the prophecy of judgment. The late orientation given to the tribal sayings by a piety characteristic of the psalms, under the influence of wisdom, is quite different; this is manifest in the two marginal additions in vv. 6a and 18. In v. 6a the pious man speaks like the man in Ps. 1 who will not keep the company of the wicked; v. 18 is a pious confession in the help that comes from Yahweh alone, and in deliberate contrast to the warrior-like attitude of the tribal sayings. This pious confession, written in the margin at least 600–700 years after the tribal sayings originated, is an impressive indication of the change that has taken place in Israel throughout the many stages of its history.

Concluding Remarks
on Genesis 37–50

1. Narrative art in the Joseph story.
2. The Joseph narrative and wisdom.
3. The individual and the group in the Joseph narrative.
4. What does the Joseph narrative say about God?
5. The Joseph narrative in the Bible and later.

1. Narrative Art in the Joseph Story

It was a natural consequence of that era of research which placed the emphasis on the question of sources, the literary layer to which a textual pericope or sentence belonged, that the same lively attention was not given to narrative style and narrative art. The exegete was concerned essentially with individual passages and not so much with the whole and its members. This is the reason why hitherto little study has been given to this aspect of the Joseph narrative; at times scarcely any attention has been paid to it. The attention I have given to it is but a beginning; it makes no claim to be complete. Nevertheless, I am sure that one can not really understand the Joseph narrative unless one attends to its narrative art.

A. The Architectonics

The structure of the Joseph narrative as a whole and in detail, from the largest to the smallest units, is aimed primarily at being heard, not at being read. This is a consequence of its being extant probably for a long time in only a few copies; it became known mainly through reading aloud and listening. But this demanded of the listeners a high degree of mental sympathy and inner participation. It is clear that the narrator presupposes this, even demands it (he remains a narrator even when he has written down the Joseph narrative). In order to retain such empathy on the part of the listeners, it was necessary that the overall narrative blueprint stand out clearly. The listeners had to know where they stood along the way between beginning and end.

Herein lies the most striking difference between the patriarchal story and the Joseph narrative. The basic element in chs. 12–36 is the individual narrative; the connecting links are the genealogy and the itinerary. By contrast chs. 37–50 are one narrative, connecting links are missing. The coherence must emerge from the narrative itself; hence the importance of the structure (see Intro., ''The Composition of the Joseph Story''). This is so transparent in chs. 37; 39–41; 42–45 as to be immediately evident to the listener. The listener in the early period of the monarchy can recognize at once that the narrative of Joseph and his brothers is embedded in the patriarchal stories, and that the story of the patriarch Jacob continues there. But this continuation is no longer a part of the patriarchal story. With Joseph's transition to the Pharaoh's court, the narrator indicates two paths which the history of Israel has followed, the period of the patriarchs and the period of the kings. He wants to say something to them about this transition, and the listener finds it at the end of the narrative, confirmed in the key sentence which brings the family history and the events at the court of the Pharaoh together under the action of God. Further, there is the structure of each of the individual parts in themselves: the sequence of the scenes in ch. 37, in chs. 39–41, the sequence of the accounts of the journeys in chs. 42–45 which reveal in part the synthesis of originally independent elements, as in chs. 39–41. Finally, each individual scene is carefully composed down to the last detail (cf. the symmetry in ch. 40; see the diagram in the comments on ch. 40 under ''Form''), so that the arc of tension of each is integrated into that of the whole with consummate narrative art.

Over and above this, the narrator makes use of yet another compositional device, that of the leitmotif. First there is the dream motif in the three pairs of dreams: Joseph's dreams, the dreams of the officials, the dreams of the Pharaoh. There is a clear line leading from the first to the third paid (cf. 40:1-23, Form); they stand in a mutual relationship to one another; the sequence could not be otherwise. The relation between dream and explanation is consciously different with each pair. The order itself of the three pairs of dreams says something to the narrative as a whole, and the listener is silently stimulated to put them in relationship with each other and to perceive their meaning for the whole. Then there is the motif of the tunic. It is characteristic of the narrator of the Joseph narrative that he never draws attention to the varied recurrence of this motif in very different contexts. One can point to other such leitmotifs; one is the greeting in word and gesture, with obeisance and the word שלום; this is of great importance in content for the narrative as a whole, as well as in form for the frame. Yet another leitmotif is the famine, whereby the narrator describes the two aspects of its importance, for the starving nomad families and for the concern of a king for his realm.

It is also part of the overall architectonics when at the conclusion the narrator has the group which was there at the beginning (father—brothers—youngest brother) come together again.

B. Doubling as an Artistic Device of the Narrator

Classical literary source criticism looked for doublets and doublings as a criterion for different literary sources. When one thought that one had found a doublet, then one was no longer occupied with it. It could not be of any real importance for the narrative because the individual literary source, J or E, ought in principle contain no doublets. But this was to misplace the question right from the start, namely, whether the narrator had any purpose in doubling a narrative element. H. Gunkel and W. Rudolf had already seen that doubling is used as a deliberate device of narrative technique; D. B. Redford and H. Donner have pursued the question further. The narrator uses it on the large scale and the small. There are two journeys in chs.

42–44 which lead to a resolution in ch. 45, and they link together the two scenes of action. Joseph, the officials, and the Pharaoh all have two dreams; the Pharaoh's dream is narrated twice, and the subtle differences between the narrator's account (41:1-7) and that of the Pharaoh (41:15-24), which leads on to the interpretation (vv. 25-52), speak very clearly. The wife tries to seduce Joseph twice (ch. 39). It is similar when different accounts of the same event are given, each determined by the situation faced, as in 42:30-34 and 43:1-7. When such differences are traced back to two sources, the purpose of the narrator is lost; he wants to elucidate the event by means of different accounts from two sides, and so at the same time quietly to emphasize it and imprint it on the listener. This "echo technique" is particularly effective in ch. 39 when virtually the same event is described in the accusation and the defense.

These repetitions in the Joseph narrative are never tiresome or boring because they are never mechanical. In many cases one could regard this device of doubling as a type of narrative parallelism, to be compared with the *parallelismus membrorum* in poetry: the repetitions in ch. 39 introduce a counterpoint between the two parallel accounts; in chs. 43 and 44 the doubling in the structure mounts steadily to the climax (44:18-34); it is similar with the dreams already mentioned in ch. 41. The device of doubling has a variety of potential. One that occurs often is the *inclusio* (see S. McEvenue, *The Narrative Style of the Priestly Writer* [1971]). The central episode in ch. 39, vv. 7-20, is framed by vv. 2-6 and vv. 21-23; with their assurance of Yahweh's assistance they stand in sharp contrast to the central part. In 43:3-5 the *inclusio* serves to strengthen the command that binds the brothers (cf. 50:5a, 6b); in 43:26-28 the greeting is framed by the obeisance of the brothers, thereby underscoring its importance.

The real purpose of this device of doubling or repetition can be understood only in the light of a narrative feature which is found throughout the OT, but which is particularly characteristic of the Joseph narrative: the narrator wants his listeners to share in the course of events that he narrates. He is concerned only with this; hence he is extremely reserved about what he himself thinks. His own thoughts must lie hidden so that the event he wants to share may come to life and speak for itself. The event is certainly meant to provoke reflection, but reflection aroused in the listeners. It is an exacting and elegant type of narrative art that will not push itself to the fore, but respects the reflective listener.

2. The Joseph Narrative and Wisdom

The concluding remark on the sapiential character of the Joseph narrative (cf. Intro. 4) is that it is neither a didactic narrative nor a wisdom narrative; the exegesis has shown this and the structure has now demonstrated it.

G. von Rad (*Wisdom in Israel* [1970; Eng. 1975] 46-47) describes the Joseph story as a didactic narrative; he says, however, that this genre cannot be marked off sharply from other genres. H. P. Müller (WO 9 [1977] 77-98) attempts to determine a genre of sapiential didactic narrative; he ascribes to it the frame of the book of Job, the Joseph narrative, the narrative that frames the Aramaic book of Ahiqar, parts of the book of Daniel, Esther, and Tobit. He specifies its function: "It presents a virtue or group of virtues as a paradigm for imitation by means of heroes who incorporate them." Following the explanation given here, this is not true of the Joseph narrative.

Only chs. 39–41 are clearly related to wisdom; but this is conditioned by the material of the narrative which deals with the wisdom of a statesman at the court of the king. Joseph is portrayed as a clever statesman and is described by Pharaoh as such (41:38-39); but his wisdom is not something acquired, not the wisdom of the schools. It is rather a wisdom directly bestowed by God (41:38) which has matured in difficult circumstances; Joseph emphasizes this in the presence of the Pharaoh (41:16) and in opposition to the defective representatives of the wisdom of the Egyptian schools. His interpretation of the dreams is different from that of the learned Egyptian interpreters (against G. von Rad, op.cit., p. 16). God has opened his eyes to the real situation. This wisdom, matured in experience, persists right through the course of the narrative, e.g., in the audience together with his brothers in the presence of the Pharaoh (47:1-12). That this wisdom is conferred immediately by God appears most clearly in the confident announcement of a severe famine; the sages did not dare to foretell it because of their dependence on the king's good pleasure. It has been shown in the Introduction 4, with special reference to D. B. Redford, that it is not a question of a wisdom motif in 39:7-20 (Potiphar's wife), nor is it a wisdom narrative. One could add that in a wisdom narrative good must be rewarded and wickedness punished in accordance with the sequence, act-consequence.

G. von Rad bases the sapiential character of the Joseph narrative above all on the two key sentences in chs. 45 and 50, especially in the essay of 1953 (Eng. 1966; see Intro., Lit. on the History. . .); however, he is more reserved in his commentary on Gen. 50:21-25 and in his *Wisdom in Israel* (1970; 1972) 200. He refers to its close relationship with Prov. 19:21 and 20:24, and sums it up, "On each occasion man's action in the first part confronts God's action in the second" (1953). But Joseph's replies to his brothers in chs. 45 and 50 are not in such general or generalizing language. They set a wicked human plan over against a good divine plan, which is not so much as hinted at in any of the proverbs (so too L. Ruppert, ad.loc.). Gen. 45 and 50 do not speak of God and man in general, timeless terms, but of a particular situation in a narrative context. Both answers in chs. 45 and 50 are structured according to an oracle of salvation, and this is not a wisdom structure. Joseph looks back in gratitude and, in order to comfort the brothers in their anxiety, speaks of God's wonderful action which both he and they have experienced. One recalls Ps. 103:3, ". . .the Lord. . .who forgives all your iniquity," rather than the proverbs. In any case Joseph's two answers, with which he comforts his brothers, do not speak the language of wisdom.

3. The Individual and the Group in the Joseph Narrative

The Joseph narrative is structured with a view to the question of the relationship between two forms of society, the family (chs. 37; 42–45) and the monarchy (chs. 39–41; 45–47). At the beginning, though only by way of hint, stands the brusque rejection of the monarchy by Joseph's brothers; at the end, the cooperation of the monarchy in saving Jacob's family (cf. comm. on 37:5-11). The narrative wants to set in relief the positive potential in the conflict over the rise of the monarchy in Israel, while at the same time making clear how the value of the family can be preserved under it.

But that is only one aspect. The Joseph narrative further shows a varied and lively interest in interhuman relations, as expressed in events and mutual relations between forms of society, on the level of the individual and the group. This interest is partly conditioned by the period in which the narrative had its origin, the early monarchy. Behind the contrast between the simple life of nomad shepherds and life at the Egyptian court, a contrast that colors the Joseph narrative, stands the experience of a profound change in life-styles which the people of Israel have lived through from the patriarchs to the kingdom of Solomon and David. This contrast comes more strongly to the fore because the author portrays simultaneously the kingdom of Egypt and the life of the patriarch Jacob and his sons. He portrays the life of the patriarchs as we know it from the patriarchal story (cf. Intro. 5), so that it is possible to insert the Joseph narrative into the Jacob story—with some modification, to be sure. The families of the patriarchs are larger; they embrace three generations, as Judah says to his father: ''. . .both we and you and also our little ones'' (43:8). There are 12 sons; differences appear between the sons of the different mothers, the eldest, the youngest, and the rest. Hence the potential for conflict is greater, coming almost to fratricide. On the other hand, the eldest acquires a responsibility within the larger circle which is already spreading out into broader forms of society.

When Joseph is sold into Egypt, the simple life of the nomad shepherds confronts, in sharp contrast, the royal court of a great kingdom. The art of the author unfolds as he allows this entirely different world to appear before his listeners in the events and figures that accompany Joseph in his rise at the royal court. It is utterly fascinating how the author never loses himself in diffuse descriptions of this strange and varied world and its brilliance, but restricts himself to people and the many-sided degrees of subordination within the court hierarchy, with all its positive and negative interrelationships. For example, there are Joseph's master, the rich and powerful official, and his distinguished wife with her attendants; the prison, where court officials rise and fall side by side. Then there is the royal court assembled in council, with the Pharaoh at the head, the Pharaoh holding audience on which fortune or fall depends, the Pharaoh celebrating, surrounded by sages and officers.

It is characteristic of the Joseph narrative that it omits entirely the external affairs and politics of the king; there is no mention of wars or of subject peoples. Attention is solely on the internal affairs of the kingdom, its social and economic situation. The king is responsible for the well-being of his people (dream and economic policy). It is this duty of the king that the author of the Joseph narrative wants to bring to the attention of his people; only the centralized power of the monarchy is capable of undertaking economic measures that can protect large numbers of people from famine. In the Joseph story it is among the circle of people around the king, among the court and its officials, that there is the phenomenon of ascendancy or its opposite, fall, demotion. It is this matter of ascendancy that is deeply suspect in the eyes of the brothers in the father's house. In the ancient patriarchal order, each has to remain in the status into which he is born. If the young brother wants to rise high, he must be stopped. But it is now said of that very one whom the brothers rejected that God was with him and caused him to rise. This ascendancy recurs after a fall; when Joseph is elevated to the position of first minister of the land, it is said again that God enabled him to interpret the dreams and advise the Pharaoh; his rise was a consequence of this. A favorable judgment is pronounced on the rise to high office of the clever and capable man in a completely different social order. It is told of others at the royal court that they rose to high positions; but the emphasis is on the risk involved (the two officials in prison). However, the author leaves no doubt about the particular danger of the misuse of power in a social order characterized by success and promotion, achievement and career. The journeys of the brothers show this; their distrust of the institution of the monarchy is completely confirmed. They are exposed to the arbitrary will of the foreign potentate, come under suspicion, and are unable to defend themselves. This appears in a different way in Joseph's experience with his master's wife. Here too the misuse of power consists in a false suspicion, against which the foreign slave cannot defend himself.

One senses here that the narrator wants to issue a warning about the grave danger of the misuse of power. There is a clear warning here to the powerful not to lay false charges against the powerless, a warning which receives its sharpest expression later in the social accusations of the prophets.

The regime of the Pharaoh and life at his court acquire a peculiarly humane trait by active attention to personal motifs, as a result of which the minister is "the brother." By means of the tensions, intrigues, enmities, and cooperation within both court and family, the narrator wanted to point out to his listeners that the new life-style under the state need not stand in complete contradiction to the ancient and traditional life-style of the family. What binds and bridges both is the action of God; God is with Joseph in the foreign land under foreign power and prospers him in his work; Joseph adheres to him even after his rise to high office, as is shown by the names in praise of God which he gives his two sons. It is God's action; it is he who is at work in Jacob's family as well as in the Pharaoh's concern to protect his people from famine.

4. What Does the Joseph Narrative Say about God?

It has been an error, often committed, to look for what the Joseph narrative says about God solely in the key sentences of chs. 45 and 50. One must look to the whole narrative. The following contexts speak about God.

a. Ch. 39:1-6, 21-23 form the theological introit to the Joseph narrative. Throughout the entire course of this initial event, God was with Joseph (vv. 2, 3, 5, 21, 23). At the end of it Joseph says, "God sent me here." God's presence with him not only affects his way of life, but also his work; it goes beyond, prospering his employer. His path leads into the depths, but God's support accompanies him even there.

b. God is also with Joseph as he undertakes to interpret the dreams, first of the officials in prison (40:8), then of the Pharaoh whose sages cannot do so; "the interpretation of dreams belongs to God" (41:16, 25, 32, 38, 39). God's action extends far beyond the personal fate of the innocent prisoner, Joseph; the interpretation of the dreams leads to the preservation of a whole people from severe famine. God can "preserve the life of a whole people" through the institution of the kingship, and he endows Joseph with the ability to carry it through. God's assistance to Joseph first had its effect on his Egyptian master; now it is at work on the Pharaoh and his kingdom. God's blessing is universal.

c. God's action also follows the steps of the brothers. The brothers realize that "God has found out the guilt of your servants" (44:16). He has gone after the guilty ones. They knew it when punishment overtook them: "What is this that God has done to us?" But first, the time must come when they confessed their guilt (44:16); only then would forgiveness be possible. But forgiveness meant their salvation. The story of the brothers is that of God's saving action as well as of his blessing; Joseph had experienced it differently as the one rejected by his brothers.

d. The key sentence compasses both, and only thus makes sense, as a comparison of the two texts 45:5-8 and 50:19-21 can show. It is spoken into the context of the brothers' fear (45:3; 50:15), which it intends to remove; and so it has the structure of an assurance of salvation. Joseph bases his plea to be calm, "do not be afraid," on God's action: "God sent me before you" (45:5, 7a); "God meant it for good" (50:20). The brothers' guilt is explicitly declared (45:5a; 50:20b); but God's action has made possible their forgiveness. God's broader intent, however, was that many people should be kept alive (45:5b; 50:20b). The differences between ch. 45 and ch. 50 are that ch. 45 is more concrete and detailed, while ch. 50 is shorter, more abstract, and has a conceptual bent. The reply in ch. 50 is a reflective and abstract reproduction of that in ch. 45 and so is particularly appropriate as a synthetic conclusion to the Joseph narrative. It presupposes the more narrative-like presentation of ch. 45; the reverse would not be possible. The key sentence in chs. 45 and 50 is, therefore, not a timeless piece of wisdom teaching; rather Joseph speaks in the context of his brothers' fear and says that God's overall action has subsumed the brothers' evil action so as to produce good. Joseph thus comforts his brothers (50:21b). The two verbs used here נחם and דבר על-לב occur also in Is. 40:1, 2, the prolog to the message of Deutero-Isaiah. Here too the words of comfort take on the form of an assurance of salvation. In both cases the same thing is meant, though the situation is different, and the forgiveness is subsumed into God's action. God's intentions (cf. Is. 55:8-9) have also included the crime against the brother; he "meant it for good," by leading the brothers along the path to repentance and reconciliation.

Joseph's words of comfort to his brothers are at the same time meant to bring together the whole event from beginning to end. It is God's action that gives unity to the whole course of happenings. All passages which in this story speak of God's action and people's reaction to it are to be brought into synthesis under this key sentence. The action is not restricted to Jacob's family, but includes "the many" who are preserved from the famine by Joseph's foresight in the service of the Pharaoh. The key sentence thus covers the whole structure that determines the Joseph narrative, constituted out of a family story, chs. 37; 42–45f., and a political story, chs. 39–41. The monarchy and its potential is taken up into God's plan to save the lives of many (this is described in a picturesque way in the brothers' audience with the Pharaoh in 47:1-6). At the same time, and by means of the key sentence, the author validates a universal outlook, the fruit of his understanding of God, which served a critical function in a period of strong nationalistic aspirations: he points to the creator who is concerned for all his creatures.

e. It has often been remarked that talk about God in the Joseph narrative is essentially different from that in the patriarchal stories of chs. 12–36; there is a complete absence of direct revelations, divine oracles, prophecies, and promises. The contrast becomes clearest in the one text where God speaks, 46:1-5; it belongs not to the Joseph narrative, but to the story of Jacob. Many exegetes trace this difference back to an enlightened piety, in particular, G. von Rad, comm. p. 438: "Its characteristic is rather a downright realism without miracle," ". . .God's saving rule, which is concealed in profound worldliness." But when one views the difference from the structure of the Joseph narrative as a whole, another explanation suggests itself. The narrator is looking at the transition from the prepolitical form of society, the family, to that determined by the state.

In this process there has been a fundamental change in what we call religion. The "religion of the patriarchs" is at an end (cf. *Genesis 12–36*, pp.

105-113). Divine oracles were communicated directly and immediately only to the patriarchs, for the patriarchal period knows nothing of the cultic or other mediator of such oracles; whatever priestly functions existed, they were exercised by the patriarch. The differentiation begins with the process of sedentarization and the advent of the state, together with a cult bound to a place. Joseph is not one of the three primal patriarchs, "Abraham, Isaac, Jacob"; hence no oracles are communicated to him and he exercises no priestly functions. And because the main part of the narrative takes place in Egypt, there is no formal worship; Joseph stands in the middle, between two epochs. This is the reason why there are no direct revelations or cult in the Joseph narrative. However, by setting Joseph as a figure between the two epochs, the narrator wanted to say something positive to his age: by what he says of God and his action, by what he suggests to people in the Joseph narrative, he is giving expression to his belief that the basic elements of relationship with God can and ought continue into the new epoch, where the form of religion is characterized in essence by cult bound to a particular place.

5. The Joseph Narrative in the Bible and Later

A. The Joseph Narrative in the Canonical and Postcanonical Writings

The Joseph narrative has found a remarkably faint echo in the writings of the OT and the NT; this makes it clear once more that Joseph is not one of the three primal fathers. He received no promise from God and so has no direct significance for the later history.

He is mentioned only once in the canonical writings of the OT, in the late historical Psalm 105, which surveys God's saving acts in the history of Israel. The story of Joseph is outlined briefly in vv. 16-23, where the emphasis is on the fulfillment of the message he announced in interpreting the dreams. The references to Joseph in the extracanonical writings, Sir. 49:15; 1 Macc. 2:53; Wis. 10:13f., and in the two NT passages, Acts 7:9-16 and Heb. 11:21f., are also in the context of a historical survey, though the viewpoints are very different. According to 1 Macc. 2:53 Joseph became master over Egypt because he kept the commandments; in Sir. 49:15 he is reckoned among the greats of Israelite history (in "praise of the fathers"); in Wis. 10:13-14 Joseph's wisdom is praised; Acts 7:9-16, in a survey of the history of Israel, gives a brief summary of the Joseph story between the stories of the patriarchs and Moses; it is similar in the chapter on faith in Heb. 11, though v. 22 highlights the promise of the exodus from Egypt (Gen. 50:24). What is common to all passages is that Joseph had his place among a distinguished series of figures in the history of Israel, and is mentioned when this series is surveyed from different points of view. L. Ruppert treats all the above mentioned passages in detail, *Die Josepherzählung der Genesis* (1965); cf. A. van Seeters, *The Use of the Story of Joseph in Scripture* (diss. Richmond, 1965).

B. The Joseph Narrative outside the Bible

In particular, cf. H. Donner, *Die literarische Gestalt. . .* (1976) 48-50. It is significant for the whole of the history of the Joseph narrative in postbiblical times that not only does the story live on, but also the figure of Joseph, though in a form that accords with the spirit of the particular age. Judaism, Christianity, and Islam see Joseph as an outstanding personality, and very often regard him as a model, whether as a breadwinner or an astute administrator or an example of chastity. In Christian writings from the Fathers to the 19th century he became the type of Christ, prefiguring his life and passion, as the citation from F. Delitzsch shows (see above, Intro., "The History of the Exegesis of Gen. 37–50"). Such an understanding concentrates entirely on time-conditioned adaptations of the figure of Joseph, and so passes on nothing of what happened between father, brothers, and brother, between family and state, and between all these and God. The Joseph narrative itself did not live on.

A concluding glance at two very widely spaced Joseph novels might serve to demonstrate this. Thomas Mann's novel, *Joseph and His Brothers* (1933–1943), which has won high status in world literature, has succeeded in arousing the fascination of the ancient biblical narrative in some of its elements so as to make it accessible and pertinent to people of the 20th century (cf. G. von Rad, "Biblische Josephgeschichte und Josephroman," *Neue Rundschau* 76 [1965] 546ff.). But this has been done by a narrative technique which is opposed to that of the biblical Joseph narrative. The narrator of the biblical story is concerned to allow the event alone to speak; Thomas Mann is preoccupied with reflections, consequences, and developments which are strongly influenced by later Jewish literature. The work is thus transplanted into a syncretistic, mythical-magical-mystical pattern of thought (H. Abts, *Das Mythologische und Religionsgeschichtliche in Thomas Manns Josephstudien* [diss. Bonn, 1949]). His work then is a later, profound, and ingenious echo of the Joseph narrative, but very far removed from it. The other narrative that takes up the Joseph story is the early Jewish narrative of Joseph and Asenath, a novel from the time of Philo, which narrates the conversion of Joseph's wife, Asenath (cf. comm. on 41:45b and lit. to ch. 41). This novel is impressed throughout by the strong missionary spirit of the Jewish diaspora of that time, and is concerned only with how Joseph's heathen wife was won over to the Jewish faith. However, the universal bias of the Joseph narrative finds expression here inasmuch as the action of the God of the Fathers is not restricted to them. There is no trace of any confrontation between the religion of Egypt and that of the Fathers. The Joseph narrative speaks differently of God and God's activity than does Jewish religious polemic, and likewise enlightened syncretism. Neither the Jewish novel from the time of Philo nor the modern novel reproduce what the Joseph narrative wants to say. Only two examples are given here; the same is true for the whole subsequent history of the Joseph narrative. The period in which the narrative itself will be heard still lies before us.

Supplement to Literature
on Genesis 1–50

General: J. C. L. Gibson (G. R. Driver, 1956), *Canaanite Myths and Legends* (1978²). O. Loretz, "Vom kanaanäischen Totenkult zur jüdischen Patriarchen- und Elternverehrung," JARG 3 (1978) 149-204. M. J. Buss, ed., *Encounter with the Text: Form and History in the Hebrew Bible* (1979). R. C. Culley, "Perspectives on OT Narratives," *Semeia* 15 (1979). M. Delcor, *Études Bibliques et Orientales de Religions Comparées* (1979). J. A. Emerton, ed., *Studies in the Historical Books of the OT*, VT.S 30 (1979). T. W. Franxman, *Genesis and the "Jewish Antiquities" of Flavius Josephus* (1979). P. Gibert, *Une théorie de la légende: Hermann Gunkel (1862–1932) et les légendes de la Bible, Bibliothèque d'Ethnologie Historique* (1979). S. Külling, "La datation de 'P' dans la Genèse," *Hokhma* 9 (1979) 17-33. F. Niedner, *The Date of the Yahvist Source of the Pentateuch and Its Role in the History of Israel* (diss. St. Louis, 1979). H. Ringgren, *Die Religionen des Alten Orients: Grundrisse zum AT* (1979). A. Strus, "La poétique sonore des récits de la Genèse," Bib 60 (1979) 1-22. Y. Aharoni, *The Land of the Bible* (rev. ed. 1980²). M. Görg, " 'Ich bin mit dir'. Gewicht und Anspruch einer Redeform im AT," ThGl 70 (1980) 214-240. N. K. Gottwald, *The Tribes of Yahweh: A Sociology of the Religion of Liberated Israel 1250–1050* (1980). O. Keel, ed., *Monotheismus im Alten Israel und seiner Umwelt*, BibB 14 (1980). B. Otzen, H. Gottlieb, and K. Jeppesen, *Myths in the OT* (1980). G. Rinaldi, " 'Territorio' e società nell' Antico Testamento," BieOr 22 (1980) 161-174. K. H. Walkenhorst, "Hochwertung der Namenserkenntnis und Gottverbundenheit in der Höhenlinie der priesterlichen Geschichtserzählung," *Annual of the Japanese Bibl. Inst.* 6 (1980) 3-28. J. Grau, *The Gentiles in Genesis: Israel and the Nations in the Primeval and Patriarchal Histories* (diss., 1980). T. J. Prewitt, "Kinship Structures and the Genesis Genealogies," JNES 40 (1981) 87-98.

Genesis 1–11: H. Gese, "Der bewachte Lebensbaum und die Heroen. Zwei mythologische Ergänzungen zur Urgeschichte der Quelle J," Fests. K. Elliger (1973) 77-85. O. Keel, *Vögel als Boten: Studien zu Ps 68,12-14; Gen 8,6-12; Koh 10,20 und dem Aussenden von Botenvögeln in Ägypten* (1977). B. W. Anderson, "From Analysis to Synthesis: The Interpretation of Gen. 1–11," JBL 97 (1978) 23-29. W. Beltz, *Das Tor der Götter: Altvorderasiatische Mythologie* (1978). T. Kronholm, *Motifs from Genesis 1–11 in the Genuine Hymns of Ephron the Syrian with Particular Reference to the Influence of Jewish Exegetical Tradition* (1978). G. May, *Schöpfung aus dem Nichts: Die Entstehung der Lehre von der creatio ex nihilo*, AKG (1978). P. D. Miller, *Genesis 1–11: Studies in Structure and Theme*, JSOT Supp 8 (1978). A. Angerstorfer, *Der Schöpfergott des AT. Herkunft und Bedeutungsentwicklung des hebräischen Terminus bara "schaffen"* (1979). R. Martin-Achard, *Et Dieu crée le ciel et la terre; Trois Etudes: Esaïe 40—Job 38-42—Genesis 1*, Essais bibliques 2 (1979). I. Rapaport, *The Babylonian Poem Enuma Elish and Genesis Chapter One* (1979). W. Strolz, ed., *Schöpfung und Sprache* (1979). A. Tsukimoto, " 'Der Mensch ist geworden wie unsereiner.' Untersuchungen zum zeitgeschichtlichen Hintergrund von Gen. 3,22-24 und 6,1-4," *Annual of the Japanese Bibl. Inst.* 5 (1979) 3-44. C. Birman, *Cain et Abel* (1980). T. E. Boomershine, "The Structure of Narrative Rhetoric in Genesis 2 and 3," *Semeia* 18 (1980) 114-129. F. H. Breukelman, "Het verhaal over de zonen Gods die zich de dochters des mensen tot vrouw namen," *Amsterdamse cahiers voor exegese en Bijbelse theol. 1* (1980) 9-21. J. Ebach, "Zum Thema: Arbeit und Ruhe," ZEE 24 (1980) 7-21. K. Jaroš, "Die Motive der Heiligen Bäume und der Schlange in Gen. 2-3," ZAW 92 (1980) 204-215. N. P. Lemche, "The Chronology in the Story of the Flood," JSOT 18 (1980) 52-62. P. Luciani, "La sorte di Enoch in un ambiguo passo targumico," BieOr 22 (1980) 125-158. M. K. Luke, *Genesis 1–3: An Exposition* (1980). D. Patte and J. Parker, "A Structural Exegesis of Genesis 2 and 3," *Semeia* 18 (1980) 55-75. H. J. Stoebe, "Sündenbekenntnis und Glaubensuniversalismus: Gedanken zur Genesis Kap. 3," ThZ 36 (1980) 197-207. A. W. Ultvedt, "Genesis 1 og dens litteraere Kilder," NTT 81 (1980) 37-54. J. Vermeylen, "Le Récit du Paradis et la question des origines du Pentateuque," Bijdr 41 (1980) 230-250. H. White, "Direct and Third Person Discourse in the Narrative of the 'Fall,'" *Semeia* 18 (1980) 91-106. P. Klemm, "Kain und die Kainiten," ZThK 78 (1981) 391-408. O. H. Steck, *Der Schöpfungsbericht der Priesterschrift: Studien zur literarkritischen und überlieferungsgeschichtlichen Problematik von Genesis 1,1—2,4a, Forschungen zur Religion* 115 (1981²).

Genesis 12–36: D. L. Petersen, "Covenant Ritual: A Tradio-Historical Perspective," BiR 22 (1977) 7-18. D. J. McCarthy, *Treaty and Covenant* (completely rev., 1978²). C. M. Carmichael, *Women, Law, and the Genesis Traditions* (1979). W. McKane, *Studies in the Patriarchal Narratives* (1979). W. Leineweber, *Die Patriarchen im Licht der archäologischen Entdeckungen: Die kritische Darstellung einer Forschungsrichtung* (1980). A. R. Millard and D. J. Wiseman, eds., *Essays on the Patriarchal Narratives* (1980). J. Van Seters, "The Religion of the Patriarchs in Genesis," Bib 61 (1980) 220-233.

Genesis 12–25: M. Anbar, "Abrahamic Covenant: Genesis 15," *Shnaton* 3 (1978) 34-52. F. Bovon and G. Rouiller, eds., *Exegesis: Problems of Method and Exercise in Reading (Genesis 22 and Luke 15)* (1978). P. R. Davies and B. D. Chilton, "The Aqedah: A Revisited Tradition History," CBQ 40 (1978) 514-546. W. Zimmerli, "Abraham," JNWSL 6 (1978) 49-60. F. Diedrich, "Zur Literarkritik von Genesis 12,1-4a," BiNot 8 (1979) 25-35. F. Guggisberg, *Die Gestalt des Mal'ak Jahwe im AT* (1979). E. Ruprecht, "Der traditionsgeschichtliche Hintergrund der einzelnen Elemente von Genesis XII 2-3," VT 29 (1979) 444-464. O. P. Robertson, "Genesis 15,6: New Covenant Expositions of an Old Covenant Text," WThJ 42 (1979/80) 259-289. L. Gaston, "Abraham and the Righteousness of God," *Horizons in BiblTheol* 2 (1980) 39-69. F. G. López, "Del 'Yahvista' al 'Deuteronomista.' Estudio critico de Genesis 24," RB 87 (1980) 243-273, 351-393, 514-559. S. Reed, *The Abrahamic Section of Genesis (11,27-25—11): A New Translation with Essays and Notes on the Text and the Theory of Biblical Translation* (diss., 1980). H. H. Schmid, "Gerechtigkeit und Glaube. Genesis 15,1-6 und sein biblisch-theologischer Kontext," EvTh 40 (1980) 396-420. E. Blum, *Die Komposition der Vätergeschichte* (diss. Heidelberg, 1981). M. E. Donaldson, "Kinship Theory in the Patriarchal Narratives: The Case of the Barren Wife," JAAR 49 (1981) 77-88. G. F. Hasel, "The Meaning of the Animal Rite in Gen. 15," JSOT 19 (1981) 61-78. R. Hayward, "The Present State of Research into the Targumic Account of the Sacrifice of Isaac," JJS 32 (1981) 127-151. D. Kellermann, "'Aštārōt—'Ašterōt Qarnayim—Qarnayim," ZDPV 97 (1981) 45-61.

Genesis 25-36: R. Aharoni, "The Literary Structure of the Jacob-Esau Drama," BetM 74 (1978) 327-340. T. Thompson, "Conflict Themes in the Jacob Narratives," *Semeia* 15 (1979) 5-26. P. Kevers, "Étude littéraire de Genèse XXXIV," RB 87 (1980) 38-87. C. Mabee, "Jacob and Laban: The Structure of Judicial Proceedings (Gen. XXXI 25-42)," VT 30 (1980) 192-207. L. T. Brodie, "Jacob's Travail (Jer. 30,1-13) and Jacob's Struggle (Gn 32,22-32)," JSOT 19 (1981) 31-60. K. A. Deurloo, "De naam en de namen (Genesis 32, 23-33)," *Amsterdamse cahiers voor exegese en Bijbelse theol.* 2 (1981). L. Eslinger, "The Case of an Immodest Lady Wrestler in Deuteronomy XXV 11-12," VT 31 (1981) 269-281.

Genesis 37-50: B. Couroyer, "*BRK* et les formules égyptiennes de salutation," RB 85 (1978) 575-585. R. Alter, "Joseph and His Brothers," *Commentary* 70,5 (1980) 59-69. G. André, *Determining the Destiny: PQD in the OT* (1980). J. B. Geyer, "The Joseph and

Moses Narratives: Folk-Tale and History," JSOT 15 (1980) 51-56; T. L. Thompson, "History and Tradition: A Response to J. B. Geyer," ibid., 57-61. E. W. Davies, "Inheritance Rights and the Hebrew Levirate Marriage, I-II," VT 31 (1981) 138-144, 257-268. D. W. Young, "A Ghost Word in the Testament of Jacob (Gen. 49,5)?" JBL 100 (1981) 335-342.

Index of Hebrew Words

Index of Greek Words

Index of Biblical References
(with Apocrypha)

Index of Biblical References

Index of Names and Subjects

267

Index of Names and Subjects